Paul, the Law, and the Covenant

Paul, the Law, and the Covenant

A. Andrew Das

B

Baker Academic

a division of Baker Publishing Group

Grand Rapids, Michigan

Published by Baker Academic
a division of Baker Publishing Group
P.O. Box 6287, Grand Rapids, MI 49516-6287
www.bakeracademic.com

Baker Academic edition published 2010
ISBN 978-0-8010-4599-8

Previously published in 2001 by Hendrickson Publishers

Printed in the United States of America

The Library of Congress has cataloged the original edition as follows:
Das, A. Andrew.
Paul, the law, and the covenant / A. Andrew Das.
p. cm.
Includes bibliographical references and index.
ISBN 1-56563-463-2 (pbk.: alk. paper)
1. Paul, the Apostle, Saint—Views on Jewish law. 2. Bible. N.T. Epistles of Paul—Criticism, interpretation, etc. 3. Jewish law—History. I. Title.
BS2655.L35 D37 2001
241′.2′092—dc21 2001004818

Cover illustration: Rembrandt van Rijn (1606–1669). *The Apostle Paul*, 1633. Victoria and Albert Museum, London, Great Britain. Erich Lessing / Art Resource, N.Y.

To Susan

Table of Contents

Acknowledgements

No one can write a work such as this without incurring an enormous debt in the process. Several years ago I had the opportunity to take a couple of Ph.D. seminars from Wayne A. Meeks at Yale. Those two seminars, early in my development as a scholar, deeply influenced me. Meeks challenged me to be cautious and exacting in my treatment of texts. During that same year I also had the opportunity to take a seminar on Galatians with J. Louis Martyn. From Martyn I learned the importance of daring and imagination. Of course, Martyn's bold construals were anchored in years of accrued knowledge and wisdom.

At Union Theological Seminary in Virginia I learned from Paul J. Achtemeier the need to strive for a synthetic interpretation of Paul. Achtemeier has never been satisfied with a Paul who is utterly riddled with inconsistencies—sometimes within the span of mere pages. The same Paul who wrote Romans 9 also wrote Romans 11, not to mention Galatians. The ultimate test of a proper understanding of Paul is whether that reading conforms to the rest of his letters. I am grateful to my *Doktorvater* for this insight.

Many others along the way have also helped me. Richard B. Hays and S. Dean McBride served as members of my committee. McBride was my conscience: the Pentateuch's stipulations must never overshadow God's grace and mercy. Hays, as an outside reader, looked afresh at the entire argument. I admire Hays for his ability to analyze an argument on its own terms and to expose vulnerabilities that need to be addressed. David M. Hay was also kind enough during a very busy semester away from Coe College to work through the manuscript in its nearly final form. John T. Carroll generously volunteered early on to be an *ex officio* member of the dissertation committee. W. Sibley Towner, amidst fond reminiscences of E. R. Goodenough, interacted with my interpretation of the intertestamental literature. I am also grateful to Jack Dean Kingsbury and William P. Brown who worked through the manuscript prior to the oral defense, as well as Kathy Davis and especially Rebecca J. Das, my mother, who both freely offered their time to read through the dissertation for style.

Finally, I would like to express a profound debt of gratitude to my beloved and long-suffering wife. We met at the beginning of my doctoral studies and pray that our sacrifice these last few years may be to God's glory! This work is dedicated to Susan, my wife.

June 3, 1998
Richmond, Virginia

Abbreviations

Secondary Sources, Bible Translations

AB	Anchor Bible
ABR	*Australian Biblical Review*
AGJU	Arbeiten zur Geschichte des antiken Judentums und des Urchristentums
AJT	*Asia Journal of Theology*
AnBib	Analecta biblica
APAT	*Die Apokryphen und Pseudepigraphen des Alten Testaments.* Translated and edited by E. Kautzsch. 2 vols. Tübingen: J.C.B. Mohr (Paul Siebeck), 1900.
APOT	*The Apocrypha and Pseudepigrapha of the Old Testament.* Edited by R. H. Charles. 2 vols. Oxford: Clarendon, 1913.
ATANT	Abhandlungen zur Theologie des Alten und Neuen Testaments
AThR	*Anglican Theological Review*
ATR	*Australasian Theological Review*
BBB	Bonner biblische Beiträge
BBET	Beiträge zur biblischen Exegese und Theologie
BBR	*Bulletin for Biblical Research*
BDF	Blass, F., A. Debrunner, and R. W. Funk. *A Greek Grammar of the New Testament and Other Early Christian Literature.* Chicago: University of Chicago Press, 1961.
BETL	Bibliotheca ephemeridum theologicarum lovaniensium
BEvT	Beiträge zur evangelischen Theologie

BHT	Beiträge zur historischen Theologie
Bib	*Biblica*
BJRL	*Bulletin of the John Rylands University Library of Manchester*
BJS	Brown Judaic Studies
BNTC	Black's New Testament Commentaries
BR	*Biblical Research*
BT	*The Bible Translator*
BTB	*Biblical Theology Bulletin*
BZAW	Beihefte zur Zeitschrift für die alttestamentliche Wissenchaft
BZNW	Beihefte zur Zeitschrift für die neutestamentliche Wissenschaft
CahRB	Cahiers de la Revue biblique
CBC	Cambridge Bible Commentary
CBQ	*Catholic Biblical Quarterly*
CRINT	Compendia rerum iudaicarum ad Novum Testamentum
CTQ	*Concordia Theological Quarterly*
EKKNT	Evangelisch-katholischer Kommentar zum Neuen Testament
ETL	*Ephemerides theologicae lovanienses*
EvQ	*Evangelical Quarterly*
EvT	*Evangelische Theologie*
ExAud	*Ex auditu*
ExpTim	*Expository Times*
FB	Forschung zur Bibel
FRLANT	Forschungen zur Religion und Literatur des Alten und Neuen Testaments
HDR	*Harvard Dissertations in Religion*
HNT	Handbuch zum Neuen Testament
HR	*History of Religions*
HSS	Harvard Semitic Studies
HTKNT	Herders theologischer Kommentar zum Neuen Testament
HTR	*Harvard Theological Review*
HUCA	*Hebrew Union College Annual*
IBC	Interpretation: A Bible Commentary for Teaching and Preaching
ICC	International Critical Commentary
IEJ	*Israel Exploration Journal*
Int	*Interpretation*

JAOS	*Journal of the American Oriental Society*
JBL	*Journal of Biblical Literature*
JBTh	Jahrbuch für Biblische Theologie
JETS	*Journal of the Evangelical Theological Society*
JJS	*Journal of Jewish Studies*
JQR	*Jewish Quarterly Review*
JSHRZ	*Jüdische Schriften aus hellenistisch-römischer Zeit*
JSJ	*Journal for the Study of Judaism in the Persian, Hellenistic, and Roman Periods*
JSJSup	Supplements to the Journal for the Study of Judaism
JSNT	*Journal for the Study of the New Testament*
JSNTSup	Journal for the Study of the New Testament: Supplement Series
JSOTSup	Journal for the Study of the Old Testament: Supplement Series
JSPSup	Journal for the Study of the Pseudepigrapha: Supplement Series
JTS	*Journal of Theological Studies*
JTSA	*Journal of Theology for Southern Africa*
Jud	*Judaica*
KD	*Kerygma und Dogma*
KEK	Kritisch-exegetischer Kommentar über das Neue Testament
LD	Lectio divina
LEC	Library of Early Christianity
LS	*Louvain Studies*
LXX	Septuagint
MT	Masoretic Text
NCB	New Century Bible
NICNT	New International Commentary on the New Testament
NICOT	New International Commentary on the Old Testament
NIGTC	New International Greek Testament Commentary
NIV	New International Version
NovT	*Novum Testamentum*
NovTSup	Supplements to Novum Testamentum
NRSV	New Revised Standard Version
NTAbh	Neutestamentliche Abhandlungen
NTS	*New Testament Studies*
OTG	Old Testament Guides

OTL	Old Testament Library
OTP	*Old Testament Pseudepigrapha.* Edited by James H. Charlesworth. 2 vols. Garden City, N.Y.: Doubleday, 1983, 1985.
PSB	*Princeton Seminary Bulletin*
PVTG	Pseudepigrapha Veteris Testamenti Graece
RB	*Revue biblique*
RechBib	Recherches bibliques
RevExp	*Review and Expositor*
RevQ	*Revue de Qumran*
RTR	*Reformed Theological Review*
SANT	Studien zum Alten und Neuen Testaments
SBLDS	Society of Biblical Literature Dissertation Series
SBLSCS	Society of Biblical Literature Septuagint and Cognate Studies
SBLSymS	Society of Biblical Literature Symposium Series
SBM	Stuttgarter biblische Monographien
SC	Sources chrétiennes
Sem	*Semitica*
SHR	Studies in the History of Religions
SJLA	Studies in Judaism in Late Antiquity
SJT	*Scottish Journal of Theology*
SNTSMS	Society for New Testament Studies Monograph Series
SP	Sacra pagina
SR	*Studies in Religion*
ST	*Studia theologica*
SVTP	Studia in Veteris Testamenti pseudepigraphica
TBl	*Theologische Blätter*
THKNT	Theologischer Handkommentar zum Neuen Testament
TJ	*Trinity Journal*
TLZ	*Theologische Literaturzeitung*
TOTC	Tyndale Old Testament Commentaries
TP	*Theologie und Philosophie*
TRu	*Theologische Rundschau*
TUGAL	Texte und Untersuchungen zur Geschichte der altchristlichen Literatur
TynBul	*Tyndale Bulletin*
TZ	*Theologische Zeitschrift*
VR	*Vox reformata*
VT	*Vetus Testamentum*

WBC	Word Biblical Commentary
WMANT	Wissenschaftliche Monographien zum Alten und Neuen Testament
WTJ	*Westminster Theological Journal*
WUNT	Wissenschaftliche Untersuchungen zum Neuen Testament
ZAW	*Zeitschrift für die alttestamentliche Wissenschaft*
ZNW	*Zeitschrift für die neutestamentliche Wissenschaft und die Kunde der älteren Kirche*
ZTK	*Zeitschrift für wissenschaftliche Theologie*

Old Testament Pseudepigrapha

Apoc. Ab.	*Apocalypse of Abraham*
As. Mos.	*Assumption of Moses*
2 Bar.	*2 Baruch (Syriac Apocalypse)*
3 Bar.	*3 Baruch (Greek Apocalypse)*
1 En.	*1 Enoch (Ethiopic Apocalypse)*
2 En.	*2 Enoch (Slavonic Apocalypse)*
Jos. Asen.	*Joseph and Aseneth*
Jub.	*Jubilees*
L.A.B.	*Liber antiquitatum biblicarum* (Pseudo-Philo)
Let. Aris.	*Letter of Aristeas*
Pr. Man.	*Prayer of Manasseh*
Pss. Sol.	*Psalms of Solomon*
Sib. Or.	*Sibylline Oracles*
T. Ab.	*Testament of Abraham*
T. Benj.	*Testament of Benjamin*
T. Jud.	*Testament of Judah*
T. Naph.	*Testament of Naphtali*

Mishnah, Talmud, and Other Rabbinic Literature

ᶜArak.	*ᶜArakin*
b.	Babylonian Talmud
B. Meṣiᶜa	*Baba Meṣiᶜa*
Ber.	*Berakot*
Exod. Rab.	*Exodus Rabbah*
Gen. Rab.	*Genesis Rabbah*
Hor.	*Horayot*
Ker.	*Kerithot*
m.	Mishnah

Mak.	*Makkot*
Mek.	*Mekilta*
Pesaḥ.	*Pesaḥim*
Qidd.	*Qiddušin*
Sanh.	*Sanhedrin*
Rabb.	*Rabbat*
Rebu.	*Rebuᶜot*
t.	Tosefta

Dead Sea Scrolls

1QH	*Thanksgiving Hymns*
1QM	*War Scroll*
1QpHab	*Pesher Habakkuk*
1QS	*Rule of the Community*
1QSa	*Rule of the Congregation*
$4QD^b$	*Damascus Document*^{b}
$4QD^c$	*Damascus Document*^{c}
4QFlor	*Florilegium*
$4QpIsa^b$	$Isaiah^b$
4QMMT	*Miqṣat Maᶜśê ha-Torah*
$4QMMT^f$	*Miqṣat Maᶜśê ha-Torah*^{f}
$4QPs^f$	*Psalms Scroll*^{f}
CD	Cairo Genizah copy of the *Damascus Document*

Philo

Abr.	*De Abrahamo*
Agr.	*De agricultura*
Cher.	*De cherubim*
Congr.	*De congressu eruditionis gratia*
Decal.	*De decalago*
Det.	*Quod deterius potiori insidari soleat*
Deus	*Quod Deus sit immutabilis*
Ebr.	*De ebrietate*
Fug.	*De fuga et inventione*
Her.	*Quis rerum divinarum heres sit*
Ios	*De Iosepho*
Leg.	*Legum allegoriae*
Legat.	*Legatio ad Gaium*
Migr.	*De migratione Abrahami*
Mos.	*De vita Mosis*

Mut.	*De mutatione nominum*
Opif.	*De opificio mundi*
Plant.	*De plantatione*
Post.	*De posteritate Caini*
Praem.	*De praemiis et poenis*
Prob.	*Quod omnis probus liber sit*
Prov.	*De providentia*
QG	*Quaestiones et solutiones in Genesin*
Sacr.	*De sacrificiis Abelis et Caini*
Somn.	*De somniis*
Spec.	*De specialibus legibus*
Virt.	*De virtutibus*

Other Ancient Sources

Ps.-Clem.	*Pseudo-Clementines*
Aristophanes	
Av.	*Aves*
Aristotle	
Rhet.	*Rhetorica*
Josephus	
Ag. Ap.	*Against Apion*
Ant.	*Jewish Antiquities*
Plato	
Phaed.	*Phaedo*
Plutarch	
Cat. Min.	*Cato Minor*
Comp. Dion. Brut.	*Comparatio Dionis et Bruti*

Introduction

Prior to 1977 and the publication of E. P. Sanders's *Paul and Palestinian Judaism,* New Testament scholarship tended to read Paul, the apostle of grace, against a backdrop of legalistic[1] Jews busily trying to earn their way into heaven by obeying the law. Ferdinand Weber's important 1880 work on Judaism propelled this understanding into the twentieth century.[2] According to Weber, an individual Jew's destiny was determined by the weighing of his or her fulfillment of the law over against transgressions, as if on a scale. Those having done more good than bad would be saved, while the rest would perish. Weber did not see God's election of the Israelite nation impacting individual salvation. Everything depended on personal accomplishment or transgression of what God had commanded.[3] This often led either to self-righteousness or to uncertainty before a God who seemed distant and unapproachable.

---

[1] "Legalism" is defined in this work as the position that one can gain God's favor apart from God's grace and mercy through the accomplishment of what the law requires.

[2] Ferdinand Weber, *System der altsynagogalen palästinischen Theologie oder Die Lehren des Talmud,* republished in *Jüdische Theologie auf Grund des Talmud und verwandter Schrifen* (ed. Franz Delitzsch and Georg Schnedermann; 2d ed.; Leipzig: Dörffling Franke, 1897). Weber's understanding dominated NT scholarship from the end of the nineteenth century through the middle of the twentieth century. Wilhelm Bousset (whose writings stayed in print longer than Weber's) championed Weber's synthesis. Hermann Strack and Paul Billerbeck's famous reference work on rabbis drew upon the synthesis. Emil Schürer's 1890 *History of the Jewish People in the Age of Jesus Christ* is still in print (trans. Sophia Taylor and Peter Christie; Peabody, Mass.: Hendrickson, 1994). Bousset's famous pupil, Rudolf Bultmann, extended Weber's influence into the latter half of the twentieth century through his own students.

[3] An individual could, however, hope for a transfer from the "treasury of merits" accrued by the Jewish patriarchs of antiquity.

Weber's synthesis did not go unchallenged. Jewish scholars such as Solomon Schechter and Claude Montefiore voiced their concern.[4] George Foot Moore also took exception in his classic *Judaism in the First Centuries of the Christian Era*.[5] Yet their work had little effect on the consensus. The dissenters faulted the Weberian school for an inadequate study of the primary sources. Their analysis of Judaism on its own terms yielded a picture very different from Weber's caricature. Unfortunately, New Testament scholarship did not take note of the critique until it arose from within its own ranks.

Building on the work of his predecessors, E. P. Sanders mapped out a picture of Judaism that was far more grace-oriented than New Testament scholarship had been willing to admit. Sanders conclusively demonstrated that the Jews were not guilty of trying to earn their way into heaven by their good works. On the contrary, the Mosaic law and its demands were always placed within the gracious framework of God's election and covenant with the nation Israel. This election *did* impact individual salvation. An often-cited passage in the Mishnah, *Sanhedrin* 10:1, says: "All Israelites have a share in the world to come." This emphasis on God's election of the people Israel is abundantly attested in the literature of intertestamental Judaism.[6] A place in the world to come was already secured merely by being a member of the elect people of Israel. The only exceptions to this rule in the Mishnah were those who deliberately forsook their relationship with God.[7] Consequently, the Jews did not agonize over salvation. Obedience to the law was to be a *response* to

---

[4] Solomon Schechter, *Aspects of Rabbinic Theology* (1909; repr., Woodstock, Vt.: Jewish Lights, 1993); C. G. Montefiore and H. Loewe, *A Rabbinic Anthology* (London: Macmillan, 1938).

[5] George Foot Moore, *Judaism in the First Centuries of the Christian Era: The Age of the Tannaim* (3 vols.; Cambridge: Harvard University Press, 1927–1930).

[6] See chs. 1 and 4, especially the discussion of *Jubilees* and the Qumran community.

[7] After saying that all Israelites have a share in the world to come, *m. Sanh.* 10:1–4 lists those who are excluded: the wicked kings Jeroboam, Ahab, and Manasseh, the individuals Balaam, Doeg, Ahithophel, and Gehazi, the flood generation, the people of the Dispersion (Gen 11), the Sodomites, the ten spies who advised against taking the land, the wilderness generation, the rebellious Korah, and the apostate cities. Those who denied the law of Moses would be excluded. The only questionable category is the denial of a place to those who reject the resurrection. On this category, see E. P. Sanders, *Paul and Palestinian Judaism: A Comparison of Patterns of Religion* (Philadelphia: Fortress, 1977), 147–52, esp. 151–52. With respect to the Qumran literature, one would have to abandon the community, whether by sin or by choice, to forfeit one's place in the world to

God's election.[8] Hardly a burden, obeying the commandments reminded the Jews that they were the chosen people and that the Lord was near.[9]

Nor need a member of God's people despair if he or she broke any of the laws. The Jews upheld a whole system of sacrifices and atonement for setting aright the situation caused by sin.[10] The laws concerning sacrifice and atonement were meant to console and encourage consciences troubled by sin. They provided a means of receiving God's mercy and grace when confronted with human failure. Even those who abandoned the covenant could be restored if they repented of their sin. E. P. Sanders coined the now famous term "covenantal nomism" to describe this perspective. The Jews' observance of the law's requirements, the "nomism," was always embedded in the framework of God's gracious election and covenant, along with the merciful provision of sacrifice and atonement for failure.[11]

Sanders's book on Judaism opened the floodgates to an entirely new way of reading Paul's letters. No longer was Paul confronting Jewish legalism.[12] Consider, for example, Gal 3:15–18. Paul says that salvation is based on God's promise to Abraham and not the law. The law came 430 years after this promise. Paul concludes that the law cannot be added on as an amendment to the promise. Nowhere does Paul's line of reasoning imply that the Jews were trying to earn their way into heaven. The problem is not with the Jews trying to do the law, or even with the Jews perverting the law.[13] Similarly, throughout Romans 2 Paul interacts with

---

come. Only the most serious sins compromised one's place among the elect in *Jubilees;* see ch. 1.

[8] See chs. 1 and 4 for references to God's election of Israel *preceding* the giving of the law.

[9] The rabbis nowhere complained about the commandments; Sanders, *Paul and Palestinian Judaism,* 110–11; Schechter, *Aspects of Rabbinic Theology,* 148–69. Of the 613 commands of the law, only a hundred or so were still applicable at the time of the Tannaim. The arrangements of the tabernacle, the conquest of Palestine, and several other commands applied only to specific groups such as priests, judges, soldiers, Nazirites, and others; Schechter, *Aspects of Rabbinic Theology,* 140–42.

[10] On the atoning value of sacrifice in Jewish literature of the period, see ch. 5.

[11] Sanders himself succinctly defines "covenantal nomism": "Briefly put, covenantal nomism is the view that one's place in God's plan is established on the basis of the covenant and that the covenant requires as the proper response of man his obedience to its commandments, while providing means of atonement for transgression" (*Paul and Palestinian Judaism,* 75).

[12] Jewish scholarship has still at times felt the need to defend itself against the charge of legalism; thus Bernard S. Jackson's "Legalism," *JJS* 30 (1979): 1–22.

[13] See ch. 3 for a discussion of this text.

a Jewish position that corresponds remarkably well with Sanders's "covenantal nomism." Paul speaks of Jews who were comfortable in their salvation and election merely by their possession of the law. The problem with the Jews was not legalism but a cheap grace that automatically granted a place in the world to come for merely being a Jew in possession of the law.[14]

If the Jews saw the Mosaic law as a response to God's grace and not a means of earning it, what then *was* the problem for Paul with the Mosaic law? The last twenty years have witnessed a barrage of works appearing on this topic almost yearly. Already in 1985 A. J. M. Wedderburn lamented: "With some NT writings we are in danger of saturation with commentaries, so that each new commentary that emerges evokes the reaction, 'Not another commentary on . . . '. At first sight it might seem almost as bad with works on Paul and the Jewish law."[15] The annual output of studies on Paul and the law has not diminished since 1985. If anything, it seems to have *increased*.[16]

The new approaches share in common an agreement with Sanders's thesis that the Jews never maintained that one had to obey God's law without any failure whatsoever. A Jew would have relied on divine election and a system of atonement for violations of the law. Such an understanding of Judaism renders comprehensible how Paul could call his own obedience of the law in Phil 3:2–9 "blameless." In Rom 2:14–15 and 2:26–27, he speaks of Gentiles who actually obey the law.[17] In Gal 5:14, Rom 8:4, and 13:8–10 the apostle envisions Christians fulfilling the law. So if Christians fulfill the Mosaic law and even pagan Gentiles are capable of doing it, how can anyone claim that Paul thought that no one could obey the law perfectly? If Paul did not see a problem with doing the law, what fault *does* he find with it?

---

[14] See ch. 7.

[15] A. J. M. Wedderburn, "Paul and the Law," *SJT* 38 (1985): 613.

[16] Since virtually every new book on Paul and the law includes a survey of the literature, I do not intend to overview all the positions and perspectives that have emerged in the last twenty years. For excellent surveys of the various books, articles, and monographs, see Stephen Westerholm, *Israel's Law and the Church's Faith: Paul and His Recent Interpreters* (Grand Rapids: Eerdmans, 1988), 1–101; Thomas R. Schreiner, *The Law and Its Fulfillment: A Pauline Theology of Law* (Grand Rapids: Baker, 1993), 13–31; Donald A. Hagner, "Paul and Judaism—The Jewish Matrix of Early Christianity: Issues in the Current Debate," *BBR* 3 (1993): 111–30; Frank Thielman, *Paul and the Law: A Contextual Approach* (Downers Grove, Ill.: InterVarsity Press, 1994), 14–47; Colin G. Kruse, *Paul, the Law, and Justification* (Peabody, Mass.: Hendrickson, 1996), 27–53.

[17] The possibility that these are Gentile Christians will be addressed in the notes to ch. 7.

Pauline scholarship is gravitating toward what has been called "the new perspective on Paul and the law." James D. G. Dunn, its leading advocate, maintains that Paul's problem with the Mosaic law is that it had been *misunderstood* so as to exclude the Gentiles from God's plan. The Jews had understood possession of the law as a boundary marker to identify the people among whom God's grace is to be found. The Gentiles would have to submit to circumcision and to Sabbath and dietary regulations if they wanted to be included in the world to come. According to Dunn, the Jews' sin (from Paul's perspective) was pride in their national and ethnic identity based on exclusive possession of the law. The Jews were forcing the Gentiles to live like Jews; God's grace was to be found only within the nation of Israel. For Paul, on the other hand, the boundary marker of God's people was not circumcision, Sabbath, or other rituals of the Mosaic law, but rather faith in Christ. Since God's grace is in Christ and not membership in an ethnic people, the Jews were wrong for their national pride. The Gentiles did not need to observe those aspects of the law that distinguish Jews from Gentiles, that is, the "works of the law." From Dunn's standpoint, when Paul speaks positively of the law, it is the law understood apart from Jewish ethnic identity or boundary markers. Whenever Paul speaks negatively of the law, he has in mind primarily these ethnic boundary markers.[18] This is a very different understanding of the problem with the law.[19] Yet it all rests on the premise that the Jews did not believe that God required people to obey the Mosaic law perfectly.

Not all scholars have found the new approach convincing. With the exception of Thomas Schreiner, most of those dissenting do not see Paul combating a legalism by which the Jews were trying to earn their way into heaven. Nevertheless, many still believe that Paul's problem with the law is that it places a legal demand on people that no one could

---

[18] For a more recent articulation of this point, see James D. G. Dunn's "Was Paul against the Law? The Law in Galatians and Romans: A Test-Case of Text in Context," in *Texts and Contexts: Biblical Texts in Their Textual and Situational Contexts* (ed. Tord Fornberg and David Hellholm; Oslo: Scandinavian University Press, 1995), 464–65.

[19] Advocates of the "new perspective" approach in recent years also include N. T. Wright, *Climax of the Covenant: Christ and the Law in Pauline Theology* (Minneapolis: Fortress, 1991); Francis Watson, *Paul, Judaism and the Gentiles: A Sociological Approach* (SNTSMS 56; Cambridge: Cambridge University Press, 1986); Michael Cranford, "Abraham in Romans 4: The Father of All Who Believe," *NTS* 41 (1995): 71–88; idem, "The Possibility of Perfect Obedience: Paul and an Implied Premise in Galatians 3:10 and 5:3," *NovT* 36 (1994): 242–58.

successfully accomplish.[20] So does Paul see doing the law as possible or impossible? This question has become the dividing line in Pauline scholarship on the law. The debate rages between those who think that Paul's understanding of the law has absolutely nothing to do with the need to obey the law perfectly and those who still think that it does.

Contrary to the "new perspective," this work will contend that the apostle does *not* see people doing all that the law requires (chs. 6–10). This does not deny that there is a strong ethnic component in Paul's thinking. The law is indeed the special possession of the Jewish people, but that insight, as valid and crucial as it is for proper understanding of Paul's thought, does not mean that the law need not be strictly obeyed.[21]

How is it possible for Paul to see doing the law as problematic given the much more optimistic outlook on the law among the Jews of his day? E. P. Sanders demonstrated that the doing of the law was always embedded within the gracious framework of God's election and covenant, what Sanders called "covenantal nomism." Whenever one failed in the performance of the law's demands, one could avail oneself of the sacrificial system, atonement, repentance, and thereby God's mercy. But Sanders himself admitted that Paul is no "covenantal nomist":

> Paul's "pattern of religion" cannot be described as "covenantal nomism," and therefore Paul presents an *essentially different type of religiousness from any found in Palestinian Jewish literature. . . . Paul in fact explicitly denies that the Jewish covenant can be effective for salvation, thus consciously denying the basis of Judaism.*[22]

---

[20] For example, Frank Thielman, *Paul and the Law,* and Stephen Westerholm, *Israel's Law and the Church's Faith.*

[21] For a recent study exploring the ethnic dimension to Paul's thinking, see Terence Donaldson, *Paul and the Gentiles: Remapping the Apostle's Convictional World* (Minneapolis: Fortress, 1997). Even while granting that Paul's thought includes a strong ethnic dimension, that does not exclude that Paul saw obeying the law as problematic. I will return to this point in chs. 8–10.

Daniel Boyarin thinks that Paul was initially troubled by the ethnic exclusivity of the law and from there moved to Christ as the solution; *A Radical Jew: Paul and the Politics of Identity* (Berkeley and Los Angeles: University of California Press, 1994), 46. His approach runs in the opposite direction of this work, which maintains that Paul's understanding of God's grace in Christ led the apostle to reevaluate the law. Boyarin's thesis depends on Dunn's "new perspective" approach to Paul; Boyarin, *Radical Jew,* 51–56, 275–77. Problems in Dunn's approach will likewise affect Boyarin's (even granting Boyarin's modifications on pp. 54–55). Nor does Boyarin seriously consider the possibility of an openness toward, and even encouragement of, proselytism; see Donaldson, *Paul and the Gentiles,* on this point.

[22] Sanders, *Paul and Palestinian Judaism,* 543, 551 (emphasis his).

It is unfortunate that this conclusion was not based on a detailed comparison of Paul and Judaism with respect to the categories Sanders deemed central to first-century Judaism, namely, election, covenant, and sacrifice. Sanders proceeded on the basis that Paul's categories of thought were simply different from those of Judaism. Yet how do the crucial elements in Jewish thinking fare in Paul the former Pharisee? If Paul had abandoned a system that can be described as "covenantal nomism," what happened to the key aspects of that system? This study will show that the key motifs of covenant, election, and sacrifice are radically redefined for Paul in terms of Christ (chs. 3–5). If the gracious framework of Judaism is denied salvific efficacy in Paul, what happens to the demands of the Mosaic law that are embedded within that system? This study contends that one should expect the law's character as a demand to come to the fore and to emerge as problematic.

Sanders wrongly minimized Judaism's belief that God intended the law to be obeyed strictly and in its entirety. Judaism maintained a balance between the need for strict obedience of the law and the possibility of atonement for God's elect, between a judgment according to works and a judgment according to mercy (ch. 1).[23] Yet when that gracious framework collapses, the law's character as a demand, the counterbalancing element, often emerges as problematic (ch. 2). Against this backdrop it is understandable that the issue in Paul would indeed revolve around doing what the law requires.

Sanders contended that a wide variety of Jewish writings from 200 B.C.E. to 200 C.E., ranging from sectarian Judaism to a more representative Judaism, manifest "covenantal nomism" as a common underlying pattern and set of assumptions. Chapter 1 of this book reviews several of these documents. While affirming with Sanders the importance of God's election and merciful regard toward the Jewish people, ch. 1 shows that Sanders did not adequately account for the tendency among Jews to regard the law as requiring strict and perfect obedience. Philo and the author of *Jubilees* upheld sinless, law-observant individuals as models for their readers. The men of the Qumran community were to strive toward the ideal of "perfect righteousness"; they were to observe "all" the law. Rabbi Akiba's statement in *m. ʾAbot* 3:16, when rightly

[23] Sanders himself recognized that one must do what the law requires, and yet one's obedience need not be perfect. When Sanders discusses the law *apart from* the gracious framework, he speaks of the legal requirement for obedience (for example, *Paul and Palestinian Judaism,* 107, 109, 112). He denies the need for strict obedience in contexts where he speaks of Judaism *as an entire system* inclusive of election, covenant, and sacrifice (see *Paul and Palestinian Judaism,* 146, 176, 204; 137, 483). I will return to this point in ch. 1.

understood, contrasts a strict judgment with a judgment that permits some sin. In covenantal nomism, as Sanders articulated it, doing what the law required (nomism) was always embedded within the grace of the covenant and God's election of Israel. Chapter 1 sharpens Sanders's tension between the embedded nomism and its gracious framework: the law requires strict and rigorous obedience. In other words, Jews *did* maintain that the law enjoins perfect obedience—contrary to the claims of many Pauline scholars.

Chapter 2 considers Jewish literature in the years following the fall of the temple in 70 C.E. as well as several works from the Diaspora, especially the apocalyptic writings. These writings depart from the pattern of covenantal nomism. Jews began to question the election of Israel after the demise of Jerusalem (e.g., *4 Ezra, 2 Baruch,* and *3 Baruch*). Likewise, Diaspora Jews, such as the authors of *2 Enoch* and the *Testament of Abraham,* were not as concerned about the ethnic privileges of an elect Israel. Yet Israel's election constitutes one of the important poles in Sanders's covenantal nomism. What is to mitigate the strict demands of the law if there is no sacrifice for sin or the grace of God's election? The recurrent picture in these documents of a strict weighing of deeds at the judgment represents the logical outcome when the gracious framework of Judaism is compromised.

The significance of Jewish works that depart from covenantal nomism is that they provide a point of comparison for Paul. Although the temple was still standing, the covenantal framework collapses (or at least is radically redefined) in Paul's writings as well. Chapter 3 evaluates the role of the Mosaic covenant in three key passages: Gal 3:15–17; Gal 4:21–31; 2 Cor 3:1–18. In each of these texts Paul was consistent in one important respect: he consistently denied any salvific or life-giving capacity in the old/Mosaic covenant. This departs radically from the function of the covenant in covenantal nomism.

Likewise, ch. 4 shows that Paul treated Israel's election in a way that compromised covenantal nomism. All Israelites do not have a share in the world to come simply by being members of Israel. The benefits of Israel's national election according to Romans 9–11 are realized only with faith in Christ. In fact, Paul's use of election language for the church shows that the church has become the true locus of saving election.

Chapter 5 addresses a final component of the gracious framework of covenantal nomism: the possibility of atoning sacrifice. While Paul spoke of Christian living as a sort of sacrifice, there is no hint that such behavior bears any relationship to the *atoning* sacrifices of the Old Testament. The scholarly community stands divided over whether Paul was alluding to the sin- or guilt-offering, or even to the Day of Atonement (e.g., Rom 8:3; 2 Cor. 5:21; Rom 3:24–25). If Paul intended such allusions, it is important to recognize that these allusions are always in the context of Christ's saving activity. Paul nowhere granted that the atoning sacrifices of the Old Testament offer any help in mitigating the effects of sin. The solution to sin resides strictly in the work of Jesus Christ. In effect, the gracious covenantal framework of Judaism has collapsed for Paul in favor of a new framework of grace grounded in the work of Christ.

Chapter 6 discusses Gal 3:10, a verse that has traditionally been understood to indicate that no one perfectly obeys all that the law commands. This chapter affirms that traditional understanding in the face of a multitude of recent alternatives. Those who maintain the traditional view typically face two important objections. Sanders contended that the Jews never believed that one had to obey the law perfectly. The law, for the Jews, was always embedded within the gracious framework of God's covenant and election. Chapters 1–5 should have dispelled that potential objection. The Jews *did* speak of perfect obedience. The gracious, mitigating framework has collapsed for Paul, leaving behind only the law and its rigorous demands. It should be no surprise that the law's requirements proved problematic to Paul. The second objection stems from the question of whether Paul saw perfect obedience as impossible elsewhere. In Phil 3 the apostle labeled his observance of the law "blameless." That objection is addressed in ch. 9.

Chapter 6 also includes a discussion of the disputed phrase "works of the law" (ἔργα νόμου) and the relationship between the law's ethnic aspects and its requirements in general. While "works of the law" in Gal 3:10 is best understood as referring to the law's requirements in a general sense, the same issue with respect to ἔργα νόμου arises in ch. 7's discussion of Rom 2. Unlike Gal 3, Rom 2 revolves around Jewish ethnic privilege. But in Rom 2 Paul critiques Jewish ethnic privilege on the basis of whether or not the Jews had done what the law requires. The demand that the law places on those who would follow it stands side by side with its function as an ethnic boundary marker. Recent Pauline scholarship has become too polarized on this point; it is a both-and relationship. The law functions both to distinguish the Jewish people and to place a burden of obedience upon them. In Rom 2 Paul questions the value of Jewish privilege based on God's election. Naturally, the embedded nomism comes to the fore. He questions whether the Jews had obeyed the law as it requires.

Chapter 8 takes up Rom 3:27–4:8, a key passage for understanding the "works of the law" as bound up with Jewish ethnic privilege. As in Rom 2, "works of the law" in Rom 3:27 (in light of the immediate context through 4:8) refers both to Jewish particularity and to the necessity of doing what the law requires. The emphasis upon achievement is clarified in Rom 4:4–5 when Paul discusses works in general. By ruling out works in general as the basis for a relationship with God, Paul can rule out the works of the Jewish law in particular. And if the Jewish law is no longer the basis for God's justifying activity, then the law can no longer serve to exclude the Gentiles from God's plan. Since Rom 4:4–5 act as a supporting premise, Paul's logic proceeds from a recognition of the "works of the law" as a human accomplishment. Paul's reasoning is understandable in light of Rom 2: Paul had denied any saving value in being a member of the elect Jewish people in possession of the Mosaic law. With the denial of the gracious framework of covenantal nomism, the law no longer acts as a sign of Jewish privilege; rather, it entails an enslaving obligation. It entails "works."

The latter half of ch. 9 discusses a passage where the enslaving function of the Mosaic law takes center stage. Paul indicates in Romans 7 that the individual who is "under the Mosaic law" struggles in vain to accomplish what the law requires. Sin and the flesh stand in the way of successful accomplishment of what the law demands. This passage corroborates the dark situation described in Rom 3:19–20 and in Gal 3:10. Humanity has proven itself incapable of living up to the high standards of the Mosaic law. Consequently, "the law of life" brings death. At the end of Rom 7 Paul must turn to Jesus Christ for a solution to the problem posed by the law's enslaving demand. Once again Paul's critique of the law focuses primarily on the necessity (and extreme difficulty, if not impossibility) of doing what it requires. Yet if Paul is serious about human inability to accomplish what the law requires, one cannot help but wonder about the apostle's statements in Phil 3. How can Paul call his observance of the law "blameless"? The first part of ch. 9 works through that question. E. P. Sanders's analysis of Judaism provides the background necessary to evaluate Paul's claim of "blamelessness." A recurrent motif in Sanders's analysis of Judaism was the consistent recognition that human beings fall short of God's will. The "righteous" are typically sinners who availed themselves of God's mercy and election even while falling short of the perfect measure toward which they were striving. Biblical figures are often characterized as "blameless" at the same time that the biblical text admits their sins. Paul can admonish his own audience to be "blameless." One ought also to note, with respect to Phil 3, that Paul's boast as a Jew included not only his Jewish identity but also his zeal for and accomplishment of the law. The law always involves the demand for rigorous obedience alongside its ethnic particularity.[24]

---

[24] Blamelessness with respect to the law ought to be distinguished from perfect obedience. Perfect obedience is unerring success in doing all that God commands in the law.

Chapter 10 analyzes a final Pauline text: Rom 9:30–10:8. This passage also discusses the law as a source of Jewish particularity. Yet even here Paul's critique consistently returns to the importance of doing what the law requires. Paul contrasts the demands of the law with the law's own witness to the necessity of faith in Christ. Paul reinterprets Deut 30:12–14's comments about the possibility of doing what the law requires by deleting the references to doing the law and turning the verses into a witness to the saving work of Jesus Christ. Paul's discussion of election in Rom 9 prepares for his contrast between doing and believing in 9:30–10:8: God's choice does not depend on human effort or accomplishment. Hence 9:30–10:8 can extend Paul's point to encompass the demands of the law. Since the covenantal framework of Judaism has collapsed in Paul's thought with the revelation of God's salvation in Christ, the law's requirements fall into the realm of a merely human endeavor. Jewish privilege has been replaced by the dilemma of living up to the rigorous standards of the law. Paul calls the attempt to attain righteousness through the requirements of the law an establishing of "one's own" or "their own" righteousness.

To summarize: the ultimate (and unanswered) problem for a reading of Paul that still sees the doing of the law's requirements as a problem or "plight" (to use Sanders's terminology) is that it was not a plight for the Jew or for Paul (Phil 3:2–9). How is it possible that Paul would see a problem in trying to do the law in light of Sanders's depiction of a more grace-oriented first-century Judaism? While first-century Judaism was certainly not legalistic in its understanding of the law, Paul's own perspective led, nevertheless, to an understanding of the works of the Mosaic law as a merely human endeavor in contrast to God's own saving activity in Christ. In effect, the gracious framework of Judaism does not produce salvation; it has been replaced by a christological framework. New Testament scholarship has not yet fully explored the consequences of a Jewish apostle (Paul) abandoning "covenantal nomism" in favor of a "christological nomism."[25]

---

[25]On the parallels between covenantal nomism and Paul's theology, see especially Morna D. Hooker, "Paul and Covenantal Nomism," in *Paul and Paulinism* (ed. M. D. Hooker and S. G. Wilson; London: SPCK, 1982), 47–56. See ch. 3 as a corrective to her treatment of covenant in Paul. While noting the general similarities between Paul and covenantal nomism, she does not explore how the shift in framework from the Mosaic law and the Sinaitic covenant to Christ might impact upon the law, precisely the issue of what follows.

No one has offered this approach. A few scholars such as Thomas Schreiner and Bruce W. Longenecker have offered hints in this direction, but no one has explored it in depth.

Chapter One

Undeserved Grace Versus Strict and Deserving Obedience in Early Judaism

Paul and Palestinian Judaism, by E. P. Sanders, marked a watershed in New Testament studies. Sanders's work was fundamentally a corrective to New Testament scholarship that had been all too ready to malign first-century and rabbinic Judaism as legalistic. Consequently, he rightly emphasized the central and significant roles that God's election and mercy played in Jewish thought.[1] Crucial to the "new perspective on Paul" has been Sanders's assertion that the Jews never understood the law to require perfect obedience. On the contrary, obedience to the law was set within the framework of God's election and covenant relationship with Israel. Should one fall short and transgress, the law itself provided means of atonement. Sanders attempted to account for material that would appear, on first glance, to indicate that the Jews saw the law as requiring rigorous or perfect obedience.

---

[1] Sanders's understanding of Judaism has garnered nearly universal assent. Even Jacob Neusner, while strongly disagreeing with Sanders on methodology, agrees that "covenantal nomism" is a correct depiction of Judaism: "So far as Sanders proposes to demonstrate the importance to all the kinds of ancient Judaism of covenantal nomism, election, atonement, and the like, his work must be pronounced a complete success" ("Comparing Judaisms," *HR* 18 [1978]: 180; see also pp. 177–78; Boyarin, *Radical Jew*, 47). Likewise in 1993: "I find myself in substantial agreement with both the classificatory language he uses ["covenantal nomism"] and the main points of his characterization of that common piety of ancient Israel in the first century" (Jacob Neusner, *Judaic Law from Jesus to the Mishnah: A Systematic Reply to Professor E. P. Sanders* [South Florida Studies in the History of Judaism 84; Atlanta: Scholars Press, 1993], x).

Klyne R. Snodgrass, on the other hand, has identified a crucial point that would significantly alter Sanders's formulation.[2] Snodgrass called attention to the sheer quantity of material in Judaism that speaks of God judging strictly on the basis of human works and accomplishment of the law. If Snodgrass's assessment is right, then intertestamental and Tannaitic Jewish thought typically hovered between two logically irreconcilable poles: God would judge the elect people according to mercy, and yet God would judge all people impartially on the basis of their works. Snodgrass points out that the *shape* of this tension differs from document to document. Some writings may emphasize God's grace and mercy, while others may emphasize God's strict judgment on the basis of law-observance. Jewish writings from this time period are distinguished in part by the balance they maintain between these two poles. In his concern to emphasize the gracious elements of Judaism, Sanders may have gone too far when he denied that there are admonitions throughout this literature to observe perfectly what God enjoins in the law. If it is true that the Jews often saw the law as requiring strict, perfect obedience, the key premise in the "new perspective on Paul" would be wrong.

I. *Jubilees*[3]

Jubilees is a showcase for Sanders's exposition of Judaism. Central to the document is Israel's election as a people before God. Written in the midst of a cultural crisis as Hellenism was making inroads into Jewish society, *Jubilees* gives detailed consideration to those laws that distinguished the elect people from the Gentiles.[4] Within the boundaries marked by these laws, one would find a gracious and merciful God. Outside of them, one would encounter strict judgment. Yet even within the gracious framework of election and mercy, *Jubilees* still maintains that God's law is strictly to be obeyed.

---

[2] Klyne R. Snodgrass, "Justification By Grace—To the Doers: An Analysis of the Place of Romans 2 in the Theology of Paul," *NTS* 32 (1986): 72–93.

[3] Citations are from the translation by O. S. Wintermute in *OTP*, 2:52–142.

[4] On the dating of *Jubilees*, see George W. E. Nickelsburg, *Jewish Literature between the Bible and the Mishnah: A Historical and Literary Introduction* (Philadelphia: Fortress, 1981), 78–79. Because of the polemic against certain Gentile practices prevalent prior to the revolt (e.g., nudity, Gentile feasts, intermarriage, and idolatry), Nickelsburg prefers a date just prior to the Maccabean revolt in 168 B.C.E.

Throughout his retelling of Gen 1 to Exod 12, the author of *Jubilees* weaves into his narrative legal concerns that betray his own situation. To begin with, Israel is God's elect people, *all* Israel (1:17–18, 25, 28; 16:17–18; 19:18; 22:11–12). Israel enjoys a special covenantal relationship with God that was bequeathed from the patriarchs (6:17–19).[5] As God's special people, it remains incumbent upon the Jews to follow those laws that distinguish them from the Gentiles (2:21). The Sabbath is not only a sign of election but also an identity marker (2:19, 31). The Jews are not to intermarry with the Gentiles or even to eat at the same table or associate with them (22:16; 30:7–8). Idolatry is forbidden (1:9; 11:16; 12:2; 20:7; 22:22; 36:5). The Jews must keep the Festivals of Weeks, Tabernacles, and Passover (6:17; 16:29; 49:4–8). They must circumcise (15:11, 25–27). They must give tithes (13:25–27). There must be no incest or nakedness (3:31; 33:10).[6] In short, the Jews must not live as the Gentiles. All the Gentiles' ways are "unrighteous" and "unclean" and lead to idolatry (22:16; 35:13). Moses at one point pleads with God that the people might never come under foreign domination lest they succumb to idolatry and pagan ways (1:19). Given this emphasis, it is no surprise that *none* of Canaan's offspring will be saved (22:20–21; 32:19). To act unrighteously is *defined* as to live and behave as a Gentile.

While all Jews number by birth among an elect people, an individual could still compromise his or her status among the elect. *Jubilees* lists a group of sins that remove one from the elect, covenant people: violations of the Feasts of Weeks (6:17) or Tabernacles (16:29–30), failure to tithe (13:25–26), nakedness (3:31), failure to observe the period of uncleanness after childbirth (3:8–11), giving the younger daughter into marriage first (28:6), adultery (39:6), and violence against a brother (4:5). Violations of these laws are "eternal errors" against the laws "writ-

---

[5] Moses renews the feast of Shabuot at Mt. Sinai. This feast is set on the fifteenth day of the third month, the very day God established the feast with Noah (6:1–21). This is also the designated date for God's covenant with Abraham (14:1–20), the changing of Abram and Sarai's names, the institution of circumcision (15:1–34), Isaac's birth and weaning (16:13; 17:1), Jacob's covenant with Laban (29:7–8), and Jacob's celebration at the Well of Oaths (44:1, 4). The shared date suggests continuity between the covenant relationship with the patriarchs and the Sinaitic legislation. There is only *one* ancient covenant between God and his people, and even the patriarchs observed the Sinaitic laws (in advance of their reception); John C. Endres, *Biblical Interpretation in the Book of Jubilees* (Washington, D.C.: Catholic Biblical Association of America, 1987), 227.

[6] Naked youths who had attempted by epispasm to conceal their circumcision participated in the games of the Jerusalem gymnasium at the height of Hellenism prior to the Maccabean era (1 Macc 1:11–15; 2 Macc 4:9, 12–14; Josephus, *Ant.* 12.240–241).

ten on the heavenly tablets." Yet *Jubilees*, as Sanders observes, does not explicitly exclude atonement for these sins.[7] However, there is no atonement for violating the Sabbath (2:27, 33), eating meat with blood (6:12–13; 21:18, 22–24), defiling one's daughter (30:10, 16), or lying with one's father's wife (33:13, 15–17). Both categories include especially egregious sins and violations of the laws maintaining Israel's unique identity. Such transgressions jeopardize one's status within the covenant.[8]

What about less serious sins? The author speaks regularly of God's mercy toward the obedient, that is, those who by their actions affirm that they wish to remain within the covenant. To those who are obedient in this covenantal sense, God is rich in mercy and may be appealed to for mercy (23:31; 31:25; 45:3). *Jubilees* fully recognizes that people sin. In light of this situation, the author praises repentance (1:22–23; 23:26; 41:23–27). Although *Jubilees* otherwise strongly opposes incest, the author's retelling of the story of Judah and Tamar specifies repentance as a mitigating factor.[9] Along with repentance, God accepts the *prayers* of a repentant heart.[10] *Jubilees* also heartily affirms the value of the sacrificial system (6:14; 50:10–11). The daily sacrifices atone for sin, and the Day of Atonement is efficacious (34:18–19).[11] Thanks to God's gracious provisions, the elect are the majority of Israel, all those who seek to remain within the covenant.

Thus one could be "righteous" even when not perfectly obedient. It would be easy to conclude from this that the law does not demand strict obedience. Nevertheless, the people's sins were never ignored but always had to be reconciled with God's will through a process of atonement and repentance. God's demands were never set aside. Indeed, it is perfection of conduct that remains the ideal. "All of his commands and his ordinances and all of his law" are to be carefully observed "without turning aside to the right or left" (23:16). In 5:19: "[God] did not show partiality, except Noah alone . . . because his heart was righteous in all of his ways just as it was commanded concerning him. And he did not transgress anything which was ordained for him." Noah, while the recipient of God's mercy (10:3), did "just as it was commanded" and was

---

[7] Sanders, *Paul and Palestinian Judaism*, 368–69.

[8] See Sanders (ibid., 367–71) for a full discussion.

[9] Or in the case of Reuben's sin, *Jubilees* maintains that the covenant was not yet fully revealed. While Reuben and Judah violated the most serious, covenant-denying sins, the author's rationalization of the ancestor's sin implicitly denies the possibility of repentance for such sins in his own day.

[10] Sanders, *Paul and Palestinian Judaism*, 379–80.

[11] Except in certain extreme instances, as mentioned above, or, for example, giving one's daughter in marriage to a Gentile (30:13–16).

"righteous in all of his ways." "He did not transgress." Jacob is "a perfect man" (27:17). Leah "was perfect and upright in all her ways," and Joseph "walked uprightly" (36:23; 40:8). While there is mercy for God's elect, the requirement of right conduct "in all things" (21:23) is still upheld and admonished through these exemplary models. While Israel enjoys an elect status, the law must still be obeyed (20:7: "to be joined to all his commands"; 1:23–24: "cleave to me and to all my commands"). Israelites' observance of the law and strict avoidance of sin is at least a partial factor in being considered "friends" of God:

> All of these words I have written for you, and I have commanded you to speak to the children of Israel that they might not commit sin or transgress the ordinances or break the covenant which was ordained for them so that they might do it and be written down as friends. But if they transgress and act in all the ways of defilement, they will be recorded in the heavenly tablets as enemies. (30:21–22)[12]

In 10:7–8 Mastema, the chief of the spirits, asks the Lord with respect to the people: "O Lord, Creator, leave some of them before me, and let them obey my voice. And let them do *everything* which I tell them." God tells Abram in 15:3 to "be pleasing before me and *be perfect*." Abraham is then praised in 23:10, since he "was *perfect in all of his actions* with the Lord and was pleasing through righteousness all of the days of his life."[13] The author therefore looks forward to the day when Israel will be *perfectly* obedient (1:22–24; 5:12; 50:5). Sanders admits from these passages: "Perfect obedience is specified."[14] He also writes: "As we have now come to expect, the emphasis on God's mercy is coupled with a strict demand to be obedient."[15] Every word of this statement must be given its due weight. What the above passages show is that, while there is provision for sin and failure, the ideal remains strict and perfect obedience of the law.

Sanders emphasizes mercy and forgiveness in *Jubilees* at the expense of the law's strict and ideal demand. He attempts to resolve the logical tension between God's mercy toward the elect and the rigorous demands of the law in favor of the former, since *Jubilees* can speak of *sin-*

---

[12] In fact, in *Jub.* 23 the nation is punished for having disobeyed God's laws; George W. E. Nickelsburg, "The Bible Rewritten and Expanded," *Jewish Writings of the Second Temple Period* (ed. Michael E. Stone; CRINT 2.2; Philadelphia: Fortress, 1984), 99–100.

[13] Nor was Abraham's obedience a matter of his own human achievement. Abraham prays for God's help with respect to his conduct in 12:20.

[14] Sanders, *Paul and Palestinian Judaism,* 381.

[15] Ibid., 383.

ners as those who are righteous by means of God's own provision for sin.[16] Therefore: "Righteousness as perfect or nearly perfect obedience is not, however, the 'soteriology' of the author."[17] While it is true that perfect or nearly perfect righteousness is not the *soteriology* of the author, it does remain the ideal with respect to the law's demand for obedience. The danger of legalism is that it downgrades God's mercy and election. The danger of Sanders's position is that he often downgrades the strict demands of the law. As much as *Jubilees* understands the law as an ethnic identity/boundary marker, and as much as *Jubilees* speaks of God's mercy toward an elect and often sinful people—unlike the strict judgment of the Gentiles (5:12–18; 23:31)—it remains true for the author that God intended the law to be obeyed *without transgression.*

II. The Qumran Literature[18]

The Qumran community called itself the "house of the law" and the "Community in law" (CD 20.10, 13; 1QS 5.2). Those who entered the community agreed to "return to the law of Moses."[19] What did this commitment to the law mean in actual practice? To begin with, it entailed unusual devotion. Wherever ten covenanters gathered, each member was required to take his turn studying and expounding the Torah so that the Torah was studied day and night without a break (1QS 6.6–8). The entire community would gather for a third of the night to study the Torah and recite the benedictions and prayers (1QS 6.6–8). Four hours of every member's day was to be spent in the Torah.[20] But even beyond

[16] Ibid., 380–83.

[17] Ibid., 382. Sanders (p. 379) argues that in fact *Jubilees* is not so strict, since it affirms repentance and God's mercy. This is a confusion, in my opinion, between the legal demand and the larger framework of Judaism, which is inclusive of God's election and mercy.

[18] All citations and quotations are from Florentino García Martínez, *The Dead Sea Scrolls Translated: The Qumran Texts in English* (trans. Wilfred G. E. Watson; 2d ed.; Leiden: E. J. Brill, 1996). Citations of 1QH will differ from Geza Vermes (*The Dead Sea Scrolls in English* [4th ed.; New York: Penguin Books, 1995]), and likewise Sanders, since I am following Martínez's numbering system. Vermes's numbers for the Thanksgiving Hymns are in parentheses.

[19] 4QD^b 17 I,3 (=CD-A 15.9, 12); 4QD^c 2 II,3–4, 6–7 (=CD-A 16.1–2, 4–5); 1QS 5.8–9.

[20] Eckhard J. Schnabel, *Law and Wisdom from Ben Sira to Paul: A Tradition History Enquiry into the Relation of Law, Wisdom, and Ethics* (Tübingen: J.C.B. Mohr [Paul Siebeck], 1985), 182.

this great devotion, to "return to the law of Moses" meant especially a commitment to perfect obedience.

A. *Observance of "All" the Law*

The Qumran documents show that there were elements in Judaism that stressed thoroughgoing obedience of the law prior to 70 C.E. In fact, the necessity of striving toward perfect fulfillment of the law is a major motif throughout the Qumran literature. The demand was strict and absolute:

> 1 QS 1.13–17: They shall not stray from any one of all God's orders concerning their appointed times; they shall not advance their appointed times nor shall they retard any one of their feasts. They shall not veer from his reliable precepts in order to go either to the right or to the left. And all those who enter in the Rule of the Community shall establish a covenant before God in order to carry out all that he commands and in order not to stray from following him.
>
> 1QS 3.9–11: May he, then, steady his steps in order to walk with perfection on all the paths of God, conforming to all he has decreed concerning the regular times of his commands and not turn aside, either left or right, nor infringe even one of his words.
>
> 1QS 5.1: This is the rule for the men of the Community who freely volunteer to convert from all evil and to keep themselves steadfast in all he prescribes in compliance with his will.
>
> 1QS 5.8: He [anyone entering the Community] shall swear with a binding oath to revert to the Law of Moses with all that it decrees, with whole heart and whole soul, in compliance with all that has been revealed concerning it to the sons of Zadok.
>
> 1QS 5.20–22: And when someone enters the covenant to behave in compliance with all these decrees, enrolling in the assembly of holiness, they shall test their spirits in the Community (discriminating) between a man and his fellow, in respect of his insight and of his deeds in law, under the authority of the sons of Aaron, those who freely volunteer in the Community to set up his covenant and to follow all the decrees which he commanded to fulfil.[21]

---

[21] See also 1QS 4.22; 8.10, 15, 18, 22; 9.9–10, 19; 10.21 with their references to "perfect" behavior. Herbert Braun tracks each use of the word "all" (כול) in its immediate context throughout the Community Rule; "Beobachtungen zur Tora-Verschärfung im häretischen Spätjudentum," *TLZ* 79 (1954): 350 n. 21. He concludes (p. 350): "alles, was Gott befohlen hat; alle Gebote sind zu halten." He

Nor is this emphasis on doing *all* the law distinctive of the *Rule of the Community* (1QS). *Damascus Document* (CD) 15.12–14 speaks of one who wishes to enter the community:

> But when he has imposed upon himself to return to the law of Moses with all his heart and all his soul [they will exact revenge] from him if he should sin. . . . And if he fulfils all that has been revealed of the law. . . .

> CD 16.6b–8: And as for what he said [Deut 23:24]: "What issues from your mouth, keep it and carry it out." Every binding oath by which anyone has pledged to fulfil the letter of the law, he should not annul, even at the price of death.

And, as with the *Rule of the Community*, there are several references to the need for "perfect" behavior (e.g., CD 2.15; 20.2, 5, 7). Even the hymns make reference to "perfection" of way (e.g., 1QH^{a} 9[=1].36).

B. Forgiveness and Atonement as Mitigating Factors

What if a member sinned and fell short of the perfection required by the law? Certain sins within the community, such as blasphemy during the reading of the law or praying, or slandering or murmuring against the community's leadership, resulted in an automatic expulsion from the community (e.g., 1QS 7.18–19). The expulsion for these sins was permanent, irrevocable, and entailed a complete loss of one's status within the elect community and no hope for a place in the world to come. Other sins led to a one- or two-year suspension, a trial period prior to readmittance to full membership (1QS 6.24–25).[22] Those who had been community members for ten years were held to a stricter standard; if they willfully sinned, they would be permanently expelled (1QS 7.22–27). There were even stricter penalties for the "men of perfect holiness" in 1QS 8. Any intentional sin on their part would result in permanent expulsion from the community (1QS 8.1–4; 8.20–9.2).[23] An

---

makes the same point with regard to the *Damascus Document* (pp. 351–52, and n. 28). See also W. D. Davies ("Paul and the Dead Sea Scrolls: Flesh and Spirit," in *The Scrolls and the New Testament* [ed. Krister Stendahl; New York: Harper & Brothers, 1957], 281 nn. 80–81), who follows Braun in locating 73 instances in the *Rule of the Community* where the word "all" is used with respect to doing the law.

[22] Seven years in the case of a Sabbath violation (CD 12.4–6).

[23] Sanders, *Paul and Palestinian Judaism*, 323–27. There is some debate, though, on the identity of this group. See Sanders, *Paul and Palestinian Judaism*, 301–3; Paul Garnet, *Salvation and Atonement in the Qumran Scrolls* (WUNT 2/3; Tübingen: J.C.B. Mohr [Paul Siebeck], 1977), 85–86; and Robert J. Daly,

inadvertent sin would lead to a two-year expulsion. Of course, the sin that always damned was a failure to accept the commandments of the law as revealed to the community. In short, the penalties for sin were in many cases quite severe.

Sanders rightly stresses the availability of a system of atonement and correction for sin at Qumran (particularly right conduct). However, far from mitigating the strict requirement of the Qumran halakah to be perfect in deed, the system of atonement confirms it. Each sin had to be atoned for in some way for the individual to be restored to a proper status as an individual of "perfect righteousness." Any sin rendered the individual impure and out of favor before God and the community until that sin had been properly rectified. For example, CD 10.2–3 says: "No-one who has consciously transgressed anything of a precept is to be believed as a witness against his fellow, until he has been purified to return."

Even with these provisions for sin, Qumran members still expressed an intense self-awareness of sin in their hymnic material.[24] Far from finding perfect obedience a matter of due course, they struggled individually with living in a fully righteous manner before God. 1QH[a] 12(=4).29–33 laments falling short of the "perfect path" required by God. Community members looked forward to the eschaton when they would be "cleansed" of this tendency toward sin (1QS 3.21–23; 4.18–22; 11.14–15; 1QH[a] 14[=6].8–10; 7[=15].15–17).[25] So then, how could they speak so insistently of "perfect righteousness"? As Sanders underscored, such status flowed out of God's gracious and merciful relations with the elect community (e.g., 1QH[a] 12[=4].37; 15[=7].30; 19[=11].29–32).[26]

Does this emphasis in the Qumran scrolls on God's mercy and graciousness rule out a strict judgment according to works? Sanders writes:

> That the requirement for legal perfection is set within a context of gratuity is made clear when one considers a group of statements concerning reward and punishment. The reward even of perfection is said to be by God's *mercy* while the wicked receive the punishment *deserved* by them. . . . *The principal point of the punishment for deeds but reward by mercy*

Christian Sacrifice: The Judaeo-Christian Background Before Origen (Studies in Christian Antiquity 18; Washington, D.C.: Catholic University of America Press, 1978), 164–67.

[24] See Sanders, *Paul and Palestinian Judaism*, 273–84.

[25] Ibid., 279–80, 283–84, 291.

[26] Sanders himself points out the dilemma between the requirement of perfect obedience and the failure to live up to the standard (ibid., 288–90). He attempts to resolve the dilemma by arguing that the failure to live up to God's standard refers to humanity's condition *before God*. Perfection must come by means of God's grace and pardon.

> *theme is that, while man can forfeit salvation by transgressions, he can never be sufficiently deserving to earn it by obedience.*[27]

For Sanders, obedience is always the response to God's grace toward his elect.[28] While God is indeed merciful, 1QS 4.6–8 is unmistakably clear, contra Sanders, that God will reward those who are obedient in their works: "And the visitation of those who walk in it [the counsels of the spirit] will be for healing, plentiful peace in a long life, fruitful offspring with all everlasting blessings, eternal enjoyment with endless life, and a crown of glory with majestic raiment in eternal light." While God is a God of compassion and mercy, he still "pays man his wages" (1QS 10.17–18). 4QPs[f] 8.4–5 says: "[Man is examined] according to his path each one is rewar[ded according to his de]eds." 1QM 11.14 asserts: "you shall carry out justice by your truthful judgment on every son of man." 1QpHab 8.1–3 says: "Its interpretation concerns all observing the Law in the House of Judah, whom God will free from punishment on account of their deeds and of their loyalty to the Teacher of Righteousness." In other words, alongside those texts that speak of God's mercy and forgiveness of sin (even at the judgment), there are passages that adhere to a strict judgment according to the standard of works.[29] Sanders resolves the tension by subordinating the passages that speak of *all* people being judged according to their works to those passages where God judges the wicked according to works but the elect with mercy and grace (e.g., 1QH[a] 13[=5].6; 14[=6].9; 17[=9].34).[30] While many Qumran passages affirm a judgment according to mercy for the elect, such passages do not exhaust *all* the evidence. The covenanters could also affirm that God would judge all people, even those of the community, on the basis of what they had earned by their works. The two motifs must be allowed to remain in tension.[31]

---

[27] Ibid., 293.

[28] Ibid., 295–96.

[29] Sanders himself recognizes the Qumran content and cites the texts, but errs, as the next sentence says, by subordinating and minimizing passages where *all* people are judged according to their works to other passages where the elect are *not* judged by their works but by grace. Ibid., 291–94, while even citing these passages.

[30] Ibid., 294. Note that these references fall *outside* the halakah in the context of the hymnic material.

[31] As Sanders himself admits with respect to the strict demand of the halakah: "from the point of view of the *halakah,* one is required to walk perfectly. From the point of view of the individual in prayer or devotional moments, he is unable to walk perfectly and must be given the perfection of way by God's grace"

C. The Distinctiveness of the Sectarian Understanding of the Law

To "return to the Law of Moses" (1 QS 5.7–9) in entering the community was to take upon oneself not only the "revealed things" that would have been clear in Moses to everyone but also the "hidden things" that would have been clear only to the "sons of Zadok" within the sect (1QS 5.8–9). Yet these "hidden things" were not concoctions of the community's imagination. Rather, they understood this revelation as embedded and preserved in the Scriptures all along, waiting to be revealed in the days of the Qumran community.[32] Since the law, from the community's standpoint, had been fully revealed only to its members, only those within the Qumran community could fulfill the law in *all* that it required (CD 14.8; 20.29; 1QSa 1.5–7; 1QS 1.7; 4.22; 5.10–12; 6.15; 9.17–21; CD 20.11, 33). This understanding of the law as, in a certain respect, their own possession no doubt strengthened their sense of God's election. Members were to be examined on the basis of their observance of this understanding of the law (1QS 5.20–24; 6.14, 17). Anyone who

---

(ibid., 288). Unfortunately, Sanders is not consistent on this point. Elsewhere he writes:

> Commandments were given which a man was to obey. Perfect obedience was the aim, and, within the tightly ordered community structure, was not considered a totally impossible goal. Infractions were punished, and the acceptance of the punishment, together with the perseverance in obedience, led to full restoration of fellowship (ibid., 286).

Sanders tries to resolve the contradiction by distinguishing between behavior monitored *within the community,* where perfect obedience is possible, as opposed to strict obedience before God, where such perfection is not possible. The problem, though, is that the Qumran material itself does not make such a neat distinction. Perfect obedience was required of *all* the law, not just what was monitored. The devotional material shows the struggles of individuals with that requirement and the need for the grace and mercy available to members of the community; see 1QH^{a} 12(=4).37; 15(=7).18–19; 1QS 10.11; 11.2–3, 12–15; Bruce W. Longenecker, *Eschatology and Covenant: A Comparison of 4 Ezra and Romans 1–11* (JSNTSup 57; Sheffield: JSOT Press, 1991), 25. Sanders has led New Testament scholars to assume that perfect obedience of the law is possible. According to the Qumran materials, perfect obedience is *required* by the *halakah,* but it is *not* necessarily possible.

[32] This reinforced their sense of divine election (1QH^{a} 6[=14].12–13, 25–26). God had entrusted to *them* the "hidden things" of his law; Sanders, *Paul and Palestinian Judaism,* 317–18. On the distinction between the "revealed things" and the "hidden things," see also Wayne O. McCready, "A Second Torah at Qumran?" *SR* 14 (1985): 5–15.

did not observe God's law, as they understood it, would be destroyed (1QH^{a} 12[=4].26–27; CD 2.6, 19–21; 1QS 5.10–13). Consequently, those outside of the community were lost. While God had established his covenant with the people of Israel, Israel had disobeyed God's law and remained apostate. The covenanters saw themselves as the rightful heirs of Israel's heritage. They were the faithful remnant of Israel.[33]

Could it be that the emphasis on "all the law" throughout the Qumran literature was intended to refer to the legal decrees *peculiar* to the community? Was the emphasis on obeying "all the law" a way of inculcating observance of the community's own sectarian interpretations and revelations? Certainly. Yet to observe the entirety of the laws as the community interpreted them was to take on a *stricter* set of obligations than the laws of the Torah as understood by the rest of Israel. Jerome Murphy-O'Connor points out that anyone who compares CD 6.11–7.4 and its elaboration in CD 9–16 will recognize that it goes *beyond* the Holiness Code of Lev 17–26 and is even more rigorous.[34] The Qumran covenanters were responsible not only for the biblical laws but also for all the additional community rules and regulations, the "hidden matters in which all Israel had gone astray" (CD 3.13–14).[35] To be committed to "all the law" meant to accept not only the new rules of the community but also the increased difficulty that such law-observance required. It *intensified* the requirement of obedience.

III. Philo[36]

Philo, unlike the rabbis or Qumran, represents a Judaism from the soil of the Diaspora, in the midst of conscious and deliberate interaction with the philosophical trends and fashions of the Gentile world. In this

---

[33] Schnabel, *Law and Wisdom,* 175–77. The community was therefore structured along the biblical parameters for historical Israel. They were a community of priests, Levites, and Israelites (CD 3:21–4:4).

[34] Jerome Murphy-O'Connor, "The New Covenant in the Letters of Paul and the Essene Documents," in *To Touch the Text: Biblical and Related Studies in Honor of Joseph A. Fitzmyer, S. J.* (ed. Maurya P. Horgan and Paul J. Kobelski; New York: Crossroad, 1989), 199–200.

[35] The community's laws are "decisions made by God Himself and are therefore absolute and binding"; Johannes A. Huntjens, "Contrasting Notions of Covenant and Law in the Texts From Qumran," *RevQ* 8 (1974): 367; see the full discussion on pp. 366–68.

[36] All citations are from the Loeb Classical Library edition published by Harvard University Press.

pluralistic environment, Philo offers an apology for the Mosaic law. Although emerging from a very different setting, certain key motifs in Philo parallel Qumran and *Jubilees:* perfect obedience of the Mosaic law is the ideal and is to be pursued. On the other hand, when an individual fails in that obedience, there remains a larger system that involves mercy and forgiveness.

A. The Law, the Requirement of Obedience, and Perfect Obedience

The figure of Moses occupies a prominent place in Philo's writings. The Jews, led by Moses, are an elect and special people who uniquely possess the law of God.[37] In his *Life of Moses* Philo depicts Moses as the supreme lawgiver, a lawgiver who ranked far above the other great lawmakers of the world. The Jews, as followers of this tradition, are to intercede with God that the Gentiles abandon their ancestral customs to follow the laws of Moses.[38] The Gentiles would thereby be delivered from the evil to the good and thus recognize the Jewish law's universal truth and meaning for their lives. Philo's writings therefore encourage Jewish faithfulness and call the Gentiles to reconsider the law of Moses as the ultimate expression of the Creator.

While Philo reflects the philosophical soil of the Gentile world, he always subordinates those ideas to an ultimately Jewish worldview. *The law of Moses* embodies the very virtues that Stoic and Platonic thinkers valued: courage, magnanimity, and justice. Philo, however, adds to the list a fourth virtue that was not recognized among the Gentiles: repentance. He defines this virtue as the abandonment of atheism, paganism, and polytheism in favor of the God of Moses. Repentant, converted Gentiles would thus join the elect people of Israel. Philo's allegorization of the Abrahamic narratives parallels in many respects Plutarch's approach to Homer's story about Penelope and her suitors. He draws upon

---

[37] *Spec.* 1.299–300, 303; E. P. Sanders, "The Covenant As a Soteriological Category and the Nature of Salvation in Palestinian and Hellenistic Judaism," in *Jews, Greeks and Christians* (ed. Robert Hamerton-Kelly and Robin Scroggs; Leiden: E. J. Brill, 1976), 26–33.

[38] *Mos.* 2.44; thus the pattern set by Abraham in *Virt.* 212–214, 219, 221, 226. See Sanders, "The Covenant As a Soteriological Category," 29–30. Similarly, Philo can use Joseph as a model of one who "strongly disapproved" of neglecting the customs of the Hebrews (*Ios.* 202–203). Onan, on the other hand, is rebuked for abandoning Hebrew customs (*Deus* 17–18); Alan Mendelson, *Philo's Jewish Identity* (BJS 161; Atlanta: Scholars Press, 1988), 22–25.

Hellenistic tools in the service of a Jewish perspective.[39] In the biblical narrative, when Abraham does not have a child by Sarah, he turns to Hagar, his Egyptian maidservant. In Philo's interpretation, Hagar represents general education, and Sarah true philosophy. Since Hagar is an Egyptian, one must look for true philosophy among the Jews, the descendants of Sarah. The general education of the Gentiles is only preparatory for the true philosophical task, the study and observance of the Jewish law (*Congr.* 1–24).[40]

Although Philo championed an allegorical approach to exegesis, he firmly resists those who take the allegories too far and deny the literal meaning. In an often-cited passage (*Migr.* 89–93) Philo attacks those who would deny the literal meaning altogether. As he puts it, circumcision does indeed point to the denial of the passions. The Sabbath does indeed point to the Unoriginated's power and the created's need for rest. Yet that does not mean that circumcision and the Sabbath are to be abandoned once their true meaning has been recognized.[41] Even as the soul is not without the body in this life, so also the higher, spiritual meaning of the law derived through allegory must never be severed from the literal meaning. There is never the one without the other.

While Philo may interpret the law in an allegorical manner and often in terms of Hellenistic philosophy, he never denies the importance of the law's prescriptions. The law of Moses mediates true philosophy and knowledge of the eternal, uncreated God.[42] Philo therefore sought to observe the law. He journeyed to Jerusalem and sacrificed (*Prov.* 2.107 [64]). He paid the temple tax and supported the custom of "first-fruits."[43] He elaborates in his writings on the Jewish festivals and synagogue customs. Finally, he urged the Jews to maintain their identity as a witness to the Gentiles. The Gentiles need to repent and adopt the law of

---

[39] In Plutarch's allegory, Penelope's chambermaids represented general education, whereas Penelope herself represented philosophy, the true and highest knowledge of nature and the universe.

[40] For a more thorough discussion of the relationship between Judaism and Greek philosophy in Philo's thought, see John M. G. Barclay, *Jews in the Mediterranean Diaspora: From Alexander to Trajan (323 B.C.E.-117 C.E.)* (Edinburgh: T&T Clark, 1996), 163–65. Barclay concludes: "But it is also true that without his faith and his sacred text Philo would never have immersed himself so deeply in philosophy. Philo reads Plato not for his own sake but for the reflection of truths he thinks he has learnt from Moses" (p. 165).

[41] Mendelson, *Philo's Jewish Identity*, 54–62.

[42] *Virt.* 64–65; *Spec.* 1.13–31; 2.164–167.

[43] *Spec.* 1.77–178; E. P. Sanders, *Jewish Law from Jesus to the Mishnah: Five Studies* (Philadelphia: Trinity Press International, 1990), 292–99.

Moses. As Peter Tomson put it, "For Philo, observance of the Jewish Law is a prerequisite to true illumination."[44]

In chastising those who allegorized the law but did not observe its precepts, Philo's wording is significant:

> There are some who, regarding laws in their literal sense in the light of symbols of matters belonging to the intellect, are overpunctilious about the latter, while treating the former with easy-going neglect. Such men I for my part should blame for handling the matter in too easy and off-hand a manner:[45] they ought to have given careful attention to both aims, to a more full and exact investigation of what is not seen and *in what is seen* [i.e., the laws' literal sense] *to be stewards without reproach. . . .*[46] It is quite true that the seventh Day is meant to teach the power of the Unoriginate and the non-action of created beings. *But let us not for this reason abrogate the laws laid down for its observance. . . .* It is true also that the Feast is a symbol of gladness of soul and of thankfulness to God, but we should not for this reason turn our backs on the general gatherings of the year's seasons. It is true that circumcision does indeed portray the excision of pleasure and all passions . . . but let us not on this account repeal the law laid down for circumcising. . . . *so we must pay heed to the letter of the laws. . . .* (*Migr.* 89–93) [emphasis mine]

Philo encourages an observance of the law in all respects. It is not enough to recognize the inner meaning behind the law and then ignore the actual observance. Even the more difficult laws, such as circumcision and the Sabbath, which most clearly distinguished the Jews from their Hellenistic neighbors and thus involved the greatest social cost, were scrupulously to be obeyed.

In *Praem.* 79–83 (especially 79 and 82, citing Deut 30:10) Philo says that it is not enough to hear or profess the precepts; one must actually do them. Mere words apart from obedient thoughts and actions will not suffice. Individuals will be weighed in the scales (e.g., *Congr.* 164; *Her.* 46). In *Deus* 162 one must not deviate to the right or to the left from the path God has prepared for humanity in the law (*Abr.* 269; *Post.*

---

[44] Peter J. Tomson, *Paul and the Jewish Law: Halakha in the Letters of the Apostle to the Gentiles* (CRINT 3.1; Minneapolis: Fortress, 1990), 44. On the other hand, one must not go so far as to make Philo an exclusive particularist who would completely deny wisdom among the Gentiles, especially among Gentile philosophers. On this point, see Barclay, *Jews*, 171–72.

[45] τῆς εὐχερείας ("handling the matter in too easy and offhand a matter") could be translated more gravely as "licentiousness," or "tolerance of/indifference to evil" (Liddell-Scott). In neglecting the visible, literal sense of the laws, they have entered into a dangerous situation.

[46] ἀνεπιλήπτου, lit. "blameless."

101–102; cf. *Leg.* 3.165; the "middle road" of *Migr.* 146). Philo praises Abraham (*Abr.* 192) since "he had not neglected any of God's commands." One's "whole life" should be one of "happy obedience to law" (*Abr.* 5–6).[47]

In *Spec.* 4.143 Philo treats the law as an organic unity when he writes regarding the command in Deut 4:2: "Another most admirable injunction is that nothing should be added or taken away, but all the laws originally ordained should be kept unaltered just as they were." Philo continues in 4.144: "if there be any adding or taking away, its whole being is changed and transformed into the opposite condition" (see also *Legat.* 117 and *QG* 3.3). Or in 4.147: "In the same way too if one adds anything small or great, . . . or on the other hand takes something away from it, in either case he will change and transform its nature." Philo sees the law in its entirety as immutable and enjoining complete obedience.[48] It is the fulfillment of *all* that the Lawgiver has provided that gives "possession of justice whole and complete" (4.144). As Philo writes in *Spec.* 4.179: "But the Jewish nation . . . lives under exceptional laws which are necessarily grave and severe, because they inculcate the highest standard of virtue."[49]

B. *The Merciful Framework and Perfect Obedience*

What about sacrifice and atonement? What about Judaism's gracious and merciful framework? Philo mirrors what one finds elsewhere in Judaism. God "ever prefers forgiveness to punishment" (*Praem.* 166). God granted to the Jews several means by which they could rectify the situation created by sin and violation of God's law. For example, Philo never denies the literal meaning of the Day of Atonement or the sacrificial system. The repentant could offer a sacrifice at the temple to ask for the remission of sins (*Spec.* 1.235–241). The ritual sacrifice and release of a

---

[47] I take the law of nature to be coordinate with the revealed, Mosaic law. See especially *Mos.* 2.52; Naomi Cohen, "The Jewish Dimension of Philo's Judaism—An Elucidation of de Spec. Leg. IV 132–150," *JJS* 38 (1987): 169–70, and Barclay, *Jews,* 172.

[48] Cohen emphasizes the strict observance required in this passage, although she oversteps the evidence with regard to the "unwritten laws" (ἄγραφοι νόμοι) in 4.150 by including also the Jewish oral law; "The Jewish Dimension of Philo's Judaism," 174–79, 185. This phrase should rather be understood as the Jewish customs peculiar to Alexandria (with John W. Martens, "Unwritten Law in Philo: A Response to Naomi G. Cohen," *JJS* 43 [1992]: 38–45).

[49] While encouraging perfect obedience of all the law, Philo did not consider all transgressions of the law equally heinous.

second goat on the Day of Atonement both effected forgiveness and purification from sin (*Spec.* 1.188–190). A long and detailed section on the various other sacrifices for sin is found in *Spec.* 1.226–256.[50] Both involuntary and voluntary sins could be forgiven through the act of sacrifice (*Spec.* 1.235–239).

Alongside sacrifice Philo upholds several other means of availing oneself of God's forgiveness. Ritual purifications are an invitation to wash the defiled soul.[51] Even the patriarchs practiced ritual purification (e.g., *Plant.* 161–162). So also the fasts on the Day of Atonement help the Jew implore God for the pardon of his or her sins (*Spec.* 2.193, 196). Likewise, *prayer* is crucial to the process of bringing about God's forgiveness (*Abr.* 6; *Mos.* 2.24; *Spec.* 2.196; *Congr.* 107). God may even apply punishments and suffering to heal an individual from the effects of sin (*Somn.* 2.293–299; *Congr.* 158–180).

Philo emphasizes the importance of participating with one's whole being in the sacrificial system. No bodily ritual is of value without the soul's participation.[52] Philo often speaks of the spiritual/symbolic meaning of the sacrifices and washings. They point toward a changed internal state.[53] Ritual purification or sacrifice is of no avail without repentance and a proper disposition.[54]

While repentance did not figure significantly in Greek thought, Philo devotes a whole section of *On the Virtues* to repentance (175–186).[55] While the Stoics were saying that the wise person does not re-

---

[50] See Jean Laporte, "Sacrifice and Forgiveness in Philo of Alexandria," in *The Studia Philonica Annual: Studies in Hellenistic Judaism* (vol. 1, ed. David T. Runia; Atlanta: Scholars Press, 1989), 36–38.

[51] Ibid., 34–35, 40. In fact, he endorses ritual washings *beyond* those prescribed by Scripture.

[52] Valentin Nikiprowetzky explains that, while Philo allegorizes the sacrificial system, his intent is to *defend* the sacrificial system and not to set any of it aside; "La Spiritualisation des Sacrifices et le Culte Sacrificiel au Temple de Jérusalem chez Philon D'Alexandrie," *Sem* 17 (1967): 97–116: "Le judaïsme de Philon a donc un aspect conservateur qu'il est très nécessaire de bien apercevoir" (p. 114).

[53] Laporte, "Sacrifice and Forgiveness," 38–39, 42.

[54] *Det.* 20–22; *Cher.* 95–96; *Mos.* 2.106–108; *Spec.* 1.67–68, 203, 227, 235–237, 272, 290; *Plant.* 108; see Mendelson, *Philo's Jewish Identity,* 65–66.

[55] David Winston, "Philo's Doctrine of Repentance," in *The School of Moses: Studies in Philo and Hellenistic Religion* (ed. John Peter Kenney; Atlanta: Scholars Press, 1995), 29–40; Ronald Williamson, *Jews in the Hellenistic World: Philo* (Cambridge Commentaries on the Writings of the Jewish and Christian World 200 BC to AD 200 1.2; Cambridge: Cambridge University Press, 1989), 248–55. See also the excellent overview of this section of Philo in Jon Nelson

pent, Philo asserts the exact opposite, since only God can be sinless (*Fug.* 157; *Virt.* 177; *Leg.* 3.106, 211).[56] The possibility of repentance flows out of God's recognition of the human tendency to sin (*Fug.* 99, 105).[57] It is as if one is ill and repentance is the only hope for a return to health (*Fug.* 160; *Abr.* 26; *Spec.* 1.236–253). The effect of sincere repentance is as if the sin had never been (*Abr.* 19; *Spec.* 1.187–188; *QG* 1.84; *Mut.* 124; *Somn.* 1.91).[58] God bestows rewards and blessings "in honor of their victory" (*Virt.* 175). Nevertheless, those who repent still bear the scars of their misdeeds (*Spec.* 1.103).

Given the human tendency to sin, the free decision to repent must be "activated and empowered" by God (*Cher.* 2). In *Abr.* 17–18 God is said to have brought about Enoch's repentance.[59] In *Leg.* 3.213 Philo says that many desire to repent but are unable to do so because God does not permit it. Repentance must be traced ultimately to the activity of God's grace. God initiates and provides a resolution for the situation caused by disobedience of the law.

Through all these means God is manifested as merciful. The Jews, though, are the *special* object of God's compassion and pity. They have been "set apart out of the whole human race" as a first fruit to God (*Spec.* 4.180).[60] While Philo affirms Israel's special status as recipients of God's mercy and affirms repentance as a means to rectify the situation caused by sin, he nevertheless commends those whose conduct is

---

Bailey, "*Metanoia* in the Writings of Philo Judaeus," in *SBL Seminar Papers, 1991* (Atlanta: Scholars Press, 1991), 135–41. He emphasizes the connection between "repentance" at conversion and the continuing life of repentance and adherence to the Mosaic law (for instance, *Virt.* 180–183).

[56] Winston, "Philo's Doctrine of Repentance," 32; Bailey, "*Metanoia,*" 140–41.

[57] Winston, "Philo's Doctrine of Repentance," 32. In his exposition of Gen 6:3 in *QG* 1.91; 2.13, Philo explains that God gave the people at the time of the flood 120 years to repent of their sin, and then seven *more* days after Noah and his family entered the ark. Such is God's patience and forbearance.

[58] Winston, "Philo's Doctrine of Repentance," 34; Bailey, "*Metanoia,*" 140. On the necessity of sincerity, see *Fug.* 160.

[59] Bailey, "*Metanoia,*" 138.

[60] Yet God's mercy and compassion have limits. Those who act freely in wickedness will receive their due punishment, since their actions "do not deserve compassion, far from it, but anger" (*Spec.* 4.76–77). When Phinehas saw his fellow Israelites flagrantly breaking the covenant, he urged the rest to take up the sword against the evildoers. They showed the evildoers no mercy or pity as they meted out justice (*Mos.* 1.302–303). Mercy and compassion within the realm of God's special dealings with Israel do not obtain apart from the intent to obey the law; Dorothy Sly, "Philo's Practical Application of Δικαιοσύνη," in *SBL Seminar Papers, 1991* (Atlanta: Scholars Press, 1991), 304.

perfect. Those who remain sinless and unblemished are superior to those who must repent and so be healed of their illness (*Abr.* 26; *Virt.* 176). Abraham achieved perfect obedience of the law (*Migr.* 127–130; *Abr.* 275–276; *Her.* 6–9).[61] Noah was "perfect" in virtue (*Deus* 117, 122, 140; *Abr.* 34, 47). In the case of Noah, however, Philo immediately qualifies the attribution of perfection (*Abr.* 36–39). Noah attained a perfection relative to his generation; he was "not good absolutely" (οὐ καθάπαξ). Philo contrasts Noah's "perfection" with other sages who possessed an "unchallenged" and "unperverted" virtue. Noah therefore won the "second prize." Although Noah is to be praised for his achievement, Philo clearly commends to his reader the "first prize" of an unqualified virtue. Moses, for instance, fell into that highest category. The Lawgiver exemplifies the attainment of the highest place of all (*Mos.* 1.162; 2.1, 8–11; *Leg.* 3.134, 140; *Ebr.* 94; *Sacr.* 8). Philo commends Moses as a model toward which his readers are to strive (*Mos.* 1.158–159).[62] Such exemplars show that perfect obedience and sinlessness remain the ideal for Philo.

Philo's ideal stands in stark contrast to his evaluation of the human ability to refrain from sin (e.g., *Mut.* 48–50, quoting Job 14:4; *Mos.* 2.147; *Agr.* 174–180). In one place at least, Philo denies that any individual can avoid sin, *including* Moses. Sinlessness is a characteristic only of God (*Virt.* 176–177 [or also the divine man]; *Fug.* 157; *Spec.* 1.252). Hilgert concludes from this that Philo is not serious about the sinless "divine man." The vast chasm between the Creator and the creature eliminates the possibility that any of Israel's heroes could be sinless.[63] Hilgert must

---

[61] The passage from *Quis rerum divinarum heres sit* is representative both as an admonition to strive toward perfect obedience as well as an expression of Abraham's attainment of that goal:

> When, then, is it that the servant speaks frankly to his master? Surely it is when his heart tells him that he has not wronged his owner, but that his words and deeds are *all* [πάντα] for that owner's benefit. And so when else should the slave of God open his mouth freely to Him Who is the ruler and master both of himself and of the All, *save when he is pure from sin* and the judgements of his conscience are loyal to his master. . . . The loyalty of Abraham's service and ministry is shewn by the concluding words of the oracle addressed to Abraham's son, ". . . Abraham thy father hearkened to My voice and kept My injunctions, My commands, My ordinances and My statutes" (Gen. xxvi. 3–5). It is the highest praise which can be given to a servant that *he neglects none* [μηδενός] *of his master's commands*. . . . [emphasis mine]

[62] Larry W. Hurtado, *One God, One Lord: Early Christian Devotion and Ancient Jewish Monotheism* (2d ed; Edinburgh: T&T Clark, 1998), 61–63.

[63] Earle Hilgert, "A Review of Previous Research on Philo's *De Virtutibus*," in *SBL Seminar Papers, 1991* (Atlanta: Scholars Press, 1991), 114, following Holladay.

therefore explain away those people Philo identifies as having been "perfect," people who have never disobeyed a single one of God's commands. A better approach is that of Ronald Williamson. For Williamson, Moses, Abraham, and others were indeed perfect and fully observant of the law. Given the human tendency to sin, their perfect lives must have been the gracious gift of a God in whom there is such perfection (*Leg.* 3.131–135; *Her.* 120–122).[64] While those who receive such perfection from God are relatively few and exceptional, they remain the ideal toward which all people are to strive.[65]

Philo thus maintains that the Jews, as an elect people, are to strive to live as virtuously and as perfectly as possible. He admits that this is very difficult. Even Enoch and Enosh were not able to live perfectly and without sin. God, on the other hand, remains a merciful God who recognizes humanity's difficulty with sin and offers abundant grace and mercy to the repentant.[66] While the emphasis in Philo is certainly upon mercy and forgiveness of sin, the law still enjoins a perfect obedience toward which all people should strive.

IV. The Tannaim

The authors of the apocalyptic literature written in the immediate aftermath of the destruction of the temple in 70 C.E. were still reeling from the lost war against the Romans.[67] By the time of the Mishnah the Jews had recovered their composure. They had begun to sift through their traditions and to understand themselves in continuity with that history. Although the temple had been destroyed, the Tannaim wanted to codify for posterity the practices and oral traditions associated with worship in the heart of Jewish space prior to its destruction. The Mishnah therefore offers a vision of the temple and nation. The rabbis viewed their day as a time of transition to that imminent, inevitable restoration of temple-centered

---

[64] As Williamson put it: "Philo did not regard the divine sinlessness, however, as incommunicable to mortal man" (p. 215). God out of free grace chooses to bestow on certain rare individuals such sinlessness and perfection (*Leg.* 3.77–79, 85, 88–89). To these exceptional individuals, there would be no need for repentance (*Virt.* 177). For the rest of humanity, on the other hand, sin remains "congenital" (*Mos.* 2.147). See the full discussion in Williamson, *Jews*, 204–7.

[65] Ibid., 205–6. There is no room in Philo for a legalistic understanding of such perfection and obedience. See, for example, *Leg.* 3.78.

[66] In *Praem.* 166–167 God prefers forgiveness to punishment. In *QG* 4.180 God judges in accordance with *our* nature and not according to the divine; Williamson, *Jews*, 37–38.

[67] See Chapter 2.

piety. Tractate *Sanhedrin* of the Mishnah carefully describes the casting of lots by priests for the performance of sacrifice and the various chambers of the temple (e.g., the wood chamber, the wheel chamber, the hewn-stone chamber). Tractate *Yoma* revolves exclusively around the temple cultus (ignoring the actual synagogue practices of its time). Tractate *Qinnim* attempts to solve the mathematical issues of the bird-sacrifices: Maccoby notes that "to study such a tractate was an academic exercise, but one which focused the mind on the messianic hope, for with the restoration of the temple these problems would become practical."[68] The Tannaim struggled to find ways to fulfill the laws regarding the temple in its temporary absence. In other words, Tannaitic Judaism's conscious return to and idealization of the situation prior to the temple's fall shared with the Second Temple period a belief in the temple's efficacy for mediating God's presence among the people. The grace and atonement that had been bound up with temple practice were still available to the people. The literature of the Tannaim therefore exhibits a continuity with the Second Temple period in affirming God's election and mercy toward Israel.

A. Rigorous and/or Perfect Obedience in the Tannaim

Several Tannaitic passages call into question Sanders's denial that the rabbis saw the law as requiring perfect obedience. For example, the rabbis spoke of the seriousness of failure to obey even one *mitzvah*. Likewise, the obedience of one command brings a reward (e.g., *m. Qidd.* 1:10a).[69] Sanders interprets these sayings as hortatory: "If God denies the land to one who transgresses, avoid transgression!"[70] Because the rabbis wanted to encourage obedience, they insisted that each command be given its proper due. But the Tosefta, elaborating on *m. Qidd.* 1:10a,

---

[68] Hyam Maccoby, *Early Rabbinic Writings* (Cambridge Commentaries on the Writings of the Jewish and Christian World 200 BC to AD 200 3; Cambridge: Cambridge University Press, 1988), 33. Lawrence H. Schiffman agrees: "[The Mishnah] was edited in an atmosphere in which the restoration of a Temple-centered reality was still a living hope, and in which the conception of sanctity still flowed from that reality, even in its absence" (*From Text to Tradition: A History of Second Temple and Rabbinic Judaism* [Hoboken, N.J.: Ktav, 1991], 194); see also Shaye J. D. Cohen, *From the Maccabees to the Mishnah* (LEC 7; Philadelphia: Westminster, 1987), 219. On the adaptation of the temple laws to a reality without the temple, see Sanders, *Paul and Palestinian Judaism*, 109, 163–64.

[69] Also *m. Mak.* 3:15. Schechter (*Aspects of Rabbinic Theology*, 164–65) takes the positive element to mean that the perfect fulfillment of one commandment would bring about salvation. Similarly Moore, *Judaism*, 1:391.

[70] Sanders, *Paul and Palestinian Judaism*, 129; so also pp. 119–20.

explains that individuals are judged according to a majority of deeds. Thus one should always consider oneself half innocent and half guilty. Every sin, then, has the potential to "destroy much good" (*t. Qidd.* 1.13–15). Far from interpreting *m. Qidd.* 1:10a as merely hortatory, the Tosefta indicates that God's judgment will be based upon whether the balance of one's deeds is good or evil. Later Amoraic rabbis followed the Tosefta and understood *m. Qidd.* 1:10 and *t. Qidd.* 1.13–15 as indicating that God would judge every individual's deeds on a scale.[71]

Sanders points to other passages in the Tosefta where a single virtuous or heinous act at the end of one's life could decisively alter the significance of all that had preceded. Sanders contends that when these passages are placed alongside those passages in the Tosefta indicating judgment according to the weight of one's deeds, the former *exclude* the weighing of deeds in the latter.[72] On the contrary, when both sets of passages are placed alongside each other, two very different Tannaitic theories of judgment emerge. Some rabbis simply held that one would be judged on the basis of a majority of deeds, while others thought that a person's whole fate could be determined by his or her last actions quite apart from such a balance of deeds.

In *m. ᵓAbot* 3:16 Rabbi Akiba asserts: "All is foreseen, but freedom of choice is given; and the world is judged by grace, yet all is according to the majority of works [that be good or evil]."[73] Like the Tosefta text, this passage also contradicts Sanders's assertion that rabbinic soteriology did not view one's place in the world to come as based on the counting or weighing of deeds.[74] Sanders's response is that this passage cannot be asserting a judgment according to the majority of works since that would be contrary to Akiba's statement in *b. Sanh.* 81a:

> When R. Gamaliel read this verse he wept, saying, "Only he who does all these things shall live, but not merely one of them!" Thereupon R. Akiba said to him, "If so, *Defile not yourselves in all these things* [Lev. 18.24].—is the prohibition against *all* [combined] only, but not against one?" [Surely not!] But it means, *in one* of these things; so here too, for doing one of these things [shall he live].[75]

---

[71] Ibid., 131; *b. Qidd.* 39b.

[72] Sanders, *Paul and Palestinian Judaism,* 130–31; so also Schechter, *Aspects of Rabbinic Theology,* 306 n. 4.

[73] As cited in Sanders, *Paul and Palestinian Judaism,* 132. I am deliberately using Sanders's translation here.

[74] Ibid., 146; Sanders openly admits: "It is true that there are some sayings which do indicate that God judges strictly according to the majority of a man's deeds" (p. 143). But Sanders claims that this is not a rabbinic doctrine.

[75] As cited in ibid., 139.

Akiba's reply, according to Sanders, denies strict judgment in favor of God's judging a person righteous by *merely one good work!* Sanders admits that *m. ʾAbot* 3:16 says that one is judged according to a majority of works. He circumvents the passage by juxtaposing a second passage from the Babylonian Talmud that seems to indicate that even one righteous work can bring about life. However, *m. ʾAbot* 3:16 is not so easily dismissed. Actually, judgment according to the weighing of one's works is a major motif that runs all through *m. ʾAbot.* In *m. ʾAbot* 2:1 Judah the Prince speaks of "a seeing eye and a hearing ear and all thy deeds written in a book."[76] In *m. ʾAbot* 4:11 Akiba's student, Eliezer ben Jacob, says that those who perform one precept receive one advocate, but one sin brings about one accuser. Further, repentance and good works are a "shield" against retribution. One must repent and multiply good works in order to cancel out the accusations. This is the language of the courtroom in the presence of the eternal judge.[77] Finally, Akiba further explicates his own comment in 3:16 when he likens God's judgment in 3:17 to a shopkeeper who offers credit and keeps his account-book open. While one may borrow against the books, payment is still required. This illustration of a shopkeeper's credits and debits serves to explain the remarks in 3:16. Even as 3:16 spoke of a judgment based on a majority of deeds, 3:17 speaks of an account-book.

The saying in *m. ʾAbot* 3:16 may pose more problems for Sanders than he recognizes.[78] The words "all is foreseen, but freedom of choice is given" present two ideas that appear contradictory and yet are both correct. God's sovereignty and human freedom of choice stand

---

[76] By context this refers to reward and loss. Further, *m. ʾAbot* 2:1 urges people to "be heedful of a light precept as of a weighty one" (see also *m. ʾAbot* 4:2). Since one does not know what reward each fulfillment brings or what loss a transgression brings, in light of the careful divine record keeping, one should obey *all* the commands. This is an excellent example where obedience of the law flows out of the awareness of God's strict judgment and not as a response to election. One might also point to *Sipre Num.* 115 (to 15:41): "Why has God given us commandments? Is it not in order that we should keep them and receive a reward?" (Paul P. Levertoff, trans., *Midrash Sifre on Numbers: Selections from Early Rabbinic Scriptural Interpretations* [London: SPCK, 1926], 110–11). Rabbi Hananiah b. Akashya (c. 150) says in his midrash on Isa 42:21 (*m. ʾAbot* 6:11 and *m. Mak.* 3:16): "The Holy One, blessed is he, was minded to grant merit to Israel; therefore hath he multiplied for them the Law and commandments." The motivation for observance of the law in these instances is the recognition of God's strict coming judgment.

[77] Charles L. Quarles, "The Soteriology of R. Akiba and E. P. Sanders' *Paul and Palestinian Judaism*," *NTS* 42 (1996): 190.

[78] Quarles, "Soteriology," 185–95.

alongside each other in a paradoxical relationship. Not surprisingly, the next statement also expresses a paradoxical relationship: "And the world is judged by grace, yet all is according to the excess of works." Divine grace stands in tension with God's judgment according to a majority of works. The problem with this understanding is that the word טוב translated as "grace" is used elsewhere in the ᵓ*Abot* tractate as "good," "good" in the sense of "righteousness" (or "justice") rather than "grace."[79] If one translates טוב as "good" (in the sense of "righteousness"), the passage would neatly correspond to the emphasis on God's righteous judgment elsewhere throughout the ᵓ*Abot* tractate (*m.* ᵓ*Abot* 3:11; 4:22). Akiba's own clarification of the term in *m.* ᵓ*Abot* 3:17 calls the "judgment" in 3:16 a "judgment of truth" (דִין אֱמֶת), thereby eliminating the notion of "grace" from contention. Both *m.* ᵓ*Abot* 3:16 and 17 are indicating that God's judgment is *just.* It is God's fair and just judgment (and not his grace) that is being contrasted with a judgment according to a majority of deeds. The contrast in *m.* ᵓ*Abot* 3.16 is between a strict divine justice that demands perfect obedience and a more tolerant judgment permitting a minority of sins in the balance.

Would this reading of *m.* ᵓ*Abot* 3:16 conflict with *b. Sanh.* 81a? In the latter Akiba and Gamaliel were discussing Ezek 18:5–9. Gamaliel read the thirteen moral commands in the biblical text and wept, supposing that only those who do "*all* these things shall live, but not merely one of them."[80] Akiba responded on the basis of Lev 18:24 that "defile not yourselves in all these things" does not refer to all these things combined but against one individually. According to Akiba, by doing one of these things [he shall live]. Sanders takes Akiba's response to mean that there is no judgment according to a majority of works; a single good deed is

---

[79] See *m.* ᵓ*Abot* 1:17; 2:29 (the "right way" as opposed to the evil way); 3:12, 15; 4:11 ("good" deeds that avert punishment), 17. In *m.* ᵓ*Abot* 5:1 the word is used for a "good" reward in the sense of "pleasant" or "precious." Yet even here the word cannot mean "grace" since it is a reward to the righteous. In *m.* ᵓ*Abot* 3:18 (quoting Jer 17:6), where the word indicates the notion of "prosperity." Never is the word used for "grace." Ibid., 187–89.

Antecedents for טוב in the sense of "fair" or "just" may extend back to the Elephantine Papyri. Yochanon Muffs has found the word used in a commercial phrase that a transaction has been fair or satisfactory. The seller is "satisfied" with the payment; *Studies in the Aramaic Legal Papyri from Elephantine* (Studia et Documenta ad Iura Orientis Antiqui Pertinentia 8; New York: Ktav, 1973).

[80] In *b. Mak.* 24a Gamaliel again bursts into tears when he reads the word "all" with respect to the 613 requirements of the law. His opponents, on the other hand, focused on one decisive fulfillment.

sufficient to live. In light of *m. ᵓAbot* 3:16, however, Akiba's response was more likely an assertion of judgment according to a majority of deeds, in which one deed could tip the scales in favor of life or death.[81] Whereas Gamaliel lamented the need for absolute perfection, Akiba took the approach that God's judgment, based on divine justice and goodness, is paradoxically compatible with a judgment according to the lesser standard of a majority of deeds. If correct, all the Tannaitic statements about one deed bringing either punishment or reward would not be merely paranetic, as Sanders claims.[82] They would show that the rabbis often thought God would judge according to a system weighing fulfillments against transgressions. A single action, for good or ill, could decisively shift the balance of one's deeds. The plethora of Amoraic statements on weighing deeds shows that the Amoraim followed Akiba on this point.[83] God's judgment on the basis of a majority of works stood, for the rabbis, in paradoxical tension *not* with mercy but with justice, a divine justice that requires strict, perfect obedience of the law. Obedience results in life, and disobedience brings about death. In the words of *m. 'Abot* 4:22: "everything is according to reckoning."

To summarize, the Tannaim held differing positions on how God would judge humanity. In some instances, they saw the law as requiring strict and perfect obedience, as Gamaliel did. In other instances, they saw God judging people on the basis of a majority of deeds, as Akiba did. Thus one should act as if every single deed could be the deciding factor on the scales of God's judgment. Sanders has written: "Human perfection was not considered realistically achievable by the Rabbis, nor was it required."[84] While most of the rabbis sided with Akiba that God does not judge strictly, *m. ᵓAbot* 3:16 shows that the rabbis *did* at times assert that God's justice requires perfect obedience.[85]

---

[81] Quarles, "Soteriology," 194. This is therefore an example of the school of Hillel adopting the "weighing" model of judgment, contra Sanders, *Paul and Palestinian Judaism,* 138 n. 61.

[82] Sanders, *Paul and Palestinian Judaism,* 141.

[83] Contra ibid., 131–32, 138.

[84] Ibid., 137.

[85] For a Jewish perspective on the "divine imperative" to do what God commands, see Gersion Appel, *A Philosophy of Mitzvot': The Religious-Ethical Concepts of Judaism, Their Roots in Biblical Law and The Oral Tradition* (New York: Ktav, 1975), 165–69. He emphasizes the obligatory nature of *all* God has commanded as an important facet of the historic Jewish perspective on the Torah (with particular emphasis on the Sefer ha-Hinnuk).

B. God's Grace and Mercy as a Mitigating Factor

If the Jews were to strive toward perfect (or a majority) fulfillment of the law, how does one account for the factors Sanders identified that indicate otherwise? For instance, the rabbis often lessened the difficulty of observing the law. They emphasized the *intent* to obey the commands. To intend to obey the command was often as important as the performance itself.[86] Yet the rabbis' emphasis on intention was never at the expense of actually fulfilling the intention. One must still strive to *do* the command and not just intend to fulfill it.[87] Thus it is a sin whenever any of the law's requirements, no matter how minor, are violated. "In their [the rabbis'] view, God had given all the commandments, and they were all to be obeyed alike. It would be presumptuous of man to determine that some should be neglected."[88] Even when the law was summarized under a few basic principles or even a *single* principle (e.g., love), the rabbis did not see the principle eliminating the need to do all of the law's commands.[89] The Tannaim also made many of the biblical commands more accessible to their contemporaries. After the destruction of the temple in 70 C.E., the temple sacrifices were no longer available. The rabbis substituted the intention of sacrificing for the sacrifice itself. One expressed this intention by substituting the study of the temple laws for the sacrifices themselves.[90] The rabbis never eliminated any of the law's commands but struggled to find ways to do what the law required in a new, contemporary setting.

One might conclude that perfect fulfillment of the law was not necessary in Tannaitic Judaism given the possibility of repentance, atonement, and sacrifice. In fact, the reverse is true. The entire system of repentance, atonement, and sacrifice was designed to rectify the situation caused by disobedience of any of God's laws and commands. The very existence of this system shows that the rabbis saw God's law as demanding perfect obedience. Failure in any respect had to be rectified and accounted for before God. Therefore, one must always strive to obey the law perfectly. Even though an individual may not fulfill the law perfectly, he or she is not free to desist from trying (R. Tarfon, *m. ʾAbot* 2:16).[91]

---

[86] Sanders, *Paul and Palestinian Judaism,* 107–9; Montefiore and Loewe, *A Rabbinic Anthology,* 272.

[87] Sanders, *Paul and Palestinian Judaism,* 109.

[88] Ibid., 112.

[89] Ibid., 114.

[90] Ibid., 109.

[91] Ibid., 176 n. 147. "Covenantal nomism" always involves a "nomism." In Tannaitic thought, the election of Israel entailed the summons to fulfill God's

Sanders often writes that the halakah does not require perfect obedience.[92] This, in my opinion, confuses the matter. The halakah always demands strict obedience. The rabbis themselves admit the difficulty of being able to do what the law requires.[93] It is the broader context of election, covenant, and the provisions for failure in atonement and sacrifice that allow for grace to prevail. While sinful people are indeed saved on the basis of God's grace and mercy, it is characteristic of Tannaitic thought that the legal demand for strict obedience still remains. The practical result of this unresolved logical tension is surely that individuals are granted a share in the world to come even when their obedience is far less than perfect. Yet the merciful provision for failure never detracts from the strict demand, even when that demand has not been realized in actual conduct.[94]

One ought not minimize halakic statements on the necessity to observe all that the law commands. God will reward good deeds and punish any violations of his law. "For one cannot obtain rewards except for deeds."[95] Sanders notes the tendency to interpret blessings as rewards

---

law and commandments (ibid., 85–86, 92–97, 99). On the importance of covenant stipulations following the establishment of a covenantal relationship in ancient suzerainty treaties, see Jon D. Levenson, "Covenant and Commandment," *Tradition* 21 (1983): 42–51. In other words, God's action on behalf of Israel and the covenant relationship *precedes* the commandments. Nevertheless, upon entry into the covenant relationship the covenant stipulations were strictly to be obeyed.

[92] For example, Sanders claims that the rabbis "consistently passed up opportunities to require legal perfection" (*Paul and Palestinian Judaism*, 138). Yet they could speak of being "completely righteous"; Montefiore and Loewe, *A Rabbinic Anthology*, 307.

[93] Sanders rightly admits: "the biblical commandments, while not necessarily more difficult to fulfil than the laws of some other societies, are nevertheless difficult or even impossible fully to obey" (ibid., 115). Elsewhere Sanders adds: "Although the term 'righteous' is primarily applied to those who obey the Torah, the Rabbis knew full well that even the righteous did not obey God's law perfectly" (p. 203).

[94] The apparent contradiction is resolved when one keeps the strict demands of the law conceptually distinct from the larger framework of God's mercy and election of Israel. The rabbis can therefore speak of how rare it is for anyone to obey God's law perfectly, that is, the commands of the law considered strictly in themselves. Yet perfect righteousness and blamelessness is quite achievable when one includes the possibility of God's forgiveness, sacrifice, and atonement. But this is not the same as actually accomplishing all that the law requires.

[95] *Mek. Pisha* 5 (to 12:6; Lauterbach, 1:34); Sanders, *Paul and Palestinian Judaism*, 117. Jacob Z. Lauterbach's text of the *Mekilta de-Rabbi Ishmael* (3 vols; Philadelphia: Jewish Publication Society of America, 1933–1935) is cited by volume and page number.

for accomplishments, even minor accomplishments.[96] Like Jesus, the rabbis narrate a parable of laborers who worked for varying lengths of time, but unlike Jesus' parable, the rabbinic moral is quite different. Those who worked longer receive a greater reward than those who worked less.[97] Sanders cautions that this doctrine of "measure for measure" recompense is counterbalanced by statements to the effect that one "light" command merits a great reward.[98] Further, God's quality of rewarding is greater than his quality of punishing.[99] Such affirmations of grace, contra Sanders, do not eliminate assertions of strict judgment. The former simply emphasize the gracious and merciful aspects of the irresolvable tension.[100]

C. The Tension between Deserving Obedience and Undeserved Mercy in the Tannaitic View of Election

In covenantal nomism, the nomism of the law's observance is embedded within the gracious framework of God's election and covenant. God's election and relationship with Israel guarantees that "all Israelites have a share in the world to come." The doing of the law takes place in the framework of grace and thanksgiving for God's provision. Yet one sees

---

[96] Sanders, *Paul and Palestinian Judaism,* 117.

[97] *Sipra Behuqotai* pereq 2 (to 26:9; Neusner, 3:354); Sanders, *Paul and Palestinian Judaism,* 118. The references to Jacob Neusner in parentheses on Sipra citations include the volume and page number from *Sifra: An Analytical Translation* (3 vols.; BJS 138–140; Atlanta: Scholars Press, 1988).

[98] Sanders, *Paul and Palestinian Judaism,* 119.

[99] *Sipra Vayyiqra Dibura Dehobah* parasha 12.10 (to 5:17; Neusner, *Sifra,* 1:327); Sanders, *Paul and Palestinian Judaism,* 123.

[100] Sanders, *Paul and Palestinian Judaism,* 124. It is precisely the gracious framework of election and the provision of atonement for failure that prevents the observance of the law from degenerating into legalism or sheer despair in the face of God's strict demands. The rabbis could therefore be optimistic about the number of Israelites with a share in the world to come. As *m. Sanh.* 10:1 says: "*All Israelites* have a share in the world to come." The passage then goes on to list those who were excluded: those who deny the resurrection of the dead, Epicureans, and those who deny that the law is from heaven. Akiba adds a few more: the wilderness generation, the ten spies, the flood generation, those who read heretical books, Jeroboam, Ahab, and Manasseh (though some rabbis dispute this, since Manasseh repented), Korah, Doeg, Ahithophel, and Gehazi. In sum, such a list shows that the vast majority of Israel is *included* in salvation. Only the most egregious of sinners forfeited their covenant membership and salvation in Israel; Sanders, *Paul and Palestinian Judaism,* 147–57. As George Foot Moore puts it: "There is no indication that pious Jews were afflicted with an inordinate preoccupation about their individual hereafter" (*Judaism,* 2:321).

the same tension between deserved reward and undeserved grace even with the gracious framework of covenantal nomism, particularly in the Tannaitic understanding of how Israel and proselytes "get in" to this special relationship with God.

The Tannaitic rationale for God's election of Israel was varied and veered in either of two directions. Either the Israelites warranted God's election on the basis of their own prior choice or obedience of God, or God's election was for his own name's sake (in view of the "merit" of the Fathers). The first approach traced God's election to the action of the Israelites themselves. Some Tannaim argued that Israel chose to accept God's commandments while the other nations did not. The descendants of Esau saw the command "Do not kill" and realized that they could not fulfill the law. Other nations could not even abide by the seven laws of Noah, let alone the laws of Mount Sinai.[101] God had given the law at Mount Sinai so that all the nations would have an opportunity to accept it. Only Israel actually did.[102] According to another Tannaitic rationale, God recognized that Israel was hard pressed for the necessary works to warrant divine election. God therefore gave the Israelites the command to obtain the paschal lamb four days prior to the first Passover in order that by this act they might display their obedience and so merit the exodus.[103] Alternatively, the Tannaim rationalized that the exodus was based on Israel's prior faith.[104] Sanders points out that the giving of the law at Mount Sinai, like the covenant to Abraham, was an unconditional covenant.[105] Still another rationalization revolved around God's election of the patriarchs. Sanders emphasizes the point that the "merit" (זְכוּת *[zekût]*) of the Fathers was traditionally misunderstood by those of the Weberian school as transferable. The "merit" of the Fathers is better translated as "for the sake of" or "by virtue of" the Fathers. זְכוּת *(zekût)*, when prefaced by the preposition ב *(bêt)*, never means "merit."

---

[101] Sanders, *Paul and Palestinian Judaism*, 88.

[102] *Mek. Bahodesh* 1 (to 19:2b; Lauterbach, *Mekilta de-Rabbi Ishmael*, 2:198–200); Sanders, *Paul and Palestininan Judaism*, 88–89.

[103] *Mek. Pisha* 5 (to 12:6; Lauterbach, *Mekilta de-Rabbi Ishmael*, 1:33–34); Sanders, *Paul and Palestinian Judaism*, 89.

[104] *Mek. Beshallah* 7 (to 14:31; Lauterbach, *Mekilta de-Rabbi Ishmael*, 1:253); Sanders, *Paul and Palestinian Judaism*, 89. Sanders (pp. 92–94) corrects misimpressions of the Tannaim's view that Israel was elected "on condition of" their future obedience. Israel did not earn their election by their future obedience, but rather the condition of their election was that they intended to adhere to the commands.

[105] Sanders, *Paul and Palestinian Judaism*, 94–95, 97. Israel's disobedience may bring about rebuke but did not set aside the Mosaic covenant. "On condition of" future obedience meant that the Israelites intended to obey it.

When *zᵉkût* (without the preposition) is used for "merit," the subject is always an earthly reward and never soteriological. The verb זָכָה *(zākâ)* often means "to act correctly" with no sense of a treasury of merits. God simply chose Israel "for the sake of" or "in view of" his promise and oath to the patriarchs.[106] The same would apply to God's election of Israel "for his name's sake."[107] Of course, the problem with this Tannaitic explanation of an election based on the patriarchs is that it only removes the issue of election one step back.[108] The question remains why the patriarchs were chosen and not others. The Tannaitic response is often that God chose the patriarchs on the basis of their own obedience or willful choice. That is why they were chosen and not others.[109]

Sanders emphasizes that these Tannaitic interpretations of Israel's election are not meant to be systematic theology. The rabbis simply wanted to defend God from seeming "capricious or arbitrary."[110] Still, such statements show that there was a genuine tension within Judaism between God's election as an act of grace and mercy, and God's election in response to human obedience and choice. Thus the rabbis could hold that "one cannot obtain rewards except for deeds" while at the same time saying "Thou hast shown us mercy, for we had no meritorious deeds."[111]

The rationale behind Israel's election is more than mere theory or an attempt to explain away God's apparent capriciousness. The same

---

[106] Sanders is following earlier scholars such as Moore, *Judaism*, 3:164; and Montefiore and Loewe, *A Rabbinic Anthology*, 221.

[107] Sanders, *Paul and Palestinian Judaism*, 90–92, 183–98; see the differing approach of Schechter, *Aspects of Rabbinic Theology*, 170–98, who takes the term to refer to a sort of imputed righteousness, although such a righteousness cannot save apart from God's grace and individual responsibility within the covenant.

[108] As Sanders himself points out (*Paul and Palestinian Judaism*, 100).

[109] See T. R. Schreiner, *The Law and Its Fulfillment*, 117–18.

[110] Sanders, *Paul and Palestinian Judaism*, 87.

[111] On the former: *Mek. Pisha* 5 (to 12:6; Lauterbach, *Mekilta de-Rabbi Ishmael*, 1:34); see also *Sipre Deut* 170 (to 18:9; Hammer, 199); 297 (to 26:1; Hammer, 287); Sanders, *Paul and Palestinian Judaism*, 89–90. The English translation cited here is Reuven Hammer's *Sifre: A Tannaitic Commentary on the Book of Deuteronomy* (Yale Judaica Series 24; New Haven: Yale University Press, 1986). On the latter: *Mek. Shirata* 9 (to 15:13; Lauterbach, *Mekilta de-Rabbi Ishmael*, 2:69); Sanders, *Paul and Palestinian Judaism*, 86, 90. One was to obey the commands "for their own sake" in view of God's election and not out of an attitude of works-righteousness or to gain a reward (*m. ᵓAbot.* 1:3; 2:12; Sanders, *Paul and Palestinian Judaism*, 120–12; Moore, *Judaism*, 2:95–100; Schechter, *Aspects of Rabbinic Theology*, 162; Montefiore and Loewe, *A Rabbinic Anthology*, 276–79).

tension manifests itself in the handling of proselytes. The Jews "get in" (as Sanders phrases it) simply by their birth or circumcision into the covenant people.[112] While "getting in" is a matter of birth and circumcision, it also involves a conscious acceptance of Israel's election and the commandments.[113] The Gentile too "gets in" by accepting the Torah.[114] Incidentally, proselytes are to obey *every single aspect* of the law.[115] The law's requirements for the proselyte are no different from those for the rest of Israel.

At times, the Tannaim see election and covenant as due to God's gracious mercy upon undeserving Israel. At other times, election and covenant are due to Israel's merit and obedience. Surely such ambiguity

---

[112] Sanders, *Paul and Palestinian Judaism,* 206–7. Elsewhere Sanders writes: "when the Rabbis did discuss how one gets in, they saw it in terms of accepting the election and the commandments" ("Puzzling Out Rabbinic Judaism," in *Approaches to Ancient Judaism* [ed. William Scott Green; 5 vols.; Chico, Calif.: Scholars Press, 1978–1985], 2:67–68).

[113] *Sipra Nedabah* parasha 2 (to 1:2; Neusner, *Sifra,* 1:78); Sanders, *Paul and Palestinian Judaism,* 84–86, 206–7, 211, 270.

[114] Sanders, *Paul and Palestinian Judaism,* 85–86, 206–7; that is, when the rabbis allowed for Gentiles in the world to come. Rabbi Eliezar said that no Gentile could be saved. From a rabbinic standpoint Gentile converts reenact Israel's initial acceptance of the covenant relationship at Sinai; Lawrence H. Schiffman, "The Rabbinic Understanding of Covenant," *RevExp* 84 (1987): 294. It is unfortunate that Sanders did not investigate more thoroughly the issue of "getting in." Timo Laato notes that entry into Judaism did indeed involve human activity; it was not a matter strictly of God's grace; *Paul and Judaism: An Anthropological Approach* (trans. T. McElwain; South Florida Studies in the History of Judaism 115; Atlanta: Scholars Press, 1995), 58–59. Likewise, "staying in" entails human obedience and is not entirely a matter of God's grace.

[115] In *t. Demai* 2.4 it says: "A proselyte ["a gentile"] who took upon himself all the obligations of the Torah and is suspected with regard to one item, even with regard to all [the obligations of] the Torah, behold, he is [deemed to be] like an apostate Israelite." *Tosefta Demai* 2.5 continues: "A proselyte who took upon himself all the obligations of the Torah except for one item—they do not accept him"; Jacob Neusner and Richard S. Sarason, eds., *The Tosefta* (6 vols.; Hoboken, N.J.: Ktav, 1977–1986), 1:82–83. The Tosefta is followed on this point by *Sipra Qedoshim* pereq 8 (to 19:32–33; Neusner, *Sifra,* 3:128) and *b. Šabb.* 31a; Alan F. Segal, *Paul the Convert: The Apostolate and Apostasy of Saul the Pharisee* (New Haven: Yale University Press, 1990), 119–20. Thus Eleazar corrected Ananias's proselytizing of the royal house of Adiabene; Izates also had to be circumcised; Segal, *Paul the Convert,* 99–102. See Sanders, *Paul and Palestinian Judaism,* 138 n. 61, 206; the proselyte is to "accept" all the laws, but to accept them all implies that there is an obligation toward all the commandments, and one will try to accomplish them. On the dating of these precepts to the Second Temple period, see Tomson, *Paul,* 88–89, 89 n. 134.

affects how one views obedience to the law *within* the system. At times, all reward is based on strict observance of the law. At other times, God is merciful and gracious, and the covenant is given gratuitously to an unworthy people. The unreconcilable logical tension must be allowed to stand.[116]

V. Conclusion

While upholding the law as a marker of Jewish ethnic identity, *Jubilees* commends Noah, Abraham, and others for their perfect obedience of the law. Philo too speaks of certain "perfect" individuals. The law, for Philo, was an immutable whole; to add or detract from it would ruin its perfection, a perfection to be mirrored in the lives of God's people. Similarly, the language of "perfect righteousness" at Qumran has a prescriptive force. Perfection was the standard by which the community members were to try to live.[117] Rabbi Akiba said that God mercifully allows for sin and failure, but the majority of one's deeds must still accord with the law. Gamaliel, on the other hand, saw God as demanding a strict and perfect obedience with little or no room for failure. Whether by perfect exemplary models or by claiming that God demands strict obedience, these documents evince a struggle with the law's strict demand. In the words of Eleazar to his torturer, Antiochus, in 4 Macc 5:20–21: "To transgress the law in matters either small or great is of equal seriousness, for in each case the law is equally despised."

At the same time, there was the virtually ubiquitous assumption that the Jews were a special people who had been favored by God. Further, *Jubilees*, Philo, and the rabbis upheld sacrifice as a means of rectifying the situation caused by sin. Along with sacrifice, there was a whole array of possible ways to ameliorate sin's effects, including suffering and repentance or, in the case of Qumran, further obedience and piety. The

116 While recognizing the logical tension, Sanders tends to resolve the matter in favor of the grace of the covenantal framework; *Paul and Palestinian Judaism*, 100–101.

117 Or to put it in terms of Josephus (*Ag. Ap.* 2.160): "to those who believe that their lives are under the eye of God all sin is intolerable [οἱ γάρ πιστεύσαντες ἐπισκοπεῖν θεὸν τοὺς ἑαυτῶν βίους οὐθὲν ἀνέχονται ἐξαμαρτεῖν]." God observes not only outward actions but also inward thoughts (2.166). The practice of the law is to be "punctilious" (2.149; πραττόμενα μετὰ πάσης ἀκριβείας). Violation of the law brings the promise of punishment (2.178, 277).

very existence of a system of atonement shows that any act contrary to God's law, even the least infraction, had to be rectified in some way; each of God's laws demands obedience. God is holy and expects the same from Israel. Perfect conduct always remained the ideal.

God's forgiving grace and the strict demand of the law represent two opposing poles of Jewish thought that persisted in logical tension.[118] It is all a matter of focus. From one perspective, the law's demands are encompassed within the framework of election and mercy. From another perspective, each of the law's commands requires obedience; fulfillment of the command leads to blessing, while disobedience leads to punishment. Or to state it differently, God will judge all people strictly according to their works, and yet God will judge Israel on the basis of mercy. For the Tannaim, this tension manifests itself even in the understanding of Israel's election. At times, election is traced to the deserving merit of the patriarchs or Israel, while at other times it is a result of God's free, unmerited grace. It is inaccurate, then, to see obedience in Tannaitic literature strictly as a response to God's election. While that is often the case, in other places the Tannaim affirm that God is not capricious and grants blessings on the basis of deserving conduct and merit. Sanders was right to stress God's grace and mercy in the system, but he stated matters too strongly when he denied that God commands strict obedience of the law.

[118] In the Prayer of Manasseh, whereas sinlessness is characteristic of only a very few such as Abraham, Isaac, and Jacob, "who did not sin against you" (v. 8), "Manasseh" admits that he is a grievous sinner (vv. 9–12). He penitently implores God for mercy and forgiveness (vv. 6–7, 13).

Chapter Two

The Compromise or Collapse of Judaism's Gracious Framework

Jubilees, Philo, and the Qumran community, though representative of the variety of pre-70 C.E. Judaism, share a common underlying theology: Israel was to observe God's law in its entirety, and yet that requirement was set within a gracious framework of divine election and mercy. The temple's destruction in 70 C.E. as well as the influence of the Diaspora on apocalyptic authors often placed stress on that system. With the shift in focus away from God's election of Israel as a nation, a corresponding increase in emphasis on a judgment according to works usually resulted. This emphasis on God's strict justice in the documents of early post-70 C.E. Judaism did not spring up suddenly and without precedent. What happens in the literature shortly after 70 C.E., particularly the apocalyptic writings, is a natural consequence of stress on a system that had held the rigorous requirement of the law's observance in tension with God's election and mercy.

I. *4 Ezra* (2 Esdras 3–14)

Written in the wake of Jerusalem's fall in 70 C.E., *4 Ezra* evinces a complete collapse in Judaism's covenantal framework.[1] The troubled "Ezra"

[1] A date in the reign of Domitian at the end of the first century is the scholarly consensus regarding this work. See Jacob M. Myers, *I and II Esdras* (AB 42; Garden City, N.Y.: Doubleday, 1974), 299–302; Michael E. Stone, *Features of the Eschatology of IV Ezra* (HSS 35; Atlanta: Scholars Press, 1989), 1–11; idem, *Fourth Ezra* (Hermeneia; Minneapolis: Fortress, 1990), 9–10; Josef Schreiner, "Das 4. Buch Esra," *Apokalypsen* (JSHRZ 5.4; Gütersloh: Gerd Mohn, 1981), 301–2.

struggles with the angel Uriel, God's representative: why did God not have mercy on the people? How could the chosen city have fallen? Throughout the dialogues in the first sections of the book, Ezra invokes God's election and covenant with Israel.[2] Yet the answer remains firm: God will judge the people strictly and impartially.[3] In the face of Ezra's repeated pleas to overlook transgression and have compassion on those of Israel who have sinned, the angel insists that the Lord will save only those who have proven themselves righteous.[4] The criterion will be perfect or nearly perfect obedience of the law (7:88–89, 94; 8:33).[5] Very few

---

[2] *Fourth Ezra* 3:12–19; 4:22–25; 5:23–30, 33; 6:54–59. With regard to the structure of the book, the first three sections (3:1–5:20; 5:21–6:34; 6:35–9:26) consist of dialogues between Ezra and the angel. The fourth section (9:27–10:59) includes both dialogue and a vision. The final three sections each describe a vision (10:60–12:51; 13:1–58; 14:1–48).

[3] *Fourth Ezra* 7:19–25, 33–38, 49–61, 70–74, 104–105. In 9:20–21 note the contrast between the grape cluster, the traditional symbol of the election of the Israelite nation, and the single grape symbolizing individual salvation by obedience; B. W. Longenecker, *Eschatology and Covenant*, 91–93.

[4] E. P. Sanders describes one such exchange:

> Perhaps, proposes the seer, the righteous can intercede for the ungodly at the judgment (7.102). The angel replies, in short, no. Only individual righteousness will count (7.104–15). The plight of man is returned to by the seer: *what is the point of the promise of salvation for obedience when everyone in fact sins?* (7.116–26). The angel again *agrees* with the seer's pessimistic appraisal of man's situation, adding the exhortation that those who are victorious (and obey the law) can receive the promised salvation (7.127–31) (*Paul and Palestinian Judaism*, 414).

The impassioned plea for mercy continues in 7:132–40 only for the angel to say: "The Most High made this world for the sake of many, but the world to come for the sake of only a few. . . . Many have been created but only a few shall be saved" (8:1–3; translations taken from the NRSV of 2 Esdras).

[5] Sanders, *Paul and Palestinian Judaism*, 416. It is hard to see what room there is for grace in *4 Ezra*'s perspective. The denial of God's mercy for those who sin leaves a soteriology based on virtual sinlessness. John J. Collins cautions that *4 Ezra* does not necessarily manifest "legalistic perfectionism" since it does not specify the requisite level of legal performance. Nevertheless, only a very few could meet *4 Ezra*'s "lofty standards." Collins explains that this reflects the "historical experience" of the author; *The Apocalyptic Imagination: An Introduction to the Jewish Apocalyptic Literature* (2d ed.; Grand Rapids: Eerdmans, 1998), 212. Collins is certainly right to stress the situationally driven perspective of the letter. On the other hand, a denial of divine mercy and atonement *does*, in fact, leave a salvation based on legal perfectionism. Sanders's assessment is correct; Collins, at other points in his discussion (for example, p. 211), admits as much: "4 Ezra does not deny that covenant but can only salvage it by buttressing it with further revelations and by reconceiving the judgment on a strict basis of individual merits, after death."

will number among the saved.[6] Ezra therefore laments that the gift of the law and election are in vain.[7] Given the evil heart that plagues all humanity, God has given Israel a law that they could not obey (3:20–22, 35–36; 9:30–37).[8] Nevertheless, the blame lies not with God but with the individual who transgresses. Only those who are righteous like Ezra will be saved (8:47–54), only those who have fully obeyed the law (7:19–25).[9] The rest who transgress will simply be condemned to torment and destruction.[10] Salvation is a matter of storing up works, or "faithfulness" (7:77; 9:7).[11]

This bleak picture leads to Ezra's final desperate and frustrated cry in 9:15–16: "There are more who perish than those who will be saved, as a wave is greater than a drop of water." Throughout the dialogues of the first part of the book, Ezra and the angel remain unreconciled. The angel insists that the Jews as a corporate people will be judged on the same

---

[6] *Fourth Ezra* 3:35–36; 7:45–48, 68–69; 8:1–3, 35, 37–41; 9:7–17, 21–22.

[7] On the essential connection between the granting of the law and God's election of Israel, see 5:27.

[8] Bruce W. Longenecker, *2 Esdras* (Guides to Apocrypha and Pseudepigrapha; Sheffield: Sheffield Academic Press, 1995), 35–36. As Collins put it: "If only 'exceptional individuals' can keep the commandments, then membership of a covenant people becomes irrelevant. This pessimistic conclusion is borne out by the actual destruction of Zion" (*Apocalyptic Imagination,* 201). B. W. Longenecker (*Eschatology and Covenant,* 54) objects that Collins is relying too much on 3:36, where Ezra asks God to compare the *other* nations to Israel in the balance. When one considers the rest of the book, as Longenecker agrees, one finds Israel itself indicted as a nation (for example, 9:30–37). Collins rightly reflects the theology of the book as a whole: the covenant does not have any practical benefit for the people apart from their own individual, strict observance of the law.

[9] Although there are two brief mentions of the possibility of repentance (7:82; 9:12), as Sanders stresses, "the point is that transgressors have not repented" (*Paul and Palestinian Judaism,* 415). The ensuing discussions reiterate that only a very few will be saved and that the criterion remains one of actual obedience of the law. Sacrifice, on the other hand, does not figure into the discussion at all.

[10] *Fourth Ezra* 7:33–38, 72–73, 79–80, 81, 127–131; 8:55–58; 9:11–12; B. W. Longenecker, *2 Esdras,* 49.

[11] In the words of Michael A. Knibb: "the author of 2 Esdras 3–14 . . . believed that by the strict observance of the law it was possible for an individual to acquire, as it were, a credit balance of good works and to earn thereby the reward in the world to come of life" ("The Second Book of Esdras," in *The First and Second Books of Esdras* [ed. R. J. Coggins and M. A. Knibb; CBC; Cambridge: Cambridge University Press, 1979], 182). B. W. Longenecker points to passages such as 7:77, 88–93 and 9:7 as proof that "extreme rigour and stringent discipline" are necessary for salvation, since divine mercy has been consistently ruled out; *2 Esdras,* 49.

basis as the Gentiles. The ethnic distinction between Jews and Gentiles on the basis of God's election is dissolved in favor of a distinction between the vast majority of sinful humanity and the tiny minority of Israelites who perfectly obey the law. The situation for most Jews before the divine Judge is no different than the Gentiles.[12]

The fourth episode in 9:27–10:59 confirms Uriel's position in the preceding dialogues. No longer is Ezra in distress lodging complaints against God. Without explicitly resolving the prior conflict, Ezra now begins to echo the angel's position.[13] Scholars therefore speak of Ezra's "conversion" to the angel's position that God is right to judge all people, including Israel, on the basis of a strict standard.[14] Gunkel suggested that Ezra's dilemma gave way in the latter part of the book to consolation—the desperate situation of Israel would be resolved in the future age and by God's justice.[15] On the other hand, Sanders rightly observes that there is nothing in the Zion vision of 9:27–10:59 that dispels the position taken in the dialogues.[16] The possibility of an amelioration must wait until the fifth part of the book.

Scholars are divided on the significance of both the eagle vision in the fifth part of the book and the Son of Man vision in the sixth.

---

[12] B. W. Longenecker, *2 Esdras,* 48–49.

[13] For example, 10:10. In this section the woman espouses Ezra's prior perspective, while Ezra adopts the angel's position; B. W. Longenecker, *2 Esdras,* 61–62; contra Walter Harrelson, "Ezra among the Wicked in 2 Esdras 3–10," in *The Divine Helmsman: Studies on God's Control of Human Events, Presented to Lou H. Silberman* (ed. James L. Crenshaw and Samuel Sandmel; New York: Ktav, 1980), 21–40. Similarly, Ezra asserts in 9:32–37 (echoing the angel in 7:20) that the people's failure to obey the law is their own responsibility and not God's (cf. 3:20–27); B. W. Longenecker, *2 Esdras,* 62–64.

[14] B. W. Longenecker, *2 Esdras,* 21–22, 59–64; Michael E. Stone, "Reactions to Destructions of the Second Temple," *JSJ* 12 (1981): 203; idem, "On Reading an Apocalypse," in *Mysteries and Revelations: Apocalyptic Studies since the Uppsala Colloquium* (ed. John J. Collins and James H. Charlesworth, JSPSup 9; Sheffield: JSOT Press, 1991), 73–74; Collins, *Apocalyptic Imagination,* 205–6. A helpful study exploring the shift in Ezra's position to that of the angel is Michael P. Knowles, "Moses, the Law, and the Unity of 4 Ezra," *NovT* 31 (1989): 257–74. The key to Ezra's transformation lies, for Knowles, in the "seed" motif. The evil "seed" in people's hearts resists the law (3:19–20, 22; 4:30). Yet Uriel speaks of the harvest of *good* seed that will change this situation (4:31–32). Even while Ezra despairs and argues with the angel, he unwittingly asks God to plant a new seed (8:6). This good seed turns out in 9:31, 33 to be the law. Knowles shows how the law has taken root in Ezra and thus effects a change; it brings about new-found fear and wisdom (Knowles, "Moses," 268–74).

[15] H. Gunkel, "Das Vierte Buch Esra" (APAT 2:331–401).

[16] *Paul and Palestinian Judaism,* 416–17.

Many see a reversion to the notions of Israel's national covenant and election, that is, Ezra's initial position, in these two visions. Both visions speak of the Jewish faithful prevailing over their heathen enemies. The multitude who are "saved" in the end, according to the visions, seems to indicate that the position of the dialogues (that few would be saved) has been overturned. This understanding has been labeled "covenantal confirmation."[17] Advocates of covenantal confirmation place emphasis on the visions that conclude the work. These visions seem to uphold the covenant relationship with national Israel. Not only is "covenantal confirmation" supported by the general thrust of the fifth and sixth visions, the position takes seriously the role of that esteemed, revered figure, Ezra, who stubbornly champions this perspective all through the dialogues.[18] In other words, proponents of this position see the dispute eventually resolved in favor of Ezra: God would be gracious and faithful to ethnic Israel even if that faithfulness is at the moment suspect.[19]

The problem with "covenantal confirmation" is that the model does not adequately consider all of the evidence. Sanders argues against emphasizing Ezra's position over the angel's: "The assumption should be that what the angel actually says is important and that the content of what is said was meant to be taken seriously. . . . But even more important, *they* [the final visions] *do not reply to the angel's answers* to 'Ezra's' complaints, and it is precisely in these answers that the negative thrust of the work is carried."[20] Even allowing for the change in tone in the visions (11:1–12:51; 13:1–58; 14:1–48; and part of 9:27–10:59), Sanders insists there is nothing in the visions that repudiates the

---

[17] B. W. Longenecker, *2 Esdras,* 31.

[18] A. P. Hayman, "The Problem of Pseudonymity in the Ezra Apocalypse," *JSJ* 6 (1975): 50–51. Nowhere does the book repudiate Ezra's position. As Michael Knibb ("Second Book of Esdras," 109) contends against views that are based entirely on the angel's position:

> It has been argued that the speeches of Ezra represent a pessimism (about the fate of Israel and of mankind) which the author wished to rebut, and that the speeches of the angel (and God) alone represent the views of the author. It is, however, nowhere made clear that what Ezra says is wrong, and it seems more likely that the dialogue form reflects a tension within the author's own mind.

So also Earl Breech, "These Fragments I Have Shored against My Ruins: The Form and Function of 4 Ezra," *JBL* 92 (1973): 273–74.

[19] One ought also to recoginize that Ezra is championing the position that most Jews in his day held—*covenantal nomism;* Sanders, *Paul and Palestinian Judaism,* 413–16.

[20] Ibid., 413.

position of the angel.[21] Since the angel is sometimes addressed as God or as if God were speaking, the angel represents the highest possible authority.[22] That it is Ezra, and not the angel, who experiences a "conversion" from his prior position rules out "covenantal confirmation" as a viable option.[23] Ezra's parting speech to the people in 14:27–36 still echoes the strict position of the angel.[24]

The evidence adduced against the "covenantal confirmation" position naturally suggests a second theory, "covenantal abrogation." According to this perspective, the visions agree with the dialogues in rejecting the efficacy of the covenant for the salvation of ethnic Israel.[25] There are two possibilities as to how the visions relate to the first part of the book. First, the visions may echo God's answer to Job; the ways of the deity are beyond the comprehension of mortal humanity (e.g., *4 Ezra* 4:2, 13–21). Second, the visions may offer an "apocalyptic

---

[21] Collins (*Apocalyptic Imagination,* 209) concurs with Sanders that in 12:34 only a remnant of the people will be saved. Similarly, Alden Lloyd Thompson writes: "Even though the final episodes are more optimistic in tone and speak of a just judge (14:32) and mercy after death (14:34), the vivid impression left by the author's complaints in episodes I-III casts a long shadow over the whole book" (*Responsibility for Evil in the Theodicy of IV Ezra* [SBLDS 29; Missoula, Mont.: Scholars Press, 1977], 356). Thompson concludes (pp. 340–42) that Ezra is forced to an "experiential solution" rather than a rational one.

[22] *Fourth Ezra* 4:38; 5:40, 41, 42; 6:6; 7:45, 58, 75; 8:47, 61; 9:18–22; Stone, *Fourth Ezra,* 16, 199.

[23] Egon Brandenburger, *Die Verborgenheit Gottes im Weltgeschehen: Das Literarische und Theologische Problem des 4. Esrabuches* (ATANT 68; Zürich: Theologischer Verlag, 1981); Wolfgang Harnisch, "Der Prophet as Widerpart und Zeuge der Offenbarung Erwägungen zur Interdependenz von Form und Sache im IV. Buch Esra," in *Apocalypticism in the Mediterrranean World and the Near East: Proceedings of the International Colloquium on Apocalypticism, Uppsala, August 12–17, 1979* (ed. David Hellholm; Tübingen: J.C.B. Mohr [Paul Siebeck], 1983), 461–64; idem, "Die Ironie der Offenbarung: Exegetische Erwägungen zur Zion vision im 4. Buch Esra," in *SBL Seminar Papers, 1981* (Chico, Calif.: Scholars Press, 1981), 79–104.

[24] The differences between the dialogues and the visions are not so fundamentally divergent as to necessitate a source theory of two distinct streams of tradition such as Sanders entertains. Sanders is not convinced of separate sources, but neither is he entirely willing to concede that the visions ultimately affirm Ezra's position in the dialogues. The consensus of recent scholarship favors the unity of the book; see Breech, "These Fragments," 267–74; Stone, "Reactions," 200–204; idem, *Fourth Ezra,* 21–23; Nickelsburg, *Jewish Literature,* 293–94; Collins, *Apocalyptic Imagination,* 196–200; Knowles, "Moses," 257–74.

[25] For example, B. W. Longenecker, *Eschatology and Covenant,* although he disavows this position in his later work, *2 Esdras.*

solution," a vision of the future that offers consolation apart from rational answers.[26]

In favor of "covenantal abrogation," the visions certainly do not dispel the harsh position of the angel in the dialogues, the position to which Ezra "converts." In fact, the role of divine mercy and election in the visions may have been overstated. God's mercy on the obedient in 12:34 may seem at first to contradict the earlier skepticism, but 7:133 had already explained that God's compassion rests upon those who strictly obey the law.[27] The mention of "faith" in *4 Ezra* 13:23 stands alongside "works" and is better translated as "faithfulness," thereby echoing the words of Uriel in 9:7–8.[28] In 13:42 the writer speaks of a returning remnant of Israel. Yet the remnant consists of people who abandoned their homes in the exile in favor of uninhabited lands where they could observe the law.[29] Further, those assembling at the end in 13:23, 33–38 are the righteous.[30] Whereas in 14:30 the law is a "law of life," in 14:32 God is a righteous judge, and in 14:28–31 people must take responsibility for their failure to observe the law—thus the admonition in 14:34 to "rule over your minds and discipline your hearts." Ezra displays none of his earlier pessimism about the possibility of successful law-ob-

---

[26] Nickelsburg, *Jewish Literature*, 293–94; Collins, *Apocalyptic Imagination*, 201, 209. The visions would therefore be integral to the work.

[27] There is no need, as does Sanders (*Paul and Palestinian Judaism*, 417), to see in the eagle vision a different *Sitz im Leben*.

[28] See B. W. Longenecker, *2 Esdras*, 80; cf. *4 Ezra* 14:34–35. Michel Desjardins emphasizes that faith in *4 Ezra* is "virtually interchangeable" with obedience to the law (see 9:7; 13:23). Those who possess a "store of good works" to be rewarded (8:36) are the same ones who have "stored up treasuries of faith" (6:5). The frequent mention of faith is a function of the problem of theodicy and yet does not contradict *4 Ezra*'s soteriology based on works; "Law in 2 Baruch and 4 Ezra," *SR* 14 (1985): 36.

[29] B. W. Longenecker, *2 Esdras*, 80. One should also keep in mind 13:37–38. These verses speak of God (or the Messiah) punishing people at the judgment by the *law*. The law will function as a measuring stick, since future reward depends on its performance; Desjardins, "Law in 2 Baruch and 4 Ezra," 35.

[30] Sanders, *Paul and Palestinian Judaism*, 417. Some see this as "all Israel" being saved (Breech), a return to traditional covenantalism. Sanders therefore proposes that the man from the sea vision is an appendage to the work. Nevertheless, while the number of people here assembled is numerous, the vision never upsets the preceding criterion of perfect obedience to the law for inclusion in that saving event. One need not excise the vision. It simply provides hope for those who endeavor to be perfect even as "Ezra" was. Ezra's earlier view of complete inability gives way to the freedom of choice maintained in the angel's position (with B. W. Longenecker).

servance.[31] In short, the answer to Ezra's plea for divine grace and mercy is the granting of the law to Israel. Perfect obedience of the law would allow the individual to stand successfully before the strict judgment seat of God. Salvation is therefore based on obedience of the law rather than God's election of the nation as a whole. Israel's advantage would simply be the possession of the divine law.

While there is good evidence for the position of "covenantal abrogation," ultimately this position too leaves something to be desired. While rightly upholding Uriel's authoritative position, Ezra remains a revered figure in Israel's history. Further, the angel never forthrightly denies Ezra's position. On the contrary, Israel *is* dearly beloved, according to 5:33 and 6:58. The problem is that the people sinned and God judges on the basis of successful observance of the law (6:26–28). Since the heathen rejected the law that God gave to beloved Israel, the Gentiles will be annihilated at the eschaton (5:27; 7:21–24; 9:7–9). God's election and covenant do not possess saving efficacy for "all Israel" but only for those of the obedient Jewish remnant who demonstrate proper and complete adherence to the law (13:39, 48). The covenant is hardly being confirmed when only a few in Israel will be saved (10:10) and when atonement and divine mercy are ineffective in an overall scheme in which God's justice prevails. Nevertheless, the angel does not entirely deny Ezra's position but modifies it: the covenant and election are still efficacious, but only for those who perfectly obey the law, that is, the remnant.[32] This position has been labeled "covenantal redefinition."[33] It acknowledges both the angel's supremely authoritative position and the merit of Ezra's appeal to election and the covenant.[34]

The position of "covenantal redefinition" shares with "covenantal abrogation" a recognition that *4 Ezra* demands legal perfectionism.[35] The law has been removed from a framework of grace and mercy. Strict

---

[31] B. W. Longenecker, *2 Esdras*, 89–90.

[32] Ibid., 45, 100.

[33] Thus B. W. Longenecker, *2 Esdras*, 98–100; contra his *Eschatology and Covenant*, where he adopts the position of "covenantal abrogation." One ought to recognize, on the other hand, that Longenecker's key point in *Eschatology and Covenant* (p. 98) remains valid; the law has been removed "from the context of God's covenant mercy."

[34] A criterion Stone emphasizes for a proper reading of the text; *Fourth Ezra*, 30.

[35] Even if one affirms that the visions overturn the position of the angel in the dialogues ("covenantal confirmation"), the dialogues would still witness to a questioning of the covenantal framework and a corresponding increase in focus on the obedience of the law.

observance of the law is required for salvation. Only a few truly obedient individuals will be saved. Only a few will be able to overcome the evil heart in all humanity that hinders the perfect obedience God requires (3:20–22, 35–36).[36] Ezra can only lament that Israel is unable to bring forth the fruit of the law (9:29–37).[37]

Sanders is certainly right to see the extreme position of *4 Ezra* as reflecting an agonizing soul-search in the wake of Jerusalem's fall. Although *4 Ezra* reflects a radically new era, its value in understanding Judaism prior to 70 C.E. cannot be ruled out. Ezra consistently represents the covenantal nomistic picture that Sanders finds elsewhere in intertestamental literature. What is different in *4 Ezra* is the angel's denial of saving efficacy to the categories of election, covenant, atonement, and mercy. There is no provision for failure, hence God's judgment upon the city. With the collapse of the gracious framework, it is only natural that the embedded demand of the law should be severed and rendered problematic. The emphasis shifts away from mercy to judgment based strictly on a perfect, divine standard.[38] *Fourth Ezra* is not unique in this respect.

II. *2 Baruch*

Scholars generally place *2 Baruch* toward the end of the first century or early second.[39] As in *4 Ezra*, the author reflects on the crushing events of 70 C.E. through a pseudepigraphic device—in this case, Jeremiah's scribe beholding the original fall of Jerusalem several centuries earlier. "Baruch" inquires about the future of Israel (3:4–6). Are God's covenantal promises to Moses still valid (3:9)? God affirms that the destruction is only a chastisement; the people and the city will be restored (e.g., 1:5; 4:1; 6:9).[40] God has not reneged on the promises (19:1–3; 22:2–23:7). In fact, the present temple is only a shadow of the heavenly

---

[36] Hence an inability to obey the law, which in turn compromises the election of Israel; cf. Stone, "Reactions," 201; Nickelsburg, *Jewish Literature*, 288.

[37] Nickelsburg, *Jewish Literature*, 291.

[38] As Sanders put it: "In IV Ezra, in short, we see an instance in which covenantal nomism has collapsed. All that is left is legalistic perfectionism" (*Paul and Palestinian Judaism*, 409).

[39] *Second Baruch* was most likely written around 95 C.E. For discussion, see Collins, *Apocalyptic Imagination*, 222–25; A. F. J. Klijn, "2 (Syriac Apocalypse of) Baruch" (*OTP* 1:616–17); and especially Pierre Bogaert, *Apocalypse de Baruch* (2 vols.; SC 144; Paris: Cerf, 1969), 1:270–95.

[40] See also Collins's discussion on this point in *Apocalyptic Imagination*, 216.

one (4:2–7). In contrast to *4 Ezra*, "God's ultimate providential care for Israel is not in doubt. The righteous are spared, the vessels protected, and even the city walls escape the indignity of violation by the Gentiles."[41]

Second Baruch draws upon a Deuteronomic pattern that implies God's continuing covenant with Israel. When the people sin, God punishes them; the people repent and are restored to the land and prosperity (31:1–32:7; 44:1–46:7; 77:1–17).[42] This covenantal pattern is part of an extensive series of Deuteronomic echoes.[43] Given the Deuteronomic framework, the proper response to this enactment of God's covenantal curses would be to repent and obey the Mosaic law more diligently.

At one key point, *2 Baruch* departs from the Deuteronomic picture. The covenantal focus shifts away from the Israelite nation as a whole toward the individual, and it is precisely in this shift that nomism begins to take precedence over the covenant. One's place in the future world is decided not on the basis of membership in the covenant people Israel but on the basis of individual obedience (*2 Bar.* 15:5–8; cf. *m. Sanh.* 10:1). Covenant membership is disavowed wherever there is disobedience (*2 Bar.* 41:3–5). "Many" Jews have been disobedient and forfeited covenant status, while only a "few" are righteous.[44] One looks in vain for a corresponding emphasis on sacrifice, atonement, or the election of the nation. As Collins writes:

> *2 Baruch* goes beyond 4 Ezra in clarifying the composition of the people who benefit from the messiah. The criterion is not ethnicity but observance of the law. Proselytes are included; apostates are not. *2 Baruch* envisages fulfillment of the covenantal promises, but in the process the covenantal people must be redefined. Conversion to Judaism is still a prerequisite for salvation, but the promises do not apply to all Jews. In view of this insistence on individual performance, it is only natural that Baruch should warn the people . . . (44:7).[45]

---

[41] Ibid., 217.

[42] Odil Hannes Steck, *Israel und das Gewaltsame Geschick der Propheten: Untersuchungen zur Überlieferung des Deuteronomistischen Geschichtsbildes im Alten Testament, Spätjudentum und Urchristentum* (WMANT 23; Neukirchen-Vluyn: Neukirchener Verlag, 1967), 180–84.

[43] See Frederick James Murphy's extensive discussion for several instances; *The Structure and Meaning of Second Baruch* (SBLDS 78; Atlanta: Scholars Press, 1985), 117–33.

[44] Gwendolyn B. Sayler, *Have the Promises Failed? A Literary Analysis of 2 Baruch* (SBLDS 72; Chico, Calif.: Scholars Press, 1984), 47–49.

[45] Collins, *Apocalyptic Imagination*, 219. Compare on p. 218: "the promises of the covenant will be fulfilled but on a different level from what we might

While mercy is present, its role is vastly reduced in favor of obedience or disobedience as the factor determining whether one is in the covenant or not. Israel is redefined as those who are obedient. One of Baruch's strongest appeals for mercy comes in 48:11–18.[46] Baruch even appeals to Israel's national election in 48:20. God's response to Baruch's plea in vv. 26–27 is telling: "You have prayed honestly, Baruch, and all your words have been heard. But my judgment asks for its own, and my Law demands its right." This divine response on the basis of the law echoes Baruch's own words earlier in v. 22: "In you we have put our trust, because, behold, your law is with us, and we know that we do not fall as long as we keep your statutes." Mercy is contingent upon obedience.[47]

This stern emphasis on a God who judges on the basis of successful observance of the law runs all through the document. All humanity stands as responsible for their actions before the Judge. In 54:14–19 the author affirms:

> And those who do not love your Law are justly perishing. And the torment of judgment will fall upon those who have not subjected themselves to your power. For, although Adam sinned first and has brought death upon all who were not in his own time, yet each of them who has been born from him has prepared for himself the coming torment. And further, each of them has chosen for himself the coming glory. . . . Adam is, therefore, not the cause, except only for himself, but each of us has become our own Adam.

Each individual is responsible as the Adam of his or her own soul and will be judged strictly according to works. Such an individualistic criterion forces the definition of true Israel to be narrowed from the nation as a whole. In 14:12–13: "For the righteous justly have good hope for the end and go away from this habitation without fear because they possess with you a store of good works which is preserved in treasuries.

---

have expected." The mention of sacrifice in 35:4 says nothing about any atoning value. Similarly, the covenant in ch. 19 leads to both life and death depending on one's obedience.

[46] "Hear your servant, and regard my appeal. For we are born in a short time, and in a short time we return. . . . Be, therefore, not angry at man because he is nothing; and do not take count of our works; for what are we? For behold, by your gift we come into the world, and we do not go of our own will. For we did not say to our parents: 'Beget us,' nor have we sent to the realm of death saying: 'Receive us.' What therefore is our strength that we can bear your wrath, or what are we that we can endure your judgment? Protect us in your grace, and in your mercy help us" (Klijn, trans., "2 Baruch," 1:636). Subsequent quotations of *2 Baruch* are taken from Klijn's translation.

[47] Collins, *Apocalyptic Imagination*, 218–19.

Therefore, they leave this world without fear and are confident of the world which you have promised to them with an expectation full of joy." On the basis of this passage Collins writes: "If many have sinned, while only a few kept the law, this is a matter of human responsibility. We must infer that the true Israel, which is heir to the promises, consists of those who keep the law."[48] In 21:11 the many who have sinned only *once* are contrasted with "many others" who "have proved themselves to be righteous."[49] The impression of an exact weighing of deeds and a judgment according to the scales does not seem far from the author's thought (e.g., 41:6). In 24:1–2: "For behold, the days are coming, and the books will be opened in which are written the sins of all those who have sinned, and moreover, also the treasuries in which are brought together the righteousness of all those who have proven themselves to be righteous." In 13:8–10: "for the judgment of the Most High is impartial. Therefore, he did not spare his own sons first, but he afflicted them as his enemies because they sinned. Therefore, they were once punished, that they might be forgiven." Forgiveness only follows after due punishment of sin.

In fact, when Baruch appeals to God for mercy, he does so on the basis of *good works.* In ch. 2 God commands Jeremiah and those like him and Baruch to retire from the city, "for your works are for this city like a firm pillar and your prayers like a strong wall." In 14:7: "Zion should have been forgiven on account of the works of those who did good works and should not have been overwhelmed because of the works of those who acted unrighteously." The fate of Israel as a whole mirrors

---

[48] Ibid., 218. On this point Collins reflects the message much more accurately than E. P. Sanders, who in his brief analysis ("The Covenant As a Soteriological Category," 18) cites references to God's mercy in *2 Baruch* (e.g., 44:14–15; 84:11) but fails to take into account prior obedience to the law as the criterion for that mercy. Michel Desjardins is more accurate: "One's attitude to the Law is the determining factor in guaranteeing salvation or punishment in the coming age." Desjardins adds: "salvation awaits those who follow the Law"; "Law in 2 Baruch and 4 Ezra," 28. Desjardins points to such passages as 32:1; 42; 44; 48:22 ("We know that we do not fall as long as we keep your statutes"); 54:13–14; 57:1–2; 84:2–11. Desjardins concludes:

> "Your law is life," says Baruch in 38:2 (cf. also 45:2; 46:3), and in chapter 57 it becomes evident that what is meant by this expression is the "promise of life" which the Law makes to those who are faithful to it. Obeying the Law does make a difference as to how one will be treated in the coming age; it is the determining factor in providing new and lasting life in the "renewed creation" ("Law in 2 Baruch and 4 Ezra," 29–30).

[49] Cf. 21:9, which also contrasts the righteous with those who sin.

that of the individual as God judges the nation itself on the scales; the good works of the righteous accrue to the nation's benefit and the sins of evildoers to its detriment. This method of judgment explains why the Jews are being punished so severely as a corporate entity with the destruction of their temple. The destruction of the temple is a result of God's chastising activity. Yet the temple's destruction is only a shadow of the judgment to come. Even as divine justice required judgment upon God's own people and temple, so the same judgment awaits the entire world, a world characterized by individuals wantonly repeating Adam's sin.

Second Baruch therefore teaches a theology of "works-righteousness" in the classic sense of the term. In 44:15 those who preserve the truth of the law will be granted a share in the world to come. In 51:2–3 those who suffer torment receive such punishment on account of their wicked actions. Those who enjoy glory do so because they "proved to be righteous on account of my law." In 63:3 Hezekiah "trusted upon his works, and hoped upon his righteousness" when he spoke with God. God heard him because of his righteousness (61:5). It is in this context that the law serves as a means to life (e.g., 38:2).[50] The law provides knowledge of God's will for the individual who chooses to obey, although it also brings a greater accountability (15:5–6; 48:22, 24). The righteous are saved by their doing of the law (51:7). This explains the incessant admonitions to respond to the crisis of the fall of Jerusalem with renewed attention to obeying the law (e.g., ch. 84). In the words of 46:5–6: "But only prepare your heart so that you obey the Law, and be subject to those who are wise and understanding with fear. And prepare your soul that you shall not depart from them. If you do this, those good tidings will come to you of which I spoke to you earlier, and you will not fall into the torment of which I spoke to you earlier." Or in 32:1: "if you prepare your minds to sow into them the fruits of the law, he shall protect you in the time in which the Mighty One shall shake the entire creation."[51] While *2 Baruch* differs from *4 Ezra* in affirming a role for God's

[50] This point was recognized already by R. H. Charles, *The Apocalypse of Baruch* (London: Adam & Charles Black, 1896), lxxxi, 26.

[51] Collins comments: "Revelation of the future puts the present in perspective. Yet the law will protect those who practice it. Observance of the law gains greater urgency in view of the coming judgment" (*Apocalyptic Imagination*, 218). In yet another series of visions in chs. 35–47, it is once again obedience of the law that brings Zion's consolation (44:3–7) and a new world that will not pass away (44:8–15). The people must be prepared to obey the law (46:4–5).

mercy (e.g., 84:11), that "mercy is evidently contingent on obedience" (e.g., 85:3).[52]

Second Baruch represents yet another document witnessing to the crisis in Judaism caused by the fall of the Jerusalem temple in 70 C.E. The questioning of God's mercy and the covenant as the law's gracious framework leads to an increased focus on the other side of the logical tension, the necessity to obey the law. Unlike *4 Ezra, 2 Baruch* does not completely deny God's mercy for the sinner. But *like 4 Ezra, 2 Baruch* gives precedence to works over mercy. While God's mercy represents the other side of chastening, it remains nevertheless predicated on the observance of the law. It is a mercy to the righteous and not to those who sin. The gracious framework of Judaism and its law has been severely compromised. The covenantal people may no longer be equated with Israel as a whole but with those Israelites whose deeds weigh in conformity with what the Mosaic law requires.

III. *3 Baruch*

Like *4 Ezra* and *2 Baruch, 3 Baruch* is reacting to the destruction of Jerusalem by the nations (1:2). Consequently, the date of this document must be after 70 C.E.[53] Chapters 4 and 11–15 include Christian insertions into an otherwise Jewish work.[54] The current consensus is that

---

[52] Collins, *Apocalyptic Imagination,* 220. Or on p. 219: "Mercy, then, only applies to those who convert and obey." On the other hand, whereas few are righteous in *4 Ezra, 2 Baruch* 21:11 says "*many* others have proved themselves to be righteous"; cf. *4 Ezra* 8:35, where the people need mercy and not the law since only a few can be saved by their good works (7:77) apart from divine compassion (7:139).

[53] John J. Collins thinks that the work was scripted not long after the fall of Jerusalem in 70 C.E.: *Between Athens and Jerusalem: Jewish Identity in the Hellenistic Diaspora* (New York: Crossroad, 1983), 232. For discussion, see also Jean-Claude Picard, *Apocalypsis Baruchi Graece* (PVTG 2; Leiden: E. J. Brill, 1967), 77; Daniel C. Harlow, *The Greek Apocalypse of Baruch (3 Baruch) in Hellenistic Judaism and Early Christianity* (SVTP 12; Leiden: E. J. Brill, 1996), 34–76; H. E. Gaylord Jr., "3 (Greek Apocalypse of) Baruch" (*OTP* 1:656).

[54] On the multitudinous connections to Judaism, see Louis Ginzberg, "Baruch, Apocalypse of (Greek)," *The Jewish Encyclopedia* (ed. Isidore Singer et al.; New York: Funk & Wagnalls, 1902, 1916), 549–51. I take 4:15, 17a; 13:4; 15:4; 16:2, 4 [Greek version] as Christian interpolations. For discussion, see Picard, *Apocalypsis Baruchi Graece,* 75–78; Ulrich Fischer, *Eschatologie und Jenseitserwartung im hellenistischen Diasporajudentum* (BZNW 44; Berlin: Walter de Gruyter, 1978), 72–73. I will be following the Greek text of *3 Baruch,* but my con-

3 Baruch originated in the Hellenistic Diaspora.[55] "Baruch" asks why God has so chastised the people before the nations, to which an angel responds promising to show him greater mysteries (1:6). Baruch is then granted a tour of the five heavens. The whole experience moves him to offer praise to God (17:3).

Throughout his vision of the heavens Baruch sees various places of reward and punishment. In the first two heavens he sees the planners and builders of the Tower of Babel being punished (*3 Bar.* 2–3). In what is most likely the third heaven, Baruch sees a serpent, or dragon, and a dreadful monster associated with Hades (*3 Bar.* 4).[56] The dragon "eats the bodies of those who pass through their lives badly" (4:5).[57] The dwelling place of the souls of the righteous is located in the fourth heaven (*3 Bar.* 10). The reference to Hades and to the punishment of the wicked in the first two heavens leads Baruch to ask about the cause of Adam's sin as well as sin in general (4:8–9, 13, 17; cf. *4 Ezra* 3:20–22; 7:117–118). The answer is that the cause of sin for both Adam and those who followed is the same: people have drunk the wine of the vine and have transgressed through sins such as murder, adultery, fornication, perjury, and theft (4:16–17). Humanity's wickedness is a major motif again in *3 Bar.* 6–8. In 8:4–5 the sun sets because its rays have been defiled during the day by such lawlessness and unrighteousness as "fornication, adultery, theft, robbery, idol-worship, drunkenness, murder, discord, jealousy, slander, murmuring, gossip, [and] divination."

Chapters 11–16 (and 17:1) form the climax of the apocalypse. Baruch sees Michael descend to the fifth heaven with a large receptacle. The accompanying angel interprets the vision (11:9): "This is where the virtues of the righteous and the good works which they do are carried, which are brought by him before the heavenly God." Three groups of angels then appear. The first group is carrying baskets filled with the flowers of human virtue (12:1–5). The second group's baskets are only half full (12:6–8). The third group is mourning and weeping over their

---

clusions are consistent with the Slavonic version. For a discussion of the versions, see Fischer, *Eschatologie*, 74–75; Gaylord, "3 Baruch," 1:656; Harlow, *3 Baruch*, 77–108.

[55] Compare, for example, *3 Baruch* 12–13 with Philo's *Somn.* 2.272. Fischer (*Eschatologie*, 75) also notes the parallels with Egyptian and Greek mythology—for instance, the Phoenix (chs. 6–8) and the Hades dragon (4:3–5).

[56] The formula in 4:1–2 compares with 2:1–2 and 3:1–2, but see 10:1, which must be the "fourth" heaven and not the third, with the fifth identified in 11:1.

[57] The Slavonic version, however, has a very different version of ch. 4. Quotations of *3 Baruch* are taken from Gaylord's translation.

empty baskets, for these angels had been assigned to evil and foolish people (13:1–4; cf. 4:17; 8:5). When the despairing angels ask to be assigned to other people, Michael consults with God and then returns (13:5–15:1). He fills the containers of the first group of angels with oil as the hundredfold reward of those who have done good deeds (15:1–2).[58] The second group receives their reward as well (15:3). The third group is commissioned to go and punish the wicked for failing to keep God's commandments (16:1–4). At this point, the gate is closed in judgement (17:1). While some of the Greek version's imagery has been reworked by a Christian interpolator to reflect the Gospels, one finds the same "measure for measure" reward in the Slavonic translation (15:2–3).

Michael's description of the third, wicked portion of humanity has covenantal overtones. They are the ones who "did not listen to my voice, nor observe my commands" (16:4). They are to be made envious and angry against "those who are no nation, against a people without understanding" (16:2). This verse (16:2) borders on a paraphrase of Deut 32:21.[59] The third group, then, is virtually identified with the Jews, and the Jewish people are to be provoked to jealousy and anger "against those who are no nation, against a people without understanding," namely, the Romans. Collins writes:

> The Jews are provoked in this way because they as a people had no merits to present to God (although the righteousness of individuals like Baruch is surely presumed). The covenant has been broken and there is no hint that it will be restored. Instead it is replaced with a system of individual rewards and punishments. This position might be seen as the logical culmination of the kind of analysis advanced by Ezra in 4 Ezra 3–9. In this context the salvation of Jerusalem is of little significance.[60]

Like *4 Ezra* and *2 Baruch*, the election and covenant with Israel have been redefined in the wake of Jerusalem's destruction. No longer do election and the covenant avail for the nation as a whole (if they ever did). There is no mention of Jerusalem ever being restored. Election and covenant have been redefined individually; they are operative only for those who do a majority of good works (a basket at least half-full) or

---

[58] Note how the righteous are called "our friends."

[59] Nickelsburg, *Jewish Literature*, 302. *Third Baruch* 16:2 hearkens back to 1:2: "And why, Lord, did you . . . [hand] us over to such heathen [ἔθνη]." The destruction of Jerusalem is therefore interpreted as *punishment for the people's sins.* As John J. Collins writes: "The Jews are provoked in this way because they as a people had no merits to present to God" (*Apocalyptic Imagination*, 251).

[60] Collins, *Apocalyptic Imagination*, 251.

better (a full basket).[61] There is no mention of sacrifice, repentance, or God's mercy.[62] There are no mitigating factors. God's recompense is on the basis of obedience or disobedience of the commandments. Those who sin "secure for themselves eternal fire" (4:16); those who are "righteous" will be saved. *Third Baruch* therefore bears witness to a Diaspora Judaism that accepted the view of eschatological judgment paralleling *m. ʾAbot* 3:16. This quantitative measurement of works is attested also in *2 Enoch* and the *Testament of Abraham.*

IV. *2 Enoch*

Second Enoch is an apocalyptic work that is extant in two different manuscript traditions, a short form and a longer one.[63] Although J. T. Milik sees the work as Christian and a product of the ninth or tenth century C.E., the consensus of current scholarship is that the work is the product of Judaism in the first century C.E.[64] Most scholars place the

---

[61] Nickelsburg, *Jewish Literature,* 302–3. He writes: "The hope for a nation reconstituted around Land and Temple is here replaced by an individualized, heavenly eschatology" (p. 303).

[62] The Slavonic text of 15:1–2 speaks of the angels with full baskets receiving "mercy." This is more likely a misreading of the Greek ἔλαιον (oil) as ἔλεος (mercy); Gaylord, "3 Baruch," 1:676–77 n. 15a.

[63] A. Vaillant, *Le Livre des Secrets d'Hénoch, texte slave et traduction française* (Textes publiés par l'Institute d'Études Slaves 4; Paris: Institut d'Études Slaves, 1952); W. R. Morfill and R. H. Charles, *The Book of the Secrets of Enoch* (Oxford: Clarendon, 1896), xii–xvi. I will be following Text A, one of the shorter versions. The English translation for what follows is that of F. I. Andersen, "2 (Slavonic Apocalypse of) Enoch" (*OTP* 1:91–221). Andersen and Christfried Böttrich (*Weltweisheit, Menschheitsethik, Urkult: Studien zum slavischen Henochbuch* [WUNT 2/50; Tübingen: J.C.B. Mohr (Paul Siebeck), 1992], 58–144) think that neither recension should necessarily be assumed as the original. One must therefore remain tentative on this matter.

[64] Many feel that Vaillant has established the shorter recension as more original; J. T. Milik, ed, *The Books of Enoch: Aramaic Fragments of Qumran Cave 4* (Oxford: Clarendon, 1976), 109–12. In favor of a first-century date (against Milik), see Fischer, *Eschatologie,* 37–41; Nevill Forbes and R. H. Charles, "The Book of the Secrets of Enoch" (*APOT* 2:426–29); Collins, *Between Athens and Jerusalem,* 243 n. 147. Of course, one cannot be dogmatic about the date; see Andersen, "2 Enoch," 1:94–98.

On the Jewish origin of the work, see Fischer, *Eschatologie.* One might note the high regard for sacrifices (see below for references). Gershom Scholem emphasizes that the "shorter" recension shows no Christian influence; *Ursprung und Anfänge der Kabbala* (Studia Judaica: Forschung zur Wissenschaft des Judentums

work's origin in Egypt.[65] The Jewish character of the work is particularly clear. First, the protagonist of the work is the Enoch of Jewish tradition. Second, the book takes a strong stand against idolatry (2:2, 34:1–2). There is only one God who created all things (47:3–6), a God who is not understood by the undiscerning (48:8). Before leaving, Enoch urges his children not to turn away from God (2:2). Probably the most compelling feature pointing to a non-Christian, Jewish origin lies in *2 Enoch*'s references to the Jewish sacrificial system (2:2; 42:6; 45:3; 59:1–3; 61:4–5; 66:2; 68:5–6).[66]

Second Enoch does not refer to the Mosaic covenant. There is no mention of circumcision or any sort of dietary restrictions, nor is there anything on Israel's special history or laws.[67] While *4 Ezra* represents a challenge to covenantal nomism, *2 Enoch* is marked by its complete absence. Given the absence of the gracious framework of covenantal nomism, one would expect God's strict justice to come to the fore, which is exactly what one finds in *2 Enoch*. On his heavenly journey, Enoch finds the rebellious angels being punished in the second heaven (7:1–4). In the northern part of the third heaven, he sees angels tormenting people who had committed godless uncleanness and witchcraft on earth. He also sees in the third heaven people who had defrauded others, starved their neighbors, and taken the clothing of the naked (10:1–6). Anyone who does not bow down to the Creator but worships idols will receive "an eternal reward" (10:6). One must stay away from unrighteous deeds (61:1–2). Enoch thus sees the various places of eternal condemnation and records all the judgments of the judged (40:13).

On the other hand, the people in the paradise of the third heaven are characterized by their good deeds. They have carried out righteous judgment, given bread to the hungry, covered the naked with clothing,

---

3; Berlin: Walter de Gruyter, 1962), 62–64. The requirement that the four legs of the sacrificial animal be tied together (*2 En.* 15, 21) is inexplicable in a Christian work.

[65] R. H. Charles lists several arguments for an Egyptian provenance (*APOT* 2:426). See also Morfill and Charles, *Secrets of Enoch,* xvii; Marc Philonenko, "La cosmogonie du 'Livre des Secrets d'Hénoch,'" in *Religions en Egypte Hellénistique et Romaine* (Paris: Presses Universitaires de France, 1969), 109–16, esp. pp. 109–10 (he admits Iranian influences as well); Fischer, *Eschatologie,* 40; and Böttrich, *Weltweisheit,* 192.

[66] However, the sacrificial practices described do not match the description one finds in rabbinic literature for those practiced in the Jerusalem temple. The four legs of an animal were not bound prior to being put to death as in *2 En.* 59 (see *m. Tamid* 4:1; *b. Tamid* 31b). This is probably due to the author's location in the Diaspora.

[67] Collins, *Apocalyptic Imagination,* 246.

helped the injured and orphans, walked ("without a defect" in MS J) before the Lord, and worshiped him alone (9:1). Chapter 42 offers a similar description of the righteous (vv. 6–9). They have been honest, compassionate, and gentle (42:12–13). Such people know and glorify the Creator (42:14). The righteous will escape torment and suffering and enjoy an eternal residence (65:11).

God's judgment, in *2 En.* 44:4–5, is based on a strict weighing of deeds on the scale:

> Happy is he who directs [his heart] toward every person, such as bringing help to him who has been condemned, and by giving support to him who has been broken, and by giving to the needy. Because on [the day of] the great judgment every deed of mankind will be restored by means of the written record. Happy is he whose measure will prove to be just and whose weight just and scales just! Because on the day of the great judgment every measure and every weight and every scale will be exposed as in the market; and each one will recognize his measure, and, according to measure, each shall receive his reward.

A similar concept of judgment is found in 49:1–3: "For I, I am swearing to you, my children, that before any person existed, a place of judgment was prepared for him, and the scale and the weight by means of which a person will be tested were prepared there ahead of time." Chapter 50 then admonishes the reader to do good deeds, since God has "put into writing the achievements of every person, [and] no one can escape." God is an "avenger" who will "repay" "on the day of the great judgment." The record of personal works recurs in 53:2–3: "You see that the works of every person, I, even I, am writing them down. And no one will destroy my handwriting, because the LORD sees everything." Chapter 52 juxtaposes the various works that bring blessing and those that bring God's curse. Verse 15 concludes: "All this will make itself known in the scales in the book on the great judgment day." The author of *2 Enoch* finds in these eschatological and cosmological scenes the crucial motivation for the ethical behavior being advocated.[68] Either God's reward and blessing or God's punishment and curse stand in the balance with every human action.[69]

---

[68] Collins, *Between Athens and Jerusalem,* 230–32; idem, *Apocalyptic Imagination,* 247; Nickelsburg, *Jewish Literature,* 186–87.

[69] Certain sins can outweigh otherwise good deeds on the scale. In 63:1–4 we are told:

> [And] a person, when he clothes the naked [and] gives his bread to the hungry, will find remuneration. But if his heart should murmur, then he makes a loss, and

Sacrifice is certainly a major motif throughout *2 Enoch*. Does sacrifice imply an element of mercy in the overall scheme? The emphasis on the priestly succession from Methuselah to Melchizedek in the later chapters, which may be an addition to the work, lends credibility to the possibility. Enoch, according to 64:5, "carries away" sin. Nevertheless, the benefits of the sacrificial system are still subordinated to a strict system of merits and scales. For example, in 2:2 sacrificing the firstborn of the herd brings about God's blessing. How the author understands this statement is clear by the parallel statements: "Do not be ungenerous with the LORD's gifts; the LORD will not be ungenerous with his donations in your storehouses." In other words, God's blessing comes about as a result of the human good deed. Similarly, 42:6's reference to "offerings of life" is in the context of the good deeds that God will reward. In 45:1: "He who is prompt with his oblations in front of the face of the LORD, the LORD will be prompt with his *compensations*" (emphasis mine). *Second Enoch* 59:1–2's mention of sacrifice is juxtaposed with evil acts that bring harm.

Although *2 Enoch* is a product of a Hellenistic Judaism influenced by Egyptian thought patterns, it is important to recognize that a strict judgment according to works corresponds neatly with the same motif elsewhere in Judaism (e.g., *m. ʾAbot*, Qumran, *4 Ezra*). The emphasis on God's strict judgment is perfectly understandable whenever God's mercy and election of Israel do not figure into the equation, as is the case in *2 Enoch*. Even sacrifice has been subordinated to a system of strict justice applied on a global scale to all humanity without exception.

V. *Testament of Abraham*[70]

The *Testament of Abraham* is extant in two recensions, a shorter version (B) and a longer one (A). George W. E. Nickelsburg has argued persuasively that *rec.* A is the more original version.[71] The parallels to Egyptian

---

nothing will be obtained. And when the poor man is satisfied, and his heart is contemptuous, then he forfeits all his good work, and he will not obtain [anything]. For the LORD detests every kind of contemptuous person.

[70]The English translation used in what follows is that of E. P. Sanders, "Testament of Abraham" (*OTP* 1:882–902). Michael Stone includes a copy of the Greek texts of both recensions with his translation in *The Testament of Abraham: The Greek Recensions* (Texts and Translations, Pseudepigrapha Series 2; Missoula, Mont.: Society of Biblical Literature, 1972).

[71]George W. E. Nickelsburg, "Structure and Message in the Testament of Abraham," in *Studies on the Testament of Abraham* (ed. George W. E. Nickels-

mythology indicate that the provenance of *rec.* A is most probably Egypt.[72] While the dating of the work is difficult to ascertain, an Egyptian provenance would require a date prior to 117 C.E., and more likely around 100 C.E.[73] The central role of Abraham indicates that this is Jewish literature.

The plot of *The Testament of Abraham* divides into two closely parallel sections: a visit by the angel Michael to take Abraham away to heaven and a visit by Death. Abraham stalls his impending death by asking Michael to show him all the world (*T. Ab.* 9). God approves the wish, and so *T. Ab.* 10 narrates the journey looking down from above the world. Abraham watches as the inhabitants of the world go about their daily routines. When Abraham sees evildoers in action, he prays that God may send wild beasts to devour them. When he sees other evildoers, he prays for the earth to swallow them up or for fire to come down from heaven and consume them. God orders Michael to stop the chariot ride: "For if [Abraham] were to see all those who pass their lives in sin, he would destroy everything that exists" (*T. Ab.* 10:13). One might note here the very skeptical estimation of human ability to remain free from sin. God points out that Abraham himself, on the other hand, had not previously sinned (10:14). At this point in the narrative Abraham can no longer claim a sinless existence. Abraham must be conducted to the place of judgments and recompenses in order that he may repent over the sinners he destroyed (10:15).

Testament of Abraham 11–13 describe the judgment scenes. At the first gate of heaven Abraham sees two passageways: one broad for the vast majority of sinful humanity and one narrow for the few judged

---

burg; SBLSCS 6; Missoula, Mont.: Scholars Press, 1972, 1976), 85–93. Nickelsburg (p. 92) explains why *rec.* A, with its better preservation of the plot of the story, is likely the more original. *Rec.* B, Nickelsburg proposes, ended up in its final form due to an intervening process of oral transmission.

[72] For example, the notion that *souls* would be weighed on scales is typically Egyptian. The document also parallels the Egyptian Jewish *Testament of Job;* Mathias Delcor, *Le Testament d'Abraham: Introduction, Traduction du Texte Grec et Commentaire de la Recension Grecque Longue* (SVTP; Leiden: E. J. Brill, 1973), 47–51, 67–68. Delcor (pp. 28–32, 59–62) traces the parallels to the Egyptian Book of the Dead. Enno Janssen's case for a Palestinian origin (*Testament Abrahams* [JSHRZ 3/2; Gütersloh: Mohn, 1975], 198–99) relies too much on evidence from the Septuagint; thus Sanders, "Testament of Abraham," *OTP* 1:875 n. 28.

[73] "Plus or minus twenty-five years," as Sanders ("Testament of Abraham," *OTP* 1:874–75) puts it, since Egyptian Judaism was not sufficiently intact after 117 C.E. for the production of such literature. The parallels to the *Testament of Job* may also point to a first-century C.E. date.

worthy. Adam sits at the gate rejoicing as angels usher souls through the narrow passage, but crying and wailing over the many going through the wide passage. The skepticism in 10:13 regarding human ability to refrain from sin is confirmed in *T. Ab.* 11:12: "For among seven thousand there is scarcely to be found one saved soul, righteous and undefiled." Michael and Abraham then proceed through the broad passage to the second gate (12:1–3). A man sits upon a throne with a table set before him. On the table is a book, and angels flank both sides of the table with papyrus, ink, and pen. The account continues (12:9–13):

> In front of the table sat a light-bearing angel, holding a balance in his hand. [On] (his) left there sat a fiery angel, altogether merciless and relentless, holding a trumpet in his hand, which contained within it an all-consuming fire (for) testing the sinners. And the wondrous man who sat on the throne was the one who judged and sentenced the souls. The two angels on the right and on the left recorded. The one on the right recorded righteous deeds, while the one on the left (recorded) sins. And the one who was in the front of the table, who was holding the balance, weighed the souls.

Michael explains to Abraham that this is the judgment and recompense. An angel then brings a soul to the judge. The books are opened, and the soul's sins and righteous deeds turn out "to be equally balanced." Abraham inquires and finds out that the judge is Abel. Michael adds (13:9–14):

> The two angels, the one on the right and the one on the left, these are those who record sins and righteous deeds. The one on the right records righteous deeds, while the one on the left (records) sins. And the sunlike angel, who holds the balance in his hand, this is the archangel Dokiel, the righteous balance-bearer, and he weighs the righteous deeds and the sins with the righteousness of God. And the fiery and merciless angel, who holds the fire in his hand, this is the archangel Purouel, who has authority over fire, and he tests the work of men through fire. And if the fire burns up the work of anyone, immediately the angel of judgment takes him and carries him away to the place of sinners, a most bitter place of punishment. But *if the fire tests the work of anyone* and does not touch it, this person is justified and the angel of righteousness takes him and carries him up to to be saved in the lot of the righteous. And thus, most righteous Abraham, all things in all people are tested by fire and balance (italics original).

Abraham inquires about the soul currently adjudged in the middle. Michael explains that "since the judge found its sins and its righteous deeds to be equal" the soul must await the judge of all (14:2). In fact, "if it could acquire one righteous deed more than (its) sins, it would enter in to be saved" (14:4). At this point, Abraham prays for the soul. God heeds the prayer and the soul is saved. Abraham then prays for those souls he had brought to a premature death and judgment (14:12–15).

Here again one finds a judgment according to a majority of deeds (like *2 Enoch, 3 Baruch,* and *m. Abot* 3:16). The notion of deeds being weighed in a balance is also paralleled in *1 En.* 41:1; 61:8; *4 Ezra* 3:34 (but here it is the weighing of Israel's deeds versus the Gentiles, and not the deeds of individuals); cf. Prov 16:2; 21:2; 24:12; *L.A.B.* 40:1; also Job 31:6; Ps 62:9; Dan 5:27. Some have argued that the *Testament of Abraham,* like *2 Enoch,* is heavily influenced by Hellenistic categories.[74] Even so, the *Testament of Abraham* reveals a Hellenistic Jew's understanding of what the eschatological judgment will be like and what God as judge will find acceptable for admission into heaven.

There is nothing in *The Testament of Abraham* about election, covenant, sacrifices, or special privileges for Abraham's progeny. The gracious framework of Judaism is clearly compromised. On the other hand, Abraham's repentance for his sin (14:12–15) does bring about God's forgiveness. Abraham is forgiven for a single sinful act, his rash judgment of humanity when viewing the world. Would repentance avail for a multitude of sins? Would one have to repent for each individual sin committed? Does repentance have a special value over against individual righteous or evil acts? Even when Abraham prays for the soul held in the balance, which resulted in the soul's salvation, there is nothing to indicate that this "merit of the Father" was only for his own elect descendants. On the contrary, Abraham intercedes

---

[74] For discussion, see George W. E. Nickelsburg, "Eschatology in the Testament of Abraham: A Study of the Judgment Scenes in the Two Recensions," in *Studies on the Testament of Abraham* (ed. George W. E. Nickelsburg, SBLSCS 6; Missoula, Mont.: Scholars Press, 1972, 1976), 32–35. E. P. Sanders notes the shift from the Egyptian notion of a weighing of souls in 12:13 to a more typically Jewish idea of the weighing of *deeds* in 13:10; "Testament of Abraham," in *Outside the Old Testament* (ed. M. De Jonge; Cambridge Commentaries on the Writings of the Jewish and Christian World 200 BC to AD 200, 4; Cambridge: Cambridge University Press, 1985), 67–68. Could it be that Egyptian motifs are being assimilated into a Jewish environment? Nickelsburg's comments vis-à-vis the Egyptian Book of the Dead are telling: "Since the Egyptian model does not account for all of the elements in the T Abr judgment scene, we may look elsewhere for their source. The most obvious place is in Jewish writings" ("Eschatology," 34). Nickelsburg (pp. 39–40) concludes that a traditional Jewish judgment scene has been modified with Egyptian elements, including the balance. That the notion of a balance could find acceptance in Judaism is reinforced by the prominence of the weighing motif elsewhere in Jewish literature.

on behalf of the souls he had prematurely judged *in general.* The patriarch's merit offers a universal benefit.[75] One may further suspect that it has value only when souls are hanging in the balance between good and evil deeds, as was the instance in question. If correct, such mercy factors into an equation that is still dominated by the weighing of deeds. Sanders points to God's mercy (e.g., 10:14).[76] Yet this mercy consists in God's patience and a delay of death so that the sinner might convert and live (see also 14:15). In the overall scheme of the document, such a conversion would surely bring about righteous deeds that would begin to tip the scales toward salvation. All humanity, whether Jew or Gentile, is judged in the same way, on the basis of a scale that measures the good against the evil done.[77] The emphasis in this section is not on a legalistic system, as Stone and Nickelsburg rightly point out, but on righteous Abraham's own shift from self-righteous condemnation of others to compassionate intercession.[78] Abraham's compassion thus mirrors God's own compassion and patient mercy that give people an opportunity to repent and turn their lives around while there is yet time.

Testament of Abraham, with its heavenly journey and judgment scenes, is a borderline example of the apocalytic genre.[79] Along with *4 Ezra, 2 Enoch,* and *2 Baruch,* this apocalyptic literature represents a type of Judaism where God's justice does not allow for mercy apart from a completely, or at least mostly, righteous life. All of these documents are characterized by a minimizing, or absence, of Israel's special privileges of election and covenant.

---

[75] Gabriele Boccaccini concludes tellingly: "Thus, even the 'merits of the fathers' acquire universal validity" (*Middle Judaism: Jewish Thought, 300 B.C.E. to 200 C.E.* [Minneapolis: Fortress, 1991], 259). He adds: "If, then, the Gentile can gain salvation by practicing the same morality that the Jew learns through the law, what sense is there in speaking about proselytism, about the repudiation of national and religious identity, about 'desertion,' and about entrance into a new people?" So also Sanders, "Testament of Abraham" (*OTP* 1:877–78).

[76] Sanders, "Testament of Abraham," in *Outside the Old Testament,* 57.

[77] Note especially that the morality implicit in Abraham's judgment in ch. 10 applies to Jews and Gentiles alike. He strikes down thieves and fornicators. As Boccaccini writes: "The unit of measure is not the law, but rather a universally applied morality" (*Middle Judaism,* 259).

[78] George W. E. Nickelsburg and Michael E. Stone, *Faith and Piety in Early Judaism: Texts and Documents* (Philadelphia: Fortress, 1983), 147.

[79] Collins, *Apocalyptic Imagination,* 251–52. The heavenly journeys and judgments scenes are crucial to the work as a whole.

VI. Conclusion

In the previous chapter several Jewish authors and documents from various times and places were adduced as evidence of a logical tension in Judaism between God's will that the law be perfectly obeyed and God's mercy granted to an elect people who often fell short of that demand. While the law was indeed a special possession of the Jewish people and a sign of their covenant identity, the ethnic, covenantal dimension of the law was never exclusive of its character as a demand. Covenant and obligation represented two sides of the same coin.

In this chapter, it has become clear that whenever covenant, election, repentance, sacrifice, and/or atonement play a reduced role (if any at all), the demands of the law come to the fore. Either absolute perfection or a majority of good works is necessary. Often God is viewed as judging on the basis of a weighing of deeds.[80] *Fourth Ezra,* in its explicit debate between the positions of covenantal nomism and legal perfectionism (or near-perfectionism), attests to what can happen when the covenantal framework collapses. Likewise *2 Enoch, 2 Baruch, 3 Baruch,* and the *Testament of Abraham* all exhibit a corresponding increase in focus on the strict demands of the law when God's election of Israel is no longer a factor. While many of these documents reflect the events of 70 C.E., the increased focus on the law's rigorous demand is a natural outgrowth of the compromise of the careful balance maintained between grace and demand in pre-70 C.E. Jewish writings.

---

[80] The position of Rabban Gamaliel (*b. Sanh.* 81a) was not unprecedented in Judaism.

Chapter Three

Would Paul the Apostle Affirm Covenantal Nomism's "(Old) Covenant"?

"Covenant," not surprisingly, is the crucial term in E. P. Sanders's formulation of "covenantal nomism": "Briefly put, covenantal nomism is the view that one's place in God's plan is established on the basis of the covenant and that the covenant requires as the proper response of man his obedience to its commandments, while providing means of atonement for transgression."[1] Sanders's thesis is that covenant and Mosaic law are two sides of the same coin. There is never a covenant without the covenantal obligations/law, and there is never law apart from the covenantal framework, a framework that attests to God's relationship with Israel.

Many of Sanders's reviewers have doubted whether covenant is as central a concept in Judaism as Sanders claims.[2] Further, Sanders fails to

---

[1] Sanders, *Paul and Palestinian Judaism,* 75.

[2] Anthony J. Saldarini in his book review of *Paul and Palestinian Judaism* criticizes Sanders for imposing a covenantal framework on the halakah: "Halaka is not derived from covenant in any concrete way in Tannaitic literature; it is itself central and primary" (*JBL* 98 [1979]: 300); likewise George Brooke, *JJS* 30 (1979): 247–50; George W. E. Nickelsburg (with Robert A. Kraft), *Early Judaism and Its Modern Interpreters* (Atlanta: Scholars Press, 1986), 20–21. Sanders does not dispute the centrality of halakah or that the term "covenant" may not always be used. Nevertheless, he insists that covenant is the conceptual framework for the halakah; *Paul and Palestinian Judaism,* 420–21; idem, "Puzzling Out Rabbinic Judaism," 66–67. Jacob Neusner has agreed with Sanders on this point in "The Use of the Later Rabbinic Evidence for the Study of Paul," in *Approaches to Ancient Judaism* (ed. William Scott Green; 5 vols.; Chico, Calif.: Scholars Press, 1978–1985), 2:43–63, esp. pp. 47–50. For an excellent further discussion and defense of Sanders's prioritizing of the covenant, see Alan F. Segal, "Covenant in Rabbinic Writings," *SR* 14 (1985): 53–62.

define the "covenant."[3] Whatever one concludes about these matters, the central thrust of Sanders's argument is that obedience to the Mosaic law is always within the gracious framework of God's election and covenant relationship with Israel. It would be helpful to trace how Paul handles the word *covenant* as opposed to covenantal nomism. Does Paul see the Jewish covenant, inclusive of the Mosaic law (as Sanders), as a gracious framework for God's people? Does the covenant relationship offer life and/or salvation?[4] In short, is Paul a covenantal nomist?

"Covenant" (διαθήκη) is used in the undisputed Pauline corpus in the eucharistic formula of 1 Cor 11:25 (cf. the Gospel parallels)[5] and repeatedly in three other passages: Gal 3–4 (3:15 and 17; 4:24), 2 Cor 3 (vv. 6, 14), and Rom 9–11 (9:4; 11:27, perhaps as a sort of inclusio). Additional references in Rom 9:4 and 11:27 will be covered in the discussion of Rom 9–11 in the next chapter. Since 1 Cor 11:25 may represent traditional material taken over by Paul, the pivotal references are Gal 3:15–18; 4:21–31; 2 Cor 3:6 and 14.

I. Galatians 3:15–17

The Jews of Paul's day often claimed that the law was eternal (e.g., Wis 18:4; *4 Ezra* 9:37; *1 En.* 99:2; Philo, *Mos.* 2.14) and that Abraham himself obeyed the law. The 430 years between Abraham and Moses were hardly "law-free." Sirach 44:19–20 says: "Abraham was the great father of a multitude of nations, and no one has been found like him in glory. He kept the law of the Most High." *Second Baruch* 57:2 says that Abraham followed the "unwritten law" and that the "works of the commandments were accomplished at that time" (so also Philo, *Abr.* 275–276; *Jub.* 11–23; *m. Qidd.* 4:14; *b. Yoma* 28b). In this light, Paul's words in Gal 3:15–17 are striking:

---

[3] For example, the Qumran community would define the covenant differently from the Tannaim. The covenant no longer defines God's relationship with the nation, but with the community. Nickelsburg (with Kraft, *Early Judaism*, 21), pointing to the discussions of Moses and Aaron in Sir 45:1–5 and 45:6–22, notes that in Joshua ben Sira the priestly covenant takes precedence over the Sinaitic covenant. The corresponding question, in terms of Paul, is whether he is speaking of an Abrahamic covenant or a Mosaic/Sinaitic covenant.

[4] Whereas there is no affirmation of life after death in, for example, Ben Sira, Paul would of course assert that salvation involves more than a right relationship with God; salvation would include resurrection and a place in the world to come.

[5] 1 Cor 11:25 indicates that a Jew would not be able to participate in the "new covenant" apart from Christ and the eucharistic blood.

> Brothers and sisters, I give an example from daily life: once a person's will [διαθήκη] has been ratified, no one adds to it or annuls it. Now the promises were made to Abraham and his offspring; it does not say, "And to offsprings," as of many; but it says, "And to your offspring," that is, to one person, who is Christ. My point is this: the law, which came four hundred thirty years later, does not annul a covenant [διαθήκη] previously ratified by God, so as to nullify the promise.

If Sanders is right that covenant and law are two sides of the same coin in "covenantal nomism," then Paul's argument here would be troubling.[6] First, Paul asserts that the law came 430 years after the promise and "covenant" (διαθήκη). Where obedience to the law, according to covenantal nomism, is grounded in the covenant relationship begun with Abraham, Paul sunders that relationship.[7] To relate the law to God's covenant with Abraham would be to add an illegal codicil to that covenant. J. Louis Martyn writes: "Separating covenant and Law in this radical manner, then, Paul is scarcely pursuing a line of thought that moves within the frame of reference properly identified as covenantal nomism. On the contrary, it explodes that frame of reference by a bill of divorce, the divorcing of covenant from Law."[8]

Second, Paul departs from the covenantal understanding of Judaism when he speaks of the singular "seed." Far from granting a special people as beneficiaries of God's covenantal dealings with Abraham, Paul envisions only one beneficiary of God's covenant: Jesus Christ. The history of God's saving work seems to skip from Abraham to Christ, finally including a very different "covenant" people, a people incorporated by faith and baptism into Christ, *the* "Seed" (Gal 3:28–29).[9]

---

[6] On the intimate connection between the covenant and the law in Jewish thought, see also the conclusions of Annie Jaubert, *La Notion D'Alliance dans le Judaïsme: Aux Abords de L'Ère Chrétienne* (Patristica Sorbonensia 6; Paris: Cerf [Editions du Seuil], 1963), 457–58.

[7] Paul's argument was moving toward this conclusion already in Gal 3:6–12. He discusses Abraham in vv. 6–9 completely apart from the law, and then discusses the law in vv. 10–12 without any reference to Abraham; Jeffrey S. Siker, *Disinheriting the Jews: Abraham in Early Christian Controversy* (Louisville: Westminster John Knox, 1991), 37.

[8] J. Louis Martyn, "Events in Galatia: Modified Covenantal Nomism versus God's Invasion of the Cosmos in the Singular Gospel," in *Thessalonians, Philippians, Galatians, Philemon* (ed. Jouette M. Bassler; vol. 1 of *Pauline Theology;* Minneapolis: Fortress, 1991), 171; likewise Erich Gräßer, *Der Alte Bund im Neuen* (WUNT 35; Tübingen: J.C.B. Mohr [Paul Siebeck], 1985), 61. Paul's reasoning would have been scandalous to Judaism and its understanding of the law.

[9] On the participatory mode of Paul's argument, see A. Andrew Das, "Oneness in Christ: The *Nexus Indivulsus* between Justification and Sanctification

Finally, it is important to note that in vv. 15–17, Paul does not employ a typically covenantal meaning of the word διαθήκη. The NRSV translates the first instance of the word as "will" and the second as "covenant," indicating the play on words in the passage. Note the legal language in v. 15: "ratify a will" (κυρόω διαθήκην), "annul a will" (ἀθετέω), "add a codicil" (ἐπιδιατάσσομαι).[10] In secular Greek usage, the word διαθήκη was used overwhelmingly as a legal term for a "last will and testament" and almost never as a "covenant" or agreement between two parties.[11] Paul's audience consisted primarily of Gentile Christians, who would not have missed the secular, legal connotations of the term.[12] The precise legal instrument that Paul has in mind has proven elusive.[13] Paul's point, though, remains clear. The legal διαθήκη cannot be altered or amended. Paul interprets the Abrahamic διαθήκη in these terms, allowing him to rule out any dependence on the later Mosaic law.

---

in Paul's Letter to the Galatians," *Concordia Journal* 21 (1995): 173–86. Paul's use of a singular seed runs counter to the collective understanding of "seed" in Judaism (and presumably the Jewish-Christianity at Galatia). On the "seed of Abraham" as an important motif in Jewish thought, see *Jub.* 16:17; 1 Macc 12:21; *Ps.-Clem., Recognitions,* 1.33.3; 1.34.1. N. T. Wright (*Climax,* 157–74) believes that "seed" here is collective, even as it is in Gal 3:29. However, the natural reading of the text is an emphatic singular seed in contrast to the plural (or collective) seed. The one seed is Jesus Christ himself. Wright proposes that Jesus is the Messiah who sums up all Israel in himself and thereby rescues the possibility of a collective "seed" here. The reading seems entirely forced and depends on Wright's understanding of Jesus as Israel's Messiah in other Pauline texts. The crucial difficulty to Wright's theory is that he must read the text backward from Gal 3:29. On a sequential reading of the text, there is nothing to indicate a collective sense in 3:16. On the contrary, it is only in v. 29 that Christians are incorporated into the one seed.

[10] J. Louis Martyn, "Covenant, Christ, and Church in Galatians," in *The Future of Christology: Essays in Honor of Leander E. Keck* (ed. Abraham J. Malherbe and Wayne A. Meeks; Minneapolis: Fortress, 1993), 141; so also Johannes Behm, "διαθήκη," *TDNT* 2:124–26.

[11] Behm, *TDNT* 2:124–25; Henry George Liddell and Robert Scott, *A Greek-English Lexicon* (9th ed.; Oxford: Oxford University Press, 1940), 394–95. The only exception in secular Greek literature is Aristophanes, *Av.* 440–441, where the word is used for a treaty between two parties.

[12] See Gal 4:8 as well as the distinction between the Galatians addressed in the second person and the Jewish-Christian outsiders addressed in the third person (1:7; 5:10, 12; 6:13); J. Louis Martyn, "A Law-Observant Mission to Gentiles: The Background of Galatians," *SJT* 38 (1985): 307–24, esp. 313.

[13] Commentators regularly note the difficulties; see, e.g., Ernst Kutsch, *Neues Testament—Neuer Bund? Eine Fehlübersetzung wird korrigiert* (Düsseldorf: Neukirchener Verlag, 1978), 137–42.

Paul frames his discussion of "covenant" strictly in terms of Abraham. There is no mention of Moses or the Mosaic covenant (quite unlike Gal 4:21–31 or 2 Cor 3). Instead, Paul presents his case in the most startling way possible for a covenantal nomist by placing the Mosaic law in a sharp antithesis with the "covenant," the *real* covenant in Paul's mind, the Abrahamic covenant. This is the only covenant of value for Paul in Galatians, and he severs any relation between it and the Mosaic law.[14]

It is understandable that the law's role is negative in this context. The Abrahamic "inheritance" does not come "from the law" in v. 18. The law does not mediate the blessings and promise of the Abrahamic covenant. In v. 10 all who are characterized by the "works of the law are under a curse." In v. 11 no one is brought into a right relationship with God by means of the law. In the most pointed statement of all, Paul says in v. 21: "For if a law had been given that could make alive, then righteousness would indeed come through the law."[15] Nowhere does Paul allow for any salvific or life-giving capacity in the law.

II. Galatians 4:21–31

Paul treats Gen 15–18 in Gal 4:21–31 in a very unusual way, particularly with regard to the Genesis covenant. Whereas Genesis spoke of a single covenant, Paul speaks of two. The one covenant in Genesis was to be with Isaac and *not* with Ishmael. Yet Paul speaks of a covenant with Isaac and *another* covenant with Ishmael. Whereas Genesis spoke of a promise to Abraham along with the command to circumcise, Paul disrupts the connection and speaks of the promise apart from Sinai, the law, and circumcision (Gal 5:1–12). Finally, whereas in Genesis Abraham promptly carried out God's command to circumcise his household—one of the most notable features of the story for Jews (and Jewish Christians)—Paul completely omits any mention of Abraham's response.[16]

Paul's departures from the Genesis understanding of the "covenant" are part of a broader series of contrasts. In Gal 4:23 he speaks of

[14] Paul can elsewhere speak of the law, in the sense of Scripture, as witnessing to God's promise (Gal 4:21; Rom 3:31), but he never says that the law itself mediates that promise or blessing. See ch. 8.

[15] Paul's depiction contrasts sharply to the estimation of the law in Judaism as offering life (Deut 28:1–14; 30:1–20; Pss 1; 119; Sir 17:1–14; 45:5; *Let. Aris.* 31, 127; *2 Bar.* 38:2; 46:3–5; 48:22; *Pss. Sol.* 14:2; *L.A.B.* 23:10).

[16] J. Louis Martyn, "The Covenants of Hagar and Sarah," in *Faith and History: Essays in Honor of Paul W. Meyer* (ed. John T. Carroll, Charles H. Cosgrove, and E. Elizabeth Johnson; Atlanta: Scholars Press, 1990), 185–86.

those begotten according to the flesh as opposed to those begotten according to the promise. In v. 24 he speaks of bearing children into slavery as opposed to being mothered by freedom in v. 26. In v. 29 Paul speaks of two children: one begotten according to the flesh and one according to the Spirit. He speaks of the present Jerusalem in contrast to the Jerusalem above. In short, flesh-slavery-present Jerusalem is contrasted with Spirit-freedom-heavenly Jerusalem. The most telling point with respect to the relationship between covenant and the law is that Paul includes Sinai on the negative side of the divide. Sinai's inclusion in the list of "negatives" prepares readers for Paul's admonitions against the law in 5:1–12. Paul disrupts the theology of Judaism and Jewish Christianity by severing the connection between the covenant and promises on one side and the Sinaitic legislation on the other. No longer does the law serve within a gracious framework.[17]

Paul's radical departures from the Genesis narrative are more understandable if interpreted in light of the conflict situation at Galatia. Paul is combating a competing missionary movement that sought to inculcate the observance of the law. The Abrahamic narratives were, in all probability, a central component of their doctrine.[18] These narratives

---

[17] Only after pronouncing this shocking divide between the Mosaic law and its gracious, covenantal framework does he speak positively of the law, but in terms of Christ and the Spirit (for example, Gal 6:2).

[18] These Jewish Christians may well have been part of a broader missionary movement that labored parallel to Paul's own missionary endeavor. Embedded within the Pseudo-Clementine literature are two documents representing Jewish Christianity in the second century, *The Ascents of James* and *The Preachings of Peter.* In *The Ascents of James* the author asserts that it is necessary that the Gentiles be converted in order to fill up the number God had promised to Abraham when many Jews failed to believe in Jesus as the Messiah (*Ps.-Clem., Recognitions* 1.42.1). This Jewish-Christian document grounds the mission to the Gentiles on God's promise of progeny or "seed" to Abraham. In *The Preachings of Peter,* the author claims to be part of a group observing the law of Moses (*The Epistle of Peter to James* 2.5). The author goes on to speak of two missions to the Gentiles, one by Peter and the other by Paul, "the enemy man" who preached a "Law-less and absurd doctrine." Further, it was Peter's mission that was the first to the Gentiles; cf. Acts 8–11. See Martyn, "Law-Observant Mission," 307–24. Given the place of Abraham in second-century Jewish Christianity, could it be that Paul is responding to the language of his opponents at Galatia and that Abraham was a subject they had raised and not Paul himself? Note especially how Paul exegetes Gal 3:6 in the following verse by answering a question that was never posed in Gen 15:6 or Gal 3:6. The unstated question, "Who is it who can be said truly to be Abraham's children?" therefore emerges out of the polemical situation at Galatia as Paul interacts with their arguments and biblical citations; Martyn, "Covenant, Christ," 139; idem, "Law-Observant Mission," 317–19;

would teach the necessity of circumcision as a sign of God's covenant relationship with his people. Further, Abraham was held by the Jews of Paul's day to be a model of law-observance. "Covenant" would have been a key term for the apostle's opponents in their discussion of Abraham. Could this be why, when Paul first uses the word in Gal 3:15, he plays with the term before returning to its theological use (but divorced from the law)?[19] Similarly, Paul radically departs in 4:21–31 from the Genesis texts that would have been used by his opponents to place the law and circumcision in the context of God's covenantal dealings with the patriarch and his descendants.[20]

In Gal 4:21–31 Paul in effect renders explicit what had remained implicit in his discussion in the preceding chapter. A covenantal nomist would have objected in Gal 3 that Paul had ignored the *covenant* God made with Moses when he gave the law, surely a covenant based on God's dealings with Abraham. Paul returns in 4:21–31 to the connection between law and covenant and draws a contrast between two covenants. The Sarah/Isaac covenant is the only one of value and is not to be associated with the Mosaic law/Sinai. The Sinaitic covenant is a covenant of slavery associated with Hagar and Ishmael. Paul therefore grants an association between the Mosaic law and an Abrahamic covenant. Unfortunately for the covenantal nomist, it is the wrong one, the covenant of slavery.

III. 2 Corinthians 3:1–18

Paul uses the word "covenant" twice in 2 Cor 3 (vv. 6, 14). In contrast to Galatians, Paul here speaks of both a "new covenant" (3:6) and

---

Charles Kingsley Barrett, *Essays on Paul* (Philadelphia: Westminster, 1982), 158–59; idem, "The Allegory of Abraham, Sarah, and Hagar in the Argument of Galatians," *Rechtfertigung: Festschrift für Ernst Käsemann zum 70. Geburtstag* (ed. Johannes Friedrich, Wolfgang Pohlmann, and Peter Stuhlmacher; Tübingen: J.C.B. Mohr [Paul Siebeck], 1976), 6–7.

[19] J. Louis Martyn, "Covenant, Christ," 141–43.

[20] First, the Abrahamic texts clearly fit the opponents' case much better, with circumcision acting as the sign of the Abrahamic covenant. One need only see how far Paul has to depart from the text of Genesis in his response. A second indication that these are texts central to an ongoing debate at Galatia is the fact that the key characters are left unnamed and assumed when Paul first broaches the matter in 4:21. Some characters never are identified except by descriptive epithets. Finally, γέγραπται is the word Paul regularly uses to introduce OT quotations. Yet here Paul is not introducing a particular text but is summarizing a large block of OT material; Barrett, "Allegory," 9–10; Richard N. Longenecker, *Galatians* (WBC 41; Dallas: Word, 1990), 207–8.

an "old covenant" (3:14). Second Corinthians 3 is a hotly disputed passage, and one cannot hope to resolve all its problems. Yet the "covenant" idea is inextricably interwoven into the fabric of the developing argument. It will therefore be necessary to take a position on some of the problems of the text prior to making comparisons with covenantal nomism.[21]

Paul writes in 2 Cor 3:6: "[God] has made us competent to be ministers of a new covenant, not of letter but of spirit; for the letter kills, but the Spirit gives life." The word for "competency" or "sufficiency" parallels the use of cognate forms in 3:5 as well in 2:16 (ἱκανόω, ἱκανός, ἱκανότης). The "letter (γράμμα)/Spirit (πνεῦμα)" language matches Paul's use of ἐγγεγραμμένη as well as πνεῦμα in 3:3. Paul's language in v. 6 therefore builds on what immediately precedes. To understand v. 6 with its reference to the "new covenant" requires taking into consideration what Paul has said in the preceding verses.

In 3:3 Paul asserts that he does not need letters of recommendation since the Corinthians themselves serve as such for the apostle. The Corinthians manifest a writing (ἐγγεγραμμένη) not with ink (μέλανι) on stone tablets but on tablets of fleshly hearts (καρδίαις σαρκίναις). Paul is being confronted by those who possess "letters of recommendation" and who are challenging his apostolic credentials.[22] In response, Paul points to the work of the Spirit in his ministry (διακονηθεῖσα ὑφ' ἡμῶν). The Spirit's activity thus validates Paul's ministry in such a way that no "letters of recommendation" are necessary.

Initially, 2 Cor 3:3 is surprising. Paul seems to contrast the Spirit's writing on fleshly hearts with the writing of "ink" on *stone tablets*. One would expect "on parchments" (ἐν μεμβράναις).[23] The difficulty is resolved if one takes the contrast between ink and the Spirit and then between the stone and the fleshly tablets as two separate and distinct comparisons that further describe the "writing" of the "letter." The

---

[21] I am indebted in the following discussion to Scott Hafemann. He has offered an exegesis of 2 Cor 3 firmly grounded in the exegesis of Exod 32–34. Also, his understanding of this difficult Pauline text is the least negative with respect to the old covenant, and he takes that covenant seriously. Hafemann's approach offers the most conservative results with regard to a comparison with Judaism.

[22] Linda Belleville, *Reflections of Glory: Paul's Polemical Use of the Moses-Doxa Tradition in 2 Corinthians 3.1–18* (JSNTSup 52; Sheffield: Sheffield Academic Press, 1991), 136–66; idem, "A Letter of Apologetic Self-Commendation: 2 Cor. 1:8–7:16," *NovT* 31 (1989): 142–63, esp. 149, 152–56. He is writing an apologetic letter of self-commendation. Note the references to the opponents in 2:17 and 4:2.

[23] Murphy-O'Connor, "New Covenant," 196.

first contrast refers to the means of writing, that is, a letter written with ordinary, human "ink" versus one written by the Spirit. The second contrast expresses the *location* of this writing: it is not on stone tablets but on fleshly hearts.[24] Paul's letter of recommendation is the Corinthians themselves, since his ministry mediated the activity of the Spirit to them.

The stone tablets allude to the Mosaic law.[25] Paul will take up the matter of the Mosaic law in his exegesis of Exod 32–34 later in the chapter. At this point, though, there seems to be no reason for the allusion. Are Paul's opponents urging observance of the Mosaic law? Quite possibly. There are, however, indications in the text that explain why Paul spoke of stone tablets here.

In vv. 5–6 Paul employs the ἱκανός word group. This is the same word used in the call of Moses in Exod 4:10 (LXX).[26] Moses objects that he is not "sufficient" for the task to which God is calling him since he is slow of speech. God responds that he will provide the words for Moses to speak and that Aaron will assist Moses. Thus God makes Moses sufficient for the calling in spite of Moses' own insufficiency. Norman Habel[27] and Wolfgang Richter[28] have shown how these elements recur in the call of the prophets. God comes to the prophet and commissions him. When the prophet objects on the basis of an inadequacy, God sufficiently provides for what is lacking.[29] Paul may be responding to the attacks of his opponents upon his credentials by citing his divine prophetic call. Where the opponents might have seen Paul's suffering (2 Cor 1:3–11; 2:14; 4:7–12, 16–18; 6:3–10) or previous persecution of the church (1 Cor 15:8–10) as a liability, Paul sees it as an insufficiency rectified by the sufficiency of

---

[24] Scott J. Hafemann, *Suffering and the Spirit: An Exegetical Study of II Cor. 2:14–3:3 within the Context of the Corinthian Correspondence* (WUNT 2/19; Tübingen: J.C.B. Mohr [Paul Siebeck], 1986), 200–201.

[25] Cf. (LXX) Exod 24:12; 31:18; 32:15; 34:1; Deut 9:10.

[26] A connection noted already in 1946 by Austin Farrar in "The Ministry in the New Testament," in *Apostolic Ministry: Essays on the History and the Doctrine of the Episcopacy* (ed. K. E. Kirk; London: Hodder & Stoughton, 1946), 115–82, esp. 171, 173.

[27] Norman Habel, "The Form and Significance of the Call Narratives," *ZAW* 77 (1965): 297–323.

[28] Wolfgang Richter, *Die sogenannten vorprophetischen Berufungsberichte: Eine literaturwissenschaftliche Studie zu 1 Sam 9,1–10, 16, Ex 3f. und Ri 6,11b–17* (Göttingen: Vandenhoeck & Ruprecht, 1970).

[29] Exod 3:1–4:16; Judg 6:11–24; Isa 6:1–7; Jer 1:4–10; Ezek 1:1–3:11; see Hafemann's overview in *Paul, Moses, and the History of Israel* (WUNT 81; Tübingen: J.C.B. Mohr [Paul Siebeck], 1995; repr. Peabody, Mass.: Hendrickson, 1996), 42–62.

God's call.[30] In fact, Paul has begun to compare his own ministry to that of Moses and the prophets already in 2:16 by an allusion to his call as apostle (ἱκανός).[31] If Paul already has Moses' prophetic call in mind, the mention of the "stone tablets" would not be so abrupt.

Another rationale for Paul's reference to "stone tablets" may lie in the apostle's OT allusions. Christian Wolff has claimed that Paul is alluding to Prov 3:3, 7:3, and Jer 17:1 in the phrase "tablet of the heart."[32] The problem with Wolff's handling of 2 Cor 3:3 is that the OT passages he has identified do not account for the activity of the Spirit upon the heart, nor for the reference to a "fleshly" heart. These two motifs point decisively to Ezek 11:19–20 and 36:26–27.[33] Ezekiel 11:20 and 36:27 indicate that the purpose of the Spirit in providing a "fleshly heart" is to enable the people to obey God's decrees and judgments, that is, the Mosaic law. Ezekiel foresees a time when Israel will be enabled by the granting of God's Spirit to observe the law. Far from disparaging the law, Ezekiel affirms it. The problem is with Israel's failure and not with the law itself. This should warn against reading the contrast between the "stone tablets" and the "tablets of fleshly hearts" in such a way as to disparage the stone tablets.[34] Throughout OT and intertestamental literature, the

---

[30] Although not drawing the parallel to Exod 4:10, N. T. Wright has emphasized the theme of Paul's Christlike sufficiency in the face of suffering and apparent weakness; *Climax*, 176.

[31] That ἱκανός is a motif associated with Paul's apostolic call, see 1 Cor 15:9–10; Victor Paul Furnish, *II Corinthians* (AB 32A; New York: Doubleday, 1984), 197.

[32] Christian Wolff, *Jeremia im Frühjudentum und Urchristentum* (Texte und Untersuchungen zur Geschichte der altchristlichen Literatur 118; Berlin: Akademie Verlag, 1976), 134–42, esp. 135. Heikki Räisänen has seized on Wolff's work to deny allusions to Jeremiah and Ezekiel in the passage, and thus to any "new covenant" motif; *Paul and the Law* (2d ed.; WUNT 29; Tübingen: J.C.B. Mohr [Paul Siebeck], 1986), 242–43, 245.

[33] A reference to Jer 38:33 LXX is questionable in 2 Cor 3:3. First, there is no mention of the Spirit in Jer 38:31–34. Second, in 2 Cor 3:3 it is the "letter of Christ" written on the heart and not the law, as in Jer 38:33. Finally, the notion of "writing" or "engraving" may be due to the allusion of God's writing of the law on the tablets of stone in the pentateuchal references. Hafemann thus cautions against seeing a reference to Jer 38 here; *Suffering and the Spirit*, 205–6.

[34] Contra Hays, *Echoes*, 129; Samuel Vollenweider, *Freiheit als neue Schöpfung: Eine Untersuchung zur Eleutheria bei Paulus und in seiner Umwelt* (FRLANT 147; Göttingen: Vandenhoeck & Ruprecht, 1989), 262. Hays (p. 131) is more to the point when he writes: "The problem with this old covenant is precisely that is it (only) written, lacking the power to effect the obedience that it demands. Since it has no power to transform the readers, it can only stand as a witness to their condemnation." Similarly, Vollenweider is correct insofar as he identifies the problem of hardened hearts.

stone tablets of the law were held in high repute. The stone tablets were the "work of God" (Exod 32:16 LXX) and written by "the finger of God" (Exod 31:18; Deut 9:18). The Lord even saw fit to give them a second time (Exod 34:1). The tablets were a sign of Israel's *glory.* This high estimation of the stone tablets as "heavenly tablets" runs all through intertestamental Jewish literature.[35] That the law was recorded on stone tablets is never a negative matter, quite unlike the hearts of stone of which Ezek 11:19 and 36:26 speak. However, Paul sees the "new age" prophesied by Ezekiel coming to fulfillment in his very ministry. Far from being a continuation of the Mosaic ministry "on stone tablets," his is the new ministry of the Spirit "on tablets of human hearts." The abrupt reference to the Mosaic law is thus necessitated by Paul's use of Ezekiel to characterize his Spirit-ministry; Paul regards his ministry as a manifestation of the eschatological age of God's Spirit.

The continued reference to the Spirit in 2 Cor 3:6 serves to confirm 3:3, particularly if one sees an allusion in the language of "new covenant" to Jer 31:31 (LXX 38:31). This is the only place in the OT where "new covenant" language is found. Like Ezekiel, Jeremiah was confronting the problem of exile as a result of Israel's hard-hearted rebellion. Indeed, Jeremiah insists that such stiff-necked rebellion has *characterized* Israel's history (Jer 7:25–26). When God offers the people a chance to repent (Jer 26:1–3; 36:1–3, 7), the leaders respond violently and negatively to the offer (26:8–11; 36:23–25). The notion of the people's "stubbornness" (שְׁרִרוּת) and their evil hearts is a motif that runs all through the book.[36] Jeremiah 11:1–11 reviews the requirement of the original covenant that the people were to obey what God decreed at Sinai; the history of the people has become the exact reverse. So Jeremiah looks forward to the day when this evil tendency will no longer characterize the people, the day of the "new covenant" after the exile. Where Israel's sin was to be written on the people's hearts in Jer 17:1, Jeremiah looks forward to a time when God will restore his people. The people of "stubborn," "uncircumcised" hearts (Jer 4:4; 9:25–26) will no longer reject the law but will have it upon their hearts. The "new covenant" will bring about a change in the people's condition so that they obey God's law. Jeremiah LXX 38 (31), even as Ezek 11 and 36, speaks of a future restoration of the exiled people in which the problem of their stubborn disobedience will be rectified (cf. Bar 3:20–33; *Jub.* 1:23–25).

---

[35] For example, *Jub.* 1:1; cf. 1:26–27; 2:1; *1 En.* 81:1–2; *T. Levi* 5:4; 7:5; *2 Bar.* 6:7–9; see Hafemann, *Suffering and the Spirit,* 208–12.

[36] For example, Jer 3:17; 7:24; 9:13; 13:10; 16:12; 17:23; 18:12; 19:15; 23:17.

By alluding to these prophetic texts (3:3 to Ezekiel and 3:6 to Jeremiah), Paul is claiming a "new covenant" ministry.[37] In contrast to the old covenant (the "letter," the ministry of Moses), Paul's ministry is capable of bringing about a change in the people's condition.[38] Unlike the old covenant, his ministry is characterized by the presence of the eschatological Spirit. Paul says that God "has made us competent to be ministers of a new covenant, not of letter but of spirit." The phrase "not of letter but of spirit" is not modifying and explaining the "new covenant" but rather Paul's *ministry.* Because Paul is a minister of the "new covenant," he is, as a consequence, a minister of the "Spirit" and not the "letter." Even as "the letter kills, but the Spirit gives life," so Paul's ministry in 2:15–16 is also capable of bringing forth life.[39]

When understood in the context of Jeremiah and Ezekiel, it is no surprise that the "letter kills." The two prophets spoke of Israel's incessant stubbornness of heart and failure to do what God's law demanded (cf. *4 Ezra* 9:28–37). They looked to the day when God's Spirit would enable the people to obey the law. The "Spirit gives life" and enables the law to function as it was originally intended. The "letter" refers to the Mosaic law functioning apart from God's promised Spirit. Paul corroborates this way of understanding the contrast between the letter and the Spirit in Romans. In Rom 2, especially vv. 27–29, Paul explains that mere possession of the "letter" is of no value apart from a corresponding obedience, an obedience rendered by the Spirit who creates a "circumcision of the heart" (cf. Deut 10:16; Jer 4:4). Romans 7:6 contrasts service in the newness of the Spirit with the oldness of the letter. The Spirit works to free the individual from the effects of being in the "flesh" (ἐν τῇ σαρκί) and the "passions of sin" (τὰ παθήματα τῶν ἁμαρτίων). No longer is the believer ruled by sin, and no longer does the law work death. What ensues in Rom 7 and 8 will develop the two sides of this letter/Spirit antithesis: Romans 7 describes the law apart from the Spirit and in the hands of sin and the flesh; Romans 8 speaks of the law in the hands of the Spirit. In the presence of the Spirit, the law no longer condemns, and it becomes possible to fulfill the law's requirement.[40]

---

[37] Hafemann, *Paul, Moses,* 146.

[38] διακόνους in 3:6 furthers διακονηθεῖσα of 3:3. See also the use of διακονία and its cognates throughout 3:7–18.

[39] Hafemann, *Paul, Moses,* 157–58. Thus 3:6 parallels 3:3 where the contrasts of ink/Spirit and stone/fleshly heart tablets independently modified "being written."

[40] See ch. 9 on Rom 7–8. Paul takes a much more negative view of human ability to do what the law demands. Where the Sinai covenant brought blessings

Second Corinthians 3:7–11, a new paragraph in Paul's line of thought, compares the ministry of Moses and the new covenant/ Spirit ministry of Paul. These verses confirm the point made in 3:6: the letter/Moses' ministry kills, but the Spirit/Paul's ministry gives life (thus confirming Paul's "sufficiency"). In v. 7 Paul calls the Mosaic law a "ministry of death," which reinforces the idea just introduced in v. 6 that "the letter kills." Yet a negative evaluation of the law itself is immediately ruled out by Paul's point that the law came "in glory." This becomes the first in a series of lesser to greater a fortiori assertions. If the Mosaic ministry of death came "in glory," then (v. 8) "how much more will the ministry of the Spirit come in glory."[41] Verse 9 is then the second in the series: "if there was glory in the ministry of condemnation, much more does the ministry of justification abound in glory!" Again Paul equates the Mosaic letter with condemnation, even while affirming its glorious nature. Verse 11 speaks of the glory that was rendered inoperative as opposed to the glory that remains. The glory of the law is not abolished, but the law's ministry is one of "condemnation" and "death." The "letter kills."

There is a tension in this argument. How can the "ministry of death/condemnation" and the letter that "kills" be a ministry that came "in glory"? The Jews held the Mosaic law as a gift offering life and not death. As Hafemann summarizes the problem: "Either the 'letter kills,' in which case its glory must seemingly be denied; or its glorious nature as the very writing of God himself, given within the context of the great Sinai theophany, makes it equally impossible to describe it as a 'ministry of death.' For his opponents, Paul cannot have it both ways."[42] Thus it is

---

for obedience and curses for disobedience, Paul sees the old covenant, because of the condition of human sin, characterized by curse; the "letter kills." The problem of anthropology is developed by Timo Laato, *Paul and Judaism.*

It is a further advantage of such a reading of 2 Cor 3 that the "letter/Spirit" contrast functions in a way that conforms to its usage elsewhere in Paul. Those who take a hermeneutical approach to the contrast—that the Spirit refers to reading Scripture through the eyes of Christ and/or the church—adopt a reading that makes little sense of the letter/Spirit contrast in the contexts of Rom 2 and 7; see Hafemann's critique of Hays; *Paul, Moses,* 414 n. 245.

[41] The argument depends on the assumed agreement that the Mosaic law was a ministry "in glory." Note the placement of δόξα consistently at the end of the clauses to draw attention to itself as the central idea of the section; Carol Kern Stockhausen, *Moses' Veil and the Glory of the New Covenant* (AnBib 116; Rome: Pontifical Biblical Institute, 1989), 97, 111; Hafemann, *Paul, Moses,* 265–66. Having established that both ministries are glorious, Paul can assert the difference between the two ministries: their results, which then becomes the focus of vv. 13–18 (where the central word group is κάλυμμα).

[42] Hafemann, *Paul, Moses,* 273–74.

incumbent upon Paul to defend how the ministry of Moses is a ministry both of "death" and yet also of "glory." Paul's support for this twofold assertion is embedded within the a fortiori comparisons. He disrupts the parallelism of the comparisons at two crucial points. First, in v. 7 the comparison is disrupted by the addition of the phrase "chiseled in letters on stone tablets" (ἐν γράμμασιν ἐντετυπωμένη λίθοις). Then, later in the same verse, Paul expands upon the phrase "the ministry of death came in glory" by adding "so that [with the result that] the people of Israel could not gaze at Moses' face because of the glory of his face, a glory now set aside."[43] These two additions explicitly invoke the account of Exod 32–34 in support of Paul's argument. The first insertion serves to support the "glory" of the Mosaic ministry, while the latter and lengthier insertion shows why the Pauline ministry is the greater one.

The first insertion, ἐν γράμμασιν ἐντετυπωμένη λίθοις, repeats the word γράμμα from v. 6. This addition shows that, although the letter kills, the letter itself is not the problem. Rather, the origin of the "letter" was always one of glory. In Exod 24:12 and 31:18 (as well as Deut 5:22; 9:9–11) these words are used for the giving of the law by God himself! The reference to the "stone" tablets of the law alludes to Exod 34:1, 4 and 29.[44] These Exodus texts narrate the second giving of the law after the golden calf incident. As in the first giving of the law, the stone tablets are received in the midst of a divine theophany (cf. 34:5–9, 28). Furthermore, this glory remained even after the giving of the stone tablets, as evidenced by Moses' face (Exod 34:29–35).[45]

The second insertion, that the children of Israel were unable to gaze intently into Moses' face because of the glory of his face (an allusion to Exod 34:29–35), points to the lesser nature of the Mosaic ministry. Paul understands in 2 Cor 3:7 that one of the consequences of the glory of the law was that the Israelites were unable to gaze at the glory on Moses' face (ὥστε + infinitive/accusative). The original text of Exodus does not mention this consequence but speaks rather of the Israelites' fear (Exod 34:30). Is Paul's reading unwarranted? The rationale for Paul's interpretation may lie in the context of Exod 32–34. Where the MT (Exod 34:29–30, 35) speaks of Moses' face "shining" (קרן), the LXX interprets the event as Moses' face being "glorified" (δεδόξασται, ἦν δεδοξασμένη). The LXX thereby explicitly links the glory on Moses' face

---

43 The NRSV's translation, "a glory now set aside," is questionable, as will be clear in a moment.

44 The giving of the tablets is a factor that unites the narrative of Exod 32–34; see 31:18; 32:15–16, 19; 34:1–4.

45 Hafemann, *Paul, Moses*, 275–78.

to God's own "glory" (δόξα) in the theophany of Exod 33 (vv. 19, 22).[46] Indeed, one of the consequences of Israel's sin according to the LXX in Exod 33:5 is the loss of their garments of "glory" (δόξα). Thus God withdrew from the people lest they be destroyed. This latter reference, in the context of Exod 32–34, holds the clue to the people's "fear" (MT) and inability to gaze into Moses' face.

Upon the first giving of the tablets in Exod 31:18, the people of Israel had begun to make a golden calf. Furious, the Lord says to Moses that the people are "stiff-necked" and that his wrath shall now consume them (32:9–10). Moses intercedes, and the Lord stays his wrath. When Moses comes down and sees the activities, he too burns with anger (32:19; cf. 32:10) and shatters the stones upon the ground, an act that symbolizes the breaking of the covenant relationship.[47] Aaron explains his actions in terms of the "evil" people (32:22). Moses destroys the calf and has the people drink water mixed with its ground remains. He then sends out the Levites to execute people. Some three thousand Israelites are killed (32:28). Moses then returns to the Lord to intercede for the people. God's response is that Moses will lead them to the promised land, but those who sinned shall have their names blotted out of the book and shall be punished (32:33–34). At this point God sends a plague on the people (32:35). So despite Moses' intercession, God still acts with judgment upon the people. God informs Moses in 33:3 that he is removing his presence from their midst lest he consume them on the way, for they are a "stiff-necked" people. The Israelites are instructed to remove their garments of "glory" (33:5 LXX). Now Moses must meet God at a tent of meeting some distance from the camp (33:7). Moses therefore asks in 33:12 whom God will send with him.[48] God's presence in the midst of his people stands in question. So Moses pleads with God for his

---

[46] Ibid., 247–48. On Moses' face as shining in the Hebrew text (versus horns or disfigurement), see Menahem Haran, "The Shining of Moses' Face: A Case Study in Biblical and Ancient Near Eastern Iconography," in *In the Shelter of Elyon: Essays on Ancient Palestinian Life and Literature in Honor of G. W. Ahlström* (ed. W. Boyd Barrick and John R. Spencer; JSOTSup 31; Sheffield: JSOT Press, 1984), 159–73.

[47] Martin Noth, *Exodus: A Commentary* (trans. J. S. Bowden; Philadelphia: Westminster, 1962), 249.

[48] God's angel was going *before* the people preparing the way and not *with* the people (as Yahweh), thus Moses' question. Further, at this point the narrative introduces a distinction between Yahweh and his angel (cf. Exod 13:21–22; 14:19–20, 24; 16:10; 23:20–28; 25:8; 29:46). No longer will Yahweh accompany his people, but the angel, which he sends, will go before them (33:2–3); Knight, *Exodus*, 193. Moses himself is to lead the people.

presence to accompany the people (33:15–16). Exodus 33:17–23 then narrates God's showing of his glory and presence privately to Moses.

The narrative highlights the inability of the Israelites to endure God's presence in their midst for "one moment" (33:3, 5; 32:9, 22). Consequently, God withdraws his presence. Now the divine presence is manifested in the "tent of meeting" some distance from the camp.[49] God reveals his presence to the people as he meets with Moses, the mediator of that presence (33:7–11). Where God had previously spoken before the people generally (Exod 19:9; 20:18, 20; 24:9–11; Deut 5:22–24), he now speaks only to Moses. His glory is manifested to Moses *alone.*[50] This is a radical reversal of God's intent to manifest his glory and presence in the very midst of his people (Exod 19:5–6; 24:9–10; 25:8; 29:45–46; Lev 26:9, 11–13). Now God's direct visitation is no longer to bless (Exod 3:16; 4:31; 13:19) but to judge (32:34; 33:3, 5).

In Exod 34:9 Moses admits that the people are "stiff-necked," but he prays nevertheless that the Lord would still pardon and deliver the people. God responds with a series of cultic commands that correspond to the cultic sin of Israel with the golden calf.[51] God restores his covenant with Israel, but the nature of his relationship to Israel has changed. Now God acts through Moses (34:10, 27). Moses acts as the mediator of

---

[49] The presence of the tent at a distance from the camp is a sharp reversal of the plan for the tent to be in the midst of the camp (cf. Exod 25:8; 27:21; 28:43; 29:4, 10, 11, 30, 32, 42; 30:16, 18, 20, 36; 31:7; see also Num 2:17). Again, God is removing his presence from their midst; Moberly, *Mountain,* 63–64. "Outside the camp" symbolizes God's separation from the people (Lev 4:12, 21; 13:46).

[50] Moses recognizes that God's answer to his pleas in Exod 33:14 is in the singular, unlike the request in v. 13, which also referred to the nation. Moses responds in vv. 15–16 again in terms of God's being pleased with both Moses and the people. See George W. Coats, "The King's Loyal Opposition: Obedience and Authority in Exodus 32–34," in *Canon and Authority: Essays in Old Testament Religion and Theology* (ed. George W. Coats and Burke O. Long; Philadelphia: Fortress, 1977), 102. Moses is clearly the people's intercessor when God speaks of his favor toward Moses but omits any mention of the people. On this basis, Moses proceeds to encounter God alone. The theophany to Moses alone is the solution to the problem of God's presence. It will be manifested through Moses. Thus Moses' face shines for the first time after an encounter with God in 34:29–35. He is acting in a new capacity as the mediator of God's glory and presence. So also William J. Dumbrell, "Paul's Use of Exodus 34 in 2 Corinthians 3," in *God Who Is Rich in Mercy* (ed. Peter T. O'Brien and David G. Peterson; Homebush West NSW, Australia: Lancer Books, 1986), 181–85.

[51] Compare especially the molten calf in ch. 32 with 34:17 and the feast of 32:5 with 34:18, 22–23, 25–26; Dale Ralph Davis, "Rebellion, Presence, and Covenant: A Study in Exodus 32–34," *WTJ* 44 (1982): 82–83; Moberly, *Mountain,* 96.

God's covenant presence to the people because of their sin; if God dealt directly with the people they would be destroyed.[52] It is in this context that the LXX interprets the "glory" on Moses' face in light of God's own theophanic glory.[53] The people can see the glory of God mediated through Moses' unveiled face for a time, but they cannot gaze on that glory because of sin.[54] Hafemann writes:

> *Against the backdrop of the explicit statements of Exod. 32:9, 22 and 33:3, 5 and the function of the tent of meeting in 33:7–11, Moses' veiling himself should be seen as an act of mercy to keep the people from being destroyed by the reflected presence of God.* The veil of Moses makes it possible for the glory of God to be in the midst of the people, albeit now mediated through Moses, without destroying them (italics original).[55]

It is therefore the divine presence mediated through Moses that causes the people to "fear" and requires Moses' veiling. It is a merciful but necessary response in light of the people's "stiff-necked" condition and the problems that their condition causes for God's presence in their midst.[56] Like the fence around Mount Sinai in Exod 19:12 or the curtain

---

[52] Moses receives the covenant alone in ch. 34 and affirms the covenant without the people adding their voice (unlike Exod 19–24); Brevard Childs, *The Book of Exodus: A Critical, Theological Commentary* (OTL; Philadelphia: Westminster, 1974), 607. It is now Moses who prepares the stone tablets of the covenant; Brichto, "The Worship of the Golden Calf," 30; Moberly, *Mountain*, 105–6; Hafemann, *Paul, Moses*, 216.

[53] Moberly notes another connection to the theophany in the repeated references to Moses' "face": "Moses sought not only that Yahweh's 'face' should go with the people but that he might see Yahweh's glory. This latter was partially granted. Now the implication is that the Israelites see the glory of Yahweh in the face of Moses" (*Mountain*, 106). He now functions as mediator.

[54] The people's fear in 34:30 is justified in the context of God's removal of the divine presence in 33:5 lest there be judgment. God's direct presence in their midst would spell destruction. While the people are mercifully allowed to encounter the divine glory through Moses as mediator, Moses does not permit them to gaze on even the mediated glory because of their sin; Hafemann, *Paul, Moses*, 222–23. Note Paul's careful use of ἀτενίζω. On this point, see note 71.

[55] *Paul, Moses*, 223; contra Stockhausen, *Moses' Veil*, 96–101, who sees the veiling in Exodus as explicitly and implicitly unmotivated, and contra Belleville (*Reflections*, 208), who sees the veiling as unmotivated in Paul. The conundrum of the veil is thus resolved on the basis of the Exodus context itself. Moberly, *Mountain*, 108, suggested this reading of Exod 34:29–35 but failed to take into consideration Exod 32:9, 22 and 33:3, 5—the problems and danger of God's presence for a "stiff-necked" people. Similarly Dumbrell, "Paul's Use of Exodus 34," 186.

[56] The Israelites' fear and hesitance to approach Moses in Exod 34:30 parallels their fear and need to stay at a distance in the presence of God in Exod 19:16, 21; 20:18–20. Fear in God's presence is also attested in God's theophany to

protecting the "holy of holies," God's glory is shielded from the people for their own protection.

Given the Exodus background of the giving of the law, it should now be clear why the "letter kills." Moses' ministry of the letter had brought God's judgment upon the rebellious people. The Exodus generation's "stiff-necked" condition guaranteed that the curses of the covenant and not its blessings would rain down upon the people. The people had no eyes to see or ears to hear (Deut 29:2–4). While God acted in mercy in response to Moses' intercessions to renew the covenant, the people had to be shielded from God's glory lest they be destroyed (Exod 32:34; 33:3, 5).[57]

The decisive advantage of understanding 2 Cor 3 in light of Exod 32–34, as Scott Hafemann has shown, is that such a reading solves many of the traditional conundrums. Chief among them is certainly the meaning of καταργέω in 2 Cor 3:7. It is common in studies of this text to see the verb taken in the sense of "to fade away."[58] Yet there is no evidence that καταργέω in any of its voices ever meant that. Further, the idea of Moses' glory fading away would introduce a notion that was totally absent in the Jewish interpretation of Exod 34 in Paul's day.[59] Given

---

Moses in Exod 3:6 and in Jacob's reaction to God's presence at Bethel in Gen 28:17. Again, the glory on Moses' face is the solution to the dilemma as to how God's presence is to be manifested in the midst of a "stiff-necked" people (Exod 33:3, 5, 7–11, 12–17). The protective aspect of the veil is also paralleled in God's own protection of Moses from seeing the full glory in Exod 33:20 or the command for the people to remain at a distance for their own protection (Exod 19:21; 20:18, 21); David A. Renwick, *Paul, the Temple, and the Presence of God* (BJS 224; Atlanta: Scholars Press, 1991), 27–29. The people are allowed to "see" but not to "gaze" at the glory, as Paul worded it. They are prevented from full exposure to that glory lest they be destroyed. It remains a partial manifestation due to the condition of the people; Vollenweider, *Freiheit*, 258.

[57] Hafemann notes that the first establishment of the Sinai covenant was broken before it had even been fully inaugurated. Thus it could not bring about God's immediate and abiding presence. The renewed covenant therefore had to be veiled as an act of mercy and as an expression of judgment (cf. Exod. 34:6–7). Because of Israel's "stiff-necked" condition manifested in the golden calf incident, the glory of God that was originally intended to sanctify Israel (cf. Exod. 19:5, 9; 20:20), would now result in destruction (cf. Exod. 33:3, 5; 34:9). The veil would protect the people but also signified a degree of separation; *Paul, Moses,* 330. The danger for the people of the divine glory on Moses' face was recognized already in 1924 by Hans Windisch, *Der zweite Korintherbrief* (ed. Georg Strecker; KEK; Göttingen: Vandenhoeck & Ruprecht, 1970), 114.

[58] For example, Windisch, Belleville.

[59] Belleville's survey of Jewish literature identified a few instances where the glory on Moses' face was understood as fading, although the majority of the tradition emphasized the permanence of the glory; *Reflections,* 24–79. Hafemann reviews and refutes Belleville's examples of a fading glory; *Paul, Moses,* 287–98.

the polemical context of this passage, it is unlikely that Paul would introduce the novelty of a fading glory.[60] The Greek verb means rather to "abolish," "bring to an end," or to "render inoperative/ineffective." If taken to mean "render inoperative/ineffective," then the focus is on the abolishing of the *effects* of a phenomenon. The passive forms of the verb carry the same meanings as the active sense.[61] The translation "rendered ineffective" makes excellent sense in 2 Cor 3. The glory on Moses' face was being rendered ineffective so that the people would not be destroyed.[62] In v. 13 Paul clarifies that it was, in fact,

---

The tradition in Paul's day uniformly supports the permanence of the glory. Likewise the OT text itself gives no reason to indicate that the glory was not a "permanent radiance"; Julian Morgenstern, "Moses with the Shining Face," *HUCA* 2 (1925): 4, 11–12. Morgenstern cites the veil as a means of preventing the Israelites from gazing at Moses' glory when he was not addressing them, even as Yahweh in his glory was not to be gazed upon. In fact, in Num 27:20 Moses transfers some of his radiance to Joshua. On the relationship between Num 27:20 and Exod 34:29–35, see Haran, "Shining," 165–67.

[60] Hays writes: "Especially if the opponents were already appealing to the Exodus story to support their own self-presentation, Paul would be putting himself in an extraordinarily weak position if he based his argument on his own fictional embellishment of the text" (*Echoes,* 218 n. 39).

[61] Hafemann, *Paul, Moses,* 301–9. But would it be possible to take καταργέω as "abolish" or "come to an end" in 2 Cor 3 in the sense that the Israelites were not to gaze at the glory's coming to an end? In other words, a gradual coming to an end would border on the meaning of "fading." Hafemann writes: "In *no* case is it appropriate to translate καταργέω with the sense of a gradual 'fading away' of that which is said to be brought to an end. The action described is decisive and clear-cut" (*Paul, Moses,* 305). The verb is used for a status of being rendered inoperative/ineffective, or a decisive act of abolishing, but never a gradual process. Such a view would require actual instances where καταργέω meant a gradual coming to an end. There are no such instances. Belleville's reading (*Reflections,* 223–24) requires this translation, although she recognizes (pp. 204–6) that "render inoperative/ineffective" is the normal meaning of this word. She cites 1 Cor 2:6 as an instance of gradual "diminishing" or "fading." The problem is that she does not consider 1 Cor 1:28 just a few verses earlier, where Paul says "God chose what is low and despised in the world, things that are not, to reduce to nothing things that are." The things that "are not" thus render ineffective/abolish "things that are." So when Paul says in 1 Cor 2:6 that the rulers of this age are τῶν καταργουμένων, he means that they are being rendered ineffective/inoperative by means of the eschatological victory realized in Christ and the present dawning of the age to come (cf. 1 Cor 13:8, 10; 15:24–26). See Hafemann (*Paul, Moses,* 306–8) and Hays (*Echoes,* 133–34) on this point. Even in 1 Cor 2:6 there is no reason to depart from the normal meaning of the word.

[62] It is hardly likely that the participle is referring to events subsequent to Moses' ministry. The entire subordinate clause beginning with the ὥστε is temporally determined by ἐγενήθη, in this case, the time of Moses; Furnish,

the veil that was "rendering (the old covenant ministry inclusive of its glory) ineffective."[63]

Paul's reference to the inability of the Israelites to gaze at the glory on Moses' face highlights the negative aspect of the Mosaic ministry, namely, why it was a ministry of death and condemnation. It was because of their sinful condition that the mediated glory of God's presence was not fully revealed lest they be destroyed. The Israelites had good reason to "fear" when they saw Moses' face. This is precisely the advantage of Paul's ministry of the Spirit (cf. 3:3). The believer now encounters the glory of God without being destroyed. Instead of bringing death, this same glory brings life.[64]

There is a shift in vv. 10–11 to neuter substantival participles. No longer is Paul referring to the two "ministries" (the feminine ἡ διακονία), or the law (the masculine ὁ νόμος) or even the "glory" of the old covenant (the feminine ἡ δόξα). The neuter signals a broadened referent. Paul is now contrasting the old covenant ministry of the "letter" with the new covenant ministry of the "Spirit," but with the "letter" and "Spirit" taken in the abstract or collective sense, that is, in light of all that has been said up to this point.[65] Paul says that in a certain respect (ἐν τούτῳ τῷ μέρει) the ministry of the old covenant has not been glorified at all, that is, when compared to the

---

II Corinthians, 203; Hafemann, *Paul, Moses,* 300. The articular participle τὴν καταργουμένην modifies τὴν δόξαν, the glory that the Israelites were unable to gaze upon. This also rules out Hays's reading of v. 10 in which the participle is taken to refer to the passing away of the old covenant in Paul's own day; *Echoes,* 134–35, 219 n. 43. Nor is this the termination of the law; contra Wright, *Climax,* 181, 191–92. See Hafemann's correction (*Paul, Moses,* 300 n. 136) of Stockhausen's argument that the participle refers to Paul's time: context determines an attributive participle's relation to the main verb. Hafemann corrects her use (*Moses' Veil,* 120 n. 60) of Moulton-Turner as well. The validity of Stockhausen's translation of τέλος as well as her reading in general depend upon her handling of καταργουμένον. There is nothing in this text to indicate a shift to a frame of reference contemporary with Paul or Christ, quite in contrast to 3:14–15, where temporal expressions clearly and explicitly indicate the shift to a contemporary reference.

[63] In 2 Cor 3:7 Paul writes: τὴν δόξαν τοῦ προσώπου αὐτοῦ τὴν καταργουμένην. In 3:11 Paul uses the neuter participle: τὸ καταργούμενον. The neuter refers back to τὸ γράμμα and/or τὸ πρόσωπον. Paul has broadened the referent of καταργέω to speak of the old covenant ministry of the letter and/or on Moses' face. Likewise the neuter δεδοξασμένον takes on a broadened referent; Hafemann, *Paul, Moses,* 323–24.

[64] Hafemann, *Paul, Moses,* 313–14.

[65] Belleville (*Reflections,* 203) identifies the old covenant with special emphasis on the Mosaic ministry; similarly Hays, *Echoes,* 135.

purpose and effects of the new covenant ministry. Where the former brought death and condemnation, the latter brings the Spirit and an abounding glory.[66]

In 3:12–18 Paul elaborates further on the significance of Exod 34:29–35 in order to emphasize the need for the veil (2 Cor 3:12–13), which is then traced to the hardening of their minds/understandings (3:14). This situation of hardened minds/understandings has remained even to Paul's own day when Moses/the "old covenant" is read (3:14–15). What is Paul saying in these verses, and how does it impact his understanding of the "old covenant"? Where vv. 7–11 emphasize the similarity in glory, vv. 12–13 contrast Moses' putting on a veil to Paul's own apostolic boldness, thus signaling the *difference* between the two ministries.[67] The language of v. 13 is parallel to v. 7, with two exceptions: the addition of εἰς τὸ τέλος prior to τοῦ καταργουμένου, and the shift of the participle from an attributive position to δόξαν (which is absent in v. 13). The traditional view is that εἰς τὸ τέλος should be taken temporally and that τοῦ καταργουμένου should refer to the fading or transitory nature (of the glory, v. 7) of Moses' ministry.[68] Others take τέλος in the sense of "goal," "outcome" (result), or even "purpose."[69] If taken as goal or purpose, Moses veiled himself to prevent the Israelites from seeing the purpose of the fading, whatever that purpose might be.

---

[66] Hafemann, *Paul, Moses,* 323–33. One may again see καταργέω as "rendered ineffective" in v. 11. This entire ministry of death and condemnation has been rendered ineffective, and it is the ministry of the Spirit that "remains" (effective).

[67] Stockhausen, *Moses' Veil,* 97, notes the key cognate group κάλυμμα in these verses.

[68] Stockhausen's translation (ibid., 88) reveals the problematic redundancy in this position: "so that the sons of Israel might not gaze upon *the end* of what is *being brought to an end*" (emphasis mine). Further, if καταργέω does not refer to a gradual fading, then τέλος would make little sense if understood temporally; Hafemann, *Paul, Moses,* 356.

[69] The Badenas-Hofius debate has shown that either termination or goal is a legitimate possibility; Robert Badenas, *Christ the End of the Law: Romans 10.4 in Pauline Perspective* (JSNTSup 10; Sheffield: JSOT Press, 1985), 38–80; Otfried Hofius, "Gesetz und Evangelium nach 2 Korinther 3," in *Paulusstudien* (WUNT 51; Tübingen: J.C.B. Mohr [Paul Siebeck], 1989), 75–120, esp. 102–3, 103 n. 175, and 110–11 n. 217. The essay was also published in *"Gesetz" als Thema Biblischer Theologie* (ed. Ingo Baldermann and Dwight R. Daniels; JBTh 4; Neukirchen-Vluyn: Neukirchener Verlag, 1989), 105–49, esp. 131–32, 132 n. 175, and 139–40 n. 217. See also Belleville, *Reflections,* 200–202.

The imperfect ἐτίθει signals the repeated action of Moses' veiling. In the context of Exod 32–34, Hafemann argues that it was due to the hard hearts of the people.[70] The resulting inability of the Israelites to gaze into Moses' face (2 Cor 3:7) required Moses to veil himself *in order that* they might not gaze (v. 13; thus the change from ὥστε + inf. to πρὸς τὸ + inf.). The final words of v. 13 indicate what the Israelites were not to gaze into: if τέλος is taken as "outcome," then the Israelites were not to gaze into the goal/outcome of that which was rendered inoperative (τοῦ καταργουμένου). The outcome of gazing into God's glory under the old ministry would have been judgment and death. The neuter participle would indicate (as with the neuter participles in vv. 10–11) that Paul is speaking here of the old covenant ministry as a whole (and not the feminine δόξα, as in v. 7).[71] The advantage of this reading is that it explains why Moses veiled himself in Exod 32–34.[72] Moses acted in this way to protect the Israelites as a "stiff-necked" people from the death and condemnation brought about under the old covenant.[73] Unlike Moses' ministry, Paul's ministry is characterized by "boldness" (v. 12) in his preaching of the "glory of God in the face of Jesus Christ" (2 Cor 4:6). The Spirit of the new covenant has radically changed the people's situation by working a change upon their hearts, the transformation predicted by Jeremiah and Ezekiel.

The opening phrase of v. 14 confirms this interpretation of vv. 12–13. Paul acted with boldness in v. 12, and he is *not* acting like Moses in v. 13. Verse 14a acts as a contrast (ἀλλὰ) not with Moses' veiling but with Paul's boldness in v. 12.[74] Paul can act with boldness because his ministry, unlike Moses', is not characterized by recipients

---

[70] Belleville's theory maintains that the people kept wanting to see the glory on Moses' face down to the last glimmer, never realizing that the fading was a sign of the temporary nature of the covenant. The problem in Exodus, as Hafemann has shown, has more to do with Israel's hardened condition and consequent inability to gaze at the glory, not their desire to look at the glory; *Paul, Moses,* 368 n. 103.

[71] Hafemann, *Paul, Moses,* 355.

[72] The veiling makes little sense if τέλος is understood christologically. See Furnish, *II Corinthians,* 207.

[73] Death would result if they were "to gaze" into Moses' face (ἀτενίζω, not ὁράω/εἶδον); Hafemann, *Paul, Moses,* 353–62; Dumbrell, "Paul's Use of Exodus 34," 186–87; contra Stockhausen and others on the usual view. Renwick, *Paul,* 140–49, independently came to the same conclusion as Hafemann.

[74] Hafemann emphasizes the οὐ . . . ἀλλά construction that governs the beginning of v. 12 through v. 13a; cf. Rom 1:32; 4:4, 13; 6:14; 7:19–20; 8:15, 26, 32; 9:8; 1 Cor 1:17; 9:12; 11:8; 12:24; 14:34; 15:10; 2 Cor 1:19; 2:23; 5:12; 10:12, 18; 12:16; Gal 4:4; *Paul, Moses,* 363–65.

whose understandings are hardened.[75] Thus v. 14a confirms the context of Exod 32–34 in Paul's argumentation: Moses had to veil himself because of the "stiff-necked" or now "hardened" condition of the people.[76]

In vv. 14b–15 Paul concludes that the "same veil" remains "to this very day" when the old covenant is read (the continuation of the Mosaic ministry).[77] The veil is "rendered ineffective" or "abolished" only in Christ. It is at this point in Paul's reasoning, when he moves from the past "to this day," that his language becomes symbolic. Hafemann takes the veil as a metonymy for Israel's hardened condition in Exod 32–34.[78] In other words, even as the glory of the Lord was veiled in the time of Moses, so it has remained for those under the old covenant ministry. Just as Moses' ministry brought death and condemnation, so the letter "kills" (present tense). Interpreted in the light of what precedes, the veil is not cognitive (failing to perceive Christ) but the problem of hardened hearts without the Spirit, hearts that are unable to bear the glory of the Lord.[79] Verse 16 then restates the fact that the veil is removed whenever someone turns to the Lord, YHWH, who is identified in v. 17 with the Spirit.[80] Those in Christ and the Spirit have an unveiled face and are being transformed into the same image of God's glory. The believer becomes like Moses, who stood before the glory of God with an unveiled face.[81]

Having reviewed 2 Cor 3:1–18 in its entirety, what can be concluded about Paul's handling of the old covenant? There is no evidence

---

[75] N. T. Wright also recognized the construction and so translated the line of thought: "we use great boldness in relation to you, unlike Moses before the Israelites, because your hearts are not like those of the Israelites, in whose presence Moses had to veil the glory" (*Climax*, 181). Wright concludes: "Paul can use boldness not because he is different from Moses but because those who belong to the new covenant are different from those who belong to the old. Moses is actually, here, in one sense a precursor of the new covenant people in 3.18, since he, alone among the Israelites, is able to look at the divine glory with unveiled face" (p. 180). Moses parallels the new covenant people and is the antithesis to the hardened status of those under the old covenant (pp. 180, 183).

[76] On the use of τὰ νοήματα, see 2 Cor 2:11; 4:4; 10:5.

[77] Temporal ἐπί; see ἡνίκα ἂν in v. 15; Hafemann, *Paul, Moses*, 370.

[78] *Paul, Moses*, 371. Cf. Isa 24:21–25:8 in light of Isa 24:5; Hafemann, *Paul, Moses*, 395.

[79] Thus the veil lies over their "heart" in v. 15. The people need a transformed heart; Hafemann, *Paul, Moses*, 374, 382, 384–85.

[80] Hafemann, *Paul, Moses*, 396; Ralph P. Martin, *2 Corinthians* (WBC 40; Dallas: Word, 1986), 46. This picks up on the theme of turning to the Lord/YHWH in the OT (Deut 4:30; 30:2, 9–10; 2 Chr 24:19; 30:9), but now understood in terms of the Spirit.

[81] Alan F. Segal, *Paul the Convert*, 34–71, esp. 59–62, 152, 156.

that the old covenant passes away, nor is there any evidence that the law passes away.[82] The veil is not to be associated with a fading, transitory glory, a notion that is otherwise unattested in Judaism. Nothing suggests that the purpose of the veil was to hide a christological meaning in the Scriptures or that the Jews of Paul's day were blind to the meaning of their own Scriptures. The ministry of Moses under the old covenant simply remains a ministry of death and condemnation because of the hardened and "stiff-necked" condition of the people. For this reason, they are hindered from gazing at the glory of the Lord lest they be destroyed. After the events of Exod 32–24, God's visitation of his people has come in wrath. Only in Christ is this hardened condition removed. Only in Christ is there a real transformation so that the glory of the Lord can be revealed boldly in Paul's own ministry of the Spirit.[83]

Paul therefore departs from a positive evaluation of the Sinaitic covenant.[84] While the "letter" or Mosaic law is here embedded within the Sinaitic (old) "covenant," the covenantal framework offers no salvific benefit. It is incapable of removing the veil of a hardened heart. The ministry of the letter under the old covenant remains one of death and condemnation because of the hard-hearted nature of the people. That the letter of the law would only bring death and condemnation contrasts sharply with the Jewish perspective on the law.[85] The "new" covenant is a decidedly *Christian* covenant. Only when the Jews turn to the *Spirit* (the Lord, YHWH, is the Spirit), as understood and at work in Paul's ministry, are they saved from their hardened state.[86]

---

[82] This follows from the translation of καταργέω as "rendered ineffective" (thus 2 Cor 3:11).

[83] N. T. Wright summarizes: "The point Paul is making is that the open-faced style of ministry he employs is *appropriate* because of *the condition that he and his hearers share,* that is, unhardened hearts and the consequent Spirit-given ability [in the new covenant] to behold the glory of God. The result is that when (vv. 16–17) someone turns to the Lord-who-is-the-Spirit, the veil is removed" (*Climax,* 184).

[84] The way Paul handles the word *covenant* in this passage, as in Galatians, may reflect the polemical contexts in which he writes. Hafemann suggests that Paul's opponents in Corinth were arguing, like his opponents in Galatia, that the Mosaic law/covenant mediated the Spirit; *Paul, Moses,* 448–49. Paul, on the other hand, sees the Spirit mediated through Christ and the "new covenant." Cf. also 2 Cor 11:15; Furnish, *II Corinthians,* 204; Charles H. Cosgrove, *The Cross and the Spirit: A Study in the Argument and Theology of Galatians* (Macon, Ga.: Mercer University Press, 1988).

[85] See the texts listed earlier in the discussion of Gal 3:15–17.

[86] On the relationship (near identification) of YHWH and the Spirit, see Linda L. Belleville, "Paul's Polemic and the Theology of the Spirit in Second Corinthians," *CBQ* 58 (1996): 298–304; Hafemann, *Paul, Moses,* 396–400, 406–11.

While the approach taken here to 2 Cor 3:1–18 is dependent on the work of Hafemann, consider for a moment the implications if one adopts one of the more traditional readings of 2 Cor 3. With Belleville the glory of the old covenant, in contrast to the permanence of the new covenant, is downgraded to a fading splendor that is coming to an end. Others, such as Westerholm, Vollenweider, and Hofius, argue that the law too (as part of the old covenant) has passed away.[87] If one takes a hermeneutical approach, with Koch or Hays, a veil stands over the reading of the law, and the Jews are blind as to the meaning of their own Scriptures.[88] Such readings of 2 Cor 3 only exacerbate the conflict with covenantal nomism and Judaism.

IV. Conclusion

A covenantal nomist, in Sanders's model, would consider the old/ Mosaic covenant a ministry of life and salvation. The Mosaic covenant would be a sign of God's gracious election of Israel, a relationship that can be traced back to God's promises to the patriarchs. In contrast, Paul refuses to admit any life-giving or salvific capacity in the Mosaic covenant and its law. Galatians 3:15–18, 4:21–31, and 2 Cor 3:1–18 all treat the Mosaic (old) covenant in a way that would consistently deny a covenantal nomistic perspective. Paul's own thinking has moved decidedly beyond covenantal nomism: no longer does the old covenant serve as a gracious, salvific framework for the law.[89]

---

[87] Vollenweider sees the freedom of 3:17 as a freedom from the law; *Freiheit,* 252, 274–77. He does not recognize that the problem has to do with human sinfulness rather than the law. Nor does Vollenweider adequately account for the fact that it is the human heart and not the law at issue in Ezek 11, 36, and Jer 31 (LXX 38); cf. Hafemann, *Paul, Moses,* 143–44 n. 163.

[88] Dietrich-Alex Koch states the matter much more pointedly with respect to the Jews than Hays, who is arguing for the appropriation of Scripture in an ecclesiological setting; *Die Schrift als Zeuge des Evangeliums: Untersuchungen zur Verwendung und zum Verständnis der Schrift bei Paulus* (BHT 69; Tübingen: J.C.B. Mohr [Paul Siebeck], 1986), 334, 339–40.

[89] Paul's devaluation of the Mosaic "covenant" does not necessarily deny a role for covenantal categories in Paul. Cf. Paul's use of δικαιοσύνη, the role of the Abrahamic covenant, and the new covenant of Jeremiah (thus Sanders, *Paul and Palestinian Judaism,* 420–21). The term itself, though, has become embroiled in a conflict with Paul's contemporaries.

Chapter Four

Would Paul the Apostle Affirm Covenantal Nomism's Emphasis on Israel's Election?

All Israelites have a share in the world to come" (*m. Sanh.* 10:1).[1] God's election of the people of Israel is a motif that courses through intertestamental and rabbinic literature.[2] According to *Jubilees* and the rabbis, only the most egregious sinners who had turned their backs on God's relationship with the people would be excluded. While the Qumran community may have isolated themselves from other ethnic Jews, they nevertheless maintained a strong sense of election, articulated in terms of the community itself.[3] "Ezra" pleads with the angel on the basis of Israel's election as a nation. The Tannaim speak of God's choice *preceding* any doing of commandments.[4]

Paul says in Rom 11:25 that *all Israel* will be saved. Romans 11:25 offers the closest Pauline parallel to the Jewish understanding of Israel's

---

[1] "I am God for all those who come into the world, nevertheless I have conferred My name particularly on My people Israel" (*Mek. Kaspa* 4 [to 23:17; Lauterbach, *Mekilta de-Rabbi Ishmael,* 3:185]).

[2] See chs. 1 and 2.

[3] For example, 1QS 3.18–25; 1QH[a] 7(=15).16–23; as well as the frequent description of the community as God's "elect."

[4] *Mishnah Berakoth* 2:2 says that one is to take on the yoke of heaven and *then* the yoke of the commandments; Sanders, *Paul and Palestinian Judaism,* 85; Schechter, *Aspects of Rabbinic Theology,* 91. In other words, God's election precedes any doing of the commandments. The Mekilta speaks of a king who acts on behalf of the people before they accept him as king in the same way that God first delivered and aided Israel prior to Mount Sinai (*Mek. Bahodesh* 5 [to 20:2; Lauterbach, *Mekilta de-Rabbi Ishmael,* 2:229–30]; Sanders, *Paul and Palestinian Judaism,* 86); similarly *Mek. Bahodesh* 6 (to 20:3; Lauterbach, *Mekilta de-Rabbi Ishmael,* 2:237–38); Sanders, *Paul and Palestinian Judaism,* 86.

national election and salvation in the world to come. The apostle explicitly addresses God's faithfulness to Israel and Israel's status as an elect people. Given the centrality of Israel's election in Jewish thought, does Paul grant ethnic Israel a share in the world to come?

I. An Overview of Romans 9–11

Romans 9–11 flow naturally from the closing thoughts of Rom 8. Paul claims in 8:28 that all things work for good for those who love God and who are called according to his purpose. Such individuals God "foreknew" (προέγνω) and "predestined" (προώρισεν, v. 29).[5] Those he predestined he then called, which in turn led to their justification and glorification. The chapter closes by concluding that neither death nor life, nor angels, nor rulers, nor things present, nor things to come, nor powers, nor height, nor depth, nor anything else in all creation will be able to separate God's people from that love. Such a theology of God's election raises a problem for Paul. If God is so faithful to the elect, what of Israel? As James Dunn puts it: "If God is not faithful to Israel, how can Paul proclaim his faithfulness to the Gentiles?"[6]

Right away one must recognize that Paul is working with a *redefinition* of the elect. While God's faithfulness to Israel is the subject of Rom 9–11, there is a clear christological shape to the way Paul frames the issue in Rom 8. The "elect" (ἐκλεκτός—8:33) are those defended by Jesus Christ. It is Christ who sits at God's right hand interceding against anyone who would accuse his people and so jeopardize their election and salvation. Romans 8:29 indicates that those God "foreknew" were "predestined to be conformed to the image of his Son." The love of God that closes the chapter in v. 39 is a love "in Christ Jesus our Lord." In other words, the problem of God's faithfulness to Israel is *subordinated*

---

[5] Similar προ- compound words will be used throughout Rom 9–11 (see 9:11, 23; 11:2), which suggests that Paul's discussion in those chapters is closely related to what he is saying about *Christians* at the end of Rom 8.

[6] James D. G. Dunn, *Romans 9–16* (WBC 38B; Dallas: Word, 1988), 530. Or as Paul Achtemeier writes: "How much comfort is there in being told that nothing can separate us from God's love when there is apparently something quite capable of separating the chosen people from God's love" (*Romans* [IBC; Louisville: John Knox, 1985], 153–54). See also Walter Gutbrod, " Ἰσραήλ," *TDNT* 3:386; E. Elizabeth Johnson, *The Function of Apocalyptic and Wisdom Traditions in Romans 9–11* (SBLDS 109; Atlanta: Scholars Press, 1989), 145; C. E. B. Cranfield, *A Critical and Exegetical Commentary on the Epistle to the Romans* (2 vols.; ICC; Edinburgh: T&T Clark, 1979), 2:446–47; Hays, *Echoes*, 63–64.

to Paul's concern for the election and salvation of those *in Christ,* an election and salvation that now also includes Gentiles.

In Rom 9:1–5 Paul resumes the discussion from 3:1: "Then what advantage has the Jew? Or what is the value of circumcision?" In ch. 3 he said "much, in every way" and cited God's entrusting to them the word before moving on to other concerns. In 9:1–5 he lists several other advantages of membership in ethnic Israel: the adoption (υἱοθεσία), the covenants (διαθῆκαι), the giving of the law, the worship, the promises, and the Fathers.[7] Note that Paul falls short of saying (with the later *m. Sanh.* 10:1) that all the Jews have a share in the world to come.[8] On the contrary, the climactic position in the list is given to the Messiah.[9] Murray J. Harris has shown that the following ascription of ὁ ὢν ἐπὶ πάντων θεὸς εὐλογητὸς εἰς τοὺς αἰῶνας modifies Christ (ὁ Χριστός).[10]

---

[7] Paul's deliberate use of the plural διαθῆκαι in Rom 9:4 is probably a nod to the Abrahamic covenant (Gal 3:15–18; Rom 4:1–22).

[8] The affirmation of Rom 11:26 does *not* occur at this point in the discussion.

[9] That the Messiah is the highlight of the list is clear by the juxtaposition of the Messiah with "the Fathers." As the Fathers begin Israel's history, so the Messiah is the climax of that history. John Piper suggests that Paul deliberately changed the grammatical construction on this final element in the series (to καὶ ἐξ ὧν) in order to emphasize it; *The Justification of God: An Exegetical and Theological Study of Romans 9:1–23* (2d ed.; Grand Rapids: Baker, 1993), 42–43.

[10] Murray J. Harris, *Jesus As God: The New Testament Use of Theos in Reference to Jesus* (Grand Rapids: Baker, 1992), 143–72; Cranfield, *Romans,* 2:464–70; Bruce Metzger, "The Punctuation of Romans 9:5," in *Christ and the Spirit in the NT* (ed. Barnabas Lindars and Stephen S. Smalley; Cambridge: Cambridge University Press, 1973), 95–112; and Dunn, *Romans 9–16,* 528–29, 535–36. First, it is more natural to maintain an identity of subject from ὁ Χριστός to ὁ ὢν. Second, it is hard to see Paul's mention of his pain and grief (λύπη, ὀδύνη) over the Jews' unbelief leading to an ascription of praise to God without an adversative. Rather, the mention of their unbelief leads more naturally to the exalted status and nature of the Messiah. Finally, the wording makes better sense as an ascription to Christ rather than God the Father. In the Greek Bible εὐλογητός always *precedes* the name of God in independent doxologies. Since εὐλογητός does not come first in Rom 9:5, an ascription to God is unlikely; see, for example, Gen 14:20; 2 Cor 1:3. ὁ ὢν is equivalent to ὅς ἐστίν if referring to Christ, but the ὢν is superfluous if referring to God (see the parallel construction in 2 Cor 11:31). Paul's doxologies are always linked to a preceding subject, but asyndeton would result here if referring to God the Father (for instance, Rom 1:25's doxology, which refers back to τὸν κτίσαντα; Rom 11:36's, which refers back to κυρίου in v. 34). In contrast to James D. G. Dunn's theory of christological development (*Christology in the Making: A New Testament Inquiry into the Origins of the Doctrine of the Incarnation* [2d ed.; Grand Rapids, Eerdmans, 1989]), see N. T. Wright's corrective in *Climax,* particularly the chapters on Phil 2:5–11, Col 1:15–20, and 1 Cor 8.

Christ is identified as the "God who is over all." A failure to believe in Jesus as the Christ would be equivalent to a rejection of the Jews' own God. Romans 9:5 casts a strong christological shadow over the discussion that ensues.

In Rom 9:6–23 Paul denies the election of ethnic Israel as a whole (or even a majority): "For not all Israelites truly belong to Israel, and not all of Abraham's children are his true descendants." Abraham's true descendants are through Isaac. The pattern repeats itself again when Rebecca is told before she gave birth that Esau would serve Jacob. For Paul natural descent and human striving do not influence God's plan. Divine election is always a sovereign matter. God is a potter who can fashion the clay in whatever way judged fitting, whether to have mercy or to harden. Paul cites Pharaoh as an instance where God acted sovereignly to harden. Alan Segal observes that there is a reversal at work of the typical patterns of Jewish thought: "for the Jew, the positive fact that God chose Isaac and Jacob is important; for Paul the converse fact is equally important: God disinherited Esau and Ishmael in spite of their ancestry." Thus: "Paul puts the non-Christian Jews of his time on the same level as Ishmael and Esau and also with Pharaoh."[11]

In 9:25–26 Paul cites the words of Hosea concerning the unworthy people of Israel. God had promised: "Those who were not my people I will call 'my people,' and her who was not beloved I will call 'beloved.' And in the very place where it was said to them, 'You are not my people,' there they shall be called children of the living God." Whereas Hosea proffered these words as hope to the people of Israel, Paul applies these words also *to the Gentiles.*[12] The OT citation justifies the statement in 9:24 that God is right to call not only the Jews but also the Gentiles. Paul's entire argument asserts that natural descent from Abraham offers no saving benefit to the Israelites. One must be a child of Abraham through *the promise.*[13] God has been working with a remnant of Israel

---

[11] Segal, *Paul the Convert,* 277; see also Hays, *Echoes,* 67.

[12] Hays writes: "Where Hosea clings to the poignant hope of Israel's privileged place despite her 'harlotry,' Paul deconstructs the oracle and dismantles Israel's privilege; with casual audacity he rereads the text as a prophecy of God's intention to embrace the Gentiles as his own people" (*Echoes,* 67). In fact, the Gentile Christian readers may have missed the "potential scandal to Jewish readers." See also William Campbell, "Favoritism and Egalitarianism: Irreconcilable Emphases in Romans?" in *SBL Seminar Papers, 1998* (Atlanta: Scholars Press, 1998), 1:23.

[13] Where Rom 9:4 lists the "patriarchs" as one of the advantages to ethnic Israel, Paul has already undercut his own argument earlier in Romans. In Rom 4 Paul explains that Abraham is a father to those *who believe.* The purpose of cir-

all along (9:27).[14] In effect, Paul is denying to ethnic Jews any saving value in the "adoption" and the "patriarchs" in themselves.[15]

In 9:30–10:4 Paul resumes the paradoxical contrast between the Jew and the Gentile that the Hosea quote raised. The Gentiles who were *not* striving for righteousness attained it while the Jews who *did* strive for righteousness did not even attain to their own law (vv. 30–31). The Jews, ignorant of the righteousness that comes from God, have been es-

---

cumcision as a sign of faith in 4:11–12 was to render Abraham the ancestor of all those who believed *apart* from circumcision. And this is clearly faith in Jesus "our Lord" (4:24–25). In other words, the argument of Rom 4 anticipates the denial of soteriological benefit on the basis of physical descent in Rom 9.

Many of the other benefits of ethnic Israel have already been granted to Gentile believers earlier in the letter. For example, Christians have received in 8:15 the "spirit of adoption" (πνεῦμα υἱοθεσίας) and are therefore "joint heirs with Christ" (συγκληρονόμοι δὲ Χριστοῦ). On "adoption" in Rom 8–9, see Brendan Byrne, *'Sons of God'—'Seed of Abraham': A Study of the Idea of the Sonship of God of All Christians in Paul against the Jewish Background* (AnBib 83; Rome: Biblical Institute, 1979), 79–140, esp. 127–29. N. T. Wright explains that all the benefits in Rom 9:1–5 have been transferred to Christ and those "in Christ" in the course of Paul's discussion in this letter: "This intensifies the irony—and, for Paul, the agony—of the present situation" (*Climax,* 237).

[14] According to Rom 9, the blessing never rested on the entirety of Abraham's seed. First God narrowed the promise to the descendants of Isaac. Then God narrowed it to those from Jacob. Thus Rom 9:8: "it is not the children of the flesh who are the children of God, but the children of the promise are counted as descendants." Isaac was the child of promise, while Ishmael was a child of the flesh, merely a natural descendant. This parallels the same line of thought in Gal 4:28–29, where Isaac and those who believe in Jesus Christ are "children of the promise" as opposed to those born "according to the flesh" according to mere physical descent. God has always chosen irrespective of human qualities and potentialities, including ethnic descent.

[15] Throughout ch. 9 Paul continues to compromise the efficacy of the benefits he listed in 9:1–5 for ethnic Jews. Paul denies that "adoption" holds any value for the "children of the flesh" in 9:6–13. Then in 9:22–23 he denies them "glory." As Heikki Räisänen writes: "And yet if the privileges listed are really meant to denote salvific possession, it is striking that these very privileges are *denied* to Israel 'according to the flesh' in what follows" ("Paul, God, and Israel: Romans 9–11 in Recent Research," in *The Social World of Formative Christianity and Judaism: Essays in Tribute to Howard Clark Kee* [ed. Jacob Neusner, Peder Borgen, Ernest S. Frerichs, and Richard Horsley; Philadelphia: Fortress, 1988], 181). See also Segal, *Paul the Convert,* 277. Hays notes the "scandalous inversions" in this chapter as "the Jewish people" "stand in the role of Ishmael, the role of Esau, and even the role of Pharaoh" (*Echoes,* 67). One must now have faith in Christ to benefit from Israel's blessings; Eldon Jay Epp, "Jewish-Gentle Continuity in Paul: Torah and/or Faith? (Romans 9:1–5)," *HTR* 79 (1986): 80–90.

tablishing their own righteousness instead (10:3). They ended up stumbling over the stone that God placed in Zion, the stone that requires belief (9:33).[16] The rationale for the Jews' failure to attain to their own law is made clear in 10:4. No matter how one chooses to read the much debated τέλος in 10:4, Christ remains central to any reading: if Christ is the end of the law, then he represents the termination point of their legal heritage. If Christ is the goal of the law, then the Jews have misinterpreted their own Scriptures and have failed to see the Scriptures' true meaning and fulfillment in Jesus Christ.[17]

As if to make the point more forcefully, Paul takes a passage from Deuteronomy that originally referred to the nearness of the law and asserts in Rom 10:6–8 that the passage was speaking in regard to Christ.[18] Verse 9 concludes: "if you confess with your lips that Jesus is Lord and believe in your heart that God raised him from the dead, you will be saved." While these words are still echoing, Paul reapplies the Isa 28:16 citation from Rom 9:33 in 10:11; the Isaiah text must be understood in connection with Christ's saving work. Paul has taken multiple OT passages and reinterpreted them as referring to Christ.[19] The Christ-centered focus of the chapter continues a few verses later where Paul asks how people will call upon and believe in the Lord unless preachers are sent. "Faith comes from what is heard, and what is heard comes through the word of Christ" (v. 17).[20]

---

[16] The identity of the stumbling stone has been fiercely debated. Reliable results can be reached only by exhausting the context of the passage itself. "Faith ἐπ' αὐτῷ" in 9:33 makes little sense as faith *in* the Mosaic law (cf. 4:24). The referent to ἐπ' αὐτῷ in 9:33 is the "stone of stumbling." Since God is the one who placed the stone, faith ἐπ' αὐτῷ cannot be faith in God. The phrase in Rom 9:33, ὁ πιστεύων ἐπ' αὐτῷ, clearly refers to Christ in 10:11. A reference to Christ already in 9:33 is not surprising given the prominence of Christ in 10:4.

[17] See ch. 10 for a detailed discussion of this verse and its context.

[18] For a detailed discussion of the logic behind this connection, see ch. 10.

[19] As Hays concludes: "The function, then, of Rom. 10:5–10 is to intensify the paradox of Israel's unbelief. Paul exposits Deuteronomy in such a way that its latent sense is alleged to be identical with the manifest claims of his own proclamation" (*Echoes*, 83). For: "the word of God, now present in the Christian gospel, is the same word of God that was always present to Israel in Torah" (pp. 82–83). Since the Torah itself proclaimed faith in Christ, Israel's unbelief is that much more culpable.

[20] Verse 17's mention of Christ follows on the heels of v. 16's quotation of Isa 53:1. As Luke Timothy Johnson has shown, throughout Romans Paul is particularly fond of quoting the Servant Songs of Isaiah. Paul therefore sees in Isa 53 a reference to the Messiah and the suffering of Jesus Christ; *Reading Romans: A Literary and Theological Commentary* (New York: Crossroad, 1997), 162–63.

Paul closes ch. 10 with a citation from Isa 65:1–2, which contrasts "a disobedient and contrary people" (Israel) with the Gentiles: God has been found by those who were not seeking (the Gentiles). God has made those who are not a nation a source of jealousy for Israel. The context of Isa 65:1–2 is telling. Israel was practicing idolatry by sacrificing in the garden (v. 3), a Canaanitish worship practice (cf. the condemnation in Isa 1:29). The people spent their time sitting "inside tombs" and "secret places" (v. 4, probably a reference to consulting the dead).[21] They were eating the flesh of swine (v. 4; cf. Lev 11:7–8; Deut 14:8). Isaiah's mention of the rotting fragments of food evokes Lev 7:18 and 19:7. Such idolatrous practices drove Israel from God's holy presence (Isa 65:5). Yet it is precisely such idolatry and disobedience that the Jews in Paul's day sought to avoid by their faithful observance of the Torah. They would be as incensed about idolatry as the prophet. But Paul's fellow Jews have fallen away from the true and proper observance of the law by denying the "goal" of the law in Christ. If Christ is the God who is over all (Rom 9:5), then a failure to follow the law to Christ would be to fall into idolatry. Paul's citation of Isaiah's condemnation of a disobedient, idolatrous people stands at the end of a passage revolving around faith *in Christ.* While Paul holds out hope for the Jews in God's concern for them (as expressed through the Isaiah citation), this hope is articulated in Paul's terms and not in terms of traditional Judaism (Rom 10:21).

Paul seems to recognize that far from resolving the plight of unbelieving Israel, the path his argument has taken in Rom 9–10 seems only to have exacerbated the problem. Paul must engage the question anew in ch. 11: "I ask, then, has God rejected his people? By no means!" Yet even at this point, he *still* cannot quite reverse the negative argument about unbelieving Israel. In Rom 11:1–10 Paul reprises the election motif of ch. 9: God has chosen a remnant within Israel. Ominously paralleling the reference to the hardening of Pharaoh in 9:17–18, Rom 11:7 says: "What then? Israel failed to obtain what it was seeking. The elect obtained it, but the rest were hardened." Paul then quotes the OT: "God gave them a sluggish spirit, eyes that would not see and ears that would not hear, down to this very day" (v. 8; Deut 29:4; Isa 29:10). The quotation from Ps 69:22–23 in vv. 9–10 is even more disturbing: "Let their table become a snare and a trap, a stumbling block and a retribution for them; let their eyes be darkened so that they cannot see, and keep their backs forever bent." Paul leaves no doubt of a judgment on unbelieving

---

[21] See the condemnation of this practice in Deut 18:11; 1 Sam 28:3; and Isa 57:9.

Israel. The elect of Israel are again distinguished from all Israel: a faithful remnant remains even as in the time of Elijah.

In Rom 11:11 and the following verses, Paul's logic takes a turn. He explains that Israel's stumbling and defeat resulted in riches for the Gentiles. Verse 12 continues: "And if [Israel's] defeat means riches for Gentiles, how much more will their full inclusion mean!" The apostle views his ministry to the Gentiles as a means of making his own people jealous (vv. 13–14). Paul then employs the analogy of Israel as an olive tree (v. 17). The Gentiles, as the wild shoot, have been grafted in where branches have been broken off on account of unbelief (vv. 19–20). The Gentiles should not become proud, though, since the tree itself still represents God's promises and relationship with Israel. God will graft the natural branches back in (v. 24). Paul concludes from the analogy in vv. 25b–26a: "I want you to understand this mystery: a hardening has come upon part of Israel, until the full number of the Gentiles has come in. And so all Israel will be saved." Verse 28 appeals to God's election of Israel, and v. 29 asserts that God's gift and calling are irrevocable. Even as God has had mercy on the disobedient Gentiles, so he will have mercy on disobedient Israel (vv. 30–31).

II. Four Approaches to Romans 11:26

Romans 11:26's "all Israel will be saved" has been a source of great controversy.[22] One school of thought maintains that there are "two covenants."[23] While a remnant in Israel is saved on the basis of God's activity

[22] Most recently, see Charles Cosgrove, *The Elusive Israel: The Puzzle of Election in Romans* (Louisville: Westminster John Knox, 1997). Cosgrove's three positions (National Israel, Ecclesial Israel, and Elect Remnant Israel) correspond to the first three options below, in that order. He considers the "Ecclesial Israel" and "Elect Remnant Israel" options plausible and/or cogent (p. 32) but does not fully address the problems with these positions. Consequently, the passage may not be as ambiguous as Cosgrove's theory of rhetorical codeliberation (pp. 32–34) requires. Furthermore, as will be clear in a moment, Cosgrove did not include in his discussion the most likely reading.

[23] Krister Stendahl observes that Paul stunningly does not mention Jesus as the Messiah in "this whole section of Romans (10:17–11:36)" (*Paul among Jews and Gentiles* [Philadelphia: Fortress, 1976], 4). Paul therefore envisions the salvation of "all Israel" at that time somehow *apart from* faith in Christ. Likewise Franz Mußner asserts: "The *parousia* Christ saves all Israel without a preceding 'conversion' of the Jews to the gospel" (*Tractate on the Jews: The Significance of Judaism for Christian Faith* [trans. Leondard Swidler; Philadelphia: Fortress, 1984], 34). Lloyd Gaston (*Paul and the Torah* [Vancouver: University of British Columbia, 1987], 147) focuses on the validity of the Israelite covenant (*m. Sanh.*

through Jesus Christ, "all Israel" will be saved on the basis of the "Torah covenant." The problem for the Jews is that they do not recognize the significance of Christ for the Gentiles and are opposing Paul's mission. Nevertheless, salvation for the Jews is still through the Torah.[24] The Gentile has through Christ what the Jew has through the Torah.

The "two covenant" theory has not fared well under scrutiny. Paul would not call Jesus the "Messiah" in Rom 9:5 unless he saw Jesus as an integral part of the Jews' own heritage[25] Paul expresses anguish in 9:1–5 about his own people and wishes himself cursed (ἀνάθεμα) and cut off from Christ (ἀπὸ τοῦ Χριστοῦ). What worse fate could there be for one who sees himself in 8:39 as ἐν Χριστῷ? It is inconceivable that Paul would even consider such extreme measures if Israel's fault were merely a lack of understanding or faithfulness with respect to God's plan for the Gentiles. "This implies that they must be 'in a plight as serious as the one he is willing to enter for their sake.' "[26] Romans 10:12–13 says that

---

10:1, following Sanders's analysis in *Paul and Palestinian Judaism*). He too rules out that the Jews will come to faith in Christ when they are saved. The Jews will be saved through a "Sonderweg." Their only problem was that they resisted the inclusion of the Gentiles; *Paul and the Torah,* 148. John R. Gager (*The Origins of Anti-Semitism: Attitudes toward Judaism in Pagan and Christian Antiquity* [Oxford: Oxford University Press, 1983], 198–99) goes so far as to speak of a Kuhnian paradigm shift in Stendahl and Gaston's position.

[24] Gaston argues that the resistance of Jews to the Gentiles' salvation in Christ has ironically worked toward their own salvation. When Paul says in Rom 11 that he wants to provoke his fellow Jews to jealousy, Gaston sees the jealousy provoking the Jews to more faithful observance of the Torah. Such Torah faithfulness then leads to their salvation; *Paul and the Torah,* 148.

[25] Heikki Räisänen, "Paul, God, and Israel," 189. N. T. Wright (*Climax,* 237) emphasizes that Jesus as the Messiah is Lord "over all," Jew and Gentile alike. Zeller connects this passage with Jesus' Davidic lineage in Rom 1:3 and 15:8, a passage in which Christ is the confirmation of the promises to the patriarchs, a "servant of the circumcised." This is the *earthly* work of Jesus and not what he accomplishes at the Parousia by means of a "Sonderweg"; Dieter Zeller, "Christus, Skandal und Hoffnung: Die Juden in den Briefen des Paulus," in *Gottesverächter und Menschenfeinde? Juden zwischen Jesus und frühchristlicher Kirche* (ed. Horst Goldstein; Düsseldorf: Patmos, 1979), 273–74. Against Mußner's theory that the Jews will be converted at the Parousia, Zeller notes tellingly that the resurrection of the dead takes place as a consequence of the reconciliation of Israel and not vice versa; "Christus, Skandal und Hoffnung," 274 n. 69.

[26] Räisänen, "Paul, God, and Israel," 180; Piper, *Justification,* 45. Paul's prayers in 10:1 for Israel's salvation implies that they are "outside of the sphere of salvation" (Räisänen, "Paul, God, and Israel," 180). Räisänen adds (p. 190): "Why the *deep sorrow* expressed by Paul in 9:1–2; 10:1? Many of Paul's statements make little sense if it was not Israel's failure to *believe in Jesus as the Christ* that was his problem."

there is no difference between Jews and Gentiles with respect to salvation. Both have the same Lord (10:12), the Lord Jesus Christ (10:9). Romans 10:8–13 explain that one is saved, whether Jew or Gentile, by believing in Jesus Christ (echoing Rom 1–4, esp. 1:16 and 3:21–31).[27] So Peter agreed in Gal 2:7 to take the gospel to the circumcised, which would have been unnecessary if salvation were possible for them otherwise. The "disobedience" of Rom 11:11–12, 19, 28a and the ἀπιστία of 11:20–23 must refer to the refusal to believe in the gospel about Christ.[28]

---

[27] Räisänen, "Paul, God, and Israel," 189; Reidar Hvalvik, "A 'Sonderweg' for Israel: A Critical Examination of a Current Interpretation of Romans 11.25–27," *JSNT* 38 (1990): 89–90. Stendahl says that "salvation" does mean faith in Christ but loses sight of the programmatic first occurrence of this term in Rom 1:16 in relation to the gospel about Jesus Christ. Dieter Sänger underscores the eight uses of the verb σῴζω and the five uses of σωτηρία. Already in Rom 1:16–17 σωτηρία, πίστις, and δικαιοσύνη stand in relation to each other. The same concepts and words dominate Paul's discussion in Rom 10:9–17 and are determinative for the apostle's meaning in 11:26; "Rettung der Heiden und Erwählung Israels: Einige vorläufige Erwägungen zu Römer 11,25–27," *KD* 32 (1986): 117. Likewise Erich Gräßer, who also notes the parallels in the language of righteousness and justification between 9:30–10:21 and earlier in the letter; "Zwei Heilswege? Zum theologischen Verhältnis von Israel und Kirche," in *Kontinuität und Einheit: Für Franz Mußner* (ed. Paul-Gerhard Müller and Werner Stenger; Freiburg: Herder, 1981), 427. One might note also the reprise in Rom 10:12 of the language of God's impartiality from Rom 2 (see ch. 7). For additional parallels, see Peter von der Osten-Sacken, *Die Heiligkeit der Tora: Studien zum Gesetz bei Paulus* (Munich: Chr. Kaiser, 1989), 33.

[28] For example, Ferdinand Hahn, "Zum Verständnis von Römer 11.26a: '. . . und so wird ganz Israel gerettet werden,'" in *Paul and Paulinism: Essays in Honour of C. K. Barrett* (ed. M. D. Hooker and S. G. Wilson; London: SPCK, 1982): 226–29. In fact, Paul expresses this Christ-centered faith in Rom 10 by means of *Old Testament* citations (Hahn, "Verständnis," 230). What does that say about the Jews' own path to God?

Gräßer adds that one cannot divorce v. 26 from the preceding discussion, especially vv. 11–12: Israel's rejection led to the salvation of the Gentiles, even as their *'acceptance'* (Annahme) will lead to ultimate salvation; "Zwei Heilswege?" 427.

The last time Paul used πίστις and ἀπιστία in tandem, as in Rom 11:20, 23, was in Rom 4:20. This verse and its context refer to Abraham's believing in God's promise of a seed, of life coming forth from a dead womb (vv. 18–19; even as God raised Jesus from the dead—vv. 24–25). This further suggests Paul has in mind belief/unbelief in Rom 11:20–23; John G. Lodge, *Romans 9–11: A Reader-Response Analysis* (University of South Florida International Studies in Formative Christianity and Judaism 8; Atlanta: Scholars Press, 1996), 187. Or as Terence L. Donaldson comments: "By the time one arrives at ch. 11, then, Paul has established a christocentric semantic range for the key vocabulary of this seemingly nonchristological discourse" (*Paul and the Gentiles*, 233).

Paul would hardly see the Gentile mission as a means of making the Jews jealous thereby leading to their salvation, if they already had their own means of salvation.[29] Romans 3:21 and 30 clearly state that God will justify the circumcised and the uncircumcised through faith in Christ. Romans 9:31–32 detail the Jew's failure to attain righteousness through the works required by the law (hardly a *Sonderweg*). The stone of stumbling for the Jews (9:33) turns out to be bound up with faith in Christ (10:11).[30] Faith, defined throughout the letter as centered on Jesus Christ, is never far from Paul's mind in Rom 11: verses 20–23 say that Israel will be restored "if they do not persist in unbelief."[31] The relationship between the Gentile mission and Israel's ultimate salvation demonstrates that there is not a separate covenant for "all Israel." Rather

---

[29] Räisänen, "Paul, God, and Israel," 190. Gräßer reasons that since the Jews will be made jealous of the Gentiles, that jealousy must surely involve *the way* the Gentiles were converted—through faith apart from works. Only a salvation through faith apart from works would have motivated their jealousy; "Zwei Heilswege?" 427 n. 54.

Dan Johnson thinks that Paul's entire line of thought breaks down if the apostle sees Jews saved by faith in Jesus Christ all throughout history only for all Israel to be saved at the end of time apart from faith in Christ; "The Structure and Meaning of Romans 11," *CBQ* 46 (1984), 102. The fates of the remnant and of "all Israel" are linked, for the believing remnant is the very basis of hope for "all Israel."

[30] If Christ is the "goal" of the law in 10:4–8, then it would be inconceivable for a Jew to find salvation in the law apart from Christ; see ch. 10 for further discussion.

[31] The language of belief is applied to both Jew and Gentile. Although Christ is not mentioned, given the lack of any further qualification, would the Jew in the same verse (11:20) be placing faith in something entirely different?

That Paul does not mention Jesus Christ in Romans 11 can be explained on other grounds—Paul is elaborating on the theme of *God's* faithfulness to "all Israel." The christological element of that faithfulness was already clarified in ch. 10; D. Johnson, "Structure," 102. Thomas R. Schreiner's response to Franz Mußner's explanation of why vv. 20 and 23 do not contradict the "Sonderweg" theory (" 'Ganz Israel wird gerettet werden' [Röm 11, 26]," *Kairos* 18 [1976]: 252) is telling. One cannot ignore the deliberately parallel construction: The Gentiles must persevere in faith or God will cut them off; unbelieving Israel is separated from God because and only as long as they do not believe. Faith is the "all-important" criterion for being grafted onto the olive tree, whether Jew or Gentile; "The Church As the New Israel and the Future of Ethnic Israel in Paul," *Studia Biblica et Theologica* 13 (1983): 31. After all, God is impartial (Rom 2). Nor does the exercise of God's sovereign power in 11:26 necessarily mean that that power will be exercised apart from the Israelites coming to faith in Christ (contra Mußner). God will simply make Jewish belief possible. What is the "power" (v. 23; δυνατός) that grafts them in again if not the "power" (δύναμις) of the gospel (Rom 1:16)? See Hvalvik, "Sonderweg," 90–91.

than being two distinct covenants, the salvation of all Israel is dependent on the evangelization of the Gentiles (11:13–16; 11:31: "*by means of* the mercy shown to you [the Gentiles], they, the Jews, will now receive mercy").[32] God's "way" for the Jews turns out to be the same as that for Gentile Christians: the way of Rom 1:16–17. The gospel of Jesus Christ is the power of salvation to *all* who believe, whether Jew or Gentile.[33]

Another approach to "all Israel will be saved" takes "all Israel" as a sort of "Israel of faith," a people of God that includes both Jewish and Gentile believers.[34] The problem with this view is that Paul has used the term *Israel* in a way that has consistently excluded Gentiles throughout the argument.[35] In Rom 9:4–5 Paul speaks of Israelites as his kindred according to the flesh to whom belong the covenants, the giving of the law, and the Fathers.[36] In 11:28 he returns to these motifs, speaking of Israel as beloved for the sake of the Fathers. The statement that "not all Israelites truly belong to Israel" (Rom 9:6) distinguishes those ethnic Israelites who believe from those who do not.[37] The contrast in Rom 11 remains

---

[32] My translation. See, e.g., Sanders, *Paul, the Law,* 194.

[33] πᾶς Ἰσραήλ in 11:26 echoes the πᾶς used in 10:11, 13 in the connection with faith in and confession of Christ whether by Jew or Gentile; James W. Aageson "Scripture and Structure in the Development of the Argument in Romans 9–11," *CBQ* 48 (1986): 285. "All" are saved through faith in Christ (Rom 3:21–22, 30); Hvalvik, "Sonderweg," 89; Ernst Käsemann, "Justification and Salvation History," in *Perspectives on Paul* (Philadelphia: Fortress, 1971), 75. When Stendahl argues that σωθήσεται (Rom 11:26) does not mean faith in Christ (*Meanings: The Bible As Document and As Guide* [Philadelphia: Fortress, 1984], 215 n. 1, 243), he loses sight of the first occurrence of "salvation" in Rom 1:16: it is a salvation that comes to everyone who has faith with respect to the gospel. Paul links salvation to the preaching of the gospel all throughout his letters (1 Cor 1:18; 15:2; 1 Thess 2:16), and this gospel is for Jew and Greek both (Gal 2:7; 1 Cor 9:20); Hvalvik, "Sonderweg," 89–90.

For a detailed critique of Gaston's and Gager's theories in their entirety, see especially E. E. Johnson, *Function of Apocalyptic,* 176–205; Heikki Räisänen, "Paul, God, and Israel," 189–92; Frank Thielman, *From Plight to Solution: A Jewish Framework for Understanding Paul's View of the Law in Galatians and Romans* (NovTSup 61; Leiden: E. J. Brill, 1989), 123–32.

[34] For example, N. T. Wright, *Climax,* 249–51; Hervé Ponsot, "Et ainsi tout Israel sauvé; Rom., XI, 26a," *RB* 89 (1982): 406–17.

[35] See, for instance, Gottlob Schrenk, "Der Segenswunsch nach der Kampfepistel," *Judaica* 6 (1950): 170–71, 173–76.

[36] Likewise, Paul maintains a distinction between Jew and Gentile all through the letter, e.g., Rom 1:16; 3:1–2; 4:11–12; 15:8–9. Paul's insistent distinction between Jew and Gentile is a recurring motif in Donaldson's study of *Paul and the Gentiles.*

[37] Romans 11:26 anticipates the healing of the rift between the remnant of believing Jews and their nonbelieving counterparts, a motif running consistently

between all ethnic Israel and a remnant within ethnic Israel (11:1–7, esp. v. 7). Even while Paul speaks of the grafting of the Gentiles into the olive tree that represents Israel, he maintains the strict distinction in language between "you [Gentiles]" and "those [Israelites]." Paul refers to "Israel" as a group distinct from the Gentiles in v. 25. In verse 28 he speaks of ethnic Israel as those who are "enemies of God" for the sake of the Gentiles and "beloved for the sake of their ancestors." Nothing in v. 26's use of "Israel" indicates a change in meaning. In contrast to ἀπὸ μέρους . . . Ἰσραὴλ in v. 25, the "all Israel" of v. 26 is the restoration promised in vv. 12 and 24, the "full inclusion" of ethnic Israel as distinct from the Gentiles.[38] The olive-branch analogy respects the distinction between Jews and Gentiles. Israel is God's chosen people, the natural branches of the olive tree. After their rejection the Gentiles are grafted in—the wild shoot. This, in turn, is followed by the restoration of the natural branches, the Jews, that is, Israel/natural branches—Gentiles/wild shoot—Israel/natural branches. Verses 25–26 build on this earlier section and the pattern remains the same: Israel—Gentiles—Israel.[39] Paul's

---

through Rom 9–11; Bruce W. Longenecker, "Different Answers to Different Issues: Israel, the Gentiles and Salvation History in Romans 9–11," *JSNT* 36 (1989): 96–107.

[38] Otfried Hofius explains that the clause πᾶς Ἰσραὴλ σωθήσεται stands in antithesis to the partial hardening on Israel in the present. Consequently only an elect "remnant" is currently saved, the "remnant" of 11:5, 7a; " 'All Israel Will Be Saved': Divine Salvation and Israel's Deliverance in Romans 9–11," *PSB* Suppl. 1 (1990): 35. "All Israel" is a corporate expression and therefore does not mean every Israelite who ever lived or even every Israelite at the time when "all Israel" is saved. It has the same meaning as the "full number" in 11:12 and is parallel to the "full number" of the Gentiles in the previous verse; Joseph A. Fitzmyer, *Romans* (AB 33; New York: Doubleday, 1993), 623.

[39] Καὶ οὕτως in v. 26 could be, grammatically, temporal; see Karl Olav Sandnes, *Paul—One of the Prophets?* (WUNT 2/43; Tübingen: J.C.B. Mohr [Paul Siebeck], 1991), 172–75. Certainly it is indisputable ἄχρι οὗ is temporal, indicating that the "fullness of the Gentiles" must come in before the hardening of Israel is removed. Nevertheless, in this context καὶ οὕτως is most probably logical; see Fitzmyer, *Romans,* 622–23; Hvalvik, "Sonderweg," 96–97; D. W. B. Robinson, "The Salvation of Israel in Romans 9–11," *RTR* 26 (1967): 94–95. The realization of the full number of the Gentiles could be in process at the very same time as God's action to bring about the salvation of "all Israel." Paul certainly hopes in his very missionary activity to the Gentiles to bring about the salvation of the Jews (11:14). In 11:30–31 Paul uses πότε only for Gentile disobedience; he uses νῦν for the Gentiles' present mercy, Israel's present disobedience but *also* for Israel's obtaining of mercy (see νῦν in both ℵ, B, and D, and the dissatisfaction with Paul's text in the later change to ὕστερον). Paul saw the time in which he was living as the "now" of hardened Israel's conversion. While the hardening will be completely removed only with the "fullness" of the Gentiles, God is already in motion

consistent distinction between "Israel" and the Gentiles throughout Rom 9–11 renders it highly unlikely that the Gentiles are included within "Israel" in 11:26.[40]

A third approach sees "all Israel" as another term for the believing Jewish remnant in Rom 9:1–23 and 11:1–10.[41] Romans 9:6b states that "not all Israelites truly belong to Israel." Perhaps "all Israel" in 11:26 need not be *all* (i.e., the vast majority of) ethnic Israel. This approach, however, would water down Paul's grand solution to the problem of his people's unbelief. The very problem that has provoked Paul's concern is precisely that the vast majority of Israel does *not* currently believe. "All Israel" (πᾶς Ἰσραὴλ, 11:26) and the "full number" (πλήρωμα, 11:12) stand in stark contrast with the "remnant" (λεῖμμα, 11:5–7), "some" (τινές, 11:17), and "part of Israel" (ἀπὸ μέρους τῷ Ἰσραὴλ, 11:25).[42] Paul's concern in this chapter has been with God's faithfulness to all Israel in spite of hardening and disobedience. As Thomas Schreiner points out, Paul's "mystery" in 11:25 is hardly a mystery if all Paul means by it is that the elect in Israel's history will be saved.[43] Verse 25 speaks of "part of Israel" being hardened, implying that another part of Israel is being saved prior to the full number of the Gentiles obtaining salvation. If by speaking of "all Israel" being saved Paul means nothing more than an elect group of Israelites, then v. 26 would say nothing be-

---

to fulfill his promises. Certainly the temporal ἄχρι οὗ does not permit N. T. Wright's equation of the eschatological "all Israel" with the remnant prior to that point.

[40] Charles M. Horne, "The Meaning of the Phrase 'and Thus All Israel Will Be Saved' (Romans 11:26)," *JETS* 21 (1978): 331–32. The focus on ethnic Israel in v. 25 is also clear in v. 28, if not also in vv. 26b–27 as the Deliverer from Zion removes impiety from *Jacob;* Daniel J.-S. Chae, *Paul As Apostle to the Gentiles: His Apostolic Self-Awareness and Its Influences on the Soteriological Argument in Romans* (Paternoster Biblical and Theological Monographs; Carlisle, Cumbria, U.K.: Paternoster, 1997), 274. This renders a switch in subject to believing Jews in v. 26 rather implausible. In fact, the subject of v. 28's "enemies with respect to the gospel" remains unexpressed and assumes the same subject as in vv. 26–27.

Christian Gentiles would be excluded from "all Israel" if OT usage is in any way determinative for the phrase. Joseph Fitzmyer points to the 148 OT occurrences of "*kol-Yisrael*" which invariably refer to "historic, ethnic Israel" (*Romans,* 623). See also William L. Osborne, "The Old Testament Background of Paul's 'All Israel' in Romans 11:26a," *AJT* 2 (1988): 284–87: "It is a collective word used for a whole people who may or may not have saving faith" (p. 287).

[41] For example, François Refoulé, ". . . *Et ainsi tout Israël sera sauvé*": *Romains 11:25–32* (LD 117; Paris: Cerf, 1984); idem, "Cohérence ou incohérence de Paul in Romains 9–11," *RB* 98 (1991): 51–79.

[42] Dunn, *Romans 9–16,* 681.

[43] T. R. Schreiner, "The Church," 26.

yond v. 25.[44] Nor does a position that sees the remnant within Israel as "all Israel" do justice to the remnant motif in the OT. The remnant within Israel was a sign of hope for Israel as a whole.[45]

This leaves a fourth approach: By "all Israel" being saved Paul refers to a future mass conversion of the Jewish people to faith in Christ.[46] The remnant of Israel all along had remained a promise of what was to come. God had not forgotten the Jewish people.[47] God always had the power to graft ethnic Israel back in (11:23), and that power will be exercised prior to the eschaton. Those of ethnic Israel who are "enemies of God for your sake [i.e., the Gentiles' sake]" are "as regards election . . . beloved, for the sake of their ancestors" (11:28). Those who are "enemies" for the moment will constitute "all Israel" at the end (11:26). Could it be that Paul viewed his own missionary activity to Spain as part of God's plan to bring in the "fullness" of the Gentiles and then to usher in the final stage in Israel's destiny?[48] Paul looks forward in Rom

---

[44] Ibid., 27. Romano Penna identifies yet another reason for seeing "all Israel" as national Israel and not a believing remnant. "All Israel" in 11:26a "is a chiastic reflection" of 9:6b's πάντες οἱ ἐξ Ἰσραήλ, "all who descend from Israel." The "all" ought therefore to be taken "in a global sense"; *Paul the Apostle: Wisdom and Folly of the Cross* (trans. Thomas P. Wahl; 2 vols.; Collegeville, Minn.: Liturgical Press, 1996), 1:318 n. 86.

[45] Paul begins Rom 9 with the Abrahamic narratives and in the early part of Rom 11 speaks of the "remnant" in Elijah's day. In the case of Abraham and Lot, and the seven thousand in Elijah's day, the remnant acted in a preserving capacity for the wicked majority. The remnant proves that God has not rejected Israel; Gerhard F. Hasel, *The Remnant: The History and Theology of the Remnant Idea from Genesis to Isaiah* (Berrien Springs, Mich.: Andrews University Press, 1972), esp. 148–52, 171–73, 389, 391; Scott Hafemann, "The Salvation of Israel in Romans 11:25–32: A Response to Krister Stendahl," *ExAud* 4 (1988): 50. The use of the remnant motif as a sign of hope for the majority of the people parallels Gen 7:23; 2 Kgs 19:30–31; Isa 11:11–12, 16; 37:31–32; Mic 2:12; 4:7; 5:7–8; Zech 8:12; D. Johnson, "Structure," 93–94; Ronald E. Clements, " 'A Remnant Chosen by Grace' (Romans 11:5): The Old Testament Background and Origin of the Remnant Concept," in *Pauline Studies* (ed. Donald A. Hagner and Murray J. Harris; Grand Rapids: Eerdmans, 1980), 106–21.

[46] See especially the defense of this position in B. W. Longenecker, "Different Answers," 95–123; so also Hahn, "Verständnis," 221–36; Dunn, *Romans 9–16*, 679–83, 690–93; Markus Barth, *The People of God* (JSNTSup 5; Sheffield: JSOT Press, 1983), 41–43.

[47] Nils Alstrup Dahl, "The Future of Israel," in *Studies in Paul* (Minneapolis: Augsburg, 1977), 151.

[48] See especially Roger D. Aus, "Paul's Travel Plans to Spain and the 'Full Number of the Gentiles' in Rom. XI 25," *NovT* 21 (1979) 232–62; also William S. Campbell, "Salvation for Jews and Gentiles: Krister Stendahl and Paul's Letter to the Romans," in *Papers on Paul and Other New Testament Authors* (vol. 3 of

11:25–26 to the grand resolution of the great "mystery" posed by the failure of so many of Israel to believe the gospel of Jesus Christ.[49]

III. Implications of Romans 9–11 for Paul's Doctrine of Election

Clearly Paul maintains two very different but related understandings of Israel's election. Israel is elect in the sense that God uniquely blessed the nation. They were the recipients of adoption, covenants, and the Fathers (9:5).[50] But the list comes to a close with the Messiah, and the ensuing verses limit salvation to the remnant within Israel. Israel's national privilege does not grant salvation apart from faith in Christ.[51] Yet this is not God's final word.

By the end of Rom 11 another understanding of Israel's election emerges.[52] God is faithful even when the chosen people are unfaithful. Paul looks beyond the present remnant to "all Israel," the full number. The gathering of the Gentiles is only a precursor to God's final act in history, the salvation of the Jews (Rom 11:15–32). This future hope for Israel remains riveted *in Christ* (e.g., Rom 10:14–17).[53] Israel's ultimate

---

Studia Biblica 1978; ed. E. A. Livingstone, JSNTSup 3; Sheffield: JSOT Press, 1980), 66.

[49] See Herman Ridderbos's articulate presentation of this position in *Paul: An Outline of His Theology* (trans. John Richard de Witt; Grand Rapids: Eerdmans, 1975), 359–60.

[50] Although adhering to the "Sonderweg" theory and therefore minimizing those aspects of Rom 9–11 calling for faith in Christ, Peter von der Osten-Sacken rightly emphasizes that Rom 9:1–5 lists genuine blessings for a special people; *Christian-Jewish Dialogue: Theological Foundations* (trans. Margaret Kohl; Philadelphia: Fortress, 1986), 19–40, 66–76, 162–63, 181–84, 188–89.

[51] Michael Cranford emphasizes this aspect of Paul's argument in "Election and Ethnicity: Paul's View of Israel in Romans 9.1–13," *JSNT* 50 (1993): 27–41. God saves in Rom 9 irrespective of Israel's ethnic identity. God's elect are not to be identified with ethnic Israel.

[52] This understanding is already hinted at by Paul's despair over those of ethnic Israel who are not benefiting from the Messiah in Rom 9:1–5. The tension between ethnic Israel's failure to believe and God's promises to them is never fully resolved until Rom 11. Jan Lambrecht is right to maintain the two themes of God's election of a remnant and the divine prerogatives to Israel as a people alongside each other in Rom 9; "Paul's Lack of Logic in Romans 9,1–13: A Response to M. Cranford's 'Election and Ethnicity,'" in *Pauline Studies* (Leuven: Leuven University Press, 1994), 55–60.

[53] Paul hopes through his very preaching to "save some of them" (Rom 11:14); Richard B. Hays, *The Moral Vision of the New Testament: A Contemporary*

fate has a decidedly christological shape.[54] The Jews in their separation from God act as a mirror for Christ's own separation from God such that as Christ rose again so also "all Israel" shall be restored prior to the eschaton. The great "mystery" for Paul is that hardened, unbelieving Israel will come to belief en masse and be saved (11:31). At that point God's faithfulness to Israel will become fully manifest for all to see.

One finds a similar redefinition of Israel's election in Rom 4. The benefits of Abraham as "our ancestor according to the flesh" accrue only to those who believe. He is the father of circumcised believers as well as uncircumcised believers (4:1–12). Ethnic descent in itself does not avail to salvation (thus the crucial importance of 4:23–25). Similarly, in Gal 3:16 Paul says that the "seed" of Abraham is not a plural seed, but the singular seed, Jesus Christ. That Jesus should be Abraham's only true seed contrasts sharply with the Jews' claim to be Abraham's seed by virtue of their physical descent and ethnic heritage. Paul then goes further in Gal 3:29 to redefine the people who are participants in the "seed of Abraham" as those who have been baptized into and put on Christ. The criterion for membership in the seed and people of Abraham is faith in Christ, the Seed. In Christ there is no longer any distinction between Jew and Gentile, slave and free, male and female. The church is therefore the ultimate locus of God's election and salvation. Paul regularly employs the language of "election" for believers in Christ.[55] Such language figures prominently at the end of Rom 8. Romans 9–11 only reinforce the point.

Introduction to New Testament Ethics (New York: HarperCollins, 1996), 435. Even preaching to the Gentiles is set within an eschatological scheme that aims ultimately at the conversion of the Jews.

[54] Hays, *Echoes,* 61; idem, *Moral Vision,* 433; Paul J. Achtemeier, "Unsearchable Judgments and Inscrutable Ways: Reflections on the Discussion of Romans," in *Looking Back, Pressing On* (ed. E. Elizabeth Johnson and David M. Hay; vol. 4 of *Pauline Theology;* SBLSymS; Atlanta: Scholars Press, 1997), 12; Terence Donaldson, " 'Riches for the Gentiles' (Rom 11:12): Israel's Rejection and Paul's Gentile Mission," *JBL* 112 (1993): 81–98, esp. 94, following Hays.

[55] Apart from Rom 8:28–39 ἐκλεκτός is used in Rom 16:13 for one of the "chosen *in the Lord.*" Paul uses ἐκλογή for the whole Christian community in 1 Thess 1:4; Karl P. Donfried, "The Theology of 1 Thessalonians," in *The Theology of the Shorter Pauline Letters* (with I. Howard Marshall; Cambridge: Cambridge University Press, 1993), 28–29. This is the Jewish Scripture's language for Israel (e.g., Deut 4:37; 7:6, 7; 10:15; 14:2; 1 Kgs 3:8; 1 Chr 16:13; Pss 89:3; 105:6, 43 [LXX 104:6, 43]; 106:5, 23 [LXX 105: 5, 23]); as well as for God's people in the future; see Isa 14:1; 42:1; 43:20; 45:4; 65:9, 15, 22, 23); also Sir 46:1; *1 En.* 91:12–17; 93:1–2, 10; *Jub.* 22:9; *2 Bar.* 21:21). Sometimes the elect would be narrowed from Israel as a whole in intertestamental material (e.g., Wis 3:9; *Apoc. Ab.* 29:13, 17; *2 Bar.* 30:2; 75:5–6). Likewise other OT terms for elect Israel are applied to the

IV. Conclusion

Israel's election, insofar as it offers a place in the world to come for an ethnic people, is probably the most crucial element in covenantal nomism's gracious framework. The concept of election has been redefined by Paul in terms of those (especially Israelites) who believe in Christ.[56] The law that had served as the mark of an elect people no longer serves that function. The law testifies instead to Christ (Rom 10:4). When Israel's national election was compromised in Jewish thought, the spotlight would shift to the law in its character as a demand.[57] It remains to be seen whether such a shift in emphasis takes place in Paul.

church: (1) *"saints"* (OT instances: Exod 19:5–6; Lev 11:44, 45; Num 16:3; Deut 33:3; Pss 16:3; 34:10; LXX 82:4; 89:6; Paul's application to the church: Rom 1:7; 12:13; 16:15; 1 Cor 1:2; 2 Cor 1:1; 6:1; 13:12; Eph 1:1; Phil 1:1; 4:21, 22; Col 1:2); (2) *"beloved"* (OT instances: Deut. 7:6–8, 13; Isa 43:3–4; 54:5–8; Jer 3:19; 31:3; Hos 1:2; 3:1; 11:1; 14:4; Mal 1:2; Paul's application to the church: Rom 1:7; 1 Thess 1:4); and (3) *"called"* (OT instances: Exod 12:16; Lev 23:2–4; Num 28:25; Isa 41:9; 42:6; 43:1; 45:3; 48:12; 49:1; 50:2; 51:2; 65:12; 66:4; Jer 7:13 [also 1QM 3.2; 4.9–11; CD 2.11; 4.3–4]; Paul's application to the church: Rom 1:6, 7; 8:28; 9:11, 12; 1 Cor 1:2, 24).

[56] Dunn is struck by how Paul's reversion to characteristic Jewish language and hope is, nevertheless, "significantly different from anything his non-Christian Jewish contemporaries cherished" (*Romans 9–16*, 692–93). Paul's eschatological solution/mystery regarding the plight of ethnic Israel parallels "solutions" in post-70 C.E. literature. Note particularly *4 Ezra* 4:35–37; 6:25; *2 Bar.* 23:4–5; 81:4; E. E. Johnson, *Function*, 124–25. These documents, like Rom 9–11, were written in the midst of questioning God's faithfulness. For Paul it was the relation of the Jews to Christ; for *4 Ezra* and *2 Baruch* it was the relation of Israel to the events of 70 C.E. All three documents question Israel's elect status, along with God's faithfulness.

[57] See chs. 1 and 2. Interestingly, Sanders (*Paul and Palestinian Judaism*, 296–98) attributes the strong emphasis in Qumran on perfect obedience of the law to the community's understanding of the narrowing of Israel's election. The result of such a shift away from Israel's election in *4 Ezra* led to outright legal perfectionism.

Chapter Five

Would Paul the Apostle Affirm Covenantal Nomism's Emphasis on Atoning Sacrifice?

The notion of sacrifice is not as living and dynamic a concept today as it was for the biblical authors, most of whom participated in or at least knew of the sacrificial cultus of the Jerusalem temple. With the passing of time and customs, much of the variety of sacrificial practice and theory has been lost. The impression of many scholarly readers is that Old Testament sacrifice was a means granted by God by which the Israelites could make amends for their transgressions. A reading of Sanders's *Paul and Palestinian Judaism* would no doubt confirm that initial impression. The way Sanders defines "covenantal nomism" places particular emphasis on sacrifice as a means by which individuals, whenever they transgressed, could be rectified in their relationship to God. Sacrifice functioned as a means of atonement through which an individual could find mercy and grace. In fact, Sanders shows that there was a means of atonement or expiatory sacrifice for just about any sin in rabbinic literature as long as the individual was willing to be restored to a relationship with the God of Israel.[1] Sanders concludes that *atoning* sacrifice occupied a central position in intertestamental and Tannaitic Judaism.

Rabbinic thought did indeed hold in high esteem the atoning value of several sacrifices.[2] The sin offering and the guilt offering effected

[1] Sanders, *Paul and Palestinian Judaism,* 157–80. I am using the term *atoning sacrifice* synonymously with *expiatory sacrifice.* Since Sanders defines covenantal nomism in terms of "atoning" sacrifice, I have followed him in terminology, but I would distinguish this from Christian theological usage. Atoning sacrifice does not necessarily imply a broken relationship with God.

[2] Sanders defines atonement in rabbinic thought as both the human act of atonement along with God's act of forgiveness; *Paul and Palestinian Judaism,* 160–61.

atonement, and the Day of Atonement functioned as the premier atoning event.[3] The rabbis often denied any value to these sacrifices if they were offered ritualistically and apart from repentance.[4] On the other hand, Sanders demonstrates that in many instances one could make a case for a sacrifice being efficacious even *without* repentance, although certainly not in a magical way.[5] Nor was the notion of atoning sacrifice unique to the rabbis.[6]

Sacrifice was not the only means of making atonement for sin in Judaism. Sanders identifies repentance, suffering, good deeds, and even death as having atoning value.[7] For example, Ben Sira upholds the atoning efficacy of sacrifice (7:29–31; 34:19; 45:16).[8] Yet sacrifice is of no value apart from repentance (7:8–9; 34:18–20 [Heb. 19–20]). Not surprisingly, then, repentance itself can atone (5:5–7a; 17:24–26, 29; 18:20). Ben Sira also upholds pious behavior, such as honoring one's father and mother and giving alms, as atoning (3:3, 14–16 [13–15], 30 [28]; 7:2; 29:12; 35:2).[9] The Qumran community upheld the validity of sacrifice (CD 4.1; 9.13–14; 11.17–12:2; 16.13), but they considered the sacrificial apparatus at Jerusalem to be controlled by evil and apostate clergy. Unable to avail themselves of the sacrificial system, the covenanters viewed righteous acts and personal piety as a substitute for the sacrificial system (1QS 5.6; 8.3–4; 9.4).[10] Similarly, repentance figured prominently. The Qumran sect was the *shabe*

---

[3] On the atoning effect of the sin and guilt offerings, see *m. Yoma* 8:8. For the atoning value of the Day of Atonement, see *m. Šebu.* 1:6–7; *m. Yoma* 8:8–9.

[4] *m. Yoma* 8:8–9; *t. Yoma* 4[5].5.

[5] Sanders, *Paul and Palestinian Judaism,* 165–68.

[6] For example, *Jub.* 6:14; 34:18–19; 50:11.

[7] The atoning value of each of these is specified in *Mek. Bahodesh* 7 (to 20:7; Lauterbach, *Mekilta de-Rabbi Ishmael,* 2:249–51). On suffering as a means of atonement, see *Pss. Sol.* 3:8–10 [7–8]; 10:1; 13:9 [10]; 1QS 8.3–4; 1QpHab 5.3–6; *Mek. Nezikin* 9 (to 21:27; Lauterbach, *Mekilta de-Rabbi Ishmael,* 3:73–74), *Mek. Bahodesh* 10 (to 20:20; Lauterbach, *Mekilta de-Rabbi Ishmael,* 2:277–80), *Sipre Deut.* 32 (to 6:5; Hammer, *Sifre,* 60). On the atoning value of death, see *m. Yoma* 8:8, *Sipre Num.* 5 (to 5:8). Death atones with repentance in *m. Sanh.* 6:2 and *t. Sanh.* 9.5. For death as atoning in certain cases *without* repentance, see *Sipre Num.* 112 (to 15:30–31; Levertoff, *Midrash Sifre,* 102). Similarly, the atoning value of suffering was often traced to its leading to repentance, e.g., *Mek. Beahodesh* 10 (to 20:20; Lauterbach, *Mekilta de-Rabbi Ishmael,* 2:277–80).

[8] Sanders, *Paul and Palestinian Judaism,* 338–39.

[9] At the same time, the fact that *good works* atone betrays the variety within Second Temple Judaism. Not all the data conveniently fits the picture of covenantal nomism. For example, there are instances in Jewish literature where one could contribute toward one's salvation; Moisés Silva, "The Law and Christianity: Dunn's New Synthesis," *WTJ* 53 (1991): 348–49.

[10] Sanders, *Paul and Palestinian Judaism,* 299–303. On the Qumran attitude toward the temple, see CD 4.17–20; 5.6–7; 6.12–13; 20.22–24; 1QpHab

Yisrael (CD 4.2; 6.4–5; 8.16) who had turned from impiety by joining the covenant community (1QH^a 2.9; 14.24; 1QS 10.20). As members of a repentant community, they were granted God's special pardon (1QH^a 14.24).[11]

A detailed analysis of each of these atoning elements in Paul is not necessary. Atoning sacrifice, given its prominence in Sanders's analysis, can function as a representative example. Before embarking on a review of atoning sacrifice in Paul, it would be helpful to review in a cursory way the variety of functions that sacrifice served in the Old Testament. Sacrifices often served as expressions of worship quite apart from the matter of atoning efficacy. Paul reflects the same diversity in his writings. The apostle describes the Christian life in terms of worship and service to God without any mention of atonement. Paul may, however, refer to atoning sacrifice when he speaks of Christ. The question must be asked whether Paul sees any value vis-à-vis sin in the atoning sacrifices of Judaism.

I. The Variety of Old Testament Sacrifice

In the Old Testament, sacrifices fulfilled a number of functions. Some sacrifices atoned, while others did not.[12] Sacrifice could be an expression

---

11.12–14; 12.7–10; Bertil Gärtner, *The Temple and the Community in Qumran and the New Testament: A Comparative Study in the Temple Symbolism of the Qumran Texts and the New Testament* (SNTSMS 1; Cambridge: Cambridge University Press, 1965), 19–20; Joseph M. Baumgarten, "Sacrifice and Worship among the Jewish Sectarians of the Dead Sea (Qumran) Scrolls," *HTR* 46 (1953): 143–45; Jean Carmignac, "L'Utilité ou L'Inutilité des Sacrifices Sanglants dans la *Regle de la Communauté* de Qumrân," *RB* 63 (1956): 531. In spite of the impurity of the Jerusalem temple cultus, the Qumran self-description as the "new temple" attests the sect's high regard for the institution itself; Georg Klinzing, *Die Umdeutung des Kultus in der Qumrangemeinde und im Neuen Testament* (Göttingen: Vandenhoeck & Ruprecht, 1971), 50–93; Daniel Jacobson Antwi, "The Death of Jesus As Atoning Sacrifice: A Study of the Sources and Purpose of New Testament Soteriology, with Particular Reference to Selected Texts" (Ph.D. diss., University of Aberdeen, 1980), 75. They looked forward to the restoration of burnt offerings, incense, and the renewal of the temple cultus at the eschaton (1QM 2:1–6); Daly, *Christian Sacrifice,* 159 n. 5, 170–71. See also Hermann Lichtenberger, "Atonement and Sacrifice in the Qumran Community," in *Approaches to Ancient Judaism* (ed. William Scott Green; BJS 9; Chico, Calif., Scholars Press, 1980), 2:159–71: "The Qumran community was not interested in devaluing the concept of sacrifice, but rather in effectively replacing it in the present time, a time devoid of legitimate sacrifice for them" (p. 162).

[11] Sanders, *Paul and Palestinian Judaism,* 305.

[12] See Ronald S. Hendel on the complexity of sacrificial ritual and the difficulties of classification, particularly from a diachronic perspective; "Sacrifice As a

of worship. Several OT texts value a worshipful inner disposition over, or at least alongside, the actual performance of sacrifice. Old Testament scholarship increasingly questions whether the "atoning" sacrifices ever expiated the sins of individuals; they may have functioned strictly to purify the temple.[13] Should a consensus emerge that the atoning sacrifices did not offer soteriological benefits for the individual, much of Sanders's thinking regarding the function of sacrifice in covenantal nomism would have to be reevaluated as well as the positions of those dependent on him. While sensitive to this debate and its implications, it remains necessary to consider the possibility that atoning sacrifice *did* offer some benefit to the individual. What are the possible atoning sacrifices in Judaism to which Paul might have referred?

The OT clearly specifies an atoning function for the sin and guilt offerings. The "sin offering" (חַטָּא) was the premier atoning sacrifice (Lev 4:1–5:13; 6:1–7, 17–23).[14] The sin offering was offered for major

---

Cultural System: The Ritual Symbolism of Exodus 24,3–8," *ZAW* 101 (1989): 366–90. The biblical witness does not itself classify sacrifices into those that atone and those that do not.

[13] Drawing on the work of Jacob Milgrom, B. H. McLean has criticized NT scholars for not recognizing that atoning sacrifices never atoned for personal sin. See McLean's *The Cursed Christ: Mediterranean Expulsion Rituals and Pauline Soteriology* (JSNTSup 126; Sheffield: Sheffield Academic Press, 1996), 27–42; idem, "The Absence of Atoning Sacrifice in Paul's Soteriology," *NTS* 38 (1992): 532–38. For a brief summary of Milgrom's thinking, which also includes a helpful overview of the various types of sacrifices, see "Sacrifices and Offerings, OT," *IDBSup* 763–71. Noam Zohar thinks that the OT sin offering *does* atone for personal sin; "Repentance and Purification: The Significance and Semantics of חטאת in the Pentateuch," *JBL* 107 (1988): 609–18. See Jacob Milgrom's vigorous response; "The *Modus Operandi* of Ḥaṭṭā᾽t: A Rejoinder," *JBL* 109 (1990): 111–13; B. H. McLean, "The Interpretation of the Levitical Sin Offering and the Scapegoat," *SR* 20 (1991): 345–56.

[14] It would be more accurate to call it a purification offering, since it was offered not only because of personal sin but also because of impurity; Jacob Milgrom, "Sin Offering or Purification Offering?" *VT* 21 (1971): 237–39, repr. in *Studies in Cultic Theology and Terminology* (SJLA 36; Leiden: E. J. Brill, 1983), 67–69; Gordon J. Wenham, *The Book of Leviticus* (NICOT; Grand Rapids: Eerdmans, 1979), 88–89; J. W. Rogerson, "Sacrifice in the Old Testament: Problems of Method and Approach," in *Sacrifice* (ed. M. F. C. Bourdillon and Meyer Fortes; London: Academic Press, 1980), 53. See also Jacob Milgrom, "Israel's Sanctuary: The Priestly 'Picture of Dorian Gray,'" *RB* 83 (1976): 390–99, repr. in *Studies in Cultic Theology and Terminology*, 75–84. On the element of God's forgiveness of the individual in atoning ritual, see esp. Lev 4:33, 35; 6:7; contra Megory Anderson and Philip Culbertson, "The Inadequacy of the Christian Doctrine of Atonement in Light of Levitical Sin Offering," *AThR* 68 (1986): 303–28. Again, one must recognize that atoning sacrifice in the OT was primarily

impurities such as childbirth (Lev 12:6, 8), skin disease (14:19, 22, 31), discharges (15:15, 30), and contact with a corpse (Num 6:11; 19:1–22). This sacrifice also effected atonement for inadvertent sins (Lev 4:2; Num 15:22–29).[15] The "guilt offering" (אָשָׁם) also had an atoning element (Lev 5:16, 18; 16:7; Num 5:8).[16] Financial compensation was a major component of this sacrifice.[17] When a party had been defrauded, the sacrifice was offered along with the payment of reparation (one fifth over the amount defrauded; Lev 5:14–16; 6:1–7; Num 5:5–10). When a Nazirite had to delay his vows due to defilement, there had to be a reparation offering (Num 6:9–12). Anyone who had a skin disease and was unable to offer sacrifices and offerings also had to make a reparation offering through the priest (Lev 14:12–14). A sort of cultic debt to the Lord had to be repaid. Like the sin offering, the guilt offering was sometimes associated with inadvertent sin (Lev 5:15, 17).[18]

---

to purify the temple from the defilement caused by sin. Early Christianity extended this to the purification of individuals (for example, Heb 9:12–14, 22, 25–26; 12:24; 1 Pet 1:2; 1 John 1:7; Rev 7:14); McLean, *Cursed Christ*, 42. Such passages from Leviticus may offer a possible explanation for the early Christian understanding, but the question remains whether *Paul* thinks of sacrifice in these terms.

[15] There was no atonement for sin "with a high hand" or deliberate sin (Num 15:30–31), a distinction reflected also at Qumran, where inadvertent sins required a two-year probationary period, whereas deliberate sin required expulsion.

[16] The guilt offering (אָשָׁם) seems to be equated with the sin offering (חַטָּא) in Lev 5:6–7. The two sacrifices are to a certain extent related. See on this point Baruch A. Levine, *In the Presence of the Lord: A Study of Cult and Some Cultic Terms in Ancient Israel* (SJLA 5; Leiden: E. J. Brill, 1974), 91–92, 98–99. Levine takes up the relationship between the two sacrifices in Lev 5:6–7 on pp. 109–10. One should also take note of Jacob Milgrom's critical remarks vis-à-vis Levine in Cult and Conscience: The Asham and the Priestly Doctrine of Repentance (SJLA 18; Leiden: E. J. Brill, 1976), 142–43.

[17] In fact, many prefer the term "reparation offering" since financial compensation is its distinguishing feature according to Lev 5:14–26. However, Leon Morris identifies several passages where the connection between the sacrifice and reparation is questionable, for example, Lev 5:17–19; 22:14–16; "ʾAsham," *EvQ* 30 (1958): 201–5.

[18] Willful sins included robbery, misappropriating a neighbor's deposit, false swearing, and oppression (Lev 6:1–7), as well as unlawful intercourse with a female slave (Lev 19:20–21). Leon Morris ("ʾAsham," 200–201) reconciles this data with the demarcation between unwilling sin and sin with the high hand in Num 15:30–31 by noting that sin with the high hand must be such that blasphemes God and despises God's word.

The significance of the burnt offering has been debated (עֹלָה; Num 28–29).[19] Some think that it was always expiatory or atoning since the death of the animal and its shed blood substituted for the one sacrificing (Lev 17:11). In many cases an atoning function is mentioned (e.g., Lev 1:4; 9:7; 14:20; 16:24).[20] The laying of hands on the victim (Lev 1:4) perhaps identified the substitute, and the victim's death then took the place of the sinner, which resulted in the sinner's acceptance before God (Lev 1:3–4, i.e., a pleasing odor, cf. 1:9). Consequently, several passages indicate that the burnt offerings dealt with sin (Gen 8:20–21; Job 1:5).[21] On the other hand, atonement was often associated with both a burnt offering and a purification offering (as in Lev 5:9–10; 9:7; 12:6–8). Perhaps only the purification offering effected atonement in these instances. Numbers 15:3 indicates that the burnt offering could be a votive or freewill offering, unlike the required atonement offering for impurity or sin. The burnt offering may be associated with a vow (Lev 22:18–25) or even a well-being offering (Lev 7:11–18; 22:21; Num 15:3). Consequently, the burnt offering could function as a *gift* to God, and the laying on of hands would merely identify the gift as that of the one sacrificing.[22] Consequently, whether the burnt offering was always atoning is debatable.[23] At the least, the sacrifice functioned as an expression of worship and of total commitment and self-surrender to God.[24]

---

[19] Philip P. Jenson, "The Levitical Sacrificial System," in *Sacrifice in the Bible* (ed. Roger T. Beckwith and Martin J. Selman; Grand Rapids: Baker, 1995), 28.

[20] On its expiatory function in these instances, see Jacob Milgrom, *Leviticus 1–16* (AB 3; New York: Doubleday, 1991), 175–77. See also 2 Sam 24:25; Job 1:5; 42:8.

[21] Gordon J. Wenham highlights Gen 8:21; "The Theology of Old Testament Sacrifice," in *Sacrifice in the Bible* (ed. Roger T. Beckwith and Martin J. Selman; Grand Rapids: Baker, 1995), 80–81. The "soothing aroma" of Noah's sacrifice had prompted a gracious response. On the use of this phrase with the burnt offering, cereal offering, well-being offering and purification offering (but *not* the reparation offering) and its significance, see Milgrom, *Leviticus 1–16*, 162–63.

[22] Thus David P. Wright, "The Gesture of Hand Placement in the Hebrew Bible and in Hittite Literature," *JAOS* 106 (1986): 433–46; Roland de Vaux, *Studies in Old Testament Sacrifice* (Cardiff: University of Wales Press, 1964), 28; also published as *Les Sacrifices de L'Ancien Testament* (CahRB 1; Paris: Gabalda, 1964), 29; Jacob Milgrom, *Leviticus 1–16*, 150–53.

[23] J. R. Porter thinks that Leviticus may reflect a later systematization where atonement became associated with any manipulation of blood (in the P document); *Leviticus* (London: Cambridge University Press, 1976), 20. See also D. P. Wright, "Gesture," 438 n. 27.

[24] Wenham, "Theology," 82–83. It is important to recognize that the expiatory dimension was not a characteristic of the sacrifice in Hellenistic times; McLean, *Cursed Christ*, 31–32.

Certainly the Day of Atonement rites functioned to effect repentance and atonement (Lev 16:30, 34).[25] Leviticus 16:5 indicates that the two goats used for the occasion are "for the purification [sin] offering," thereby associating the animals with atoning sacrifice. Similarly, Num 29:11 indicates that the scapegoat was the purification offering of atonement. One goat's blood was sprinkled on the center of sacred space, the cover of the ark in the holy of holies. The other goat was then driven out of the camp into a place that signified major impurity and separation from God's people (cf. Num 5:1–3). The Day of Atonement ritual availed even for the high priest, who put aside his normal ceremonial garments to wear a simple linen (Lev 16:4, 6).[26] Both aspects of the Day of Atonement, the blood ritual and the scapegoat, were ascribed atoning significance (Lev 16:9–10, 16, 21).[27]

The institution of the Passover is sometimes identified as a sacrifice (Exod 12:27).[28] A year-old male sheep or goat was slain (Exod 12:5; 29:1; Lev 1:3, 10; 3:1, 6–7; 9:3), but the bones were not broken (Exod 12:46). The meat was roasted over the fire and then consumed (Exod 12:8–10). The blood was smeared on the door-frames of the house. The smeared blood functioned apotropaically to ward off the destroyer (Exod 12:7, 13, 22–23).[29] The OT never specifies the Passover as atoning.[30] The Passover sacrifice was associated with God's activity as Israel's

---

[25] On the high view of the Day of Atonement's atoning power in rabbinic thought, see *m. Yoma* 8:8; *b. Ker.* 7a.

[26] Jenson writes: "Only when atonement has been successfully performed is the normal hierarchical order reestablished and the distinctive high priestly garments once again donned (v.24)" ("Levitical Sacrificial System," 34).

[27] Scholars debate the precise significance of the blood ritual and the scapegoat. For discussion, see N. Kiuchi, *The Purification Offering in the Priestly Literature: Its Meaning and Function* (Sheffield: Sheffield Academic Press, 1987), 143–59; Jenson, "Levitical Sacrificial System," 36, 40 n. 34. On the atoning significance of these rites from a rabbinic perspective, see *m. Šebu.* 1:6–7; *m. Yoma* 8:8–9.

[28] Notker Füglister, *Die Heilsbedeutung des Pascha* (SANT 8; Munich: Kösel-Verlag, 1963), 71–72.

[29] Van Seters suggests that the blood also purified the Israelite homes. The use of hyssop (Exod 12:22), associated elsewhere with ritual purification, supports this supposition (Lev 14:4, 6, 49, 51, 52; Num 19:6, 18; Ps 51:7; Heb 9:19); "The Place of the Yahwist in the History of Passover and Massot," *ZAW* 95 (1983): 180–81. However, one must be cautious not to overextend the biblical evidence as to the precise function of the blood rite.

[30] For discussion, see Füglister, *Die Heilsbedeutung,* 75–105. On the frequent misunderstanding of the Passover as an atoning sacrifice, see McLean, *Cursed Christ,* 34–35.

Redeemer (Exod 6:6). In Exod 13:13–16 the male firstborns were to be redeemed in commemoration of the Passover. A substitutionary sacrifice was required for the lives of firstborn male humans and animals. With provision of a sheep as a substitute, the firstborn donkey had to be put to death (13:13). The Passover was therefore a celebration of God's redemption and deliverance of Israel.[31] In Exod 12:14 the Passover is to be celebrated as a "memorial." In Exod 12:25–26 the Israelites are instructed to tell their children once they are in the promised land how God spared their homes that night. Philo and Josephus understood the Passover as a celebration of thanksgiving for the exodus (e.g., *Spec.* 2.27; *Ant.* 2.313). Exodus 13:8 specifies that the Israelites are to narrate the Passover to their children in the first person: "It is because of what the LORD did for *me*, when *I* came out of Egypt." This recital was taken up by the Mishnah (*m. Pesaḥ.* 10:4–5): "Therefore are we bound to give thanks, to praise, to glorify, to honour, to exalt, to extol, and to bless him who wrought all these wonders for our fathers and for *us*. He brought *us* out from bondage to freedom." In the Mishnah the Passover memorial was more than a remembrance of God's deliverance of the firstborn of Israel from the destroying angel; it came to signify the entirety of God's saving deliverance of Israel from the bondage and oppression of Egypt. As Exod 13:8 and the Mishnah show, the Passover is a celebration of God's saving activity *in the present* and of God's *continued* redemption of Israel.[32]

Sacrifices could function in a variety of ways. The "peace offering" (שְׁלָם) is an example of a nonatoning sacrifice.[33] In Lev 7:11–21 three different types of "peace offerings" are identified: the thanksgiving offering, the offering made in fulfillment of a vow, and the freewill offering. The occasion for the sacrifice could be to give thanks to God for something or simply to honor the Lord. Likewise the "meal" or "cereal offering" of Lev 2 and 6:14–18 did not atone. The Psalms emphasize the nonatoning aspects of sacrifice. Sacrifice was typically understood as an

---

[31] Of course, the Exodus texts depict the *original* Passover, which took place in individual homes. Passover rituals were soon taken over by the priests and Levites at the central sanctuary (Deut 16:1–8; 2 Chr 30:1–27; 35).

[32] Likewise in *Jub.* 49 the Passover brought about God's *continued* blessing in the form of a freedom from plagues in the coming year.

[33] On the basis of Lev 17:11, Wenham argues that *all* sacrifices involving blood must be considered as atoning. There is always an element of substitution at work; "Theology," 82. See also Rogerson, "Sacrifice," 53. Nevertheless, the element of atonement is specified for other sacrifices and not for the "peace offering." For an explanation of Lev 17:11 that respects the nonatoning nature of the "peace offering," see Jacob Milgrom, "A Prolegomenon to Leviticus 17:11," *JBL* 90 (1971): 149–56, repr. in *Studies in Cultic Theology and Terminology*, 96–103.

expression of worship (e.g., Pss 27:6b; 119:108; 141:2). Sacrifice served as a means of thanksgiving to God (e.g., Pss 54:6 [8]; 107:22; 116:12, 17). The psalmists place more value on the proper inner disposition of the worshiper than on the act of sacrifice (e.g., Pss 40:6–8 [7–9]; 50:14, 23; 51:16–19 [18–21]; 69:30–31 [31–32]). When atoning sacrifice is mentioned in Ps 40:6, the sacrifice takes second place to an obedient and worshipful disposition. Where sin was an issue, it was God who acted to forgive (e.g., Ps 65:1–3 [2–4]). In Ps 51 sacrifice is an expression of thankful and receptive hearts for the God who had acted to forgive sin. In the Psalms an individual's prayer or confession, a contrite spirit, or even godly instruction (e.g., Pss 25; 32) leads to God's forgiveness.[34] The prophetic literature places the same emphasis on sacrifice as an expression of one's whole way of being and of a proper disposition toward God. Repeatedly the prophets urge that sacrifice be an expression of the worship of one's entire life (e.g., Isa 1:10–17; Jer 7:21–23; Hos 6:6; Amos 4:4–5; 5:25; Mic 6:6–8; Hag 2:10–19; Mal 1:7, 11; 2:13–16).[35] Atonement is therefore only one aspect of sacrifice: sacrifice functioned especially as an expression of worship and thanksgiving.

---

[34] Nigel B. Courtman, "Sacrifice in the Psalms," in *Sacrifice in the Bible* (ed. Roger T. Beckwith and Martin J. Selman; Grand Rapids: Baker, 1995), 54–55; Henry McKeating, "Divine Forgiveness in the Psalms," *SJT* 18 (1965): 78–81. In fact, McKeating (p. 82) asserts that nowhere is there any hint "that forgiveness is mediated or achieved through sacrifice." The psalms of forgiveness never mention sacrifice and the psalms mentioning sacrifice never speak of forgiveness. Psalm 51 is the exception that proves the rule. Here sacrifice and forgiveness are both mentioned, but the sacrifice follows upon the forgiveness as a means of praise, and vv. 18–19 (16–17) indicate that God does not require sacrifice.

[35] The relationship need not be antagonistic; it could be complementary; Ernest C. Lucas, "Sacrifice in the Prophets," in *Sacrifice in the Bible* (ed. Roger T. Beckwith and Martin J. Selman; Grand Rapids: Baker, 1995), 70–72. On this point, see Milgrom's analysis of Jer 7:21–23 ("Concerning Jeremiah's Repudiation of Sacrifice," *ZAW* 89 [1977]: 273–75, repr. in *Studies in Cultic Theology and Terminology* [SJLA 36; Leiden: E. J. Brill, 1983], 119–21), as well as Meir Weiss's skepticism that Amos is antagonistic toward cultic practices; "Concerning Amos' Repudiation of the Cult," in *Pomegranates and Golden Bells: Studies in Biblical, Jewish, and Near Eastern Ritual, Law, and Literature in Honor of Jacob Milgrom* (ed. David P. Wright, David Noel Freedman, and Avi Hurvitz; Winona Lake, Ind.: Eisenbrauns, 1995), 213–14. Weiss (p. 214) writes that Amos is directing his attack against *specific* practices and not the cult in general: cultic acts are of no value when not accompanied by justice and righteousness. Finally, see Baruch A. Levine, "An Essay on Prophetic Attitudes toward Temple and Cult in Biblical Israel," in *Minḥah le-Naḥum: Biblical and Other Studies Presented to Nahum M. Sarna in Honour of His 70th Birthday* (ed. Marc Brettler and Michael Fishbane; JSOTSup 154; Sheffield: JSOT Press, 1993), 202–25.

II. Christian Sacrifice in Paul

Judaism never jettisoned the importance of actual sacrifice. While sacrifice was increasingly spiritualized, the ritual act itself still played a major role when accompanied by the proper, repentant disposition. Paul's understanding of sacrifice, on the other hand, is entirely spiritualized. One looks in vain to find a role for the actual performance of sacrifice. Sacrificial language is related to the work of Christ and Christian existence, quite apart from any actual sacrifices. That actual sacrifice no longer plays any role suggests that the framework of covenantal nomism has collapsed. No longer does the performance of sacrifice act as a means of availing oneself of God's mercy for sin.

Paul occasionally uses the language of sacrifice for Christian existence. In Rom 12:1–2 he says: "I appeal to you therefore, brothers and sisters, by the mercies of God, to present your bodies as a living sacrifice, holy and acceptable to God, which is your spiritual worship." Paul sees the offering up of one's entire person to the Lord as a sort of sacrifice. The sacrifice of the Christian has no atoning significance but is "spiritual worship" (τὴν λογικὴν λατρείαν).[36] The thanksgiving and response character of this worshipful sacrifice is clear from its position in the letter. Romans 12:1–2 begins the parenetic section where Paul discusses the proper Christian response to what God has done, as described in chs. 1–11 and in the climactic hymn of praise in 11:33–36.[37] Likewise, the Philippians' gifts to Paul (Phil 4:18) act as a pleasing sacrifice to God. These gifts betoken the worshipful surrender of one's whole life and being to the Lord. In Rom 15:16 Paul describes himself in cultic terms, as a priest offering up the Gentiles as a sacrifice to God.[38] The lives of the

---

[36] T. K. Abbott points to the variety of ways sacrifice was understood. Substitution, atonement, and forgiveness were not always present, nor is there anything to suggest such ideas in Rom 12:1 (or 15:16; Phil 2:17); *A Critical and Exegetical Commentary on the Epistles to the Ephesians and to the Colossians* (ICC; Edinburgh: T&T Clark, 1897), 147–48.

[37] Commentators have frequently noted the connections between Rom 12:1–2 and what precedes; e.g., Christopher Evans identifies several connections to Rom 1–2; "Romans 12.1–2: The True Worship," in *Dimensions de la Vie Chrétienne (Rm 12–13)* (ed. Lorenzo De Lorenzi; Série Monographique de "Bendedicta" 4; Rome: Abbaye de S. Paul h.l.m., 1979), 30–33. One need only consult a concordance to see the extensive overlapping of key ideas: e.g., σεβάζεσθαι, λατρεύειν, ἀσέβεια, νοῦς, ἐπίγνωσις, σῶμα, and οἰκτιρμῶν.

[38] Note the cluster of sacrificial terms: "priestly service" (ἱερουργοῦντα), "offering" (προσφορὰ), "acceptable" (εὐπρόσδεκτος), and "sanctified" (ἡγιασ-

Gentiles are therefore a sacrifice; Rom 15:16 parallels what Paul says in Rom 12:1–2. In 2 Cor 2:14–15 Paul views his own apostolic ministry in sacrificial terms. His ministry offers up the aroma of Christ to God. He offers his life as an act of worshipful service to God.[39] In Phil 2:17 Paul describes himself as "poured out as a libation over the sacrifice and the offering of your faith." The sacrificial description of Christian existence and Paul's ministry may parallel such language in connection with Christ's death.[40] Nevertheless, Paul does not specify that his own self-sacrifice or the self-sacrifice of Christians serves to *atone* for sin. The sacrificial language Paul uses for himself and his Christian communities is the language of worship, thanksgiving, and personal service to God.

III. The Sacrificial Significance of Christ's Work

While the sacrifice of Christians is an expression of worship and self-surrender with no atoning function for sin, many scholars think Paul describes Christ's ministry in the terms of atoning sacrifice. The potential instances are not particularly numerous. First Corinthians 5:7 may identify Christ with the Passover sacrifice. Paul may be stating the benefits of the Eucharist in 1 Cor 10 and in 11:23–25 in terms of atoning sacrifice. Paul may be speaking of Christ's work in terms of the sin or guilt offering in Rom 8:3 and 2 Cor 5:21. Romans 3:24–25 may be explaining Christ's saving activity as a sort of Day of Atonement sacrifice. These potential allusions are significant since they may be articulating Christ's work in the language of *atoning* sacrifice. It is necessary to examine whether these passages do, in fact, treat Christ's work as atoning for sin.

μένη). λειτουργός is used in the LXX for priestly service to God (2 Chr 11:14; Joel 2:17; Ezek 45:4); Steve Walton, "Sacrifice and Priesthood in Relation to the Christian Life and Church in the New Testament," in *Sacrifice in the Bible* (ed. Roget T. Beckwith and Martin J. Selman; Grand Rapids: Baker, 1995), 139. See also Isa 66:20.

[39] Paul's use of ὀσμή and εὐωδία is probably an allusion to sacrifice. These two words are also used together in Phil 4:18 and Eph 5:2 in clearly sacrificial contexts; Renwick, *Paul,* 78, 85–86. On the other hand, see Furnish, *II Corinthians,* 176–77, 187–88; Alfred Plummer, *A Critical and Exegetical Commentary on the Second Epistle of St. Paul to the Corinthians* (ICC; Edinburgh: T&T Clark, 1915), 71.

[40] Renwick, *Paul,* 80; with J.-F. Collange, *Enigmes de la Deuxieme Épitre de Paul aux Corinthiens: Étude Exégetique de 2 Cor. 2:14–7:4* (Cambridge: Cambridge University Press, 1972), 33; and C. K. Barrett, *A Commentary on the Second Epistle to the Corinthians* (New York: Harper & Row, 1973), 100.

If so, they may suggest a positive role for the Jewish atoning sacrifices within Paul's thought.

A. 1 Corinthians 5:7—The Paschal Lamb

Paul may refer to Christ's saving work as a sort of paschal lamb offering for sin in 1 Cor 5:7. In 1 Cor 5 he demands the excommunication of a man involved in incest in the hope that the man will be restored. It grieves Paul that the congregation has tolerated the situation. How can the congregation boast in its divine gifts and spirituality when it is tolerating such gross immorality? Paul says in v. 6 that a little leaven leavens the whole lump. The man's incest and the community's toleration of the act have become the leaven that is ruining the Corinthian church. Paul's words recall the Jewish Feast of Unleavened Bread, when the old leaven was to be completely discarded lest there be any impurity (Exod 12:18–20). The Corinthian community is to be like a pure lump of unleavened bread in its conduct. Paul then says, in v. 7b, that Christ is the paschal lamb that has been sacrificed.[41] After the lamb was sacrificed, the Jews were not to eat the old leaven (Deut 16:6; Mark 14:12; Luke 22:7). Even as Christ has been sacrificed as the paschal lamb, the community must live in a way that properly reflects the significance of that event. The Corinthians must avoid the leaven of immorality (v. 8). Christ's paschal work has inaugurated a festival celebration, the Christian life.

Paul's reference to the paschal lamb is more telling than his passing mention would suggest. Paul treats Christ in relation to one of the supreme institutions of Jewish sacrifice. Paul's brief reference to the paschal lamb indicates that he took the identification of Christ with the sacrificial lamb for granted and assumed the Corinthian community would identify the two as well.[42] Yet as quickly as Paul raises the topic, he departs from it and returns to parenesis that centers far more on the leaven than on the paschal lamb. Nor does Paul emphasize the sacrificial blood

---

[41] θύω is a term normally used for animal sacrifice. Note the aorist tense signifying a one-time event. That the word could be an allusion to the paschal lamb, see Dean O. Wenthe, "An Exegetical Study of I Corinthians 5:7b," *Springfielder* 38 (1974): 134–40; and Raymond Corriveau, *The Liturgy of Life: A Study of the Ethical Thought of St. Paul in His Letters to the Early Christian Communities* (Studia Travaux de recherche 25; Paris: Desclée de Brouwer, 1970), 73–83, esp. 78; cf. Exod 12:21; Deut 16:2, 5.

[42] Joachim Jeremias, "πάσχα," *TDNT* 5:900. The identification may therefore antedate Paul.

of Christ in this context, even though Exod 12:22 (and the use of Exod 12 in Jewish tradition) might lend itself well to such an emphasis.[43] Jewish literature from the Old Testament through the end of the first century C.E. never considered the paschal lamb to have an atoning function.[44] Likewise, Paul does not elaborate on the significance of Christ's sacrifice as an atonement for or redemption from sin.

B. The Eucharist

In his discussion of the Lord's Supper in 1 Cor 10 Paul urges the Corinthians to avoid food sacrificed to idols. The Lord's Supper and the pagan sacrifices are mutually exclusive. The comparison suggests that the Eucharist is a sacrificial event. This impression is confirmed by 1 Cor 11:23–25, where Paul passes on the tradition of the eucharistic sacrifice of Christ's body and blood in death. But Paul does not handle the Eucharist in the manner one would expect of a sacrifice. The point of the comparison in 1 Cor 10 is not between the pagan sacrificial food and the Lord's Supper as a sacrifice, but between the spiritual realities that stand behind the respective meals. Those who eat food sacrificed to idols share in the demonic realities present with the pagan altar, even as those who partake of the bread and cup participate in the Lord Jesus Christ. Because Christians participate in a union with Christ, they are not to participate in a union with demons by partaking of food sacrificed to idols.[45] Paul develops a participatory, rather than sacrificial, understanding of the eucharist in 1 Cor 10.[46]

Similarly 1 Cor 11 departs from a sacrificial understanding of the Eucharist. Whereas the eucharistic tradition in Matthew, Mark, and Luke speaks of the cup being "poured out" (ἐκχυννόμενον) and uses the expiatory phrase "for many/you" (ὑπὲρ πολλῶν/ὑμῶν), Paul omits both phrases. Paul places "blood" (with Luke) in a modifying phrase within the predicate ("This cup is the new covenant in my blood"), whereas

---

[43] For example, *Exod. Rab.* 15:3 (on Exod 12:10).

[44] McLean, *Cursed Christ,* 34–35; however, a connection between the paschal sacrifice and atonement for sin is clear in Ezek 45:18–25, where the Passover is celebrated alongside a sin offering. Yet it is the sin offering and not the Passover lamb that should be understood as atoning.

[45] Sanders, *Paul and Palestinian Judaism,* 455–56.

[46] Note too that Paul makes his point by means of the bread of the Eucharist and not the cup or the blood. It is the one loaf that unites the church into one body. Paul passes up an opportunity to develop the idea of the shedding of sacrificial blood; Romano Penna, *Paul the Apostle,* 2:41.

Mark and Matthew treat "blood" as the direct predicate ("this is my blood of the covenant"). Penna thus writes:

> Apart from any other considerations, it is obvious that this [Paul's] formulation gives priority to the effect or result mediated by the blood rather than the instrument or cause that brought it about, i.e., the "new covenant" rather than the "blood" of Christ, even though the two are linked precisely as cause (or instrument) and effect.[47]

Further, this is the blood of a "new" covenant, which calls to mind Jer 31 rather than Exod 24:8, as in Matthew and Mark.[48] Far from emphasizing the sacrificial aspects of the Eucharist, Paul develops the tradition along a different trajectory. Paul warns of sinning against the Lord's body and blood by an unworthy communion, an idea that makes sense within the participatory schema of 1 Cor 10. As in the preceding chapter, Paul is concerned in 1 Cor 11 with the danger of violating the hidden reality in which one participates by means of the sacrament.[49] While Paul utilizes a tradition that mediated Jesus' sacrifice of his body and blood in death, Paul retells the tradition in language that does not emphasize the sacrificial motif, but rather employs the tradition in support of a more participatory motif.[50]

C. The Sin Offering—Romans 8:3; 2 Corinthians 5:21

Commentators have been historically divided over whether Paul is alluding in Rom 8:3 to the OT "sin offering." The Hebrew word (חטאת) can refer to "sin" or to the "sin offering."[51] The Greek phrase περὶ τῆς

---

[47] Ibid., 2:29.

[48] Ibid., 2:30.

[49] For a detailed analysis of the eucharistic texts from this perspective, see A. Andrew Das, "1 Corinthians 11:17–34 Revisited," *CTQ* 62 (1998): 187–208.

[50] Interpreters have traditionally taken ὑπὲρ ἡμῶν (as in Gal. 3:13) as a reference to sacrificial (expiatory) death; Daly, *Christian Sacrifice,* 237; Leon Morris, *The Apostolic Preaching of the Cross* (Grand Rapids: Eerdmans, 1956), 59. The problem is that there are other ways of understanding the phrase. Vincent Taylor thinks that when Paul uses ὑπέρ and περί rather than ἀντί, he is straying away from a substitutionary understanding; *The Atonement in New Testament Teaching* (London: Epworth, 1940), 86. Paul may be speaking, rather, of an identity transfer; Jesus enters into solidarity with the human situation of curse, in order that we might enjoy participation in the liberation from that situation found "in Christ." The emphasis may be on participation; Sanders, *Paul and Palestinian Judaism,* 464; Richard B. Hays, "Christology and Ethics in Galatians," *CBQ* 49 (1987): 268–90; Das, "Oneness in Christ," 173–86. It is therefore best to rely on Paul's explicit references to atoning sacrifice.

[51] On the concept of sin offering, see Lev 4:1–5, 13.

ἁμαρτίας in the LXX usually translates the Hebrew phrase "for sin" (עלחטאת and לחטאת). The Greek phrase τὸ περὶ τῆς ἁμαρτίας usually translates "sin offering."[52] That leaves περὶ ἁμαρτίας (as in Rom 8:3), which in the LXX is used for both "sin" *and* "sin offering." In at least forty-four of the fifty-four usages, περὶ ἁμαρτίας stands parallel to εἰς ὁλοκαύτωμα, εἰς θυσίαν σωτηρίου, and similar sacrificial phrases. In other words, in the majority of instances the phrase indicates the "sin offering" and parallels the articular counterpart when the phrase is used in connection with the burnt offering or some other sacrifice. Given the Septuagintal usage, N. T. Wright believes that the presumption should rest with taking περὶ ἁμαρτίας as "sin offering."[53] Wright also points out that the nature of the OT sin offering has not been properly weighed. The sin offering was provided as a means of dealing with unwilling sins or sins of ignorance and not the sin committed "with a high hand" (for such sin there is no sacrifice but only removal from the covenant people).[54] Hebrews 10:26 says that the sin offering does not avail for one who sins willingly. In Rom 7:7–25 Paul discusses *unwilling sin.* "For I do not do what I want, but I do the very thing I hate. . . . I can will what is right, but I cannot do it. For I do not do the good I want, but the evil I do not want is what I do. . . . For I delight in the law of God in my inmost self, but I see in my members another law at war with the law of my mind" (vv. 15, 18–19, 22–23). Such unwilling sin renders more likely the possibility that Paul is speaking of Christ in terms of the "sin offering."[55]

Wright has demonstrated the possibility of an allusion to the sin offering, but the allusion is by no means certain. Paul speaks in Rom 7 and 8 more in terms of cosmic powers: sin and death on the one hand and the power of the Spirit on the other. The Spirit liberates the Christian from the law in the hands of sin and death. The categories of discussion are cosmic rather than cultic.[56] There is no clear indication in the context that Paul has the cultic sin offering in mind.[57] Paul uses ἁμαρτία

---

[52] McLean (*Cursed Christ*, 46) contends that the sin offering in the Septuagint always included the use of the article. If this is true, Rom 8:3 cannot refer to the OT sacrifice unless there were very strong contextual reasons to suggest otherwise.

[53] N. T. Wright, *Climax*, 221–22.

[54] Numbers 15:30–31, a distinction reflected in later Judaism as well: *m. Sanh.* 7:8; *m. Hor.* 2:1–6.

[55] N. T. Wright, *Climax*, 223–24.

[56] David Seeley, *The Noble Death: Graeco-Roman Martyrology and Paul's Concept of Salvation* (JSNTSup 28; Sheffield: Sheffield Academic Press, 1990), 29.

[57] C. Breytenbach, "Versöhnung, Stellvertretung und Sühne: Semantische und Traditiongeschichtliche Bemerkungen am Beispiel der Paulinischen Briefe,"

elsewhere in Rom 8:2–3 for anything but the sin offering (ἀπὸ τοῦ νόμου τῆς ἁμαρτίας, ἐν ὁμοιώματι σαρκὸς ἁμαρτίας). That περὶ ἁμαρτίας should refer to the sin offering would require a shift in meaning for ἁμαρτίας in the space of a few words. A sin offering allusion is therefore unlikely.

N. T. Wright has identified a second potential reference to the "sin offering" in 2 Cor 5:21.[58] The text reads: "For our sake [God] made him to be sin [sin offering] who knew no sin, so that in him we might become the righteousness of God." If one were to recognize an allusion to the sin offering in Rom 8:3, the likelihood of additional allusions would increase. As with Rom 8:3, Wright sees contextual clues for translating ἁμαρτία as "sin offering" in 2 Cor 5:21. The focus of this section is on Paul's apostolic ministry, a ministry of weakness and suffering.[59] The appearance of Paul's ministry in 4:7, 10–12 is likened to a fragile earthen vessel that may seem disgraceful and shameful.[60] Wright says: "Insofar as this ministry is a thing of shame and dishonor, it is so despite Paul's intention, and the sin-offering is the right means of dealing with such a problem."[61] Wright's reasoning is not compelling. Paul's seemingly weak and shameful appearance is weak and disgraceful only from a human point of view. God, the author of Paul's ministry, certainly would not be offended by Paul's ministry. Why would a "sin offering," a means of rectifying one's relationship to God, be necessary for the outward appearance of Paul's ministry from a mistaken *human* standpoint? Wright argues more persuasively that 2 Cor 5 identifies God and the divine ambassador: Paul, as the gospel minister, "becomes" the very "righteousness of God" in his ministry. To grant Wright's premise does not necessarily lead to a reference to the sin offering. Wright does not rule out alternative construals to his own model of Paul as a sin offering, for

---

NTS 39 (1993): 73. As T. C. G. Thornton objects, there is nothing alongside περὶ ἁμαρτίας to indicate a sacrifice as there are in other NT uses of περὶ ἁμαρτίας for the sin offering (e.g., Heb 10:18; 13:11); "The Meaning of καὶ περὶ ἁμαρτίας in Romans viii. 3," *JTS* 22 (1971): 516. Even in the OT usage that N. T. Wright cites as support, περὶ ἁμαρτίας referred to the "sin offering" only when sacrifical terminology was used alongside the phrase, precisely what is lacking in Rom 8:3.

[58] N. T. Wright, "On Becoming the Righteousness of God: 2 Corinthians 5:21," in *1 and 2 Corinthians* (ed. David M. Hay; vol. 2 of *Pauline Theology;* SBLSymS; Minneapolis: Fortress, 1993), 200–208. ἁμαρτία is often used to translate "sin offering" in the LXX; see Exod 29:14; Lev 4:24; 5:9 (12); 6:18–25; Num 6:14.

[59] Paul begins this line of thought already in 2:14.

[60] See also 5:13, 16.

[61] N. T. Wright, "On Becoming the Righteousness of God," 208.

instance, Morna Hooker's. She suggests an "interchange" approach: Christ takes on the minister's condition, including his sinfulness, in order that the minister might share in Christ's condition and so become the righteousness of God.[62] Certainly 2 Cor 5:21 uses the language of "for us" alongside the more participatory (or perhaps representative) "in him" language.[63]

Charles Talbert also affirms a sin-offering allusion in 2 Cor 5:21.[64] He too points out that ἁμαρτία is used in the LXX for both the sin offering (Exod 29:14; Lev 4:24; 5:12; Num 6:14) and the guilt/reparation offering (Num 18:9). Likewise, περὶ ἁμαρτίας is used for both (Lev 5:9; 6:18–25—sin offering; Lev 7:1–10; Isa 53:10—guilt offering). The idea of a guilt or reparation offering would fit the context of 2 Cor 5:21: Christ's sacrificial death has brought about reparation to God as the wounded party. The verse would offer a *mechanism* for how God's reconciliation with the world takes place. Talbert also believes that the OT provides a precedent for translating ἁμαρτία with two different senses in 2 Cor 5:21 (as "sin" and then as "guilt [or sin] offering"); one finds the same multiple usage in Lev 4:3: "let him offer for *sin* [ἁμαρτίας] which he has committed a young bull without blemish to the Lord *for a sin offering* [περὶ ἁμαρτίας]."

Talbert's case is not compelling either. First, the translation of ἁμαρτία as "sin offering" or "reparation offering" is only one *possible* understanding of 2 Cor 5:21. That ἁμαρτία was occasionally used that way in the LXX does not mean that Paul is using it for "sin offering" or "reparation offering" here. And as indicated above, in light of competing alternatives (e.g., Hooker's interchange model), it is not enough merely to suggest a possible mechanism by which Christ's work effects atonement. The most serious problem for Talbert's view is precisely the one he seeks to avoid: ἁμαρτία must take two very different senses within the same verse. The reference to Leviticus does not help, since the Leviticus context clearly indicates a sacrifice ("a young bull without blemish"). Such indicators are lacking in 2 Cor 5:21. Further, the περὶ

---

[62] Morna D. Hooker, *From Adam to Christ: Essays on Paul* (Cambridge: Cambridge University Press, 1990), 13–25. "Knowing no sin" does not necessarily refer, then, to the blameless sacrificial victim.

[63] Stephen H. Travis, "Christ As Bearer of Divine Judgment in Paul's Thought about the Atonement," in *Atonement Today: A Symposium at St John's College, Nottingham* (ed. John Goldingay; London: SPCK, 1995), 26–27; cf. Rom 5:19; 6:10–11.

[64] Charles H. Talbert, *Reading Corinthians: A Literary and Theological Commentary on 1 and 2 Corinthians* (New York: Crossroad, 1989), 167–68.

ἁμαρτίας and ἁμαρτίας of Lev 4:3 are two *different* expressions. Wright has shown in his work on Rom 8:3 that περὶ ἁμαρτίας was the usual way of referring to the sin offering. Since 2 Cor 5:21 does not use περὶ ἁμαρτίας, a reference to the sin offering is less likely, and the problem of two usages of ἁμαρτία with differing meanings in the same verse remains.[65]

Many have thought that Paul is drawing upon Jewish traditional material in 2 Cor 5:21. The use of traditional material would increase the probability of a sacrificial reference in this verse.[66] Collange points to the tenuous link between v. 20 and v. 21 and the rhythmic and striking character of v. 21.[67] The concept of "sin" is not used here as a power but rather as a transgression and its consequence. Paul does not elsewhere in his extant writings reflect on Jesus' sinlessness.[68] Departures from Paul's own thought and language increase the likelihood that Paul may be drawing upon traditional language. The works of N. T.

[65] Stanislas Lyonnet and Leopold Sabourin try to answer this argument by supposing that Paul did not use the full prepositional phrase in order to maintain a contrast with the "righteousness of God"; *Sin, Redemption, and Sacrifice: A Biblical and Patristic Study* (AnBib 48: Rome: Biblical Institute Press, 1970), 251–52. Nevertheless, this remains an attempt to explain away the *absence* of sin-offering language as one finds it in Rom 8:3 (assuming a reference there). They also point to the verb ποιέω as a Septuagintal word for "making/offering a sacrifice" (p. 252 n. 24). D. Philipp Bachmann, on the other hand, points to less ambiguous words for sacrifice that Paul did *not* choose to use: ἔδωκεν, ἀνήγαγεν, προσήνεγκεν, παρέστησεν, παρέδωκεν, ἀνήνεγκεν; *Der zweite Brief des Paulus an die Korinther* (3d ed.; Leipzig: A. Deichertsche Verlagsbuchhandlung Werner Scholl, 1918), 273.

[66] Ralph Martin sees a citation of a Jewish-Christian fragment; *2 Corinthians*, 138–41, 156–57. Furnish does not assert an actual citation in 5:21 but at least the use of traditional material; *II Corinthians*, 351.

[67] Collange, *Enigmes*, 275; Ernst Käsemann says the "participial predicates" "undoubtedly breathe a liturgical spirit"; "Some Thoughts on the Theme 'The Doctrine of Reconciliation in the New Testament,'" in *The Future of Our Religious Past: Essays in Honour of Rudolf Bultmann* (ed. James M. Robinson; trans. Charles E. Carlston and Robert P. Scharlemann; New York: Harper & Row, 1971), 52.

[68] Käsemann, "Some Thoughts," 53. While Peter Stuhlmacher attempts to refute Käsemann's argumentation in *Gerechtigkeit Gottes bei Paulus* (Göttingen: Vandenhoeck & Ruprecht, 1965), 77–78 n. 2, he is elsewhere supportive of seeing Jewish-Christian traditional material behind this verse. See Stuhlmacher's essays, "Jesus' Resurrection and the View of Righteousness in the Pre-Pauline Mission Congregations" and "The Apostle Paul's View of Righteousness" in *Reconciliation, Law, and Righteousness: Essays in Biblical Theology* (Philadelphia: Fortress, 1986).

Wright and Hooker show that many scholars see continuity between 2 Cor 5:21 and its context.[69] One might also note the paradoxical expressions here that so typify 2 Corinthians: the one who knew no sin became sin (cf. power through weakness, 12:9; life through death, 4:12; wealth through poverty, 8:9).[70] Finally, Reimund Bieringer and Margaret Thrall have both demonstrated that the various arguments for pre-Pauline material in 2 Cor 5:19–21 do not stand the test of critical scrutiny.[71]

Possibly 2 Cor 5:21 makes use of Isa 53.[72] In 2 Cor 5:21 Christ has done no wrong but is made an offering for sin in order that there might be a right relationship with God. This parallels the Suffering Servant in Isa 53 who also did no wrong (v. 9) but gave his life as an offering (v. 10) so that through this suffering many would be justified (v. 11). The Suffering Servant's sacrifice corresponds to the אָשָׁם, the guilt/reparation offering of Lev 7:1–10.[73] If Isa 53 stands behind 2 Cor 5:21, a Jewish-Christian background and a reference to the guilt/reparation offering may be indicated.[74]

Renwick argues for a sacrificial reference by pointing to the cultic language that runs throughout this section of 2 Corinthians. Not only does Paul speak of ἁμαρτία in 2 Cor 5:21, but he also speaks of his ministry as an "odor and fragrance" in 2 Cor 2:14–16 (ὀσμή, εὐωδία). These words occur together in the context of sacrifice throughout the OT as

---

[69] For example, if Wright's understanding of the passage is correct, one need not see "righteousness of God" as differing from Paul's other usages, as R. P. Martin claims in his case (*2 Corinthians*, 140) for traditional material.

[70] Travis, "Christ As Bearer of Divine Judgment," 26, who thereby qualifies the probability that Paul is reworking traditional language.

[71] Reimund Bieringer, "2 Kor 5,19a und die Versöhnung der Welt," *ETL* 63 (1987): 312–23; Margaret E. Thrall, *A Critical and Exegetical Commentary on the Second Epistle to the Corinthians* (2 vols.; ICC; Edinburgh: T&T Clark, 1994), 1:445–49.

[72] Lyonnet and Sabourin, *Sin;* Leopold Sabourin, *Rédemption Sacrificielle: Une Enquete Exégétique* (Studia 11; Bruges: Desclée de Brouwer, 1961), 156–59; and especially the arguments of Otfried Hofius, "Erwägung zur Gestalt und Herkunft des paulinischen Versöhnungsgedankens," *ZTK* 77 (1980): 186–99, esp. 196–99.

[73] The same word, אָשָׁם, is used in both passages; Lyonnet and Sabourin, *Sin*, 253–56.

[74] Ralph Martin (*2 Corinthians*, 140) follows Reginald Fuller in arguing that Isa 53 indicates pre-Pauline material. The argument requires, though, that one show that all Paul's other references to Isa 53 are pre-Pauline as well, a difficult proposition. Seeley, *Noble Death*, 39–57, thinks that many of the alleged Pauline references to Isa 53 do not actually refer to it.

well as in Paul.[75] In 2 Cor 4:7–11 Paul speaks of the Christian's body as an "earthen vessel" (ὀστρακίνοις σκεύεσιν). This term is used in the OT for the vessel used to bear the remains of the sin offering after the animal has been sacrificed (Lev 6:28; LXX, 6:21; cf. 6:25–27, LXX 6:18–21) or to contain the remains of sacrificial birds killed for the cleansing of leprosy (Lev 14:50). Such sacrificial allusions earlier in the letter increase the likelihood of a sin-offering reference in 2 Cor 5:21.[76]

Nevertheless, translating ἁμαρτία as "sin offering" still requires a different sense for the same word in the same verse.[77] Translating ἁμαρτία as "sin offering" ruins the chiastic contrast between a sinless Christ being "made sin" in contrast to the sinful Christian becoming the "righteousness of God." "Sin" and "righteousness of God" are in an antithetical relationship, which would not be possible if one were to take ἁμαρτία as "sin offering."[78] The evidence is not very compelling that Paul is alluding to the sin and/or guilt offering in Rom 8:3 and 2 Cor 5:21. If he is, he has metaphorically reinterpreted the OT rite in terms of Christ. The rites themselves do not offer any real solution to the problem of sin. Only in Christ does one find true atonement for sin. If Paul is *not* referring to OT atoning sacrifices in Rom 8:3 and 2 Cor 5:21, then Paul would be ignoring a key salvific component of the Jewish thought of his day. Either scenario involves a departure from the crucial role of atoning sacrifice in Sanders's articulation of covenantal nomism.

D. Day of Atonement—Romans 3:24–25

In the course of describing God's saving activity in Jesus Christ in Rom 3:21–26, Paul uses a word that cannot be found in any of his other let-

---

[75] See Gen 8:21; Exod 29:18, 25, 41; Lev 1:9, 13, 17; 2:2, 9, 12; 3:5, 11, 16; 4:31; 6:15; 8:21, 28; 17:4, 6; 23:13, 18; Num 15:3, 4, 7, 10, 13, 14, 24; 18:17; 28:2, 6, 8, 11, 13, 24, 27; 29:2, 6, 8, 11, 13, 36; Ezra 6:10; Ezek 6:13; 16:19; 20:28, 41; Dan 2:41; 4:37a; Eph 5:2; Phil 4:17–18.

[76] Renwick, *Paul,* 75–86.

[77] Gerhard Friedrich cannot conceive of ἁμαρτία occurring three times within the verse and yet the middle instance having a completely different meaning from the preceding and following ones; *Die Verkündigung des Todes Jesu im Neuen Testament* (Biblisch Theologische Studien 6; Neukirchen-Vluyn: Neukirchener Verlag, 1982), 70. Paul would surely have clarified his usage in order to avoid the possible confusion; Collange, *Enigmes,* 278. Leopold Sabourin's reference (*Rédemption Sacrificielle,* 155) to κεφαλή in 1 Cor 11:4 is not helpful since the change in meaning is clearly warranted by the context of the verse.

[78] Bachmann, *Der zweite Brief,* 273; Philip Edgcumbe Hughes, *Paul's Second Epistle to the Corinthians* (NICNT; Grand Rapids: Eerdmans, 1962), 215; Thrall, *Second Corinthians,* 1:441; McLean, *Cursed Christ,* 109.

ters, ἱλαστήριον. What renders this word so striking is that in twenty-one of its twenty-seven occurrences in the LXX, it is used as the Greek translation of כַּפֹּרֶת, the golden lid over the ark of the covenant. Annually on the Day of Atonement the high priest sprinkled the blood of the sacrifice onto the lid of the ark for the forgiveness of the people's sins (Exod 25:10–22; Lev 16). By using ἱλαστήριον Paul may be describing Jesus' saving work in terms of the Day of Atonement. Unfortunately, Rom 3:25's potential allusion to the Day of Atonement is yet another hotly disputed issue. One has to reckon (again) with the possibility that Paul is using traditional or creedal material in these verses. If Paul is drawing upon traditional or creedal language, the possibility of a "mercy seat" reference would significantly increase.[79] Before assessing the case for a reference to the "mercy-seat" in Rom 3:25, the possibility of pre-Pauline material must be considered.

1) A Traditional or Creedal Fragment. Rudolf Bultmann was the first to propose that Paul is citing an early creedal fragment.[80] Not all who have followed Bultmann on this point have agreed with him that the beginning of the creedal fragment is located in v. 24. Since the studies of Eduard Lohse and Klaus Wengst, most have identified the pre-Pauline fragment as 3:25–26a. In favor of beginning the fragment with v. 24 is the awkward transition from v. 23 to v. 24. The emphatic πάντες ("all") in v. 23 does not have an antithetical counterpart in v. 24.[81] Verse 24 does not begin with the grammatical construction one would expect in Paul (e.g., an aorist participle, a third instance of πάντες, or an indicative construction with a conjunction).[82] Verse 24 does not, then,

---

[79] This was Judaism's supreme atoning event. The use of ἱλαστήριον in a Jewish-Christian environment may well refer to the Day of Atonement ritual.

[80] Bultmann first suggested pre-Pauline material in 3:24–25 in "Neueste Paulusforschung," *TRu* 8 (1936): 11–12. He developed the reasoning for this conclusion in his *Theology of the New Testament* (trans. Kendrick Grobel; 2 vols.; New York: Charles Scribner's Sons, 1951), 1:46–47.

[81] Ernst Käsemann, "Zum Verständnis von Römer 3.24–26," *ZNW* 43 (1950–1951): 150, repr. in *Exegetische Versuche und Besinnungen*, vol. 1 (Göttingen: Vandenhoeck & Ruprecht, 1960), 96–100, esp. 96.

[82] John Reumann, who sides with Bultmann, writes:

> We should expect something like, "All men sinned . . . , but all men are declared righteous by God's grace." But one does not get *dikaiountai de,* or any indicative form like it. Instead there is a participle, and no conjunction at all. Since verse 25 begins with a relative pronoun, and the passage proceeds with two parallel clauses . . . , and a final clause . . . , one must say that the construction in verse 23 never is completed as it ought to be. Verse 24 begins an intrusion, as if from another context ("The Gospel of the Righteousness of God: Pauline Reinterpretation in Romans 3:21–31," *Int* 20 [1966]: 435).

smoothly complete the sense of the previous phrase. However, those who begin the citation with v. 25 are not persuaded by these arguments. Wengst points out that Paul commonly continues a sentence with a coordinating participle after a finite verb.[83] The πάντες in v. 23, which refers back to πάντας τοὺς πιστεύοντας ("all who believe") in v. 22, does not need a counterpart in v. 24. The subject of the circumstantial participle, given its referent, would remain "all who believe." A repetition of πάντες would be unnecessary.[84]

Following Bultmann, proponents of a pre-Pauline fragment have typically identified non-Pauline terminology in vv. 24–26: πάρεσις, προγεγονότων, ἁμάρτημα, προτίθεσθαι, ἀπολύτρωσις, ἔνδειξις, ἀνοχή, and δικαιοσύνη in the attributive sense.[85] ἱλαστήριον is non-Pauline; the use of αἷμα is non-Pauline, since Paul refers to Christ's death by means of the word σταυρός.[86] These peculiarities of vocabulary, with the exception of ἀπολύτρωσις, are limited to vv. 25–26a, and ἀπολύτρωσις is not a Pauline *hapax* (Rom 8:23; 1 Cor 1:30). The list of non-Pauline vocabulary is therefore limited to vv. 25–26. The creedal material ought to begin, then, with the relative clause in v. 25. The use of the relative pronoun is a common way of introducing cited material (e.g., Phil 2:5; 1 Pet 2:23; 1 Tim 3:16).[87]

But in fact the case for pre-Pauline material in vv. 25–26 is not compelling either. Most of the reputedly non-Pauline words occur elsewhere in Paul: ἀνοχή (Rom 2:4); ἔνδειξις (2 Cor 8:24; Phil 1:28); ἁμάρτημα (1 Cor 6:18). With respect to Paul's preference for σταυρός over αἷμα, Paul prefers αἷμα in Rom 5:9.[88] The difficulty posed by δικαιοσύνη in v. 24–25 can be resolved by taking it in the same way as the three other instances of δικαιοσύνη in the context.[89] The only remaining candidates for non-Pauline words are: πάρεσις, ἱλαστήριον,

---

[83] See BDF § 468 (p. 245) on this point; cf. 2 Cor 5:12; 7:5; 10:14–15.

[84] Klaus Wengst, *Christologische Formeln und Lieder des Urchristentums* (Gütersloh: Gerd Mohn, 1972) 87. So also Cranfield, *Romans,* 1:205.

[85] Käsemann, "Zum Verständnis," 150–51; Reumann, "The Gospel," 436–37.

[86] 1 Cor 10:16; 11:25, 27 are all allegedly based on pre-Pauline tradition, leaving only Rom 5:9 as an exception to this rule; Bultmann, *Theology,* 1:46–47.

[87] Eduard Lohse, *Märtyrer und Gottesknectt: Untersuchungen zur urchristlichen Verkündigung vom Sühntod Jesu Christi* (2d ed.; Göttingen: Vandenhoeck & Ruprecht, 1963), 149–50.

[88] Proponents of the pre-Pauline theory are therefore forced to argue that Rom 5:9 is also pre-Pauline, although there is far less evidence in 5:9 than in Rom 3:25–26.

[89] Douglas A. Campbell, *The Rhetoric of Righteousness in Romans 3.21–26* (JSNTSup 65; Sheffield: Sheffield Academic Press, 1992), 52.

and προγεγονότων, a ratio of three out of seventeen words in Rom 3:25–26a (17.6 percent). As Douglas Campbell has pointed out, *hapax legomena* average 17.4 percent in Paul's letters as a whole.[90] There is nothing about this vocabulary that might necessitate a pre-Pauline fragment hypothesis.[91]

Käsemann notes the "Near Eastern hymnic-liturgical" style of Rom 3:24–26 with its high concentration of genitival and prepositional constructions.[92] However, if one were to exclude v. 24 from consideration (in agreement with Lohse and Wengst), and if one were to eliminate διὰ τῆς πίστεως, a phrase typically ascribed to Paul's editing of the tradition, then the number of prepositional phrases would be reduced from seven to four. One of the seven genitives would also be eliminated. Campbell notes that a profuse use of prepositions and genitives characterizes all of 3:21–26, not just the supposed pre-Pauline verses.[93] Once one excises the Pauline διὰ τῆς πίστεως, the pre-Pauline "hymnic-liturgical style" appears rather clumsy.[94]

---

[90] D. A. Campbell, *Rhetoric,* 53.

[91] Cf. the vice list in Rom 1:29–31 with a ratio of 12:26, nearly fifty percent. Yet this passage is typically considered Pauline; D. A. Campbell, *Rhetoric,* 53 n. 2.

[92] "Stil aus der hymnisch-liturgischen Überlieferung des vorderen Orients"; Käsemann, "Zum Verständnis," 151.

[93] D. A. Campbell, *Rhetoric,* 55.

[94] A fact that motivates Charles Talbert's work on reconstructing the pre-Pauline fragment; "A Non-Pauline Fragment at Romans 3.24–26?" *JBL* 85 (1966): 287–96. By *excluding* ten of the forty-eight words (διὰ πίστεως [3:25], τὸν ἐκ πίστεως Ἰησοῦ [3:26], and ἐν τῷ νῦν καιρῷ [3:26]), Charles Talbert has discovered a symmetrical pattern in vv. 25–26 (p. 290). Yet the resulting symmetrical pattern breaks up words and phrases that should be understood together. For example, Talbert severs ἱλαστήριον from its natural relation to ἐν τῷ αὐτοῦ αἵματι ("in his blood") and places the reference to Christ's blood into a less than convincing parallel with ἐν τῇ ἀνοχῇ τοῦ θεοῦ, a reference to God and his patience. George E. Howard notes that Talbert inserts an understood "we" into his reconstruction of the link between vv. 24 and 27 without any contextual indication and disrupts the more natural relationship between the participle δικαιούμενοι and v. 23's πάντες; "Romans 3:21–31 and the Inclusion of the Gentiles," *HTR* 63 (1970): 225. See D. A. Campbell for additional syntactical problems with Talbert's reconstruction; *Rhetoric,* 44 n. 1. Sam K. Williams observes that Talbert's reconstruction involves syntactical relations that are completely unparalleled in the rest of the New Testament; *Jesus' Death As Saving Event: The Background and Origin of a Concept* (HDR 2; Missoula, Mont.: Scholars Press, 1975), 8–9. Of much more questionable value is Talbert's hypothesis that 3:25–26 is a post-Pauline interpolation. Williams (pp. 6–11) shows how both Talbert as well as Gottfried Fitzer's post-Pauline hypotheses ("Der Ort der Versöhnung nach Paulus: Zu der Frage des Sühnopfers Jesu," *TZ* 22 [1966]: 161–83) lack in evidence.

Many advocates of pre-Pauline material in vv. 25–26 have pointed to the unusual theology of these verses.[95] Paul does not refer to Jesus' death as a ἱλαστήριον anywhere else. Paul tends to describe Jesus' death in terms of the cross rather than "blood."[96] Paul does not speak anywhere else of God's righteousness requiring expiation for former sins. The assertion in v. 25 that God had "passed over" former sins is difficult in view of what precedes in Rom 1:18–3:20. The preceding material in Romans indicates that God's wrath stood over all equally because of sin, hardly a situation of forbearance. Käsemann therefore maintains that there is a tension between v. 25c–d and v. 26b–c. Paul is essentially *correcting* the pre-Pauline citation. πάρεσις, in the citation, referred to the passing over or overlooking of past sins. Such a statement, Käsemann said, could not be Pauline, since Paul was not interested in a covenant restoration or atonement after a period of divine patience. Paul's perspective was radically eschatological and discontinuous (thus the apostle's interpretive ἐν τῷ καιρῷ). God's δικαιοσύνη is not his patience but his eschatological power. Paul had appropriated the tradition only because it had used δικαιοσύνη in relation to the work of Christ, but he immediately had to qualify the citation.[97]

The argument from non-Pauline theology is not decisive either. For example, consider Käsemann's argument from πάρεσις. Käsemann assumes that the word means "passing over" or "overlook": God simply ignored the sin of former times. Werner Kümmel's essay on πάρεσις renders the translation "passing over" or "overlook" less likely since the word may also be translated as "remission" or "forgiveness." If so, πάρεσις would not refer to a passing over of previous sins but to a *present* forgiveness of sins. A present forgiveness of sins in v. 25 would conform with the other present actions in its context.[98] πάρεσις only occurs here in the New Testament and four times in classical literature.[99] The

---

[95] Bultmann, *Theology,* 1:46–47; Käsemann, "Zum Verständnis," 151–54.

[96] For this argument to be compelling, one must also argue a pre-Pauline background for the exceptions: 1 Cor 10:16; 11:25, 27 and Rom 5:9, not all of which are necessarily likely.

[97] Fitzer, "Ort der Versöhnung," 163, notes the troubling lack of a particle, δέ for instance, to signal a corrective.

[98] Werner Georg Kümmel, "Πάρεσις und ἔνδειξις: Ein Beitrag zum Verständnis der paulinischen Rechtfertigungslehre," *ZTK* 49 (1952): 154–67, repr. in *Heilsgeschehen und Geschichte: Gesammelte Aufsätze, 1933–1964,* vol. 1 (Marburg: N. G. Elwert, 1965), 260–70.

[99] Plutarch, *Comp. Dion. Brut.* 2; Dio Chrysostom, *Thirtieth Discourse: Charidemus* 80 [30], 19; Dionysius of Halicarnassus, *The Roman Antiquities* 7.37.2; Appian, *Basilica* 13.1.

first three classical instances do not at all mean "overlook" or "pass over" but rather "release" (with the last two of the three leaning more toward the idea of forgiveness). Douglas Campbell located the final instance of πάρεσις in Appian, and there it *does* mean "overlook" or "pass over." Thus the nonbiblical evidence is divided. The translation of πάρεσις must be decided on the basis of the context of Rom 3. However, what is basic to all the classical instances of πάρεσις is the notion of "release." "Release" is less specific than "forgiveness," and the latter is not clearly required by extrabiblical usage. The idea of "release" would also make excellent sense in Rom 3 if ἀπολύτρωσις is taken as "deliverance" (paralleling Paul's usage in Rom 8:23). πάρεσις makes much better sense in this context as "release" (or perhaps "forgiveness"), since it is employed because of and alongside "deliverance" (ἀπολύτρωσις). διά with the accusative usually has a causal force and would therefore ground the manifestation of God's righteousness in the preceding phrase, a righteousness that brings about salvation in Christ. "Forgiveness" would be the basis for God's saving righteousness (lit., "to demonstrate his righteousness on account of the forgiveness of sins committed beforehand," εἰς ἔνδειξιν τῆς δικαιοσύνης αὐτοῦ διὰ τὴν πάρεσιν τῶν προγεγονότων ἁμαρτημάτων).[100] If πάρεσις is understood in this way, vv. 25–26a would no longer conflict theologically with their context, and one of the main arguments for a pre-Pauline fragment would dissipate. Since the arguments in favor of a pre-Pauline fragment are not decisive, the case for a reference to the Day of Atonement "mercy seat" must be decided on other grounds.[101]

2) ἱλαστήριον as "mercy seat." ἱλαστήριον was the normal Greek word used to translate the lid of the ark of the covenant. *Yom Kippur* was the preeminent atonement ritual in Judaism as well as one of its major annual festivals. The Mishnah says that on the Day of Atonement Lev 16, 23:26–32, and Num 29:7–11 were read. Leviticus 16 (LXX) uses the word ἱλαστήριον seven times (for כַּפֹּרֶת). After describing the dilemma

---

[100] D. A. Campbell, *Rhetoric,* 48–49. He adds further that vv. 25c–26a are constructed in an almost perfect parallelism to vv. 26b–c, with the latter referring to the present. A present "forgiveness" in vv. 25c–26a would match much better the parallel in vv. 26b–c than "overlook," an action regarding *past* sins.

[101] What of the argument for a pre-Pauline fragment based on the use of the relative pronoun at the beginning of v. 25? The relative pronoun is confirmatory only alongside other factors indicating a quoted fragment. Otherwise ὅν remains a mere relative pronoun, a device used to avoid the unnecessary repetition of nouns. One might also note that the relative pronoun is in the accusative case here, whereas it is nominative in the other proposed instances (Phil 2:6; 1 Tim 3:16; 1 Pet 2:23).

caused by sin in Rom 1:18–3:20, Paul turns to God's activity in Christ. As a Jewish Christian steeped in the OT Scriptures, it would be hard not to think of Jesus in terms of the OT solution to sin: the Day of Atonement ritual. In fact, Paul says in 3:21 that God's righteousness and salvation were witnessed to by the Scriptures. While one must be cautious about seeing a reference to the "mercy seat," certainly a *Yom Kippur* allusion would strengthen the ties of the gospel to the OT.[102] Paul does assume a certain level of familiarity with the Greek OT on the part of his audience (e.g., Rom 4:1; 7:1; 9–11), a familiarity that would surely include a knowledge of the Day of Atonement.

That the word ἱλαστήριον refers to the "mercy seat" has been hotly disputed.[103] The first occurrence of ἱλαστήριον in the Septuagint, Exod 25:16 (17), does not refer to the mercy seat but acts as an adjective for the word that does, ἐπίθεμα.[104] Ezekiel 43 uses τὸ ἱλαστήριον five times to translate the ledge(s) envisioned on the great altar (the עֲזָרָה, *not* the כַּפֹּרֶת).[105] The term is used throughout extrabiblical Greek to denote propitiatory monuments, sacrifices, actions, or objects. Both Dio Chrysostom and the inscriptions from the island of Cos speak of votive gifts

[102] Note D. A. Campbell's caution (*Rhetoric,* 130–33) regarding ἱλαστήριον as a reference to the mercy seat; cf. Büchsel's (*TDNT* 3:322–23). Campbell (p. 132) points to Paul's use of Levitical, cultic language throughout Romans. He notes Rom 8:3 and the sin offering (see above). Romans 8:34 says that Christ intercedes for his people at the right hand of God. He provides "access" (προσαγωγή) to God in Rom 5:2. Romans 12:1–2 speaks of the Christian life in terms of sacrifice. In Rom 15:16 Paul describes himself as λειτουργὸν Χριστοῦ Ἰησοῦ εἰς τὰ ἔθνη, ἱερουργοῦντα τὸ εὐαγγέλιον τοῦ θεοῦ, ἵνα γένηται ἡ προσφορὰ τῶν ἐθνῶν εὐπρόσδεκτος, ἡγιασμένη. The verb ἱερουργέω is often used for performing a holy service such as sacrifice; Antwi, "Death of Jesus," 327. This evidence increases the likelihood of a reference to the mercy seat in Rom 3:25.

[103] In fact, since Adolf Deissmann German scholarship has remained largely unpersuaded of a "mercy-seat" reference. Deissmann's position was championed in the English-speaking world by Leon Morris.

[104] Adolf Deissmann, *Bible Studies* (2d ed.; trans. Alexander Grieve; Edinburgh: T&T Clark, 1909), 125–26. Deissmann later saw ἱλαστήριον as "propitiatory thing" and ἐπίθεμα as specifying the object in question; "ΙΛΑΣΤΗΡΙΟΣ und ΙΛΑΣΤΗΡΙΟΝ," *ZNW* 4 (1903): 207–8. T. W. Manson, in his attempt to answer this argument, was forced to emend the Hebrew text; " ἹΛΑΣΤΗΡΙΟΝ," *JTS* 46 (1945): 3. Leon Morris comments on Manson's attempt to avoid the difficulty: "not sufficient weight has been attached to the maxim *difficilior lectio potior.* In view of the absence of ἐπίθεμα everywhere else it is difficult to see how the great majority of MSS, should support the longer text unless it be original"; "The Meaning of ἹΛΑΣΤΗΡΙΟΝ in Romans III. 25," *NTS* 2 (1955–1956): 35.

[105] The Septuagint in 1 Chr 28:11 translates כַּפֹּרֶת with ἐξιλασμός and not ἱλαστήριον.

brought to the deity in order to induce a favorable reaction.[106] In light of this extrabiblical usage, that Symmachus translates Noah's ark using ἱλαστήριον should not be surprising. Similarly, Josephus uses ἱλαστήριον not in reference to the כַּפֹּרֶת but as an adjective for a propitiatory monument of white stone (*Ant.* 16.7). Fourth Maccabees 17:22 uses the term in a context of martyrdom where a reference to the mercy seat is unlikely.

The 4 Macc 17:22 reference has been the source of particular debate. Many see this text as a witness to martyr theology. One finds associated with the death of a martyr the same cluster of motifs elsewhere associated with sacrfice: substitution, purification, atonement, and blood.[107] Since the martyr Eleazar was also a priest, the book could be alluding to a replacement of temple sacrifice with martyrdom.[108] Similarly, James Dunn believes that in the Diaspora, at a distance from the Jerusalem temple, the death of martyrs came to have an atoning significance in place of the temple sacrifices.[109] However, the cultic terms are employed in a *noncultic* situation and context (cf. also 4 Macc 6:29).[110] Sam K. Williams points out that 4 Maccabees utilizes

---

[106] Deissmann, *Bible Studies,* 130–31. If ἱλαστήριον is interpreted as a gift to God on the basis of these parallels, it would make better sense of προέθετο in Rom 3. God publicly displays Christ as the gift that humanity itself could not provide. This would rule out a sacrificial reference; McLean, *Cursed Christ,* 45–46.

[107] For example, Lohse, *Märtyrer,* 152–53; Seeley, *Noble Death,* 19–27, 83–112; John S. Pobee, *Persecution and Martyrdom in the Theology of Paul* (JSNTSup 6; Sheffield: JSOT Press, 1985), 61–63; Williams, *Jesus' Death;* Morris, *Apostolic Preaching,* 170.

[108] D. A. Campbell, *Rhetoric,* 111 n. 1.

[109] James D. G. Dunn, "Paul's Understanding of the Death of Jesus," in *Reconciliation and Hope: New Testament Essays on Atonement and Eschatology* (ed. Robert Banks; Exeter: Paternoster, 1974), 131–32; idem, *Romans 9–16,* 171, 180. Martyr allusions are therefore complementary rather than exclusive of a Day of Atonement reference in Rom 3:25. The problem, though, is that the cluster of terms in 4 Macc 17:22, ἱλαστήριον, αἷμα, and ἀντίψυχον, matches the language of Lev 16–17. The rare term ἀντίψυχον combines two words in Lev 17:11 on the atoning value of blood, ἀντί . . . ψυχῆς. Further, both 4 Macc 6:28–29 and 17:21 say that the deaths were to serve as a "ransom" (ἀντίψυχον) and "purification" (καθάρσιον) for sin, i.e., cultic terminology; Bruce Chilton, *A Feast of Meanings: Eucharistic Theologies from Jesus through Johannine Circles* (NovTSup 72; Leiden: E. J. Brill, 1994), 192. This points to a sacrificial background, particularly the Day of Atonement; D. A. Campbell, *Rhetoric,* 220, also notes that the lack of ἀντίψυχον in Romans demonstrates that 4 Maccabees was not the source of Paul's imagery.

[110] Penna, *Paul the Apostle,* 2:32.

cultic terminology in these two passages in a *metaphorical* fashion.[111] Is the use of ἱλαστήριον in 4 Macc 17:22, in the context of martyrdom, paradigmatic for the interpretation of Rom 3:25? In Rom 3:25 *God* presents the ἱλαστήριον and not the martyr.[112] Also, a second-century dating of 4 Maccabees, if correct, would rule out its value for the interpretation of Romans.[113] Certainly to Jewish Christians interpreting the death of Christ, the notion of the Day of Atonement would have been of immensely greater significance than the deaths of martyrs.[114] What this discussion of 4 Macc 17:22 does show with respect to Rom 3:25 is that ἱλαστήριον had a broader range of usage than just the "mercy seat." Translating ἱλαστήριον as "propitiatory" or "means of propitiation"

---

[111] Thus 17:21–22 says the martyrs became ὥσπερ ἀντίψυχον; Williams, *Jesus' Death*, 179–82. The martyrs are not literally sacrificial victims or ransoms, and sacrificial terms and benefits are ascribed to other actions besides sacrifice (as in Pss 51:7; 141:2; 1QS 9.4–5; Wis 3:4–6). Stanley Stowers (*A Rereading of Romans: Justice, Jews, and Gentiles* [New Haven: Yale University Press, 1994], 212–13), echoing Williams, has strongly objected to Dunn's notion that 4 Maccabees attests to the sacrificial death of human martyrs. There is no mention of sacrifice or the temple cult in the text. God was angered by the apostasy of his people and had sent Antiochus to punish them (4:19, 21). Yet many of the Jews were in fact faithful, including the seven martyrs. As a result of their enduring perseverance and piety, God's anger against the people's unfaithfulness was assuaged (see also 2 Macc 7:32–38). The martyrs' endurance served as a ἱλαστήριον. Or perhaps, alternatively, their endurance proved an example for their compatriots leading to Antiochus's defeat and the nation's return to the Lord in repentance (4 Macc 17:20–24; cf. vv. 7–19; 1:11; 18:4–5). The central feature of the text is not the shedding of the martyrs' blood but rather their faithful example, which leads to atonement before God and faithful action from their fellow Jews.

[112] Dunn, "Paul's Understanding," 132; Travis, "Christ As Bearer of Divine Judgment," 30. And as D. E. H. Whitely points out, the substitutionary death of the Maccabean martyrs is "explicitly stated," whereas in Rom 3:23–26 "the language is allusive and ambiguous"; *The Theology of St. Paul* (Oxford: Basil Blackwell, 1964), 146.

[113] After demonstrating that Bickerman's case for a first-century date is flawed, D. A. Campbell (*Rhetoric*, 219–28) points to terminology attested in second-century descriptions of torture (e.g., τροχαντήρ), the striking parallel in descriptive detail with Talmudic literature on the martyrdoms under Hadrian, and the similarities with second-century Christian martyrologies, all of which indicate a second-century date.

[114] With Peter Stuhlmacher, "Recent Exegesis on Romans 3:24–26," in *Reconciliation, Law and Righteousness* (Philadelphia: Fortress, 1986), 102–3. Certainly in a context dominated by the problem of sin (and with the words ἐν τῷ αἵματι), it is more natural to think of the supreme value of the Day of Atonement now seen in terms of Christ. Cf. n. 112.

better reflects the diversity of usage. Such a translation, on the other hand, would render less likely an allusion to the Day of Atonement.[115]

Wherever ἱλαστήριον in the Septuagint translates the Hebrew כַּפֹּרֶת, something in the context always specifies the ark of the covenant, whether a mention of the ark itself, a reference to the cherubim on the ark, or both.[116] When the term is used with *other* objects (such as Noah's ark in Symmachus's text of Gen 6:16 [15], or Ezekiel's altar), the object is specified. Similarly, when Philo uses ἱλαστήριον for the ark of the covenant, he specifies the ark in the context. Romans 3 offers no such contextual indication. One ought, then, to take ἱλαστήριον in a more general sense.[117] The word could be used for a broad range of objects. Indeed, Stowers thinks that the matter should be closed on this note. Any ordinary speaker of the Greek language would have recognized ἱλαστήριον as a word typically used for conciliation or propitiation of someone's wrath (e.g., Philo, *Spec.* 1.237; Plato, *Phaed.* 1C; Plutarch *Cat. Min.* 61). The word was used in both cultic and noncultic contexts with no sense of sacrifice.[118] Campbell suggests that the LXX used the article with ἱλαστήριον precisely because Greek-speaking Jews were aware of pagan propitiatory rites and objects.[119] For the Jews the כַּפֹּרֶת was *the* propitiatory.

Perhaps one cannot absolutely rule out an allusion to the mercy seat in Rom 3:25. While there were various possible meanings of

---

[115] Morris is persuaded by Deissmann's evidence and, given the lack of any other reference in this text to the Day of Atonement (the reference to blood could be taken along the lines of the martyrs in 4 Macc 17), asserts that the more general sense of "means of propitiation" should be favored; *Apostolic Preaching,* 172. Wolfgang Kraus recognizes the variety of usage and argues that ἱλαστήριον means "place of atonement" with particular reference to Lev 16 and also (!) Ezek 43 (in terms of the temple dedication); *Der Tod Jesu als Heiligtumsweihe: Eine Untersuchung zum Umfeld der Sühnevorstellung in Römer 3.25–26a* (WMANT 66; Neukirchen-Vluyn: Neukirchener Verlag, 1991).

[116] Morris writes: "In the one place where כַּפֹּרֶת occurs without mention of the ark, etc., namely I Chron. xxviii. 11, the LXX renders with ἐξιλασμός, a reading which raises difficulties of its own, but the point is that ἱλαστήριον by itself was evidently not regarded as definite enough to point us to the כַּפֹּרֶת"; "ἹΛΑΣΤΗΡΙΟΝ," 36.

[117] For example, "propitiatory."

[118] Stowers, *A Rereading of Romans,* 210.

[119] D. A. Campbell, *Rhetoric,* 112. Interestingly, Campbell does not see a typological comparison with the mercy seat, and yet he maintains that there is an allusion to the Day of Atonement in Rom 3. If the text does not refer to the mercy seat (Campbell agreeing with Deissmann), what else is there in the text to suggest the Day of Atonement?

ἱλαστήριον in the ancient world, that variety did not prevent the Greek fathers from unanimously discerning a reference to the mercy seat in Rom 3:25.[120] The Jews also tended to use ἱλαστήριον for the mercy seat, a usage that begins already with the OT (Exod 25:17–22; Lev 16:2, 12–16). Philo refers to the angels who incline their wings toward τὸ ἱλαστήριον in *Cher.* 8.25. In *Mos.* 2.95 and 97 Philo refers to the "*epithema* as the cover which in the sacred books is called *hilasterion*," and to the "*epithema* which is called *hilasterion*."[121] Deissmann points out, nevertheless, that Philo's description and explanations of the term show that the Greek ἱλαστήριον did not automatically bring the mercy seat to his readers' minds.[122] Hence Philo had to specify the mercy seat in the context.[123]

To summarize, it is unlikely that ἱλαστήριον refers to the mercy seat, or more generally, to the Day of Atonement. If Paul had in mind the events of the Day of Atonement, he unfortunately did not develop the idea further in the context of Rom 3:25.[124] If Paul *does* mean by ἱλαστήριον the "mercy seat," Peter Stuhlmacher outlines the implications: "The cultic celebration of the Day of Atonement is abolished and superseded by virtue of this act of God, because the atonement granted definitively by God in Christ once and for all renders superfluous further cultic atonement ritual."[125] If Paul refers or alludes to the OT rites that resolved the issue of human sin, he sees these rites in terms of Christ and never ascribes saving efficacy or value to the rites themselves.

---

[120] Lyonnet and Sabourin, *Sin,* 160 n. 33; Morris emphasizes, in response, the distance of the Greek fathers from the time of the Apostles; "ἹΛΑΣΤΗΡΙΟΝ," 38.

[121] Note the lack of the article even as in Rom 3:25; see also Philo's references in *Fug.* 19.100. Although Philo uses ἱλαστήριον to refer to the "mercy seat" in all six occurrences, the problem is that these pasages from Philo are all in the context of his exposition of the Scriptures.

[122] Deissmann, *Bible Studies,* 128; Morris, "ἹΛΑΣΤΗΡΙΟΝ," 40.

[123] Friedrich points out that the absence of the article in Rom 3:25 with ἱλαστήριον is indeed a problem for the "mercy-seat" proponents; *Die Verkündigung,* 62–63. The Blass-Debrunner-Rehkopf (14th edition) grammar cites the rule that the predicate nominative is anarthrous when it designates an abstract quality attributed to an item but is articular when refering to the item itself; contra Stuhlmacher, "Recent Exegesis," 99.

[124] Morris, "ἹΛΑΣΤΗΡΙΟΝ," 41. Similarly, W. D. Davies points out that the only references to the Day of Atonement here are the use of the terms "blood" and ἱλαστήριον, and "Paul does not develop these but leaves them inchoate" (*Paul and Rabbinic Judaism: Some Rabbinic Elements in Pauline Theology* [London: SPCK, 1955], 242).

[125] Stuhlmacher, "Recent Exegesis," 104.

IV. An Apotropaic Ritual

Perhaps a better model for Paul's understanding Christ's saving work is not sacrifice but an apotropaic ritual.[126] Unlike a sacrifice, an apotropaic ritual involves substitutionary representation. The Day of Atonement ritual includes an apotropaic component. While the Israelites sacrificed one of the animals and placed its blood on the mercy seat to purify the temple, another animal was driven off into the wilderness. The animal driven off into the wilderness functioned apotropaically to carry away the sins of the people. B. H. McLean offers an extensive case that Jesus' saving activity ought to be understood against this background.[127] If he is correct, sacrifice would not be the basis for Paul's understanding of Jesus' saving work. Should Christ's work be taken as an apotropaic act, it remains *Christ* who is the agent of deliverance; no analogous OT ritual would bear saving efficacy.[128]

V. Conclusion

Paul nowhere recognizes any salvific value to the atoning offerings and sacrifices of Judaism. While Paul may on occasion speak of Christ in terms of the OT atoning sacrifices, he is only illustrating the significance of *Christ's* saving work. A more likely option is that Paul understood Christ's activity not in terms of a sacrifice but an apotropaic ritual such as the Day of Atonement scapegoat.[129] Yet even if Christ's work is being treated in apotropaic terms, it is Christ who is the effective agent. The Lord's death is effective, for Paul, in a way that the OT rituals were not; otherwise, his death would not have been necessary (Gal 2:21; 3:21). The

[126] On the difference between the two, see McLean, *Cursed Christ,* 75–76. For example, death is not the significant element in a sacrifice, but rather the *blood.*

[127] McLean, *Cursed Christ,* 41–52, 65–145; see esp. McLean's interpretation of 2 Cor 5:21, Gal 3:13, and Rom 8:3 in light of apotropaic rituals.

[128] A scapegoat allusion would account for the more participatory dimension of Paul's thought, but it is not clear that Paul is borrowing from the OT ritual per se. Apotropaic rituals were simply a commonplace in the Hellenistic world, for both Jews and Gentiles; McLean, *Cursed Christ,* 103–4.

[129] The participation would be the means whereby the curse was transferred from the individual to Christ. It would also explain why atoning sacrifice does not figure prominently in Paul, a question raised already by Taylor, *Atonement,* 94.

sacrificial apparatus does not function as a gracious mitigating factor for the demands of the law as it would in Jewish thought. If Paul does not affirm a role for atoning sacrifice in his thought, the implications of this for Paul's view of the law are far-reaching. Dunn claims that perfect obedience of the law is attainable for the Jew by appealing to the sacrificial system and atonement *as a component of the law.* The Jew could therefore find forgiveness even in the law itself. (See chs. 6 and 8.) Most recently, Michael Cranford has advocated Dunn's view of the law as inclusive of sacrifice and atonement. But if the law's provisions no longer atone for sin, then the Jew has no place to turn for forgiveness of violations of the law.

Atoning sacrifice plays no greater role in Paul's thought than did the Jewish covenant and election (chs. 3 and 4). None of the three elements are seen as saving or efficacious. Jewish thought held in tension the just and strict demands of God's law on the one hand and God's gracious election and mercy on the other (ch. 1). Paul does not see God's election and mercy availing for the Jew apart from Christ. When election and covenant were compromised in Jewish thought, emphasis shifted to strict, legal (or broadly ethical) obedience of God's will (ch. 2). One would expect a similar shift in emphasis in Paul. In other words, Paul's denial of the efficacy of sacrifice, election, and covenant leads him into the sort of dilemma that other Jewish groups felt who no longer had available to them the temple (post-70 C.E. Judaism) or an efficacious covenant with ethnic Israel (Qumran). Accepting Christ as the sole mediator of God's grace forced Paul to reconceptualize Judaism's gracious framework. Consequently, the law's demands would take on greater importance since the rigorous requirements of the law were mitigated by that framework. Paul is saying that the Jew who disobeys the law has no effective path to resolve the situation caused by sin, since its resolution can be found only in Christ. The Mosaic law has been severed from its context and forced to function as an empty series of demands requiring obedience with no solution for failure—hence, Paul's negative view of the law, the subject of the following chapters.

Chapter Six

Galatians 3:10: The Necessity of Perfect Obedience

Pauline scholarship prior to 1977 generally understood Judaism to teach that one must rigorously obey the law, and that Paul concurred. E. P. Sanders's *Paul and Palestinian Judaism* questioned whether the Jews actually held such a view: the older Pauline scholarship had failed to reckon adequately with the strong sense of election and covenant operative in Judaism. The law was embedded within a gracious framework such that less than perfect obedience was possible. Chapters 1 and 2 modified Sanders's model. The Jews affirmed that God commands "perfection of way," even while the gracious framework of God's election and mercy mitigated that strict demand from a practical standpoint. Nevertheless, Sanders denied that perfect obedience was a factor in Jewish thought.[1] Scholars naturally began to question whether *Paul* regarded the law as requiring perfect obedience.[2] The watershed text in the debate has been Gal 3:10 and its citation of Deut 27:26: "For all who rely on the works of the law are under a curse; for it is written, 'Cursed is

---

[1] After all, if the law provides means of atonement for transgressions, perhaps what is at issue in Gal 3:10 is something other than perfect fulfillment of the law.

[2] Sanders was already struggling with this issue in *Paul and Palestinian Judaism* (p. 137; see also 551). In his section on the Tannaim, he refers to the "legal perfection" that Paul sees the law requiring in Gal 3:10, a view quite unlike that found in Tannaitic exegesis of Deut 27:26. Yet in *Paul, the Law, and the Jewish People* (pp. 21–23) Sanders rejects his former position, arguing instead that Paul would agree with his fellow Jews that the law could indeed be obeyed (for example, Phil 3:3–11). See chs. 1 and 2 for instances where the Jews did understand the law to require strict obedience, contra Sanders.

everyone who does not observe and obey all the things written in the book of the law.' "

In Gal 3:10 Paul supplies only one of the premises of an enthymeme and its conclusion:

> Premise: Cursed is everyone who does not observe and obey all the things written in the book of the law.
>
> Conclusion: All who rely on the works of the law are under a curse.

The implied premise, if reconstructed from the stated premise and conclusion as closely as possible, would read:

> All who rely on the works of the law do not observe and obey all the things written in the book of the law.[3]

Given this implied premise, Paul could be saying that no one can fulfill the law perfectly, or he could simply be stating an empirical fact that no one does all that is written in the book of the law.[4] Either way, the problem with the law for Paul is that it requires perfect obedience, an obedience that no one has attained.

While the traditional view granted an implied premise specifying the necessity of perfect obedience of the law, scholars since 1977 have begun to construe Gal 3:10 very differently so that perfect obedience is no longer a factor. Christopher Stanley and Joseph Braswell think that

---

[3] It was a common practice in antiquity to omit a premise in an enthymeme, particularly when that premise would have been obvious to the hearer/reader. Aristotle writes: "For if any of these [premises of an enthymeme] is well known, there is no need to mention it, for the hearer can add it himself" (*Rhet.* 1.2.13 [1357a], translation from LCL). In *Rhet.* 2.22.3 (1395b), "nor should [an enthymeme] include all the steps of the argument . . . it is simply a waste of words, because it states much that is obvious." See also *Rhet.* 3.18.2, 4 (1419a); Epictetus, *Discourses* 1.8.1–4; Quintilian 5.14.24; 5.10.3. For a first-century example, see *The "Progymnasmata" of Theon*, III, 104–109 (trans. James R. Butts; Ann Arbor, Mich.: University Microfilms International, 1986), 198–201. On the frequent omission of one of the terms of a syllogism in the Synoptic Gospels, see Richard B. Vinson, "A Comparative Study of the Use of Enthymemes in the Synoptic Gospels," in *Persuasive Artistry: Studies in New Testament Rhetoric in Honor of George A. Kennedy* (ed. Duane F. Watson; JSNTSup 50; Sheffield: Sheffield Academic Press, 1991), 119–41. The implied premise would have been obvious in Gal 3:10; Albrecht Oepke, *Der Brief des Paulus an die Galater* (3d ed.; THKNT; Berlin: Evangelische Verlagsanstalt, 1973), 105.

[4] Aristotle distinguishes logical syllogisms from rhetorical enthymemes; *Rhet.* 1.2.14–15 (1357a). The latter's premises may only indicate what is *generally* true; Kjell Arne Moreland, *The Rhetoric of Curse in Galatians* (Emory Studies in Early Christianity 5; Atlanta: Scholars Press, 1995), 118 n. 22, 204.

the implied premise is not really necessary. N. T. Wright and James Scott contend that Gal 3:10 has more to do with Israel as a whole than with individual obedience of the law. James Dunn considers perfect obedience of the law irrelevant since by "works of the law" Paul does not mean the law in its entirety but only certain aspects of the law that distinguish the Jews from Gentiles. Daniel Fuller thinks that Paul's argument is limited to the legalistic misuse of the law. E. P. Sanders argues that the word "all" (implying perfect obedience) is merely incidental since the word derives from Paul's OT quote, and the key words in Paul's line of reasoning in Gal 3:6–14 do not emphasize strict obedience. Still other scholars think that the phrase "*all* the book of the law" directs attention to the narrative portions of the Pentateuch, particularly Abraham's faith; the law therefore directs the Christian to have faith even as Abraham believed. Each of these possibilities would jeopardize the premise that Paul sees the law requiring strict obedience of its demands. The soundness of the simple syllogism stated above, particularly the implied premise regarding perfect obedience, depends upon the successful elimination of these alternatives.

I. Omitting the Implied Premise

Christopher D. Stanley[5] and Joseph P. Braswell[6] have proposed an ingenious way to read Gal. 3:10:

> Premise: All who fail to do the whole Torah are subject to a curse.
>
> Conclusion: Therefore all who rely on "the works of the law" are *under the threat of* this curse.

If this reading is correct, Paul is not asserting that no one is able to keep the law. He is concerned about the possibility of falling short under the law and thus coming under its curse (a possibility that does not exist for those in Christ). Paul's real argument with regard to the law is in vv. 11–12: the law is not based on faith.

The most serious problem with Stanley's and Braswell's reconstruction of Paul's logic is that the apostle states the more forceful conclusion. The issue is not that the threat of the curse will become effective

---

[5] " 'Under a Curse': A Fresh Reading of Galatians 3.10–14," *NTS* 36 (1990): 481–511, esp. 500–501, 508–11.

[6] " 'The Blessing of Abraham' versus 'The Curse of the Law': Another Look at Gal 3:10–13," *WTJ* 53 (1991): 73–91, esp. 75–77.

at some future point. The issue is that those who rely on the works of the law are *currently* under the curse. The two instances of εἰσίν in 3:10a reinforce the sense of the present actuality of the curse.[7] The history of Israel shows that the covenant curses did indeed come about. In 3:13 Christ's death takes place in order to redeem those actually suffering from the law's curse; v. 13 therefore resolves the situation described in v. 10. Christ did not take the curse upon himself because of the mere threat of a curse upon humanity.[8]

II. Deuteronomy 27:26—The Curse of the Exile on Corporate Israel

Paul cites Deut 27:26 as a premise in his Gal 3:10 enthymeme, but his exact wording reflects the broader context of Deut 27–30:

> Deut 27:26: τοῖς λόγοις τοῦ νόμου τούτου
>
> Gal 3:10: τοῖς γεγραμμένοις ἐν τῷ βιβλίῳ τοῦ νόμου
>
> Deut 28:58: τὰ γεγραμμένα ἐν τῷ βιβλίῳ τούτῳ
>
> Deut 28:61: τὴν μὴ γεγραμμένην ἐν τῷ βιβλίῳ τοῦ νόμου τούτου
>
> Deut 29:19: αἱ γεγραμμέναι ἐν τῷ βιβλίῳ τοῦ νόμου τούτου
>
> Deut 29:20: τὰς γεγραμμένας ἐν τῷ βιβλίῳ τοῦ νόμου τούτου
> (29:20 is identical with 29:26 and 30:10)

---

[7] Moreland, *Rhetoric*, 201–3. Moreland (p. 203) points to Paul's opponents, in their reliance upon the law, as those especially under the curse; cf. Gal 1:8–9.

[8] These problems plague Norman H. Young's approach as well; "Who's Cursed—And Why? (Galatians 3:10–14)," *JBL* 117 (1988): 86–87. He contends that the curse of obeying the law is merely a potential one. The Galatians will suffer the Mosaic curse if they choose to adhere to some of the stipulations of the law and not to others. In other words, those who rely on what the law requires would *not* be under a curse as long as they did not abandon any of its precepts. This is precisely the opposite to the conclusion that Paul actually draws. Young's exegesis of vv. 11–14 hinges on his conclusions with regard to v. 10. Verses 10–14 would provide no argument against observance of the law per se. Contra Young, there is no reason why Paul's opponents would not have agreed that one needed to be faithful to the law's precepts. God's plan would simply be a matter of faith in Christ alongside faithfulness to the law.

Note especially the addition of the phrase ἐν τῷ βιβλίῳ and the alteration of λόγοις to γεγραμμένοις.[9] Paul's citation of Deut 27:26 must therefore be considered within the broader context of Deut 27–30, if not also Deut 31 and 32.[10] To understand James Scott's and N. T. Wright's corporate approach to Gal 3:10, the focus of this section, one must appreciate the context of Deut 27:26.

At various points throughout Deut 27–32, God threatens to invoke the covenantal curses if Israel fails to obey the law.[11] Deuteronomy 28, for example, is divided into a series of blessings in vv. 1–14 and a series of curses in vv. 15–68. Many of the curses refer to the exile (vv. 32, 36, 37, 41, 48, 63, 64, 68). The passage predicts that Israel will become subject to a foreign power (28:49–52) and exiled from the land (28:64–68; so also 29:24–28; 30:1; 31:16–22). According to Deut 28:58 these curses would come about because Israel would "not diligently observe all the words of this law that are written in this book." In the covenant established in the plains of Moab in Deut 29:1–28, disobedience would bring about its covenantal curses. The Song of Moses in Deut 32:1–43 reminds Israel yet again that disobedience would result in punishment (cf. vv. 26, 47).

Deuteronomy 27–32 parallels Lev 26 in content and logic: the covenant curses would ensue upon failure to obey the law. Israel would be destroyed and left in ruins, and the survivors scattered among the

---

[9] On Paul's omission of τούτου, see below. For a thorough discussion of the relationship between Paul's text and its OT precursors, see Christopher D. Stanley, *Paul and the Language of Scripture: Citation Technique in the Pauline Epistles and Contemporary Literature* (SNTSMS 69; Cambridge: Cambridge University Press, 1992), 238–43.

[10] Hans-Joachim Eckstein, *Verheißung und Gesetz: Eine exegetische Untersuchung zu Galater 2,15–4,7* (WUNT 86; Tübingen: J.C.B. Mohr [Paul Siebeck], 1996), 124–28. From a critical perspective, Deut 27–32 is a composite text. On this point, see A. D. H. Mayes, *Deuteronomy* (NCB; London: Marshall, Morgan & Scott, 1979), 337, 343–46, 348–51, 358–59, 367–68, 371–72, 374–76, 379–82. On the secondary nature of Deut 27:26 itself, see also Gerhard Wallis, "Der Vollbürgereid in Deuteronomium 27, 15–26," *HUCA* 45 (1974): 48. Paul is not the first to treat Deut 27 within a broader context. *Jubilees* 23 draws upon the pattern of sin, punishment, repentance/turning point, and salvation, the very pattern that one sees in Deut 27–32. *Jubilees* 23:32 even refers to Moses, and the command to write down the words is reminiscent of Deut 31:19. The same fourfold pattern recurs in *Testament of Moses* (compare especially *T. Mos.* 9:6 and Deut 32:43). For the intertestamental parallels to Deut 27–32, see Nickelsburg, *Jewish Literature*, 77–78, 80–82. Given this pattern, it is possible that Paul may have in mind not just Deut 27–30 but also chs. 31–32.

[11] Note the emphasis in Deut 27:26 on "doing" with τοῦ . . . ποιῆσαι αὐτούς in the emphatic position at the end of the sentence (so also Gal 3:10).

nations (Lev 26:27–39). This threat of exile is taken up elsewhere in the Old Testament as well. Joshua warns that unfaithfulness will lead to a loss of the land (Josh 23:14–16). Second Kings 17:7–23 attributes the exile to Israel's forsaking the Lord to serve other gods. Isaiah 42:24 attributes the nation's fall to sin against Yahweh and failure to obey his law. Jeremiah 11:3–4 pronounces a curse (ἐπικατάρατος) upon the people for disobeying the covenant commandments that God gave after Israel departed from Egypt, that is, the Sinaitic legislation. The emphasis in Jeremiah (as in Deuteronomy) is on doing *all* the commandments of the law (v. 4; cf. v. 8 on Israel's failure). Daniel 9:11 traces the cause of Israel's exile to transgression and failure to obey the law of Moses. From the prophetic perspective the curse (κατάρα) has fallen upon the people for their transgression of the law.

Yet the curse of the exile for Israel's disobedience in the OT was not without hope. The dark picture is ameliorated in Deut 30:1–8 by God's promise of a restoration to the land after the exile. This promised restoration is mentioned also in 32:34–43. Similarly, Deut 4:26–31 foretells the exile, the people's repentance, and their return from exile. Daniel prays on the basis of God's mercy that the Lord would deliver and restore the people just as he had delivered Israel from Egypt (Dan 9:15–19). Gabriel responds to Daniel's prayer with the prophecy of the seventy weeks (9:20–27), a prophecy that corresponds to Jer 25:11–12's and 29:10's seventy years. Daniel's seventy weeks, however, suggests a much longer exile of 490 years.[12] This tradition of the prolongation of the exile may be attested also in Bar 1:15–21, where the curse that God declared through Moses still stands over the people for their disobedience. Second Maccabees 7:33 refers to the disaster befallen Israel as lasting for "a little while" (cf. Dan 9:24). God is rebuking the nation prior to his compassion "as Moses declared in his song" (2 Macc 7:6; Deut 32:26). *First Enoch* 85–90 (esp. 89:59–74) speaks of seventy angelic shepherds, one for each period of time until the kingdom of God comes. The same pattern of sin, exile, and then restoration is attested in *T. Levi* 16:1–2, 5. The Qumran community understood itself as the fulfillment of the promised return from the exile. *Damascus Document* 1.3–11a refers to the 430 years of exile in Ezek 4:4–8. The Qumran covenanters saw that period as coming to an end shortly after the founding of the community under the Teacher of Righteousness.

James Scott argues from the intertestamental literature regarding the prolongation of Deut 27–32's exile that many in the intertestamental

---

[12] With respect to the sevenfold increase, see Lev 26:18, 21, 24, 28.

period saw Israel as still under the curse of the exile. Such a viewpoint, for Scott, stands behind Gal 3:10: "[Paul] could therefore confidently posit in Gal 3.10 that the threatened curse of Deut. 27.26 had not only come upon Israel historically but also that it continued to abide on the people to his day."[13] Scott argues further that what is at issue in Gal 3:10 is *not* individual disobedience. Galatians 3:10 has nothing to do with individual failure to obey perfectly the Mosaic law; the issue has to do with Israel *as a whole* under the law.[14] N. T. Wright develops the logic as follows:

> a) All who embrace Torah are thereby embracing Israel's national way of life.
>
> b) Israel as a nation has suffered, historically, the curse that the Torah held out for her if she did not keep it.
>
> c) Therefore all who embrace Torah now are under this curse.

Wright points out that this argument rests on the prior assumption that:

> a) Israel as a whole is under the curse if she fails to keep Torah.
>
> b) Israel as a whole failed to keep Torah.
>
> c) Therefore Israel is under the curse.[15]

Like Scott, Wright sees Deut 27–32 speaking about the fate of the nation of Israel *as a whole* and not about individuals sinning or failing to keep the law.[16]

That the law was given to Israel as a whole does not deny individual responsibility to abide by the law. It is not an either/or matter, as

---

[13] James M. Scott, " 'For as Many as Are of Works of the Law Are Under a Curse' (Galatians 3.10)," in *Paul and the Scriptures of Israel* (ed. Craig A. Evans and James A. Sanders; JSNTSup 83; Sheffield: Sheffield Academic Press, 1993), 214–15.

[14] Ibid., 214 n. 89.

[15] N. T. Wright, *Climax*, 147.

[16] Joel Kaminsky's study of the interrelationship between the Israelite individual and the nation as a whole in the OT reinforces Wright and Scott's point; *Corporate Responsibility in the Hebrew Bible* (JSOTSup 196; Sheffield: Sheffield Academic Press, 1995), 120. Deuteronomy stresses the solidarity of the Israelite nation as a whole (Deut 7:6–11; 28:1–32:43). Individuals find their ultimate significance in relation to the nation as a whole and not singly (Deut 26:16–19). The Deuteronomistic History retains this corporate focus on the nation (Josh 22:20 and 1 Kgs 8).

Scott's and Wright's analyses suggest. The fate of the nation as a corporate whole cannot be abstracted from the conduct of its individual members. The sin of individual Israelites accrues to Israel as a whole. Deuteronomy 27, for instance, does not address the corporate fate of Israel to the neglect of individual accountability. Deuteronomy 27:26 is the twelfth in a series of curses (27:15–26). Two of the twelve curses are explicitly identified as sins committed "in secret" (vv. 15, 24).[17] Four more curses involve sexual sins that would also be committed privately (vv. 20–24). Likewise, no one would move a boundary marker in public (v. 17). A blind man would never be able to testify that he had been led astray (v. 18).[18] Bellefontaine explains that when the Levites pronounced the curse and the community responded in affirmation during the ceremony envisioned in Deut 27, the community was guaranteeing that sins committed by individuals in secret would not bring about God's vengeance on the community as a whole (e.g., Achan in Josh 7). God would curse the guilty criminal, and the community would no longer be liable.[19] Deuteronomy 27:26 is therefore situated in the context of a section concerned with the retributive divine curse that falls upon *individual* law-breakers for secret sins.

A similar tension between individual fulfillment of the law and the fate of the nation runs throughout the following chapters in Deuteronomy as well. While Deut 28:1–14 predicts that God will establish Israel as a people and nation in the midst of the nations, God will bless the people with children, livestock and crops. These blessings accrue to individuals.[20] Deuteronomy 28:16–19 speaks of misfortunes that affect the individual whether in the city or in the field, whereas the curses throughout the rest of the chapter are set within the context of God's judgment of the nation as a whole.[21] Joel Kaminsky's study of corporate versus individual responsibility cites Deut 29:15–20 as yet another text that specifically focuses upon the individual Israelite. The individual Israelite who serves an idol will have his or her name blotted out from under heaven. The Lord will single out that individual for punishment.

---

[17] Elizabeth Bellefontaine, "The Curses of Deuteronomy 27: Their Relationship to the Prohibitives," in *A Song of Power and the Power of Song* (ed. Duane L. Christensen; Winona Lake, Ind.: Eisenbrauns, 1993), 260.

[18] Ibid., 262.

[19] Ibid., 267; see also Albrecht Alt, "The Origins of Israelite Law," in *Essays on Old Testament History and Religion* (trans. R. A. Wilson; Garden City, N.Y.: Doubleday, 1966), 115.

[20] Josef G. Plöger, *Literarkritische, formgeschichtliche und stilkritische Untersuchungen zum Deuteronomium* (BBB 26; Bonn: Peter Hanstein, 1967), 193–94.

[21] Moreland, *Rhetoric*, 35.

Then in the verses that follow 29:15–20, the emphasis shifts again to the corporate.[22] Deuteronomy 27–30 therefore manifests an interplay between individual and collective emphases.[23] The curses against individual disobedience of the law are set in the midst of the responsibility of the nation as a whole. While Wright and Scott have corrected the tendency of scholarship to overindividualize, the fate of corporate Israel must not be abstracted from the deeds of its individual members. The exile of Israel testifies to the conduct of individual Israelites under the law.

Contrary to Wright's and Scott's overemphasis on the corporate dimension, Gal 3:12 focuses upon the *individual* who lives by what the law requires. In fact, one sees an interplay between corporate and individual motifs later in Paul's letter that bears striking resemblance to the pattern in Deut 27–30. As John M. G. Barclay has shown, Gal 5:25–6:10 is structured on the basis of corporate responsibility alternating with individual accountability: vv. 6:1a, 2, 6, and 9–10 stress the responsibilities of the community as a whole, while the remaining verses, vv. 1b, 3–5, and 7–8, emphasize the actions of individuals.[24]

Apart from an overemphasis on the corporate dimension, the Wright-Scott approach to Gal 3:10 points to the belief in certain segments of intertestamental Judaism that the nation of Israel was still experiencing the curse of the exile for its disobedience. Certainly Paul's opponents did not share that viewpoint. Paul is confronting throughout Romans and Galatians a Jewish Christianity that placed far more emphasis on the *blessings* God had bestowed upon Israel and the Jews. The opponents were urging the Gentile Christians to join in the heritage of God's people Israel through circumcision. The Jewish dialogue partner of Rom 2:17–29 likewise sees salvific value in being a member of the Jewish people. Paul's own former boasts as a Jew in Phil 3:6 relied upon an effective relationship between God and Israel. In other words, Paul is battling a Jewish Christianity that has more in common with Sanders's

---

[22] Kaminsky, *Corporate Responsibility*, 133–36.

[23] As S. Dean McBride has observed, quite apart from the *content* of these chapters, one must account for the alternation of second person singular and plural forms of address in Deuteronomy. Regarding Deut 27:16–25 in particular, Volker Wagner notes interest in the private individual (vv. 17–20), the family (vv. 15–16, 20–25), as well as the community as a whole (vv. 16–25); *Rechtssätze in gebundener Sprache und Rechtssatzreihen im israelitischen Recht: Ein Beitrag zur Gattungsforschung* (BZAW 127; Berlin: Walter de Gruyter, 1972), 32–39, esp. 38 n. 32.

[24] John M. G. Barclay, *Obeying the Truth: Paul's Ethics in Galatians* (Minneapolis: Fortress, 1988), 149–50.

covenantal nomism than with the pessimistic view of those who considered the curse of the exile as still in progress.[25] Galatians 3:10 functions best in a context where the covenant is standing and efficacious. Paul's opponents were trying to convince the Galatians to practice circumcision (5:3; 6:13) and the Jewish law (3:1–5) with its sacred days (4:8–10) and other prescriptions. Deuteronomy 27:26 with its curse upon those who do not fulfill the law would have been an excellent text for Paul's opponents, for encouraging observance of the law.[26]

Wright's and Scott's thinking may be more helpful in deciphering Paul's response. Deuteronomy 27:26 pronounces a curse upon those who do not fulfill the commands of the law. How can Paul turn this text upside down to curse those who do practice the law? The answer would lie in Israel's past inability to avoid the curse of exile. If *Israel* had been unable to fulfill the law and thereby avoid its curse, why would the Gentile Galatians want to rely on the law? Israel's curse would thus serve as a warning to any individual (or group) who would hope to enter into a right relationship with God through the law. At the same time, Paul omits the key premise necessary for his new, very different conclusion. He leaves it to the Galatians to figure it out for themselves. In light of Israel's history Paul's premise should have been obvious: all who rely on

---

[25] Wright's and Scott's evidence for the continuation of the exile has been contested. As Mark A. Seifrid points out, Baruch's "today" is part of the *literary* setting of the work and offers little proof that the author saw the exile as having continued; "Blind Alleys in the Controversy over the Paul of History," *TynBul* 45 (1994): 86–89. Nor does 2 Maccabees support Scott's and Wright's case. The prayer for return from exile (2 Macc 1:27–29), as Seifrid shows, has been answered already by 15:37. The *Damascus Document* indicates that the curse of the exile had already ended through the Qumran community's formation. Josephus (*Ant.* 4.312–314) refers to Deut 27–30 and yet speaks of *several* exiles! *Exile: Old Testament, Jewish, and Christian Conceptions* (ed. James M. Scott; JSJSup 56; Leiden: E. J. Brill, 1997) is a compilation of very useful essays on the continuation of the exile in places such as Galatians, Josephus, the rabbis, Qumran, and apocalyptic literature.

[26] Deuteronomy, like Paul's Jewish-Christian opponents, places the law within a framework of God's covenant and grace. See Georg Braulik, "The Development of the Doctrine of Justification in the Redactional Strata of the Book of Deuteronomy," in *The Theology of Deuteronomy: Collected Essays of Georg Braulik, O. S. B.* (trans. Ulrika Lindblad; N. Richland Hills, Tex.: BIBAL, 1994), 151–64. That the OT texts in Gal 3:10–14 may have been prooftexts for Paul's opponents, see the discussion in ch. 3 of Gal 3:16–19 and 4:21–31, as well as Barrett, *Essays on Paul,* 158–59; idem, "Allegory," 6–7; and most recently, J. Louis Martyn, *Galatians* (AB 33A; New York: Doubleday, 1997), 309. This would explain the tension in Gal 3:10 between Paul's conclusion and the text he quotes in support.

the works of the law (Israel and anyone else who would try) fail (and failed) to observe and obey all that is written in the book of the law. Of course, Paul could have argued more straightforwardly: "All who do *not* comply with the law's demands are under a curse, for the law itself invokes a curse on those who do not obey it."[27] But how would the Galatians have taken that? Surely Paul's wording would have appeared to be a challenge to observe the law more scrupulously. By omitting the key premise Paul avoids saying anything that might be construed as an invitation to obey the law and at the same time forces the Galatians to supply the missing premise *on their own.* Paul rhetorically forces the Galatians into a mental process that would lead them to recognize the plight of human disobedience and inability with respect to the law.

III. "Works of the Law"

James D. G. Dunn disagrees with the traditional understanding of Gal 3:10: Paul does not claim in this verse that the Mosaic law must be perfectly obeyed. On the contrary, Paul uses the technical term "works of the law," which, according to Dunn, refers to those works required by the law that distinguish the Jews from Gentiles, such as circumcision, Sabbath observance, and the food laws.[28] Under pressure from his critics, Dunn has modified his position: the phrase "works of the law" refers to all that the law requires, but the primary focus of the expression is still on those laws that act as national and ethnic boundary markers.[29] Either way, Paul has in mind particularly those aspects of the law that served as

---

[27] Daniel P. Fuller, "Paul and 'The Works of the Law,'" *WTJ* 38 (1975–1976): 32.

[28] James D. G. Dunn, *Romans 1–8* (WBC 38A; Dallas: Word, 1988), lxxi–lxxii, 186–87, 190–94.

[29] See, for example, Dunn's article, "Paul and Justification by Faith," in *The Road from Damascus: The Impact of Paul's Conversion on His Life, Thought, and Ministry* (ed. Richard N. Longenecker; Grand Rapids: Eerdmans, 1997), 96–97.

Dunn sometimes expands the understanding of "works of the law" to serve as a shorthand for "covenantal nomism," the law's commands *inclusive* of Judaism's gracious covenantal framework; James D. G. Dunn, "Yet Once More—'The Works of the Law': A Response," *JSNT* 46 (1992): 100–101; idem, *The Theology of Paul the Apostle* (Grand Rapids: Eerdmans, 1998), 355, 358. This extrapolation depends on "works of the law" referring primarily to the boundary-marking features of the law. If "works of the law" of itself simply refers to what the law commands, apart from an emphasis on particular commands (*context* would be a different matter!), then such an extrapolation would be gratuitous.

signs of Jewish ethnic identity. One of the strongest passages for Dunn's thesis is Gal 2:16. In v. 16 Paul says that no one is justified by the "works of the law" but rather by faith in (the faithfulness of?) Jesus Christ. What does Paul mean by "works of the law"? In the preceding verses (2:11–14) Paul recalls the dispute with Peter at Antioch over whether the Gentiles must live like Jews. The dispute was over the food laws that distinguished the Jews from Gentiles. Dunn believes, then, that "works of the law" must refer to the boundary-marking aspects of the law. Galatians 3:10 could be paraphrased: "those who rely on their Jewish ethnic identity are under a curse." In Dunn's paradigm Gal 3:10 pronounces guilty those relying on their ethnic heritage, since they deny that God's plan in Christ includes the uncircumcised Gentile as well. By insisting on the "works of the law," such individuals are guilty of nationalistically excluding the Gentiles from God's people.[30]

Pauline scholarship is indebted to Dunn for underscoring Paul's understanding of the law as the unique possession of the Jews (e.g., Rom 2:12). Nor can one deny in a passage such as Rom 3:28–29 that "works of the law" is associated with Jewish ethnic identity.[31] On the other hand, to accept with Dunn that the law is the unique and special possession of the Jewish people does not rule out that this law must also be obeyed strictly and in its entirety.[32] One must again avoid the pitfall of "either/or" thinking. Consider Dunn's analysis of Gal 2:16. Paul continues in Gal 2:21: "for if justification comes through the law, then Christ died for nothing." Paul's statement here parallels his claim a few verses earlier that no is justified by the "works of the law." Likewise v. 19: "For through the law I died to the law, so that I might live to God." Paul's elaboration in the ensuing verses seems to have more to do with the law as a whole than with a focus on only a part of the law.[33] Paul's point is that the law

---

[30] James D. G. Dunn, *The Epistle to the Galatians* (BNTC; Peabody, Mass.: Hendrickson, 1993), 172; idem, *Jesus, Paul, and the Law: Studies in Mark and Galatians* (Louisville: Westminster John Knox, 1990), 231.

[31] Rom 3:28–29 will be the topic of ch. 8. Since many of Dunn's supporting texts are in Romans, the proper understanding of "works of the law" will be a recurrent issue in the treatment of Romans in the ensuing chapters.

[32] See the final section of ch. 7 (on Rom 2) as well as ch. 8 on "works of the law" in Rom 3.

[33] Against Dunn's view that the Jews *misunderstood* the law in overly ethnic terms, Räisänen objects on the basis of Gal 3: "And it is altogether impossible to read ch. 3 as an attack on just a particular *attitude* to the law. Why should the death of Christ have been necessary to liberate men from an attitude of theirs?" Rather: "The problem of the 'identity markers' may well once have been the starting point for Paul's theologizing about the law, but finally he arrived at very

as such cannot justify. A better approach would begin not with the boundary-marking features of the law but with the law in its entirety: obedience to the law requires obedience of *all* that it commands, which would certainly include those aspects that distinguish the Jews from the Gentiles. Conversely, to take on part of what the law requires, the food laws, entails the whole law. Thus Paul can move very naturally from a review of his critique of Peter at Antioch over the food laws to a discussion of the law itself. Paul sees no point in forcing the Gentiles to live like Jews under the law since the law does not offer a right relationship with God (vv. 15–16).

Paul's citation in Gal 3:10 shows that he has in mind by the phrase "works of the law" more than just the ethnic aspects of the law. Deuteronomy 27–30 is full of curses against all sorts of legal violations: illicit sexual relations, misleading the blind, changing borders, following other gods, even withholding justice from widows and orphans. Obedience of the law brings blessings, and disobedience curses. The summaries in Deut 27:26; 28:1, 15, 58, 61; 30:10 consistently emphasize obedience of *all* that God commands in the law. The language is comprehensive; the law is an organic whole, and all of it must be obeyed.[34] One comes to a similar conclusion with respect to Deut 27:15–26: the laws are not limited to Israel's distinctiveness. The prohibitions in this section exemplify pentateuchal law in general. Each of the commands in 27:15–26 matches corresponding injunctions elsewhere in the Mosaic corpus. The first curse against the carving and establishing of images and idols is based on the prohibition in Exod 20:4 (see also Exod 34:10–17; Deut 12:2–4).

---

negative statements on the law *as such* and *as a whole*" ("Galatians 2.16 and Paul's Break with Judaism," in *Jesus, Paul and Torah: Collected Essays* [trans. David E. Orton; JSNTSup 43; Sheffield: Sheffield Academic Press, 1992], 122).

[34] A similar context greets the reader in Leviticus. Paul cites Lev 18:5 in Gal 3:12. Leviticus 18:5 in its immediate context of vv. 3–5 requires Israel not to live as Egypt or Canaan. Israel must remain separate from those people. Leviticus 18:24–28 says that the land will eject anyone who pollutes it. To avoid being expelled from the land as the Canaanites before them, Israel must "do" "all my statutes and all my ordinances." The law is based on the principle of *doing what it requires.* The emphasis in the LXX on doing "all" that is commanded (πάντα τὰ προστάγματά μου, καὶ πάντα τὰ κρίματά μου; so also Lev 20:22; 26:15) parallels the repeated emphasis on doing *all* that is commanded in Deuteronomy. And so, Lev 20:22 and 26:14–43 (as with Deut 27:26) foretell the exile that will come because of Israel's disobedience and failure to do the law. Certainly this is how Ezek 20 (vv. 11, 13, 16, 21, 23–24) and Neh 9 (vv. 27, 29, 30, 33–34, 36–37) understand Lev 18:5: Israel failed to obey the commandments. The history of Israel would have shown for Paul, quite unlike his Jewish-Christian opponents, that the promise of life through the observance of the law is an illusory one.

The curse for dishonoring one's father and mother (v. 16) parallels Exod 20:12; 21:17; Lev 19:3; and 20:9. The curse against moving landmarks (v. 17) reflects Deut 19:14. The curse for misleading the blind (v. 18) parallels Lev 19:14. So also the rights of widows, orphans, and foreigners (v. 19) compare with Exod 22:20–23; 23:9; Lev 19:33–34; Deut 1:17; 10:18–19; 24:17–18. The other curses in Deut 27:15–26 likewise correspond to prohibitions elsewhere in the Sinaitic legislation.[35] That Paul cites a summary verse for a series of admonitions that are paralleled elsewhere in the Pentateuch suggests that he had in mind obedience to the law *in general.* Deuteronomy 27:15–26, however, extend these prohibitions into the private and secret arena not accessible to the community's ordinary legal process. Deuteronomy 27:26 and 28:1 require obedience of all the commands of the law in the context of secret sins.[36] When Paul uses the phrase "works of the law" in Gal 3:10 and cites Deut 27:26 (in a composite quote drawing on other summary statements in Deut 27–30), the Deuteronomy context indicates that Paul has in mind the law in its *entirety,* including even actions done in private. Nothing suggests any particular emphasis on covenantal boundary markers as such.

The Qumran manuscript 4QMMT offers a rare independent attestation in Hebrew of Paul's phrase "works of the Law" (מעשׂי תורה). In an otherwise helpful discussion of this document, Dunn contends that the phrase מעשׂי תורה refers to the observance of those aspects of the law that distinguished the Qumran community from other Jewish groups.[37] This analysis is unduly restricted by Dunn's "either/or" formulation. The phrase must be understood to include *all* that the law requires. Whenever an individual chose to depart from God's law on a particular point (as understood by the Qumran community), in the community's judgment that Jew had apostasized. From the community's perspective, to neglect any aspect of the law would bring into play the curses of Deut 27–30 and the need for separation (as Dunn himself shows). In other words, the "works of the law" always refers primarily to what the law requires *in general and in its entirety.* Only secondarily does it focus on particular boundary-defining strictures. Dunn reverses the rightful emphases. Because the focus is primarily upon the law as a whole, the particular laws referred to by the phrase can vary from one

---

[35] See Bellefontaine's discussion ("Curses") for the remaining curses, as well as Wallis, "Der Vollbürgereid," 50–51.

[36] See the discussion of this point in the preceding section.

[37] James D. G. Dunn, "4QMMT and Galatians," *NTS* 43 (1997): 147–53; idem, "Paul and Justification," 98.

conflict situation to another. In the face of a wrongful departure from the entirety of God's law, the specific laws that have been violated must come to the fore and serve as a mark of separation. By esteeming and obeying those laws the community showed itself devoted to the entirety of God's counsel. Certain regulations served as distinguishing features precisely because the community was devoted to the entirety of the law. Since *all* the "works of the law" must be obeyed, "some" must be highlighted.[38]

The *Rule of the Community* at Qumran confirms this interpretation of 4QMMT. The *Rule of the Community* calls members to "return to

---

[38]The heading of 4QMMT indicates that it must address "*some* of the works of the law." "Works of the law" must therefore go *beyond* those aspects in dispute within the document to include the *entirety* of the law; Ben Witherington III, *Grace in Galatia: A Commentary on Paul's Letter to the Galatians* (Grand Rapids: Eerdmans, 1998), 176–77. Joseph A. Fitzmyer is worth quoting at length with regard to Dunn's thesis:

> Yet it is now seen in the light of this Qumran text that "works of the law" cannot be so restricted [to those aspects of the law serving as badges to mark out God's people—AAD]. The text of 4QMMT does single out about twenty halakhot, but they are not limited to circumcision and food laws; they are moreover associated by the Jewish leader who wrote this letter with the status of "righteousness" before God. There are, indeed, food regulations among the precepts singled out, but they include many others, e.g., regulations about sacrifices, about the impurity of members, tithes to be paid, etc. In fact, it makes explicit mention of "the Book of Moses and the words of the prophets and David." Given such a broad outlook, it is difficult to see how the restriction of the phrase that Paul uses can be understood in Dunn's sense ("Paul's Jewish Background and the Deeds of the Law," in *According to Paul: Studies in the Theology of the Apostle* [Mahwah, N.J.: Paulist, 1993], 23).

Fitzmyer then adds that the sloganlike phrase had a legalistic connotation since righteousness in God's sight depended on observance of these precepts (see especially the epilogue to the document; 4QMMT^{f}/4Q399). Fitzmyer repeatedly emphasizes that "works of the law" at Qumran must be taken in a general sense (pp. 19–24).

4QFlor 1.7 may use the Heb. equivalent to "works of the law" (מַעֲשֵׂי תּוֹרָה). Many believe that the original text was actually מעשי תודה, "acts of thanksgiving"; see John Kampen, "4QMMT and New Testament Studies," in *Reading 4QMMT: New Perspectives on Qumran Law and History* (ed. John Kampen and Moshe J. Bernstein; SBLSymS; Atlanta: Scholars Press, 1996), 138–39 n. 40; Florentino García Martínez, "4QMMT in a Qumran Context," in *Reading 4QMMT: New Perspectives on Qumran Law and History* (ed. John Kampen and Moshe J. Bernstein; SBLSymS; Atlanta: Scholars Press, 1996), 24. If "works of the law" is the correct reading, the text refers to deeds the law requires as a sort of incense to the Lord. These deeds would distinguish the law-observant from others. There is, again, a sense of "both/and" in this text. Israel is distinguished from the nations by the "works of the law" and at the same time is obligated to perform these works as their worship of God.

the law of Moses according to *all* that he commanded" (1QS 5.8). In 1QS 5.21 individuals are examined upon entry into the community with respect to their "works of the law," whether they were careful "to walk according to *all* these precepts" (see also 1QS 6.18). The precepts include the "avoidance of anger, impatience, hatred, insulting elders, blasphemy, malice, foolish talk, and nakedness" (1QS 5.25–26; 6.24–7.18).[39] Circumcision, observance of the Sabbath, and the food laws are therefore only the starting point. Membership in God's people on the basis of the law requires obedience to *all* that the law demands. The Qumran parallels suggest that Paul has in mind in Gal 3:10 more than just the ethnic or boundary-marking components of the law.

Dunn thinks that in Gal 3:10 Paul is critiquing an overly nationalistic *attitude* (or misunderstanding) on the part of the Jewish Christians with respect to the ethnic aspects of the law.[40] The problem, though, can hardly be a misunderstanding of the law, since the law itself distinguishes between the Jew and the Gentile (Rom 2:12; 1 Cor 9:21). Paul sees far more in Christ's work and deliverance from the curse of the law than a deliverance from a mere nationalistic misunderstanding (or abuse) of the law.[41] Christ's death effected a release from *eschatological powers* (e.g., sin, flesh, death; cf. Rom 7). Paul's problem with the law, on the other hand, is that it is fundamentally unable to bring about a right relationship with God (Gal 2:21; 3:21).

---

[39] These parallels argue against Lloyd Gaston's suggestion that "works of the law" should be taken as a subjective genitive, "works that the law does"; "Works of Law As a Subjective Genitive," *SR* 13 (1984): 39–46. See also ch. 8 and the parallel between Rom 3:28, "works of the law," and 4:2, where Abraham was not justified by his "works." Abraham's own deeds are in view (thus also 4:4–5).

[40] Dunn admits that he is arguing a "quite narrow and specific" position that may seem a "surprisingly narrow understanding of the redemptive effect of Christ's death" (*Jesus, Paul, and the Law,* 229). He is also explicit that the sin bringing about the curse of the law is an "attitude"; idem, *Galatians,* 172. It may confuse the issue when Dunn answers his objectors (in Rom 2–3!) that Paul is not attacking only a false attitude to the law. Yet even in his discussion there, the primary problem is not Jewish disobedience (as Rom 2–3 actually say) but "the Jewish attitude to the law"; "Yet Once More," 108–9.

[41] Dunn, *Galatians,* 176–79; idem, *Jesus, Paul, and the Law,* 229. Räisänen rightly points out that Gal 2:19 makes little sense if Paul's problem with the law had only been with a misunderstanding in wrongly excluding the Gentiles or an overly zealous emphasis on its ethnic boundary features; "Galatians 2.16," 121–22. The language of dying to the law (2:19) and the law coming 430 years after the promise (3:17) suggest that the issue is with the law itself. Or for that matter, Gal 3:12 indicates that the problem with the law is that it is *not based on faith.*

IV. Legalism

Dunn is not the only scholar to distinguish "works of the law" (ἔργα νόμου) and "law" (νόμος) in Gal 3:10. Daniel P. Fuller has championed in recent years the position that Paul uses ἔργα νόμου in order to specify a legalistic misuse of the law as opposed to the law itself. Since the "works of the law" are often contrasted with faith, Fuller concludes that ἔργα νόμου must refer to trying to earn God's favor by legalistic observance of the law, that is, to "bribe God" by means of one's good works.[42] Fuller rightly recognizes that the implied premise in Gal 3:10 refers to perfect obedience to the law. That Paul should understand the law as impossible or nearly impossible to do does not, on the other hand, imply that the Jews were legalistic in their observance of the law.

Fuller's distinction between ἔργα νόμου and νόμος does not hold. Paul uses these terms interchangeably, as a comparison with Gal 3:11 shows.[43] Even in 3:10 Paul defines ἔργα νόμου *in relation to* "the book of the law" (ἐν τῷ βιβλίῳ τοῦ νόμου) in his OT citation. Similarly in Rom 3:21a: no one is justified by "the works of the law" (χωρὶς νόμου; cf. 3:20). This negative statement is closely coordinated with the immediately preceding positive statement of what the *law* accomplishes; it brings the knowledge of sin. "Law" and "works of the law" are coterminous.[44] Those who argue that legalism stands behind ἔργα νόμου in Gal 3:10 and its context are hard pressed to explain why Paul does not use that phrasing elsewhere in the

---

[42] Daniel P. Fuller, "Paul and 'The Works of the Law,'" 33–37, 42; see also Ernest De Witt Burton, *A Critical and Exegetical Commentary on the Epistle to the Galatians* (ICC; Edinburgh: T&T Clark, 1921), 120; Charles H. Cosgrove, "The Mosaic Law Preaches Faith: A Study in Galatians 3," *WTJ* 41 (1978–1979): 146–64. Note also that in eliminating the implied premise that those who rely on the law do not do all that the law requires, Fuller adds *two* propositions: a) A works-based salvation is bribery. b) Those who bribe are under a curse. Therefore, anyone who relies on a works-based salvation is under a curse. Yet nowhere does Paul (or any Jewish writer) describe legalism as bribery; Moisés Silva, "Is the Law against the Promises? The Significance of Galatians 3:21 for Covenant Continuity," in *Theonomy: A Reformed Critique* (ed. William S. Barker and W. Robert Godfrey; Grand Rapids: Zondervan, 1990), 159–60 n. 12. See also Andrew John Bandstra's critique of the legalist position in Gal 3:10–14 (*The Law and the Elements of the World: An Exegetical Study in Aspects of Paul's Teaching* [Kampen: J. H. Kok, 1964], 116) as well as Douglas Moo's critique of Fuller's *Gospel and Law: Contrast or Continuum?* (*TJ* 3 NS [1982]: 101–2).

[43] See Gal 2:16, with 3:21 and 5:4.

[44] This is also a problem for Dunn's distinction between ἔργα νόμου and νόμου. Paul has in mind, given these parallel descriptions, more than a few statutes or a misunderstanding but what the law requires in its entirety.

argument of Gal 3 if it is the key to his point. Verse 12 states rather bluntly that it is the law, not a misunderstanding of it or a wrong attitude, that is opposed to faith.[45] Paul's citation of Deut 27:26 in v. 10 condemns the *failure* to obey the law, not obedience of the law in the wrong spirit.[46] The law simply does not offer an effective means of salvation (thus Gal 2:21; 3:21).

A survey of Gal 3:1–14 will help show why the concept of legalism is completely absent from Paul's reasoning. In 3:1–5 Paul asks the Galatians how they received the Spirit. Was it through the observance of the law or through the message that evoked faith? Paul's question implies that the opponents were teaching that the Spirit is somehow associated with the law. It is as if Paul's opponents had represented his gospel message as lacking and requiring supplementation through the Mosaic law: the obedience of the law would bring about a Spirit-filled life. Such a teaching would be understandable given the connection between the observance of the law and God's Spirit in Judaism.[47] The outsiders apparently were urging the Galatians on to a fuller experience of the Spirit through their observance of the Mosaic law (hardly a legalistic motivation). The law was a source of blessing. In Gal 3:6–9 Paul argues that the blessing of the Gentiles through Abraham takes place by faith. That the blessing comes about by faith hearkens back to the denial of the law as a source of blessing in 3:1–5. J. Louis Martyn directs attention to two second-century Jewish-Christian documents, *The Ascents of James* and *The Preachings of Peter* (embedded in the Pseudo-Clementine literature), which affirm the law as well as a Gentile mission.[48] The explicit rationale for the law-observant Gentile mission is that the full number promised to Abraham might be fulfilled. *The Preachings of Peter* even claims that Peter's law-observant mission to the Gentiles *preceded* Paul's. Such literature offers a helpful backdrop for Paul's conflict at Galatia. Paul's argument against his opponents in Gal 3:6–9 revolves around the issue of how the Abrahamic blessing is to be mediated to the Gentiles, namely,

---

[45] In light of this, it is understandable that Charles H. Cosgrove reversed himself on his earlier support of Fuller's interpretation of 3:10–14 in terms of legalism; *The Cross and the Spirit,* 53–54, esp. 53 n. 31.

[46] This poses difficulties for Rudolf Bultmann's formulation as well. His problem with the law was that it led to one's own "self-powered striving" "in forgetfulness of his creaturely existence;" *Theology,* 1:264; Heinrich Schlier, *Der Brief an die Galater* (14th ed.; KEK 7; Göttingen: Vandenhoeck & Ruprecht, 1971), 89–95. Again, the issue for Paul is not the doing of the law but failing to do it.

[47] The obedience of the law would hasten the arrival of the eschaton (1QS 8.13–16; 9.19–20) and thus also the granting of the Spirit at that time (1QS 9.3; cf. 1QS 4.20–21; *T. Jud.* 23–24; *Mek.* on Exod 14:3 and 15:1; Cosgrove, *The Cross and the Spirit,* 99–101.

[48] Martyn, "Law-Observant Mission," 307–24.

whether it is mediated by the law (3:1–5) or by faith (3:1–9).[49] The Jews traditionally saw Abraham as a paradigm of faithfulness to the law.[50] Paul, on the other hand, sees Abraham as a paradigm of faith in the promise. Paul excludes a role for the law in the mediation of Abraham's blessing to the nations. What is at issue has nothing to do with legalism but rather whether the law is God's means of blessing for the Gentiles. Paul's return to the law in v. 10 shows that it had never been far from his mind in the immediately preceding verses. Even as legalism does not figure in vv. 6–9, it does not figure in vv. 10–12.

V. Obeying "All" the Works of the Law

In *Paul, the Law, and the Jewish People,* E. P. Sanders lists three reasons why Paul cannot be referring to "legal perfection" in Gal 3:10, asserting that Paul does not insist upon perfect obedience of the law. While the word "all" in 3:10 might suggest otherwise, Sanders explains in his first point that Paul uses the word only because it occurred in the Deuteronomy quotation. What prompted the citation, though, was the apostle's desire to link two of the key words in his argument, "law" and "curse." Deuteronomy 27:26 is the only place in the OT where "law" and "curse" occur together. The word "all" was merely incidental. This key-word citation technique, according to Sanders, runs all through this section of Galatians. Paul's central argument is in the first part of Galatians 3:8 (and note the key terms): the *Gentiles* would be *righteoused* by *faith.* Paul's citation of Gen 15:6 in v. 6 combines the terms "*faith*" (πίστις) and "*righteoused*" (the δικ- word group). The only other instance where these two words are used together in the OT is Hab 2:4 (cf. Gal 3:11!). Galatians 3:8b (citing Gen 18:18) adds the third key word: *Gentiles.* Paul is therefore "proving" his points by quoting texts that include the key terms. His interest lies strictly in the key terms and not the rest of the citation.[51] The problem with Sanders's point is that Paul's citation of the

[49] That 3:6 is to be understood with 3:1–5, see Sam K. Williams, "Justification and the Spirit in Galatians," *JSNT* 29 (1987): 93–94. The καθώς of v. 6 links that verse with vv. 1–5. To the question "Does he who supplies the Spirit to you and works wonders among you do so on the basis of the obedience of the law or the message that evokes faith?" Paul's implied answer is: "Of course it is on the basis of the message that evokes faith." Verse 6 continues: "Just as Abraham believed. . . ." I have translated v. 5 differently from Williams; see Das, "Oneness in Christ," 178 n. 12.

[50] See the documentation and discussion of this point in ch. 8.

[51] Sanders, *Paul, the Law,* 21.

Abrahamic narratives is more than incidental to the apostle's reasoning.[52] Paul understands Abraham as the prototype of justification by faith (cf. Rom 4). It is unlikely, then, that the texts are cited merely for the words they use.[53] On the other hand, the Abrahamic texts were probably favorites for Paul's opponents as a basis for their law-observant message to the Gentiles: the Genesis texts provided a way of understanding how Gentiles were to be incorporated into the covenant relationship through circumcision (Gen 17).[54] The Abrahamic texts would therefore have been significant *both* to Paul and his opponents. Whereas the opponents would have emphasized the Gentiles and circumcision, Paul completely avoided mention of circumcision in favor of Abraham's faith. Paul employs the text in a way that would be deliberately contrary to his opponents' understanding.[55] Paul's selection of OT passages has less to do with a key-word technique and more to do with the constraints of the situation. For the opponents, Deut 27:26 would encourage thorough observance of "all" that God's law requires, whereas for Paul the text highlights the difficulty of what the law demands.

Sanders's second point is that Paul's own words should say more about what the apostle intends to communicate than the prooftexts he employs. Since Paul does not elaborate on Deut 27:26's "all," the word must not have been crucial for the point he was making. Paul merely wants to connect the key ideas of "law" and "curse."[56] But the word "all" in Deut 27:26 *is* crucial to Paul's point. Each of Paul's citations in 3:10–12 explains and undergirds in some way Paul's own argument. Deuteronomy 27:26 is cited in Gal 3:10 to provide a *reason* (γάρ) why those relying on the works of the law are under a curse: the law demanded that all its precepts be obeyed.[57] Paul implies that the precepts

---

[52] See his usage of the Abrahamic material elsewhere in Gal 4:21–31 and Rom 4.

[53] In-Gyu Hong, *The Law in Galatians* (JSNTSup 81; Sheffield: Sheffield Academic Press, 1993), 137.

[54] Martyn, "Law-Observant Mission," 307–24; also Hong, *Law in Galatians*, 136–37.

[55] As Michael Cranford writes: "What Sanders overlooks is that any mishandling of the text on Paul's part would provide his opponents the opportunity to discount his use of the text and therefore the argument on which it rests" ("Possibility of Perfect Obedience," 246). Cranford also points to Gal 5:3 and 5:14, where Paul uses similar language, which suggests that πᾶσιν was significant also in 3:10.

[56] Sanders, *Paul, the Law*, 21–22.

[57] The word "all" reverberates throughout Deut 27–30 (e.g., 28:1, 15, 58; 30:10 LXX); Ronald Y. K. Fung, *The Epistle to the Galatians* (NICNT; Grand Rapids: Eerdmans, 1988), 142. Its importance in Deuteronomy lends cre-

have not been fully obeyed and that the curse has come into effect.[58] When Paul says in v. 11 that no one can be justified by the law, he cites Hab 2:4 to explain why: a right relationship with God is brought about by *faith*.[59] Lest anyone respond that the law and faith are compatible, Paul uses Lev 18:5 to show that the law is not based on faith but on ac-

---

dence to a similar importance in Paul, if Paul is not following a key-word citation method.

[58] Thomas R. Schreiner writes:

> But if one follows Sanders' interpretation, Paul never divulges why the law is to be excluded as a way of salvation. He simply asserts that since salvation is through Christ, it cannot be through the law. I do not see how such an argument would have convinced the Galatians, for the argument of the Judaizers was that salvation was attained through Christ *and the law*. Paul likely would have needed reasons to counterattack successfully the Judaizers. Sanders' interpretation amounts to Paul insisting his view is true simply because he said so (*The Law and Its Fulfillment*, 46).

[59] Hab 2:4 acts as a premise to support the conclusion stated in 3:11a:

> Premise: He who is just/righteous by faith will live (3:11b).
> Premise: But the law does not enjoin faith (3:12a).
> Conclusion: Therefore, no one is justified by the law (3:11a).

See Moreland, *Rhetoric*, 212; Jan Lambrecht, "Curse and Blessing: A Study of Galatians 3,10–14," in *Pauline Studies* (Leuven: Leuven University Press, 1994), 283. The syllogism was recognized already by Thomas Aquinas; John Bligh, *Galatians: A Discussion of St Paul's Epistle* (London: St Paul Publications, 1969), 262. That Paul states the conclusion *first* (3:11a) parallels 3:10, where the conclusion is also stated first. This parallelism in v. 10 and then vv. 11–12a would correspond with the pattern Gerhard Ebeling identified in vv. 6–9: Scripture quote (vv. 6, 8) followed by conclusion (vv. 7, 9); *The Truth of the Gospel: An Exposition of Galatians* (trans. David Green; Philadelphia: Fortress, 1985), 168–69. Note also the parallel structure in these conclusions (οἱ ἐκ πίστεως, followed by predications related to Abraham).

However, there is a competing theory as to the logic of 3:11. Hermann Hanse points out that some take δῆλον with the ὅτι that immediately follows (δῆλον ὅτι) instead of with the ὅτι that preceded at the beginning of the clause (ὅτι . . . δῆλον); "ΔΗΛΟΝ (Zu Gal 3[11])," *ZNW* 34 (1935): 299–303. What this means is that 3:11a could act as support for the Scripture quote in 3:11b instead of the Scripture quote in 3:11b acting as support for 3:11a (as in the NIV: "Clearly no one is justified before God by the law [ὅτι . . . δῆλον], because [ὅτι] 'The righteous will live by faith.'"). The alternative translation reads: "But because [ὅτι] no one is justified before God by the law, it is obvious that [δῆλον ὅτι] 'The just shall live by faith'"; thus Thielman, *Paul and the Law*, 127; Cosgrove, *The Cross and the Spirit*, 54 n. 32; N. T. Wright, *Climax*, 149 n. 42. The latter translation does not break up the δῆλον ὅτι. It also allows Paul's argument to build very naturally from v. 10 rather than introducing an entirely new argument that justification comes through faith and not the law. It is not clear, though, how v. 12b would function in this understanding. Also, it seems strange that a scriptural quote would act as a *conclusion* to an argument rather than a supporting premise, quite

complishing its requirements ("to do them"). Deuteronomy 21:23 in v. 13 explains *how* Christ became a curse for the believer (by dying on a tree).[60] Without the citations Paul's line of thought would be considerably weakened if not ruined.[61]

Sanders's third reason is based on the structure of Gal 3:6–14. Verses 10–13 are subordinated to v. 8, the main proposition of the entire argument: God righteouses the Gentiles by faith. In v. 8b when Paul cites Gen 18:18, which uses the word "blessed," the citation naturally leads him to consider the opposite word, "cursed." Galatians 3:10 is thus the negative proof of the positive assertion in 3:8. Whereas faith brings blessing, the law brings a curse. Galatians 3:11–12 flow naturally out of the preceding verses: the law is not of faith. Verse 13 then speaks of the removal of the curse. Verse 14 sums up the argument from 3:8 with the blessing of Abraham coming to the Gentiles. Verses 10–13 are therefore subordinated to the argument of 3:8.[62] The subordination of the "curse" in 3:10–13 to the "blessing" of 3:8 shows that Paul is not developing a new argument in these verses; he is not asserting the impossibility of keeping the law. The usage of "all" is only incidental. Salvation comes by Christ and not by the law. The problem with Sanders's third point is that vv. 10–13 introduce a crucial new element, the curse, such that Christ's redemption must resolve the situation (vv. 13–14) before the promised blessing of v. 8 can be fulfilled. Failing to do what the law requires brings about the curse of the law and the necessity of Christ's death. Once the

---

unlike what is the case throughout the rest of the passage; Burton, *Galatians*, 166. Further, Hanse (p. 302) points out that it is very common for the δῆλον to be separated from the preceding ὅτι in a construction indicating a conclusion. Had Paul intended δῆλον to go with the immediately following ὅτι and thus indicating that the Hab 2:4 citation in Gal 3:11*b* is the conclusion, he could have begun 3:10a with εἰ, εἴπερ, ἐπεί, ἐπειδή, or ὥσπερ.

[60] Thomas R. Schreiner, "Paul and Perfect Obedience to the Law: An Evaluation of the View of E. P. Sanders," *WTJ* 47(1985): 257–58.

[61] In Sanders's scheme, Paul seems merely to be *asserting* that salvation is by Christ and not the law without ever explaining why; T. R. Schreiner, "Paul and Perfect Obedience," 259.

One might also note that Sanders himself does not consistently abide by his second principle. Not only do Paul's own words in 3:10a mention the curse; Paul also speaks of those who are ἐξ ἔργων νόμου. Whereas Paul's citation speaks only of obedience to the law, Paul's *own words* include also the term ἔργα. As Robert H. Gundry writes: " 'Works' shows that he has in mind performance, which relates to the bulk of the quotation, 'everyone who does not continue in all things written in the book of the law, so as to do them' "; "Grace,Works, and Staying Saved in Paul," *Bib* 66 (1985): 24. See also Douglas Moo, " 'Law,' 'Works of the Law,' and Legalism in Paul," *WTJ* 45 (1983): 90–99.

[62] Sanders, *Paul, the Law*, 22.

curse is removed, the promise can proceed unhindered to the Gentiles.[63] Yet the curse as a necessary link in the progressing argument is not easily subsumed under v. 8's statement that God "righteouses" the Gentiles by faith. None of Sanders's points, then, effectively challenges a reference to legal perfection in Gal 3:10.

VI. The Law and Faith

When Paul quotes Deut 27:26 in 3:10, not only does he add ἐν τῷ βιβλίῳ (thereby reflecting Deut 28:58, 61; 29:19, 20, 26, and 30:10), he also omits the word "this" (τούτου) from the phrase "this book of the law." Paul may be making these changes in order to extend and universalize the curse to the entire Sinaitic legislation in all its prescriptions. Kjell Arne Moreland concludes that Paul has in mind not just the necessity to obey the law perfectly, but a *particular* failure. By omitting τούτου, Paul alludes to the *narrative* portion of the Pentateuch (see Gal 3:8–9, and 4:21, where "law" is inclusive of the pentateuchal narratives). The narrative portions of the law concerning Abraham inculcate faith.[64] The particular sin of Paul's opponents is that when they deny the role of faith they have failed to abide by *all* the law. The problem with Moreland's proposal is that Paul's thinking about the law in Gal 3 never swerves from the law's requirements and strictures. See not only v. 10's citation of Deut 27:26 but also the citation of Lev 18:5 in v. 12. Paul speaks of the law in vv. 15–18 as coming 430 years *after* the Abrahamic promise. In other words, there is a fundamental distinction throughout this passage between faith as indicated in the Abrahamic narrative and the demands and requirements of the Sinaitic legislation (thus vv. 12, 15–18).[65] One is justified by one or the other but not both. To interpret the law here as enjoining faith mitigates the force of that antithesis. Nor does the omission of τούτου in the Deut 27:26 citation necessarily lead one to consider the narrative portions of the Pentateuch. As Christopher Stanley explains, to repeat the τούτου of Deut 27:26 in Gal 3:10 would sever the

---

[63] Stanley, "Under a Curse," 485–86; see also Gundry's critique ("Grace," 24–25). Just because vv. 10–13 are subordinate to vv. 8 and 14 does not mean that they do not introduce strong, new supporting ideas, including the curse on those not perfectly obeying the law; T. R. Schreiner, "Paul and Perfect Obedience," 259.

[64] Moreland, *Rhetoric,* 206–10; so also Braswell, "Blessing," 78–79.

[65] Thus also Bandstra (*Law,* 118), against Ragnar Bring. Bring (*Commentary on Galatians* [trans. Eric Wahlstrom; Philadelphia: Muhlenberg, 1961], 115–25), like Moreland (see *Rhetoric,* 210), sees the failure of Gal 3:10 as a lack of faith.

word from its antecedent earlier in the Deuteronomy text. The omission would remove the ambiguity. It may also be that the removal of τούτου conformed better to Paul's emphasis on the law in the absolute sense, the law per se. Or τούτου may not have been omitted at all: according to the external evidence, the text of Deut 27:26 available to Paul may not have had τούτου.[66]

VII. "All" the Law Elsewhere in Galatians

Galatians 3:10 is not unique with regard to the law requiring perfect obedience. Paul returns to this idea later in Galatians. In Gal 5:3 Paul warns: "Once again I testify to every man who lets himself be circumcised that he is obliged to obey the entire law" (ὅλον τὸν νόμον).[67] One has to understand 5:3 in light of the rhetorical situation of the letter. Galatians 5:3 is precisely what *Paul's opponents* would have said to encourage a thoroughgoing observance of the law. Circumcision was only the first step to the whole law. The Galatians' seriousness about taking on the observance of the law as a whole is suggested by 4:21: Paul addresses them as those "who desire to be subject to the law." Where the opponents would have urged the Galatians to obey the whole law, Paul is reversing the teaching of the opponents. The only way 5:3 can function as a technique of *dissuasion* is if obeying the whole law is difficult or impossible (i.e., Gal 3:10). Κατάρα would still be echoing in their ears from 3:10, which itself hearkens back to the language of 1:8: ἀνάθεμα, the dark language of curse. Paul wants the Galatians to be absolutely certain as to what adopting circumcision and the law involves.[68] Obeying the entirety of the law is no easy endeavor. They will be submitting again to a yoke of bondage and oppression that brings with it the curse for failure. One comes to a similar conclusion in Gal 6:13's charge: "Even the circumcised do not themselves obey the law." This is a highly polemical denigration of Paul's opponents. The rhetorical value of the statement lies in its power to shock the Galatians. Paul's statement would not be effective,

---

[66] Stanley, *Paul and the Language of Scripture*, 241–42.

[67] "Once again" in 5:3 (πάλιν) probably links 5:3 to the admonition of 5:2, even as 1:9 repeats 1:8. Several scholars, like Barclay (*Obeying the Truth*, 64) and T. R. Schreiner (*The Law and Its Fulfillment*, 63–64), see the "again" linking 5:3 with Gal 3:10. Even if the "again" (πάλιν) cannot bear the weight that this connection requires, certainly the content of 5:3 mirrors 3:10, even as 5:2 echoes 2:21: Christ will be of no value to those who are circumcised. Rather, one is justified *either* by the law *or* by faith in Christ (5:4).

[68] Barclay, *Obeying the Truth*, 64.

rhetorically, if the opponents had never required strict obedience of the law or attempted as much.[69] In his rhetoric Paul implies that the outsiders at Galatia are right: the law does, in fact, require strict, perfect obedience. The opponents are ironically implicated by their own teachings.[70] The rhetorical force of Gal 6:13 must not be underestimated. If even those Jewish Christians who prize the law are unable to meet its demands, how much less would the Gentile Galatians be able to do it! If a curse falls on those who do not meet the law's demands (and is falling upon the Jewish-Christian outsiders), how much more will the Galatians be liable to the law's curse if they continue on their present path? The force of the argument depends upon the high degree of devotion to the law exhibited by the Jewish-Christian teachers.

VIII. Conclusion

In Gal 2:15 Paul writes in the language of his opponents: "We ourselves are Jews by birth and not Gentile sinners." Paul, like his fellow Jewish Christians, employs the term "sinner" in a way that would exclude law-observant Jews. Paul revisits this matter in Gal 3:10: a neat distinction between the righteous, law-observant Jew and the Gentile "sinner" is not possible.[71] Those under the Mosaic law are subject to its curse for any

---

[69] Hong, *Law in Galatians*, 108; Barclay, *Obeying the Truth*, 64–65. This also rules out the view of Sanders (*Paul, the Law*, 23) that the opponents were introducing the law only gradually. For a detailed refutation of the possibilities that Paul's opponents were taking a gradual approach with the Gentiles, see Barclay, *Obeying the Truth*, 60–69. Further, Sanders's focus on Peter in Gal 2 is misplaced. It was not Peter who initially raised the question of law-observance but other Jewish Christians, the ones who, in their strict view of the law, had objected to Peter's laxity. It is *these* Jewish Christians' view that most resembles Paul's Galatian opponents'.

[70] Cranford ("Possibility of Perfect Obedience," 255) thinks that Paul's opponents were advocating circumcision for the Gentiles but were not keeping the rest of the law. That Paul indicts the Galatians in 4:21 for wanting to be under the law suggests that the teachers were advocating a more complete observance than just circumcision. Galatians 2 suggests also the food laws. Circumcision, food laws, and special days (Gal 4:10) were the most distinctive (and difficult) elements of Jewish observance of the law for Gentiles. If the Galatians were instructed to observe these elements, it is inconceivable that the Jewish-Christian teachers would have neglected the rest of the law. For Paul's line of reasoning to have effectively indicted his opponents, the issue must have involved observing the whole law, the very problem he identified in 3:10.

[71] Actually Paul revisits it already in Gal 2:17 when he asks: "But if, in our effort to be justified in Christ, we ourselves have been found to be sinners, is

infraction of its strict requirements. Alan Segal is right to see Gal 3:10 as a first-century Pharisaic witness to the second-century rabbinic tradition of legal perfectionism represented by Gamaliel in *m. ʾAbot* 3:16.[72] The situation for the law-observant Jew is no different than for "Gentile sinners."[73] "For if a law had been given that could make alive, then righteousness would indeed come through the law" (Gal 3:21). The curse of the law demonstrates that those under the law are entrapped with the Gentiles in "the present evil age" (Gal 1:4). The answer to humanity's plight in this dire cosmic situation is Jesus Christ, "who gave himself for our sins" (1:4). What Christ did would have been meaningless if it were possible for people to find a right relationship with God through the law (2:21).

Christ then a servant of sin? Certainly not! (μὴ γένοιτο)." Since the apodosis is missing a verb and ἄν, the whole sentence is grammatically referring to a real situation; Robert C. Tannehill, *Dying and Rising with Christ: A Study in Pauline Theology* (Berlin: Alfred Töpelmann, 1967), 55; followed by Vincent M. Smiles, *The Gospel and the Law in Galatia: Paul's Response to Jewish-Christian Separatism and the Threat of Galatian Apostasy* (Collegeville, Minn.: Liturgical Press, 1998), 152–53. In all thirteen other instances where Paul uses the phrase μὴ γένοιτο to deny the claim of a real or imaginary opponent in a diatribe, he "denies a conclusion that an opponent improperly draws from *premises that Paul takes to be correct*" (Smiles, *Gospel*, 154). In other words, the premise "we ourselves have been found to be sinners" is true. The subject of the "we" has remained unchanged since v. 15: "we Jews by birth." Paul places the Jew in the same category that the Jew had applied to the Gentile: "sinner." Galatians 3:10 provides crucial support for Paul's logic. There can be no ethnic division between Jews and Gentiles with respect to the category of sin, since even the Jew falls short of the law's rigorous demand. The Jew's situation is no different from the Gentile's.

[72] Segal, *Paul the Convert*, 119–20. See also pp. 98, 333 n. 7. One of the typical objections to this understanding of Gal 3:10 has been, in light of Sanders's work, that the Jews never saw the law as requiring perfect obedience. Chapters 1 and 2 demonstrated that the Jews *did* quite often speak of perfect obedience. Cranford ("Possibility of Perfect Obedience," 242–44, 249) and Young ("Who's Cursed," 83) assume that perfect obedience was not an issue in Judaism as the foundation for their exegesis of Gal 3:10. Young even cites the availability of the sacrificial system. Neither author, however, recognizes the collapse of the gracious framework of the law when God's mercy is located in Christ. These shifts would create a problem for the observance of the law as far as Paul was concerned, a problem that would not have existed for covenantal nomists like Paul's opponents.

[73] Paul says that he was blameless in his observance of the law in Phil 3:2–11. How can this be if the implied premise in Gal 3:10 states that *no one* perfectly obeys the law? An answer to this objection will be proposed in chapter 9. Galatians 3:10, considered in and of itself, teaches that the law requires strict and perfect obedience and that no one achieves such legal perfection.

Chapter Seven

Romans 1:18–2:29: Judgment according to Works Apart from Ethnic Privileges

Romans 1:18–2:29 consists of three distinct phases of argument. In Rom 1:18–2:11 Paul establishes that all humanity is without excuse before God's judgment, since God judges all people impartially on the basis of their works. In Rom 2:12–16 Paul speaks of the Mosaic law for the first time in this letter. The law functions, to the extent that all people possess it, as the *means* by which God impartially judges all people. Romans 2:17–29 addresses the Jew who thinks that circumcision and Jewish ethnic identity provide a mitigating factor so that God should be more favorably disposed toward him or her as a Jew. Certain elements of Paul's thinking deserve further consideration. While recognizing the law's ethnic character as the special possession of the Jews, Paul sees the law primarily in terms of its legal demands and obligations, on the basis of which God will judge the world. The Jew possesses no special advantage by virtue of his or her Jewish ethnic identity that would mitigate God's strict and impartial judgment according to works.

I. Romans 1:18–2:11

Whether the end of Rom 1 forms a unified section with the beginning of Rom 2 has been debated. Many scholars have argued that Rom 1:18–32 is directed toward the Gentiles, while Rom 2:1–29 is aimed toward the Jews.[1] Paul's language of condemnation with respect to idolatry and

---

[1] For example, M.-J. Lagrange, *Saint Paul Épitre aux Romains* (*Etudes bibliques;* Paris: Librairie Lecoffre, 1950), 21–47; Gunther Bornkamm, "Gesetz

perverse sexual sin would fit the Gentiles far better than the Jews. Paul's language parallels Jewish texts polemicizing against Gentile idolatry and immorality. The sudden address in 2:1 of the one who judges would therefore turn the tables on Jewish moral superiority. The indictment of the Gentiles would broaden to include also the Jews at this point. This understanding, however, does not account for all the evidence. While 1:18–32 does implicate the Gentiles, the verses are not aimed *exclusively* at the Gentiles. Paul does not single out the Gentiles as such in 1:18–32. Nor does Paul directly address the Jews until 2:17.[2]

One reason 1:18–32 is not limited to the Gentiles and 2:1–11 to the Jews is the chiastic structural arrangement that unifies these two sections:

A Ἰουδαίῳ τε πρῶτον καὶ Ἕλληνι (1:16)
B ἀποκαλύπτεται γὰρ ὀργὴ θεοῦ (1:18)
C εἰς τὸ εἶναι αὐτοὺς ἀναπολογήτους (1:20)
C′ διὸ ἀναπολόγητος εἶ (2:1)
B′ ἐν ἡμέρᾳ ὀργῆς καὶ ἀποκαλύψεως δικαιοκρισίας τοῦ θεοῦ (2:5)
A′ Ἰουδαίῳ τε πρῶτον καὶ Ἕλληνι[3] (2:9–10)

Several other features reinforce the chiasm. The phrase "to the Jew first and also to the Greek" in 1:16 and 2:10 is accompanied by a grammatical parallelism (e.g., παντὶ τῷ πιστεύοντι, 1:16; παντὶ τῷ ἐργαζομένῳ, 2:10). The prepositional phrase ἐπὶ πᾶσαν in 2:9 (as opposed to the dative [+ *reward*] in 2:7, 8, 10) echoes 1:18 with its ἐπὶ πᾶσαν (which proclaims

---

und Natur. Röm 2:14–16," in *Studien zu Antike und Urchristentum* (BevT 28; Munich: Chr. Kaiser, 1959), 2:93–97; Dunn, *Romans 1–8,* 51; Thomas H. Tobin, "Controversy and Continuity in Romans 1:18–30," *CBQ* 55 (1993): 298–318.

[2] If Paul had meant to turn to the Jew in 2:1, one should find the direct address of the Jew in 2:1 and not later, in 2:17; Paul J. Achtemeier, "St. Paul, Accommodation or Confrontation: A Tradition- and Context-Analysis of Romans 1.18–32 and 2.14–15, Attempting to Determine Whether or Not Paul Is Seeking to Accommodate the Thought of These Verses to the Hellenistic Mentality" (Th.D. diss., Union Theological Seminary, New York, 1957), 135.

[3] Jouette M. Bassler, *Divine Impartiality: Paul and a Theological Axiom* (SBLDS 59; Chico, Calif.; Scholars Press, 1982), 124–25, who was building on the work of Max Pohlenz, "Paulus und die Stoa," *ZNW* 42 (1949): 70–75, esp. 73–74. These considerations render unlikely Calvin L. Porter's view that 2:1–16 is a refutation of 1:18–32; "Romans 1.18–32: Its Role in the Developing Argument," *NTS* 40 (1994): 210–28. Against viewing 1:18–32 as an indictment of the Gentiles, thereby reinforcing Jewish separation (with Porter), see below.

Romans 1:18 begins with γάρ, thereby indicating a continuity in Paul's line of thought from 1:16–17 to 1:18; 1:16–17 are transitional; Bassler, *Divine Impartiality,* 126–28; Paul Schubert, *Form and Function of the Pauline Thanksgivings* (BZNW 20; Berlin: Alfred Töpelmann, 1939), 32; P. J. Achtemeier, *Romans,* 35.

divine *wrath* even as 2:9 does). "Wrath" (ὀργή), "truth" (ἀλήθεια) and "wickedness" (ἀδικία) in 1:18 correspond to the same words in 2:5, 8: "truth," "wickedness" and "wrath." The chiastic structure places emphasis on God's wrath being revealed against *all people* irrespective of whether they are Jews or Gentiles.

Paul Achtemeier's analysis of 1:18–31 has confirmed that these verses deal not only with Gentile sin but also with Jewish failure. James Dunn notes the parallel between Rom 1:18–32 and Wis 13:1–14:27, a Jewish critique of the Gentiles, but Achtemeier shows that Wisdom of Solomon is only one of several Jewish texts that parallel Rom 1:18–32. One must also take into consideration Jer 10:12–15; Isa 40:18–22 (also vv. 26, 28); Isa 45:18–20 (cf. Rom 14:11 and Isa 45:23); *Sib. Or.* Fragment iii, 3–31 and Book 3:8–41; *2 En.* 10:4–6 and 34:1–2. These texts share a common pattern with Rom 1:18–32: God, the Creator of the world, has not been properly acknowledged by humanity. People have, instead, turned away from God to idols, which resulted in misery, moral perversity, and vice.[4] Jeremiah 10:12–15, the OT text that most closely parallels Rom 1:18–32, depicts "*everyone*" as involved in the difficulties described (v. 14). Isaiah 40:18–20 speaks to the Jews, while Isa 45:18–22, 26, 28 addresses all the "nations," that is, the Gentiles. *Second Enoch* 34 indicts the idolaters of the generations before Noah, while *2 En.* 10 speaks of "those who dishonor God." Nothing in *2 En.* 10 excludes the Jews who do such things from condemnation.[5] *Sibylline Oracles* Fragment iii, 3–31 does not identify the people concerned, and *Sib. Or.* 3:8–41 addresses humanity without any distinction.[6] *Sibylline Oracles* 3:8–41 closely resembles Rom 1:18–32, "containing all the elements of the Pauline formulation in

---

[4] P. J. Achtemeier, "St. Paul," 126. The pattern is: a) God is Creator; b) God is not acknowledged; c) People foolishly turn to idols; d) This results in misery and vices. Jeremiah 10:12–15 and Isa 40:18 do not have the catalogue of vices. *Second Enoch* 34:1–2 omits mention of God as Creator.

[5] P. J. Achtemeier, "St. Paul," 132.

[6] Rolf Dabelstein points to passages in the *Sibylline Oracles* warning the Jews of those sins that characterize the Gentiles (for example, *Sib. Or.* 3:763–765). Further, such vice catalogues were typically used to differentiate the righteous from the wicked *within* Israel (for instance, 1QS 4.2–14); *Die Beurteilung der 'Heiden' bei Paulus* (BBET 14; Frankfurt: Peter D. Lang, 1981), 85. Paul picks vicesthat apply to *all* humanity and "undercuts in the most sweeping manner any potential claims of individual, group, or national exceptionalism. No group can claim a position of superiority with regard to honor . . ." (Robert Jewett, "Honor and Shame in the Argument of Romans," in *Putting Body and Soul Together: Essays in Honor of Robin Scroggs* [ed. Virginia Wiles, Alexandra Brown, and Graydon F. Snyder; Valley Forge, Pa.: Trinity Press International, 1997], 266–68).

[7] P. J. Achtemeier, "St. Paul," 133.

identical order."[7] Wisdom 13:1–14:27 also addresses all humanity, although clearly non-Jews are especially in mind.[8] While the emphasis is sometimes on the Gentiles, and at other times on the Jews, Achtemeier concludes that this tradition tends to indict "all people" or "everyone."[9] In addition to the texts Achtemeier mentions, *T. Naph.* 3–4 deserves comment. The author appeals to the order manifest in the sun, moon, and stars. The Gentiles have chosen to "change the order" and "devote themselves to stones and sticks, patterning themselves after wandering spirits." The author admonishes those with the law of God, basing his admonition on the creation: "In the firmament, in the earth, and in the sea, in all the products of his workmanship discern the Lord who made all things, so that you do not become like Sodom, which departed from the order of nature." The writer then indicates that they too will "stray from the Lord, living in accord with every wickedness of the Gentiles and committing every lawlessness of Sodom." A general indictment of humanity, as one finds in such texts, would function well in Rom 1:18–32, since both "Jews and Gentiles" are identified in 1:16–17 and in 2:9–10.

While Rom 1:18–32 describe sins that more often typify the Gentiles, Paul's indictment could, for the most part, include the Jews as well. Paul's condemnation of idolatry in 1:21–25 and the consequent immorality (in the following verses) does not exclude the Jews. Romans 1:23 contains language that alludes to Jer 2:11 and Ps 106 (LXX 105):20.[10]

---

[8] Even if addressing sins more typical of Gentiles, the admonitions would serve also as a warning for the Jews; Dabelstein, *Beurteilung*, 85.

[9] P. J. Achtemeier, "St. Paul," 133. Dunn argues from Wisdom of Solomon that Paul is using a Jewish tradition that indicted the Gentiles; *Romans 1–8*, 53, 56–57, 72. Dunn does not consider how this pattern is used in Jewish literature outside the Wisdom of Solomon; it is employed not just to indict the Gentile. Dunn is more on target when he writes: "The evil against which the divine wrath is initially directed is described in the most general and all-embracing terms: against *all* disregard or contempt for God and for the rights of our fellow human beings. . . . Here again the description is as broad and as inescapable as possible" (*Romans 1–8*, 70).

[10] Romans 1:21 also parallels Jer 2:5. The parallels to Ps 106 (LXX 105):20 are striking: καὶ ἠλλάξαντο τὴν δόξαν αὐτῶν ἐν ὁμοιώματι μόσχου ἔσθοντος χόρτον. The reference to "their glory" ought to be understood in light of the people being unable to behold God's glory (cf. Exod 32–34 and the sin of the people—see ch. 3). Jacob Jervell (*Imago Dei: Gen 1,26f. im Spätjudentum, in der Gnosis und in den paulinischen Briefen* [FRLANT 76; Göttingen: Vandenhoeck & Ruprecht, 1960], 312–31, esp. 319–22), Morna Hooker ("Adam in Romans 1," *NTS* 6 [1959–1960]: 297–306; idem, "A Further Note on Romans 1," *NTS* 13 [1967]: 181–83) and Niels Hyldahl ("A Reminiscence of the Old Testament at Romans i. 23," *NTS* 2 [1956]: 285–88) all see further allusions to Genesis. Bassler (*Divine Impartiality*, 196) disagrees: the primary focus in this verse is on Israel's

These OT passages speak of *Israel's* apostasy and idolatry, especially the golden calf incident of Exod 32.[11] Bassler notes how the refusal to honor or glorify (ἐδόξασαν) God in 1:21–22 neatly parallels the charge in 2:23 against the Jew who "dishonors" (ἀτιμάζω). The suppression of the truth mentioned in 1:18 parallels the Jew in 2:21–24 who has knowledge and truth in the law and yet still does what is wrong.[12] Romans 1:18 therefore forms an excellent heading for vv. 18–32: the wrath of God is being revealed against *all* the godlessness and wickedness of humanity.[13]

Romans 1:18–32 functions within a broader unit that ends at 2:11. Assertions of divine impartiality open and close this section (1:16; 2:9–11). The strongest expression of this is the statement: "For God shows no partiality" (2:11). God's impartial dealings are manifested in how God responds to human sin. In 1:23 people exchange the glory (δόξα) of God for images. In v. 24 God hands the people over (παρέδωκεν)

---

idolatry. If Genesis allusions are present, they merely indicate that the apostasy of Israel in the golden calf incident "was regarded as a reenactment of the fall of Adam." The Genesis allusion would be secondary. Daniel Chae critiques Hyldahl at length for omitting important parallels between Rom 1:18–32 and Deut 4:15–18 in favor of a relationship between Gen 1 and Rom 1; *Paul As Apostle*, 75–78.

[11] Bassler, *Divine Impartiality*, 122, 195–97, 249. Bassler (p. 122) writes: "Although he [Paul] employs an argument traditionally directed against the Gentiles, he clearly signals that it was also, if not primarily appropriate to the Jews." Again Dunn recognizes the importance of the allusion even while inconsistently maintaining that Paul is concerned almost exclusively with Gentiles in 1:18–32:

> But it would probably not escape notice that the illustration Paul uses to document the typical Jewish polemic against idolatry is Israel itself! It is Israel who stands as a perpetual warning of how quickly man can turn from God and lose himself in things. The most devastating example of humankind's folly in turning its back on God is given by Paul's own people. Those among his largely Gentile audience who recognized the allusion would probably appreciate this unexpected twist in the Pauline emphasis—"Jew first and also Greek" (*Romans 1–8*, 73).

[12] Bassler, *Divine Impartiality*, 250 n. 4; for example, adultery and stealing, much as in Rom 1's catalogue.

[13] Rolf Dabelstein (*Beurteilung*, 75–76) emphasizes this verse as determinative for what follows. God's condemnation stands over *all* godlessness and wickedness. Nor does Paul ever specify in these verses or at the beginning of Rom 2 that he is speaking of Gentiles and then of Jews. For instance, *1 En.* 91:7 uses the same language in its indictment of all who sin in the midst of a parenetic section that has nothing to do with matters of ethnicity; Dabelstein, *Beurteilung*, 76. Dabelstein then works through 1:19–32 showing how elements typically thought to indict the Gentiles are paralleled in similar indictments of the Jews themselves. For example, compare Rom 1:20–21 with *2 Bar.* 54:17–18's indictment of the Jews on the basis of the knowledge of God in creation; similarly, *T. Naph.* 3:2–4; 4:1; *1 En.* 80–82; Dabelstein, *Beurteilung*, 78–79, 81.

to "dishonor" (ἀτιμάζεσθαι) their own bodies, the very opposite of "glory."[14] In v. 25 the people exchange (μετήλλαξαν) the truth of God for a lie. God then hands them over (παρέδωκεν) to their own punishment and allows them to exchange (μετήλλαξαν) natural sexual relations for the unnatural. In 1:28 the people "did not think it worthwhile to retain the knowledge of God" (my translation, οὐκ ἐδοκίμασαν τὸν θεὸν), so God gives them over (παρέδωκεν) to an ἀδόκιμον νοῦν ("a depraved mind"). In each section an appropriate punishment follows the sin.[15] This general pattern of divine retribution is maintained in 1:32 through the beginning of ch. 2. In 2:1 the one who judges (ὦ ἄνθρωπε πᾶς ὁ κρίνων) ends up, by means of God's appropriate retribution, "condemning" himself or herself (σεαυτὸν κατακρίσεις).[16] Paul's words would apply to *anyone* who judges others for doing the things mentioned in 1:18–32.[17] Indeed, God's carefully measured response to sin forms an ironic contrast to the hypocritical judge of 2:1–3: "So when you, a mere man, pass judgment on them and yet do the same things, do you think you will escape God's judgment?" (NIV). Unlike the hypocrite God's judgment is impartial and truthful (2:6–11). According to Rom

---

[14] Morna D. Hooker shows how "glory" and "dishonor" are used by Paul as opposites; "A Further Note on Romans 1," 182.

[15] On the structure of these verses, see Douglas Moo, *The Epistle to the Romans* (NICNT; Grand Rapids: Eerdmans, 1996), 96; Bassler, *Divine Impartiality,* 132; E. Klostermann, "Die adäquate Vergeltung in Rm 1:22–31," *ZNW* 32 (1933): 1–6 (Rom 1:22–24, 1:25–27, 1:28–21; 1:32–2:1ff.); Fitzmyer, *Romans,* 276. Regardless of one's estimation of Bassler or Moo's structure, it is certainly indisputable that these sections are characterized by God's impartial and just retribution of sin. See the Jewish parallels in Joachim Jeremias ("Zu Rm 1.22–32," *ZNW* 45 [1954]: 119–21) and Klostermann (pp. 3–5).

[16] Achtemeier observes that 2:1 applies to the individual what 1:32 applies more generally; "St. Paul," 135. διό in 2:1 deliberately parallels the structure of 1:18–32 (cf. διό in 1:24 and διὰ τοῦτο in 1:26; see also 1:21, 28); Achtemeier, "St. Paul," 135. Bassler (*Divine Impartiality,* 131–32) identifies several other points of continuity across the chapter division: the theme of adequate retribution, the verbs πράσσειν and ποιεῖν, κριν-words in 2:1–3 bracketed by the δικαίωμα in 1:32 and δικαιοκρισίας in 2:5. With regard to the διό and the mention of Jews and Gentiles together in 2:9–10, see also Roman Heiligenthal, *Werke als Zeichen: Untersuchungen zur Bedeutung der menschlischen Taten im Frühjudentum, Neuen Testament und Frühchristentum* (WUNT 2/9; Tübingen: J.C.B. Mohr [Paul Siebeck], 1983), 165–67.

[17] Some have postulated a hypothetical Jew standing behind 1:18–32 who is polemicizing against the Gentiles only to have the tables turned in 2:1. Thomas Schmeller has enthusiastically endorsed this position; *Paulus und die 'Diatribe': Eine vergleichende Stilinterpretation* (NTAbh 19; Münster: Aschendorf, 1987), 225–86. However, it is *God* who judges and condemns sin in 1:18–32; Neil Elliot, *The Rhetoric of Romans: Argumentative Constraint and Strategy and Paul's Dia-*

2:6–11 all people are accountable for their actions, and God will repay according to what each person has done (2:6: ὃς ἀποδώσει ἑκάστῳ κατὰ τὰ ἔργα αὐτοῦ). Verses 7–9 contrast the fate of those who do good as opposed to those who do evil. God will reward the former and will pour out wrath and anger against the latter (cf. 2:5). The criterion of judgement will be "according to each one's deeds" (κατὰ τὰ ἔργα αὐτοῦ). In vv. 9–10 Paul emphasizes that *all* will be judged according to their deeds, whether Jew or Gentile.[18] Kendrick Grobel's chiastic arrangement of these verses only reinforces the impartial nature of God's judgment:

A God will judge everyone equitably (v. 6)
B Those who do good will attain eternal life (v. 7)
C Those who do evil will suffer wrath (v. 8)
C′ Wrath for those who do evil (v. 9)
B′ Glory for those who do good (v. 10)
A′ God judges impartially[19]

---

logue with Judaism (JSNTSup 45; Sheffield: Sheffield Academic Press, 1990), 183–84. Schmeller (pp. 279–80) has to insert cues lacking in the text itself to make a change in voice explicit in 2:1. It is not the moral superiority of a supposed Jewish speaker in 1:18–32 that Paul attacks, but rather the presumption of escaping judgment for doing the same things (2:3–4); Elliot, 184–85. The sudden twist leads the reader to question whether he or she is the hypocrite of 2:1. Paul's warning is that God will still judge according to one's works; Elliot, 125–26. Paul's use of διό elsewhere (21 other occurrences; plus 8 in Acts) always maintains the same subject in the following material as in what preceded; Chae, *Paul As Apostle*, 97. Paul would have used ὡσαύτως rather than διό had he wanted "to connect the *same* thing/manner/action" with "*different* people/objects" in what follows; see Rom 8:22–26, 1 Cor 11:25, and elsewhere in the NT; Chae, *Paul As Apostle*, 98. Stanley Kent Stowers points to Greco-Roman diatribe, where a speaker or writer turns to address an imaginary dialogue partner directly; *The Diatribe and Paul's Letter to the Romans* (SBLDS 57; Chico, Calif.: Scholars Press, 1981), 110–12. The guilty one judging others directly addressed in 2:1–2 would correspond to the very personality described in 1:29–31. This individual is insolent (ὑβριστής), arrogant (ὑπερήφανος), and pretentious (ἀλαζών). Elsewhere, Stowers points to the oldest chapter divisions in the *kephalaia majora* and Codex Vaticanus, both of which consider 1:18–2:12 a unit. A break at 2:1 would not establish itself in the manuscript tradition until later; "Text As Interpretation," in *Judaic and Christian Interpretations of Texts: Contents and Contexts* (ed. J. Neusner and E. Frerichs; vol. 3 of *New Perspectives on Ancient Judaism;* Lanham, Md.: University Press of America, 1987), 20–27.

[18] The twofold repetition of both πᾶς and Ἰουδαίῳ τε πρῶτον καὶ Ἕλληνι underscores how "each one" (ἑκάστῳ) will be judged in the same way; Bassler, *Divine Impartiality*, 126.

[19] Kendrick Grobel, "A Chiastic Retribution-Formula in Romans 2," in *Zeit und Geschichte. Dankesgabe an Rudolf Bultmann zum 80. Geburtstag* (ed.

II. Romans 2:12–16

Paul declares in Rom 1:16–17 that the gospel is the power of God's salvation to everyone who believes, to the Jew first and to the Gentile. This tantalizingly brief mention of Jews and Gentiles invites some development, particularly given God's special dealings with the Jews. Paul says in Rom 1:16–2:11 that no one has an excuse before God's judgment. God will impartially judge each individual on the basis of his or her works, whether a Jew or Gentile.[20] God does not show favoritism (2:11). This leads to an obvious objection. Did not God give the law to the Jews and not the Gentiles? Surely that introduces an unfair inequality into God's dealings with humanity. Paul again mentions Jews and Gentiles in 2:9–10 before finally turning to the matter of possession or non-possession of the Mosaic law in 2:12–16.[21] Romans 2:12–16 therefore flows naturally out of what precedes.[22]

Erich Dinkler; Tübingen: J.C.B. Mohr [Paul Siebeck], 1964), 255–61; cited here as modified by Moo (*Romans*, 135) and Fitzmyer (*Romans*, 303). Note also that this is *not* a pre-Christian situation. These verses are stating axiomatically the basis for God's judgment. God's wrath "is being revealed" (present tense) against ungodliness and unrighteousness (1:18). Likewise, several passages in Paul speak of Christians being judged according to their works (e.g., 1 Cor 3:13–15; 2 Cor 9:24–27; Gal 6:8).

[20] Bassler (*Divine Impartiality*, 131) identifies the theme of this section that "God recompenses all impartially according to their actions." Elliot (*Rhetoric*, 122) points out, contra Bassler, that this statement is not a conclusion in and of itself. Rather, divine impartiality is used as a premise (γάρ, 2:11) to support the conclusion that "there is no excuse before God's judgment" (cf. 1:20; 2:1). On divine impartiality in Judaism, see Deut 10:17; 2 Chr 19:7; *Jub.* 5:15–16; Sir 35:15; *Pss. Sol.* 2:16–18; *m.* *ʾAbot* 4:22 and the overview in Heiligenthal, *Werke als Zeichen*, 143–99 (as impacting Rom 2:1–11).

[21] That Paul is referring to the *Mosaic* law is clear from the division of humanity in these verses into Jew and Gentile. The law is that which distinguishes the Jew "in the law" (ἐν νόμῳ) from those who are "law-less" (ἀνόμως) and "without the law" (τὰ μὴ νόμον ἔχοντα, v. 14).

[22] Bassler (*Divine Impartiality*, 121–37) makes too sharp a break after v. 11. Further, Bassler (pp. 137, 152) sees v. 11 as a thematic introduction to vv. 12–29. The line of argument, though, runs in the reverse. Verses 12–29 work to show the accountability of all people before God's impartial judgment, whether Gentile (vv. 14–16) or Jew (vv. 17–29). Elliot (*Werke als Zeichen*, 122 n. 2) rightly notes the grammatical subordination of 2:12–16 to what precedes (γάρ, 2:12). What follows in the chapter reinforces that *all people* are accountable before God's judgment and that no one has any special advantage lest God be less than impartial.

How can God's judgment be impartial if there is a division in humanity based on the possession or nonpossession of God's law? Paul responds by saying that both Jew (those "in the law") and Gentile (those "apart from the law") will be impartially judged according to the standard of whether they have *done* the law.[23] Verse 13 proclaims: "For it is not the hearers of the law who are righteous in God's sight, but the doers of the law who will be justified."[24] Verses 14–15 then provide the anticipated clarification of how Gentiles who do not possess the law will be judged according to it:

> When Gentiles, who do not possess the law, do instinctively what the law requires, these, though not having the law, are a law to themselves. They show that what the law requires is written on their hearts, to which their own conscience also bears witness; and their conflicting thoughts will accuse or perhaps excuse them.[25]

In vv. 15–16 the Gentiles' conscience acts to accuse and defend them; they are a law to themselves even though they do not have the law.[26] Having dispelled a potential objection, Paul can return in v. 16 to the language of the divine tribunal that dominated vv. 1–5.[27]

---

[23] Paul uses ἀνόμως for lack of possession of the law in 1 Cor 9:21. Although Stowers notes that this meaning is not as widely attested as the sense of behavior contrary to the law, he admits Isocrates' *Panegyricus* 39 as an instance of ἀνόμως for lack of possession of the law (but see Stowers's full discussion); *A Rereading of Romans,* 134–38. Note the parallels between this verse and v. 14's ἔθνη τὰ μὴ νόμον ἔχοντα (i.e., further evidence for the traditional view). If one accepts Stowers's view, v. 12 would divide humanity into those who live wantonly (whether Jew or Gentile) and those who attempt to live according to the law: "For all who have sinned in a lawless manner shall perish in a manner befitting lawlessness. All who have sinned while living within the law, shall have their case judged by the law"; Stowers, *A Rereading of Romans,* 139.

[24] *Mishnah ʾAbot* 1:17 says: "Not the expounding of the Law is the chief thing but the doing of it"; see also Wis 6:18–20; Josephus, *Ant.* 20.44; 1 Macc 2:67.

[25] The first line could be translated: "For whenever Gentiles, who do not have by nature the law, do what the law requires . . ."

[26] Bassler, *Divine Impartiality,* 148–49. Although the Gentiles do not possess the law, what they have, by reason of their conscience (a law to themselves), is comparable to the Mosaic law, at least to the extent of rendering God's judgment impartial; Andrea van Dülmen, *Die Theologie des Gesetzes bei Paulus* (SBM 5; Stuttgart: Katholisches Bibelwerk, 1968), 77. See esp. Philo, *Ios.* 29; *Mos.* 1.162; 2.12, 14, 37, 52; *Spec.* 2.13; *Prob.* 46; *Opif.* 3. Philo says that Abraham kept the "unwritten law" that is clear even from Nature (*Abr.* 5–6, 60, 275–276).

[27] Verse 16 links vv. 12–16 with what precedes in vv. 1–5; Moo, *Romans,* 144. The difficult phrase that the judgment will be κατὰ τὸ εὐαγγέλιόν μου in 2:16 is also to be explained on the basis of divine impartiality, as Bassler has shown

Much ink has been spilt over the question of the identity of the Gentiles in these verses. Paul does not elaborate on how Gentiles "do the things of the law." Rather he *assumes* this notion in support of God's impartial judgment and hence that no one has an excuse. Certain clues in the text suggest what sort of Gentiles Paul has in mind.[28] The work of the law in v. 15 also leads to *accusing* thoughts on the day of judgment, which would hardly befit a Gentile Christian.[29] If vv. 12–16 are intended to further support the statement of v. 11 and what preceded (γάρ, v. 12),

---

(*Divine Impartiality*, 157–58). Few would see the gospel as the norm of God's judgment. It is hard to see how impartial judgment, a doctrine shared also by the Jews, could be part of the *Christian* gospel (1:16–17). Bassler (p. 157) thus reasons that God's impartial judgment according to works is in accordance with God's same impartiality with respect to the message of salvation. Even as God's salvation does not depend on one being a Jew or Gentile, so also God's judgment.

[28] Some think that "by nature" (φύσει) is adverbial and modifies "do" (ποιῶσιν); Dunn, *Romans 1–8*, 98; Fitzmyer, *Romans*, 310 (cf. 1 Cor 11:14); Räisänen, *Paul and the Law*, 104; Moo, *Romans*, 149–50. If so, these individuals *cannot* be Gentile Christians, since Christians do not do the law "by nature," but by means of *the Spirit* (cf. Rom 8:4; Gal 5:22–23); Bornkamm, "Gesetz und Natur," 109. φύσει is more likely adjectival modifying ἔχοντα in the phrase "those who do not have the law." Word order favors the adjectival usage since adverbs are not usually separated from their verbs; Glenn N. Davies (*Faith and Obedience in Romans: A Study in Romans 1–4* [JSNTSup 39; Sheffield: Sheffield Academic Press, 1990], 62 n. 5), following Adrio König, "Gentiles or Gentile Christians? On the Meaning of Romans 2:12–16," *JTSA* 15 (1976): 58. Davies admits that the argument from word order is by no means decisive. For a substantival participle *followed* by a modifying dative, see Rom 14:1: τὸν δὲ ἀσθενοῦντα τῇ πίστει προσλαμβάνεσθε where τῇ πίστει modifies the substantive and not the verb προσλαμβάνω. More compellingly, when Paul uses φύσις in his letters, he normally uses it to express Gentile or Jewish identity (see Rom 2:27; Gal 2:15; Eph 2:3); Cranfield, *Romans*, 1:156–57; Paul J. Achtemeier, " 'Some Things in Them Hard to Understand': Reflections on an Approach to Paul," *Int* 38 (1984): 257–58. Cranfield, unlike Achtemeier, takes "not having the law by nature" to be a reference to Gentile Christians. Achtemeier points out another problem for taking "by nature" (φύσις) adverbially with "do the law" (ποιῶσιν):

> If gentiles know by nature what is good and then do it, they are morally superior to the Jews, who need the law to tell them what is good and how to do it. Such inherent moral superiority of gentiles over Jews not only makes the chosen people morally inferior to all others but it also makes nonsense of Paul's argument, which intends to show that all people are equally under condemnation (see 3:9) (*Romans*, 45).

[29] This aspect of the text is not fully appreciated by N. T. Wright, who speaks of Gentiles "vindicated at the judgment"; "The Law in Romans 2," in *Paul and the Mosaic Law* (ed. James D. G. Dunn; WUNT 89; Tübingen: J.C.B. Mohr [Paul Siebeck], 1996), 148. This is no mere "inner conflict," as Wright supposes (p. 146), but an objective accountability on the basis of the "work of the law" before God's judgment.

then the Jews and Gentiles here must be the same as those in 2:10, that is, Jews and Gentiles in general.[30] It is hard to see Gentile Christians as "not having the law" (τὰ μὴ νόμον ἔχοντα, οὗτοι νόμον μὴ ἔχοντες, v. 14), given the place of the Old Testament in early Christianity.[31] If Rom 2:14–15 are not referring to Gentile Christians, is Paul saying that there are *pagan* Gentiles who have done all that the law requires?[32] Nothing in the text indicates that the Gentiles in question have actually done what the law requires. If they had, they would no longer be Gentiles. The Gentiles' consciences not only "defend" them, but their consciences also "accuse" them, which implies a less than adequate doing of the law.[33] The conjunction (ὅταν) in v. 14 more properly means "whenever," which also suggests occasional, less than rigorous Gentile obedience.[34] Some would connect v. 14 to v. 13b and argue that the Gentiles of v. 14 are the "doers of the law" mentioned in v. 13b.[35] However, v. 13 is best seen as a parallel to v. 12b's "those under the law," even as v. 14 is a parallel to v. 12a's "those apart from the law." The chiastic structure of the verses reinforces the parallelism:

A Gentile—without the law (v. 12a)
  B Jew—with the Law (v. 12b)
  B′ Jew—not the hearers of the law but the doers (v. 13)
A′ Gentile—without the law who does the things of the law (v. 14)[36]

---

[30] Friedrich Kuhr ("Römer 2.14f. und die Verheissung bei Jeremia 31.31ff," *ZNW* 55 [1964]: 253). Kuhr (p. 254) rightly adds that it is precisely the point of vv. 12–16 to show that the Gentiles *in general* are not exempt from God's judgment even though they do not possess the Mosaic law. A reference to Gentile Christians here would be out of place; so also Rolf Walker, "Die Heiden und das Gericht: Zur Auslegung von Römer 2, 12–16," *EvT* 20 (1960): 302–6.

[31] "Not having the law" is too close in thought to being ἀνόμως in v. 12 for this to be a separate and distinct group of Gentile Christians in v. 14 as opposed to Gentiles in general in v. 12; contra N. T. Wright. One ought also to consider Paul's description of Gentile Christians in 1 Cor 9:21: μὴ ὢν ἄνομως θεοῦ ἀλλ' ἔννομος χριστοῦ.

[32] Räisänen takes this approach; *Paul and the Law,* 101–6.

[33] In fact, the emphasis is primarily upon accusation. Dunn writes: "The implication of the ἢ καί, 'or even,' is that Paul expects the former to be more the rule and the latter more the exception" (*Romans 1–8,* 102).

[34] John W. Martens stresses the indefinite aspect of ὅταν and cites instances where its meaning bordered on a conditional; "Romans 2.14–16: A Stoic Reading," *NTS* 40 (1994): 62–64.

[35] Cranfield, *Romans,* 1:155; König, "Gentiles or Gentile Christians," 56.

[36] Even if one is not persuaded by the chiasm, v. 14 need not be taken to expound on who the "doers of the law" are. Verse 14 could just as easily go with the

Paul's point is that the one who hears the law and thus would be indicted by not doing it is the Jew and not the Gentile. The connections between v. 14 and what precedes do not indicate that the Gentiles actually do the law.[37] Paul writes in v. 14 that the Gentiles do τὰ τοῦ νόμου (he does not use τὸν νόμον ποιεῖν πληροῦν or v. 27's τὸν νόμον τελοῦσα). Far from saying that the Gentiles fulfill the entire law, Paul is simply saying that the Gentiles occasionally do things that the law requires.[38] By their occasional fulfilling of the law, the Gentiles show that they are a law to themselves; the work of the law is written on their hearts. They are accountable before God, just as the Jews who have the law.[39] Nonpossession of the law is no excuse.

III. Romans 2:17–29

Romans 2:17 introduces a new section as Paul specifically turns to the "Jew." Yet this section is an integral part of the developing argument.[40]

first part of v. 13: The Gentiles, even though they do not have the Mosaic law, are a law to themselves (v. 14). They have, to the degree necessary for God's judgment to be impartial, "heard" the law (v. 13a); thus T. R. Schreiner, *The Law and Its Fulfillment,* 194.

[37] G. N. Davies (*Faith and Obedience,* 64) objects that the γάρ would lose its connective force (so also König, "Gentiles or Gentile Christians," 56). Not so: the connection would simply be to v. 12. Nor can Davies see why Paul would refer to the Gentiles' knowledge of God again here if the Gentile was already accountable in 1:18–32. But it is the introduction of the law that necessitates the restatement: God still judges impartially, even when the law is factored in, since the Gentile has its requirements written on the heart. Davies needs v. 14 to link with v. 13 in order to support his theory that Paul has in mind pre-Christian Gentile believers.

[38] Fitzmyer, *Romans,* 309; Bassler, *Divine Impartiality,* 145–46; Laato, *Paul and Judaism,* 81–83. Räisänen argues that Gentile fulfillment of only some of what the law requires would hardly condemn the Jew (thus 2:27); *Paul and the Law,* 103. However, Paul's point in 2:12–16 is not to shame and condemn the Jew by Gentile fulfillment of the law (as in v. 27) but rather that all people are accountable to God whether they have the law or not, including the Gentile.

[39] Thus also Bornkamm, "Gesetz und Natur," 2:99–101; Bassler, *Divine Impartiality,* 146–49; Laato, *Paul and Judaism,* 80–82; T. R. Schreiner, *The Law and Its Fulfillment,* 193–96.

[40] The law remains a key component of the discussion, even as in 2:12–16. Alongside the Mosaic law, Paul begins to elaborate on "circumcision" (περιτομή) and "uncircumcision" (ἀκροβυστία). Paul's description in v. 29 of the "secret Jew" (ὁ ἐν τῷ κρυπτῷ Ἰουδαῖος) who receives God's praise, picks up the reference to God's judgment of the people's secrets (τὰ κρυπτὰ τῶν ἀνθρώπων) in 2:16. The reference to "circumcision of the heart" (περιτομὴ καρδίας) recalls the work of the law written in the Gentiles' hearts in v. 15 (τὸ ἔργον τοῦ νόμου γραπτὸν ἐν ταῖς καρδίαις αὐτῶν); Bassler, *Divine Impartiality,* 127–28, 137–39. Verse 29's οὗ ὁ

Verses 14–16 expounded on v. 12a: those without the law will perish without it, since their consciences attest that the work of the law is written on their hearts. Verses 17–29 build on vv. 12b–13: it is not enough to hear the law, the Jew must also *do it*.[41] Verses 12–13 reveal that the law is the criterion of God's impartial judgment, and vv. 28–29 return to this impartial judgment of what is in people's hearts. Paul shows that *everyone* is accountable to God, *even the Jew*. People will be judged on the basis of whether they have done what the law requires. Mere possession of the law and circumcision are not enough (vv. 17–24).[42]

Everything mentioned in these verses is typical of Jewish self-understanding. Either one calls oneself, or is called, a Jew (v. 17). The Jew relies on the law and boasts in God (v. 17).[43] As a result of possession and instruction in the law, the Jew knows God's will and approves what is excellent (v. 18). The Jew is described as a leader of the blind, a light for those in darkness, a corrector of the foolish, and a teacher of children (vv. 19–20). The Jew possesses the embodiment of knowledge and the truth in the law (v. 20).[44] Paul is not describing here legalists trying to earn their way into heaven.[45] Rather, Paul is describing someone who believes that being a Jew and possessing God's law and the knowledge that the law provides will save him or her at the judgment. Paul's "Jew" fits the description of Sanders's covenantal nomist; this is an individual who considers himself or herself a member of a chosen and elect people who will be saved.

ἔπαινος οὐκ ἐξ ἀνθρώπων ἀλλ' ἐκ τοῦ θεοῦ hearkens back to the impartiality theme from earlier in 2:11 (ibid., 139).

41 Verse 17 and what follows seems to build on v. 13, that it is not the hearers of the law who will be justified. If so, it acts as further support of Paul's statement there, and vv. 17–29 would likewise be subordinated to the statement of God's impartial judgment in vv. 9–11. Building on v. 13, vv. 14–16 show that the Gentile is accountable before God, even as vv. 17–29 show that the Jew is also accountable.

42 Verses 17–24 are tightly structured as Bassler (*Divine Impartiality*, 262 n. 100) notes:

A Ἐπονομάζειν (v. 17)
  B ἐπαναπαύῃ νόμῳ and καυχᾶσαι ἐν θεῷ (v. 17)
  B′ ἐν νόμῳ καυχᾶσαι and τὸν θεὸν ἀτιμάζειν (v. 23)
A′ ὄνομα τοῦ θεοῦ (v. 24)

43 An ironic contrast to those identified in 1:21, 23, 25, 32.

44 In contrast to those in 1:18, 21. In fact, all the advantages of the Jew in these verses can be traced to possession of the Mosaic law; L. T. Johnson, *Reading Romans*, 40.

45 Rather, Paul's critique is not that they are legalistically trying to do the law but that they *transgress* it.

Paul's entire tone changes in v. 21, where the protasis of vv. 17–20 is followed by a series of rhetorical questions. Paul asks if those who teach others have taught themselves the law. He asks if those who say that one is not to steal or commit adultery do these things themselves. They teach the abhorrence of idols, but do they rob temples? While the Jews pride themselves as the teachers and leaders of the blind and those in darkness, they have caused God's name to be blasphemed among the nations (v. 24). While they boast of being in the law (cf. v. 17), Paul questions if the Jews actually dishonor God by their disobedience of the law (v. 23). Instead of leading the Gentiles to God, the Jews have led the Gentiles to dishonor and blaspheme God by not practicing the truth they know. In these verses Paul critiques the Jewish understanding of their privilege as a people. Paul asserts that it is not enough to be a Jew, to possess the law, and to be circumcised. One must also *do* what the law requires.[46]

Verses 25–29 build on Paul's critique in vv. 17–24. Verse 25 says that circumcision is therefore of value only if there is a simultaneous "doing" of the law.[47] If one transgresses the law, one's circumcision has become uncircumcision. Obedience is the ultimate criterion. If the uncircumcised does the "requirements of the law," he or she will be regarded as circumcised (v. 26). Verse 27 asserts that the outwardly cir-

---

[46] Elliot (*Rhetoric,* 130–32) recognizes a major difference between 2:1–5 and the sharp questions of 2:21–24. In 2:1–5 Paul *presumes* the guilt of the one he addresses (likewise 3:9–20). In 2:21–24 Paul states the matter in terms of rhetorical questions. He never denies the Jews' privileges (cf. 3:1–9) but asks whether there has been the accompanying obedience. The interrogation of the Jew thus serves to demonstrate that no one is exempt from accountability before God's impartial judgment. See especially Elliot, *Rhetoric,* 134–35, 196–201: Paul's point, then, is not to indict every Jew of these particular sins (contra Räisänen, *Paul and the Law,* 106) but to show that the Jews are accountable because of the law, the very source of their ethnic distinctiveness (2:12–13). Klyne R. Snodgrass rightly notes that Paul does not use the word ἁμαρτία until Rom 3:9–29 ("Justification by Grace," 76). While the concept itself is present (for example, 1:18–31; T. R. Schreiner, *The Law and Its Fulfillment,* 68), the primary point is that *all are accountable to God for their actions.* Consequently, sin in 3:9–20 is truly a problem requiring a solution, requiring a source of mercy and deliverance. For a similar conclusion regarding equal accountability before God in Rom 2, see Jean-Noël Aletti, "Rm 1,18–3,20: Incohérence ou cohérence de l'argumentation paulinienne?" *Bib* 69 (1988) 47–62. Aletti considers the obedient individuals of Rom 2 strictly hypothetical.

[47] The emphasis in vv. 25–29 on circumcision, an ethnic identity marker, confirms that Paul is responding to Jewish national identity and privilege; Dunn (*Romans 1–8,* 119–20) and Barclay (*Obeying the Truth,* 245). In other words, to be a member of the Jewish people marked by circumcision is not satisfactory for a right relationship with God, contrary to common Jewish belief.

cumcised but transgressing Jew will be judged by one who is not circumcised by nature but fulfills (τελοῦσα) the law.[48] Verses 28–29 conclude that outward circumcision does not make a Jew, but the inward circumcision that comes through the Spirit.[49] Verses 25–29 are thus the last stage in a series of statements that takes Jewish presumption on the

---

[48] It would hardly carry any persuasive value to say that only a hypothetical Gentile judges the Jew. Why bother? On the other hand, *actual* Gentile obedience and *actual* Gentile judges would shame the Jew; contra Richard H. Bell, *No One Seeks for God: An Exegetical and Theological Study of Romans 1.18–3.20* (WUNT 106; Tübingen: J.C.B. Mohr [Paul Siebeck], 1998), 194; Otto Kuss, *Der Römerbrief übersetzt und erklärt* (Regensburg: Friedrich Pustet, 1957), 1:64–65, 90; Hans Lietzmann, *Einführung in die Textgeschichte der Paulusbriefe an die Römer* (4th ed.; HNT 8; Tübingen: J.C.B. Mohr [Paul Siebeck], 1933), 42–44; van Dülmen, *Theologie*, 77, 82. Kuss is followed by Thielman (*Paul and the Law*, 172–74), although Thielman (p. 174) admits the possibility that Paul has in mind actual Gentiles while not identifying them at this point in the letter.

[49] The entire description of the true Jew draws upon language that Paul will later use to describe *Christians;* Heinrich Schlier, *Der Römerbrief* (HTKNT 6; Freiburg: Herder, 1977), 88–89; Laato, *Paul and Judaism*, 84; Soucek, "Exegese," 103–4; and T. R. Schreiner, *The Law and Its Fulfillment*, 197–98. In v. 26 Paul speaks of τὰ δικαιώματα τοῦ νόμου, the same phrase used in the singular in Rom 8:4, where those who walk by the Spirit fulfill this "just requirement of the law" (cf. Gentile disobedience of God's δικαίωμα in 1:32). The contrast in v. 29 of the "Spirit" and the "letter" recurs in Rom 7:5–6 (and 8:1–4) and 2 Cor 3:6–7. Paul contrasts the new, eschatological situation of those in Christ who have the Spirit with those in the letter of the law who do not have the Spirit (see chs. 3 and 8). This jeopardizes G. N. Davies's case that Paul has in mind OT believers; *Faith and Obedience*, 69–70. Similarly, in Phil 3:3, those who worship in the Spirit are the "true circumcision." In v. 26 the uncircumcised are *"reckoned"* as circumcised, language used throughout Rom 3 and 4 for those reckoned righteous on the basis of faith (3:28; 4:3, 4, 5, 6, 8, 9, 10, 11, 22, 23, 24; 9:8; Gal 3:6; 2 Cor 5:19). Circumcision will be a sign of faith in Rom 4. There Paul will reinterpret circumcision in terms of Abraham rather than the law (which he allows for the sake of argument here).

So if Paul had in mind Gentile *Christians* in his description of the Gentile in Rom 2, why doesn't Paul identify them as such? The reason is that Paul does not turn to Christ's work until 3:21–26. A precise identification at this point would be irrelevant. All that matters at this point in Rom 2 is that God's judgment is objective and impartial. Nor does Paul definitively assert that there *are* such Gentiles. He says "if" in Rom 2:25. Paul leaves matters at the level of suggestion (although he does say that such people will "judge" the Jew in v. 27, a function of Christians; see 1 Cor 6:2). Similarly, questions about whom Paul has in mind in vv. 6–10 are irrelevant. Paul is simply laying down the criteria of God's just judgment. He does not actually identify anyone falling into the category of the good, although the language again is suggestive of Christians.

Nevertheless, Paul is using language that anticipates his unfolding argument. As Paul proceeds, it will become clear that those Gentiles judged righteous on the final day are Gentiles *in Christ.* His argument, essentially, is looping back on

basis of the law and circumcision and turns it on its head. There are Gentiles circumcised in heart who do what is good (2:7, 10, 12–16, 25–29). The Gentiles are proof that God's judgment is impartial and that it is based on actions and not on the mere possession of the law or circumcision. All people are accountable before God's judgment.[50]

No Jew would have had a problem with Paul's assertion that one must do the law. The Jews too said that God would judge according to one's actual works.[51] Further, Paul never denies all the privileges of being a Jew. He simply says that these privileges are valid only when accompanied by obedience (2:12–13, 25–27). Paul departs from Judaism when he denies any salvific privilege or benefit to being a Jew.[52] As dis-

---

itself. In light of what comes later, it will become clear that 2:6–10 and 2:26–29 had truly included *all* people, even Gentiles in *Christ*. That these two passages should be read together is suggested by the mention of eschatological praise in 2:29 paralleling the reward to those who do good works in 2:6–10. Yet the language of 2:25–29 begins to prepare the reader for the ensuing verbal parallels and a recognition that it is the Christian Gentile who so fulfills the law. Not surprisingly, then, Paul speaks of *Christians* being judged according to their works throughout the rest of his letters (for instance, 1 Cor 6:9–10; 9:24–27; Gal 5:21; 6:8).

[50] Douglas A. Campbell thinks that Rom 2:9–3:20 functions as a *reductio ad absurdum* of judgment according to works, thereby showing that God really justifies by faith; "A Rhetorical Suggestion concerning Romans 2," *SBL Seminar Papers, 1995* (Atlanta: Scholars Press, 1995), 140–67. Jean-Noël Aletti has extensively critiqued Campbell's theory; "Romains 2. Sa Cohérence et sa fonction," *Bib* 77 (1996): 158–65. Campbell does not attach sufficient importance to the fact that judgment according to works is a *biblical* principle. Further, Rom 1:24–28 affirms (three times) that God's judgment has already begun. God is already punishing on the basis of works; Aletti, "Romains 2," 159–60. How can Paul say that one is justified only in Christ without first addressing the possibility of salvation in Judaism through covenantal privileges? Paul's answer is that God's judgment according to works eliminates Jewish privilege. Thus, contra Campbell, judgment according to works is a serious motif that stretches well beyond 2:1–8 into the entirety of the chapter; Aletti, "Romains 2," 161–62.

[51] Pss 28:4; 62:12 (LXX 61:13); Prov 24:12; Job 34:11; Jer 17:10; 25:14; 32:19; 51:24; Ezek 33:20; Hos 12:2; Sir 16:12–14; *1 En.* 1:7–9; 100:7; 1QS 10.16–18; 1QH[a] 18.12–13; 1QpHab 8.1–2; *4 Ezra* 6:19; 7:17, 33–44; *Pss. Sol.* 2:15–18, 33–35; 9:4–5; *2 Bar.* 13:8–9; 44:4; 54:21; *Jub.* 5:12–19; 21:4; 33:18; *T. Levi* 3:2; 4:1; *T. Gad* 7:5; *T. Benj.* 10:7–9; *As. Mos.* 12:10–11; *Sib. Or.* 4:183–185; *Jos. Asen.* 28:3; *L.A.B.* 3:10; cf. Matt 16:27; 2 Cor 5:10; Col 3:25; 2 Tim 4:14; 1 Pet 1:17; Rev 2:23. Verse 6 even alludes to Ps 62:12. Sometimes God's people are judged with mercy in contrast to the strict judgment of the Gentiles. At other times, the Jews are judged strictly by their deeds as well.

[52] For example, when he denies that physical circumcision brought one into the elect people and thus into salvation. In Jewish tradition, failure to circumcise excluded one from God's people and saving plan (*Jub.* 15:25–34; Josephus, *Ant.* 13.257–258; 13.318; see also 1 Macc 1:48, 60–61; 2:46; 2 Macc 6:10).

cussed in chapters 1 and 2, the Jews held God's judgment according to works in tension with his election and mercy toward his people.[53] Paul disrupts the irreconcilable tension between the two poles of Jewish thought by weighing judgment over mercy.[54] Paul dismisses the Jews' special status as a chosen and elect people and places them on the same level as the Gentiles. Paul resolves the tension between judgment according to works and God's mercy to the people by affirming the former while denying any saving value in the latter. In his own thinking Paul has clearly moved away from covenantal nomism.[55] Surely a Jewish reader would object: "What about God's mercy?" "What about the sacrificial system, which atones for failure and sin?" "What about circumcision as a sign of Israel's election?" In short, a Jew would fault Paul for denying God's mercy in the equation.[56] Romans 3 responds to that potential objection: there is hope for Israel.[57] In 3:21–26 Paul shows that saving

---

[53] Snodgrass, "Justification by Grace," 78.

[54] Romans 2:4 speaks of "kindness," "forbearance," and "patience." These are all terms used in Jewish literature for God's dealings toward his covenant people. Wisdom 15:1–2, after condemning Gentile idolatry and sin (chs. 11–14), says: "But you, our God, are kind and true, patient [μακρόθυμος], and ruling all things in mercy. For even if we sin we are yours, knowing your power." *Psalms of Solomon* 9–10 also stress God's mercy toward his covenant people. Quite often Jewish literature affirms both sides of the tension within the same breath, for example, *Pss. Sol.* 15:8, which says that "those who act lawlessly shall not escape the Lord's judgment" only to turn around and exempt the "righteous" from that judgment.

[55] Moo rightly recognizes that Paul is denying the Jewish covenantal framework for dealing with sin. The vast human dilemma caused by sin required a more potent system than the traditional Jewish covenantal framework; *Romans,* 157.

[56] George P. Carras's comments ("Romans 2,1–29: A Dialogue on Jewish Ideals," *Bib* 73 [1992]: 195) are helpful in understanding how Paul as a Jew could come to this critique: the Jews depended on their privileged status for mercy. Paul, however, critiques that privileged position as an impugning of God's impartiality. For Paul, the "Jew" adopts a different standard for himself with the covenant and mercy than for others and so violates God's impartial judgment of both the Jews and the Gentiles; Carras, 206. Nevertheless (against Carras), the Jew would surely have objected that Scripture itself, alongside impartial judgment, speaks of God offering mercy to a repentant Israel. With the proper disposition, one would receive mercy. Paul ignores this, preferring to pit God's impartial justice against the traditional means of mercy.

[57] Paul asks in 3:1 if the Jew has any advantage. Paul answers affirmatively and begins to list their advantages, then digresses. He does not return to the Jews' advantages until Rom 9. However, Paul does say in 3:9 that whatever advantages the Jews have, they are still under the power of sin.

Hays (*Echoes,* 44–46) thinks that Rom 9–11 builds on Rom 2. The quotation of Isa 52:5 LXX in Rom 2:24 is not only a reminder that the Jews' sins have brought God's name into disrepute among the Gentiles; it is also a passage of

righteousness is to be found *in Christ.*[58] Apart from Christ the law is reduced to legal obligation and a standard of performance for Paul. The law's ethnic component becomes merely an ethnic distinction and nothing more; it is no longer a sign of God's grace.[59] Once the gracious framework of Judaism is compromised, the law in its character as God's demand and the criterion for the judgment comes to the fore.

IV. Excursus on "Works of the Law"

In Rom 3:19–20 Paul, summarizing the line of thought that began in 1:18, employs the phrase ἔργα νόμου. James D. G. Dunn, N. T. Wright, and others have asserted that this phrase (as in Gal 3:10) means especially those aspects of the Mosaic law such as circumcision that distinguish Jews from Gentiles and mark national identity. A proper understanding of ἔργα νόμου necessarily involves Rom 2 since Paul addresses there the ethnic presumption of those who are circumcised and who call themselves Jews (2:17, 25). Perhaps the context of Paul's discussion in Rom 2 indicates that ἔργα νόμου in 3:20 refers especially to those works that distinguish Jews from Gentiles.

In Rom 2:6 God will judge each individual according to his or her "deeds" (κατὰ τὰ ἔργα αὐτοῦ). The deeds may be good (ἔργου ἀγαθοῦ, v. 7) or bad (ἀδικίᾳ, v. 8). Nothing suggests that Paul has Jewish ethnic

---

hope for Israel. In other words, even while affirming Israel's sinfulness and denying any salvific benefit in Jewish ethnic identity per se, the "echoes of Scripture" foreshadow Israel's inclusion among the Messiah's people later in Romans (esp. 9:5 and 11:26–27). While suggestive, would the Gentile readers of Romans have picked up on this point? Also, God's covenant faithfulness to Israel will be manifested *in Christ,* the Messiah. Even in Rom 9–11 the saving value of the covenant and election are of no avail apart from faith in the Messiah (see ch. 4 on Rom 9–11).

[58] Even though one's relationship to God is restored by faith in Jesus Christ, 3:21–26 never overturns the principle of Rom 2 that God will judge according to one's works.

[59] If it is a matter of performance and not possession, Paul opens the door for the Gentiles; Bassler, *Divine Impartiality,* 141. The Jews and Gentiles would be on an equal footing before God; van Dülmen, *Theologie,* 74. Moo is absolutely right:

> This argument is an outright attack on the "covenantal nomism" that Sanders has sketched. The denial of special status to the Jews is an implicit rejection of the election that was the foundation for "covenantal nomism. . . ." Jewish works, then, are no different from Gentile works, once the larger framework of the covenant—as usually understood in first-century Judaism—is eliminated (*Romans,* 214–15).

identity markers in mind.[60] Paul is elaborating on the basis for God's judgment of "all" people (2:9–10). In 2:10 Paul uses the verb ἐργάζομαι for the actions of all who do good whether Jew or Gentile (παντὶ τῷ ἐργαζομένῳ τὸ ἀγαθόν, Ἰουδαίῳ τε πρῶτον καὶ Ἕλληνι).[61] In Rom 2:15 Paul speaks of the "work of the law" (τὸ ἔργον τοῦ νόμου) written on the heart of the Gentiles. Here "work" (ἔργον) is qualified by νόμος. Paul certainly does not have Jewish identity markers in mind here. The Gentile remains a Gentile even while doing (ποιέω, 2:14) the work of the law. ἔργον thus signifies human activity and doing of the law apart from any notion of Jewish, ethnic distinction.

Paul's use of ἔργα apart from νόμου, the singular ἔργον, and the verb ἐργάζομαι all indicate human activity and doing in general, with no reference to Jewish identity markers per se. Dunn distinguishes ἔργα νόμου from these other uses of ἔργον and its cognate verb; ἔργα νόμου acts *uniquely* as a technical term for the ethnic, boundary-marking aspects of the law. This helps Dunn resolve the contradiction between 2:13 ("the doers of the law . . . will be justified") and 3:20a ("by the works of the law, no flesh will be justified," my translation). Dunn can say that "works of the law" in 3:20a refers to the boundary-marking aspects of the law, while 2:13 refers to the law in its entirety.[62] Dunn has to distinguish sharply between the singular "work of the law" (τὸ ἔργον τοῦ νόμου) in 2:15 and the plural ἔργα νόμου. The singular refers to the Gentiles' accomplishment of the law but hardly its ethnic markers. Where the singular has a positive force, the plural ἔργα νόμου has a negative force (e.g., Rom 3:20, 28; Gal 2:16; 3:2, 5, 10). Yet it is difficult to see the plural ἔργα νόμου carrying a technical sense so different from the meaning of the singular τὸ ἔργον τοῦ νόμου.[63] A better solution to the contradiction between 2:13 and 3:20a is simply that while in principle

---

[60] Cf. Rom 13:12, where Christians are to cast off the "works (ἔργα) of darkness" and act as citizens of the day. This is an admonition to do good works and to act in a right fashion. Again, there is nothing to suggest Jewish boundary markers.

[61] There is nothing in v. 6 or its context to suggest "covenant obligations" such as acts of charity or the ritual law as Dunn (*Romans 1–8*, 85) suggests. Paul simply asserts that people's actions, whether Jew or Gentile, are the basis for God's judgment.

[62] So also Watson, 119–20.

[63] Akio Ito stresses that both the plural and singular forms have a neutral force in themselves. It is the context that suggests a negative force for the plural and a positive force for the singular. Ito therefore concludes that the plural and singular phrases are "synonymous and general expressions which the contexts define more narrowly"; "Romans 2: A Deuteronomistic Reading," *JSNT* 59 (1995): 28–29.

the one who does the law is justified, no one, in fact, does the law (thus Rom 3:9, 19–20).[64] Dunn claims that ἔργα νόμου—with its distinct focus on the ethnic, boundary-marking aspects of the law—is entirely negative from Paul's perspective. But if that were the case, surely Paul would have made clear his attitude while discussing Jewish ethnic privileges in Rom 2. In Rom 2:17–29, however, Paul sees absolutely no problem with Jewish ethnic identity markers as long as they are accompanied by full observance of the law.[65] If ἔργα νόμου in 3:20 is intended to summarize what preceded in the discussion of the law in Rom 2, the phrase must take into account that Paul is consistently using "works" *in a more general fashion:* to signify human activity and doing, *in opposition to mere Jewish privilege.* The Jew must actually do what the law requires in its totality. One should not be surprised that the "works of the law" (so to speak) that Paul identifies are the moral failures on the part of the Jews: robbing temples, adultery, and stealing, hardly its ethnic aspects. The sins of the Jews turn out to parallel those of all humanity in 1:18–32 (cf. 2:2–3).

In Rom 2 Paul employs the word "work" (ἔργον) and its cognates so often in order to hammer home his point that it is not enough to possess the law; one must do it (cf. Gal 3:10). Paul is using "work" and its cognates in this more natural sense. Doing what the law requires will be the criterion of God's judgment (Rom 2:22–23, 25, 26, 27), whether one possesses the law or not (2:14–16, 17–29). One's identity as a Jew or Gentile will not influence God at the judgment. It is what the individual *does* that makes a Gentile out of a Jew or a true Jew out of a Gentile. In light of Paul's whole thrust in ch. 2, the summary expression in 3:20, ἔργα νόμου should be understood in the more natural sense of the works that the law requires and without any special focus on the ethnic aspects of the law.[66]

---

[64] Or at least no one does the law apart from Christ.

[65] This point is fatal for Dunn. Romans 2:17–29 does not reflect the negative view of Jewish ethnic identity markers that Dunn's overall theory would lead one to expect. See Thomas R. Schreiner, " 'Works of the Law' in Paul," *NovT* 33 (1991): 226–28; contra Dunn and N. T. Wright. Note also that it is *the context* of 2:17–29 that identifies Jewish ethnic/national privilege and *not* the phrase ἔργα νόμου.

[66] And if one sees the context of usage of ἔργα νόμου in 3:20 as negative, unlike Rom 2, the answer in *this* context would be that 3:20 refers to doing what the law requires *in the light of* human sinfulness and failure, whereas Rom 2 was speaking strictly in terms of the law's requirement and human accountability; so also Snodgrass, "Justification by Grace," 84.

V. Conclusion

Paul denies that Jewish ethnic privilege and identity (as attested by circumcision and possession of God's law) mitigate God's strict judgment of all people according to their works. God will judge the Jew no differently from the Gentile and without granting any special leniency or mercy.[67] Paul therefore compromises the gracious framework of covenantal nomism in favor of a universal judgment according to one's deeds. The law correspondingly functions as the legal standard of what God requires of humanity.

[67] Ulrich Wilckens, *Der Brief an die Römer* (3 vols.; EKKNT 6/1–3; Neukirchen-Vluyn: Neukirchener Verlag, 1978), 1:177.

Chapter Eight

Romans 3:27–4:8: Justified by God's Grace or by the Doing of the Mosaic Law?

Recent scholarship has focused on the ethnic dimensions of Rom 3:27–4:8.[1] Like the line of thought in Rom 2, Paul again confronts the ethnic advantage posed by the Jews' possession of the Mosaic law. Romans 3:27–4:8 focuses on works in a manner similar to the insistence in Rom 2 that God will judge all people equally on the basis of their works. Since God justifies through faith, human efforts are excluded, including the doing of the Mosaic law. If doing the Mosaic law is not a factor in God's justifying on the basis of faith, then the Gentiles may be justified by faith as well. While Paul's critique of the law's division of humanity is certainly central to these verses, that critique is grounded in an understanding of the law as based on human effort. Such an understanding of Paul's logic assumes that νόμος in Rom 3:27–31 refers to the Mosaic law. It also assumes that Rom 4 supports Paul's thinking in 3:27–31, particularly the reference to "works" in 4:4–5. Each of these assumptions has been vigorously contested in the scholarly literature.

I. The "Law of Works" and the "Law of Faith"

Many scholars do not think that νόμος in Rom 3:27–31 refers to the Mosaic law. The word νόμος in 3:27 could have the more general meaning "order," or "principle." Heikki Räisänen has shown that νόμος had a

---

[1] For example, Cranford, "Abraham in Romans 4," 71–88. Although the focus of this chapter is on Rom 3:27–4:8, Paul's unit of thought extends beyond 4:8 to the end of the chapter. The following discussion will also address the relationship between 4:4–8 and 4:9–25.

broad range of potential meanings in first-century Greek usage.[2] When Paul asks "By *what law* is boasting excluded?" the question could very well be a play on words. There certainly are not two separate Mosaic laws. In asking "by what law?" Paul must be comparing the *principle* of works with that of faith (cf. the following queries: "[a law/principle] of works?" or "a law/principle of faith?").

Gerhard Friedrich contends that νόμος in v. 27 does in fact refer to the Mosaic law (and not "order" or "principle"). νόμος is used eleven times in Rom 3:19–31. Paul consistently uses νόμος for the Mosaic Torah throughout these verses. Why should v. 27 be different?[3] Räisänen objects to this argument and points to Rom 7:21–25 and Rom 8:2 as instances where Paul uses νόμος in a more general sense.[4] His objection loses force if one takes νόμος as a reference to the Mosaic law in 7:21–25 and 8:2 as well.[5] The consistent usage of the term in the immediate context places the burden of proof on those arguing for the more general sense. Some think that if "by what law?" (3:27) is taken as the Mosaic law one would have to posit two different Mosaic laws, which would be absurd. Friedrich responds that Paul could just as easily be asking not "which" but "of what nature."[6] Paul uses this word (ποῖος) elsewhere only in 1 Cor 15:35, where he asks with "what kind of body" will the dead be raised. Rather than asking "which," Paul is asking "what kind."[7] The question "by what kind of law?" could be referring to the law from

---

[2] Heikki Räisänen, "Paul's Word-Play on νόμος: A Linguistic Study," in *Jesus, Paul and Torah: Collected Essays* (trans. David E. Orton; JSNTSup 43; Sheffield: Sheffield Academic Press, 1992), 69–94.

[3] Gerhard Friedrich, "Das Gesetz des Glaubens Röm. 3,27," *TZ* 10 (1954): 404–5: until v. 27 νόμος always refers to the Torah, as it does as well as in vv. 28–31. Friedrich cannot understand why νόμος in v. 27 must suddenly mean something different. In fact, νόμος has consistently meant the Mosaic law in *every instance* throughout Romans up to this point; G. N. Davies, *Faith and Obedience,* 135.

[4] Räisänen, "The 'Law' of Faith and the Spirit," in *Jesus, Paul and Torah: Collected Essays* (trans. David E. Orton; JSNTSup 43; Sheffield: Sheffield Academic Press, 1992), 55. In fact, as Räisänen observes, most scholars see a more general usage in these two passages.

[5] See the discussion of the meaning of νόμος in Rom 7:21–25 in ch. 9 following, particularly the arguments of P. J. Achtemeier, "Unsearchable Judgments." On 8:2 (and various other passages), see C. F. D. Moule, "Justification in Its Relation to the Condition κατὰ πνεῦμα (Rom. 8:1–11)," in *Battesimo e Giustizia in Rom 6 e 8* (ed. L. de Lorenzi; Rome: St. Paul Abbey, 1974), 177–87.

[6] Friedrich, "Das Gesetz," 414–15.

[7] C. Thomas Rhyne emphasizes this point as well; *Faith Establishes the Law* (SBLDS 55; Chico, Calif.: Scholars Press, 1981), 151 n. 21. James D. G. Dunn phrases the question: "What kind of understanding of the law?"; *Romans 1–8,* 186. See the same type of usage in Acts 7:49.

differing perspectives. The law could be understood in terms of the works that it prescribes (ἐξ ἔργων) or in terms of the faith to which it bears witness (ἐκ πίστεως).[8] Understanding the Mosaic law from two different perspectives is not a notion that just springs forth out of thin air in v. 27. On the contrary, this tension within the law is manifested already in vv. 21–22: one is saved "*apart from the law*," and yet "*the law*" (along with the prophets) can testify to God's righteousness and faith in/of Christ. Romans 3:27 builds on this tension as the Mosaic law is viewed from differing angles. Negatively, salvation is apart from its works. Positively, it bears witness to the righteousness that comes through faith.[9] The advantage of understanding νόμος as the Mosaic law from differing perspectives is that the meaning of νόμος remains consistent all through this section (3:21–31).

Some have questioned whether the genitive modifiers of νόμος in 3:27 will allow for the interpretation that Friedrich and those following him have proposed.[10] As much as Räisänen disagrees with seeing a refer-

---

[8] Glenn N. Davies disagrees: "Certainly one objection to Friedrich's translation of 3.27c is that it is somewhat unnatural to ask 'What kind of Law (of Moses)?' To ask the question 'What kind of Law?' is different from asking 'Which perspective on the Law?'" (*Faith and Obedience*, 136). Davies therefore prefers the translation of νόμος as "principle." Yet he is not entirely sure of his position. In spite of his translation, he acknowledges that the twenty uses of νόμος for the Mosaic law prior to 3:27 must bear weight for one's understanding. The "principle" must be understood *in light of the Torah*. Davies's final position thus resembles in a peculiar way the very position he had been opposing. Why not be consistent and simply translate νόμος as the Mosaic law?

[9] Rhyne, *Faith*, 70. Friedrich's literary parallels ("Das Gesetz," 415) between vv. 21–22 and 27–28 are not compelling, as Räisänen has shown; "The 'Law' of Faith and the Spirit," 57. Friedrich wants to take νόμου πίστεως in v. 27 as a parallel to μαρτυρουμένη ὑπὸ τοῦ νόμου in v. 21b but does not answer why it could not go with διὰ πίστεως in v. 22 instead. While Friedrich's parallel structure is wanting, the overall thrust of his argument could still be correct: Paul is developing further what he had to say about the Mosaic law in the immediately preceding context (vv. 21–22).

Paul in v. 27 probably drops the reference to the prophets (v. 21) in order to sharpen rhetorically a contrast that in vv. 21–22 had already revolved around the word "law." Dunn emphasizes that one must not dissect the law (v. 27) into some core apart from its Jewish ritual requirements; *Romans 1–8*, 186–87. Paul is treating the law as a whole here, understood either from the point of view of the works that it requires (and for Dunn, particularly those that set the Jews apart as a people) or from the point of view of faith. When understood in terms of the latter, the works that it requires become secondary.

[10] For example, Ulrich Luz, *Das Geschichtsverständnis des Paulus* (BevT 49; Munich: Chr. Kaiser, 1968), 173 n. 143. Luz thinks that Friedrich's reading is a little too complicated, and what sort of genitive would be τῆς πίστεως?

ence to the Mosaic law in v. 27, he still cautions with respect to the genitives: "But one would be wise not to give too much weight to this formal argument."[11] He points to Rom 9:31, where there is a similarly difficult genitive relationship, νόμον δικαιοσύνης. Yet most would accept that 9:31 is a reference to the Mosaic law. Räisänen cites Turner approvingly: "The relationship expressed by the gen[itive] is so vague that it is only by means of the context and wider considerations that it can be made definitive."[12] Klyne R. Snodgrass writes:

> The words in the genitive are not incidental "add-ons" for Paul, but often carry as much or more force than the noun they qualify. When Paul asks "What kind of law?", the options he offers are "law characterized by works" and "law characterized by faith". I do not think that we can avoid a reference to the Torah with these expressions.[13]

In other words, the context must ultimately decide the relationship of the genitive to the noun it modifies.

Along with Paul's consistent use of νόμος for the Mosaic law prior to 3:27, another important consideration is the relationship between the phrase "[law] of works" and boasting. In Rom 2:17 and 2:23 Paul speaks of the Jews' pride in their special relationship to God. The basis for that "boast" is their possession of the νόμος, the Torah/Scriptures (2:23: ὃς ἐν νόμῳ καυχᾶσαι). The Jew "relies on the law" (ἐπαναπαύῃ νόμῳ, 2:17), is instructed by the law (κατηχούμενος ἐκ τοῦ νόμου, 2:18), and has the embodiment of knowledge and truth in the law (τῆς γνώσεως καὶ τῆς ἀληθείας ἐν τῷ νόμῳ, 2:20). Bruce W. Longenecker concludes:

> Already, then, Paul has established an intricate connection between Jewish boasting and their possession of the biblical texts—ὁ νόμος. (The Jews are, after all, ἐν νόμῳ.) When the two terms appear again in 3.27, the reference of each is presumably the same as in 2.17–23 unless otherwise clarified. But Paul does not indicate that the references have changed.[14]

Longenecker adds: had Paul wished to avoid speaking of the Mosaic law at this point, given his precedent in ch. 2, all he had to do was omit the

---

[11] Räisänen, "The 'Law' of Faith and the Spirit," 57 n. 1.

[12] Nigel Turner (and James Hope Moulton), *Syntax*, vol. 3 of *A Grammar of New Testament Greek* (Edinburgh: T&T Clark, 1963), 207. Moule ("Justification," 181) calls the use of the genitive "notoriously flexible and pregnant"; contra Michael Winger, "Meaning and Law," *JBL* 117 (1998): 108–9.

[13] "Spheres of Influence: A Possible Solution to the Problem of Paul and the Law," *JSNT* 32 (1988): 101.

[14] B. W. Longenecker, *Eschatology and Covenant*, 208. On this point, Longenecker is following Snodgrass, "Spheres of Influence," 101; so also Osten-Sacken, *Heiligkeit*, 23–24.

word νόμος (ποῦ οὖν ἡ καύχησις; ἐξεκλείσθη. διὰ τῶν ἔργων; οὐχί, ἀλλὰ διὰ πίστεως).[15] It is therefore no surprise when Paul asks in Rom 3:29 whether God is the God only of the Jews. Paul had been speaking in terms of the Mosaic law, the very source of division between the Jews and the Gentiles. Romans 3:29 conclusively proves that Paul had been thinking in v. 27 in terms of the Mosaic law (and not some "principle" of works) by the phrase "law of works."[16]

If "law of works" must mean the Mosaic law in 3:27, so also must "law of faith." Either "law of works" and "law of faith" both refer to the Mosaic law, or they must both be translated as "principle." It would be difficult to read the "[*law*] of works" *(Mosaic law)* alongside the "*law* of faith" *(a principle)*. That would require two totally different meanings of νόμος in the immediate context posed in answer to the singular νόμος in the question "by what sort of law?"[17] Also, it would be hard to see νόμος as Mosaic law consistently through the other ten instances of the term in vv. 19–31 and then an isolated exception in v. 27b.[18]

In spite of these difficulties, some have interpreted "law of faith" as the principle of faith even while they have maintained that the "law of works" is the Mosaic law.[19] Paul excludes the Mosaic law from God's justifying activity through faith (e.g., "apart from the law," "apart from the works of the law"). Such a sharp antithesis ultimately leads Paul to ask if the law has been nullified through faith (v. 31a). Douglas Moo thinks that the apostle's question would make sense only if the preceding verses had remained utterly negative about the law. If that were so, v. 27's *positive* phrase "law of faith" would mean something *other* than the Mosaic

---

[15] In fact, as Snodgrass writes on Räisänen's understanding of v. 27, particularly in relation to v. 31's reaffirmation of the Mosaic law:

> On his view, for all intents and purposes, the word νόμος could just as easily have been omitted in 3.27. Further, Räisänen ends up claiming that Paul sees the order of the Torah being replaced by another law, which is the *opposite* of what Paul claims to be saying in 3.31. Räisänen has to conclude that Paul makes the positive comment on the law in 3.31 *blitzartig* ("Spheres of Influence," 101).

Räisänen himself ("The 'Law' of Faith and the Spirit," 63) describes the switch to a positive construal in 3:31 as taking place "quite suddenly."

[16] James D. G. Dunn, " 'The Law of Faith,' 'the Law of the Spirit' and 'the Law of Christ,' " in *Theology and Ethics in Paul and His Interpreters* (ed. Eugene H. Lovering Jr. and Jerry L. Sumney; Nashville: Abingdon, 1996), 65–66.

[17] It is at least consistent to understand νόμος to mean "principle" *all through* this verse.

[18] Friedrich's objection takes on added force; "Das Gesetz," 404–5.

[19] While understanding the "law of works" as the Mosaic law does not depend on the "law of faith" being the Mosaic law, the question is still worth pursuing.

law, that is, two different principles.[20] One must not only consider the *negative* question, "Is the law abolished?" (with Moo) but also the corresponding *positive* answer: "The law is *established* through faith." Verse 31 requires not only a negative dimension in the immediately preceding verses regarding the Mosaic law but also a *positive* dimension.[21] Paul can speak of the Mosaic law alongside faith in a positive connection in v. 31—only a few verses after v. 27. If νόμος means the Mosaic law and is juxtaposed with faith in v. 31, then it must also mean the Mosaic law in connection with faith in v. 27.[22] Just as a negative construal of the Mosaic law in vv. 27–28 leads to the question "Is the law abolished?" so also a corresponding positive construal of the Mosaic law alongside faith is necessary to sustain the response that "the law is established through faith." That positive construal surely resides in v. 27's phrase "law of faith," that is, the Mosaic law from the vantage point of faith. Verse 27 therefore prepares for the positive and negative thrusts regarding the law in v. 31, even as vv. 21–22 prepared for the dual thrust in v. 27.[23] To

---

[20] Moo, *Romans,* 248–49.

[21] Moo did not recognize this positive strand in Paul's argument concerning the law.

[22] Dunn, "The Law of Faith," 66: "Paul can speak of the 'the *law* of *faith*' because he believed that *faith* establishes the *law.* In such a direct and integrated line of argument the νόμος of 3:27 cannot be other than the νόμος of 3:31." Räisänen ("The 'Law' of Faith and the Spirit," 63) recognizes this positive usage of the law but ignores the implications of this data for his own position. See the above note on his mishandling of v. 27 in light of v. 31.

[23] Westerholm finds it telling that such a crucial distinction should emerge where Paul is not even concerned with the law as his subject. Paul is concerned about boasting, and the law drops out of view in ch. 4; *Israel's Law and the Church's Faith,* 125. Yet Paul did not introduce the distinction here but rather in vv. 21–22, where he had emphasized the law's role as a witness to the very faith that excludes boasting (thus the οὖν in v. 27). Further, it is the discussion of the law at the end of Rom 3 that motivates Paul to provide an extended example from that law in Rom 4.

Jan Lambrecht and Richard W. Thompson object to taking νόμος (v. 31) as the Mosaic law in the sense of Scripture; *Justification By Faith: The Implications of Romans 3:27–31* (Zacchaeus Studies; Wilmington, Del.: Michael Glazier, 1989), 27–28, 47–48; also Richard W. Thompson, "Paul's Double Critique of Jewish Boasting: A Study of Rom 3,27 in Its Context," *Bib* 67 (1986): 530–31. That νόμος *could* be an equivalent at times to γραφή, see Rom 3:19 in the context of the Scriptural catena in 3:10–18, as well as Gal 4:21 and 1 Cor 14:21; Richard B. Hays, "Three Dramatic Roles: The Law in Romans 3–4," in *Paul and the Mosaic Law* (ed. James D. G. Dunn; WUNT 89; Tübingen: J.C.B. Mohr [Paul Siebeck], 1996), 156. If νόμος is taken as the Scriptures, then the answer of v. 31 makes perfect sense: "We uphold the law," that is, the Mosaic Scriptures. The problem for Lambrecht and Thompson lies in the *question:* "Do we then overthrow the law by

understand "law of faith" as a further reference to the Mosaic law is well grounded in the immediate context.

In Rom 4 Paul can cite Abraham as an example of the positive dimension of the Mosaic law, that is, as the law's own witness to faith.[24] Douglas Moo downplays this connection to 3:27–31. He questions why Paul does not use νόμος positively in Rom 4 had there been a positive reference to "the law of faith" in Rom 3:27–31.[25] Westerholm writes: "But are we really to assume that Paul thought his readers would identify the two ["law of faith" and "promise"] with the Mosaic Law when he explicitly

---

this faith?" What would provoke Paul to ask: "Do we overthrow the law/Scripture?" What in the context suggests that the *Scriptures* are in jeopardy? Paul has been attacking, rather, the law as a *legal corpus and demand.* But Lambrecht and Thompson are forced to see an isolated use of νόμος for something other than the Mosaic law in v. 27b. Further, they do not take into account the parallelism between Paul's negative statements and his positive statements. On the one hand is *the witness of the law* (and the prophets) *to God's righteousness in Christ by faith* (vv. 21–22), the "law of faith" (v. 27); "we establish the law" (v. 31). On the other hand is *the law as antithetical to faith* (vv. 21–22), the "law of works" (v. 27); the question "Do we overthrow the law?" (v. 31). In fact, v. 21's "witness" of the "law and prophets" to the "righteousness of faith" shows that the law itself does not convey that righteousness (the negative aspect) but witnesses to it (the positive aspect). The elements of "law" and "faith" recur in v. 27, even as "law" and "works" parallels v. 21's χωρὶς νόμου. Paul has been playing on these two aspects of the law since 3:21, thereby paving the way for the play on the word νόμος in 3:31. Far from abolishing the Mosaic law and its demands, Paul is upholding it in its witness to the most crucial demand of all, in its witness to the need for faith, a need that only God can resolve (Rom 3:21–26; 4:17). Indeed, Paul does not eliminate the law and its demands in Rom 4. Circumcision is still maintained, but it becomes subservient to faith whether one is circumcised or not; see Lambrecht and Thompson, *Justification By Faith*, 56–59. Circumcision is thus given its true value as a sign of faith, the very role that the law itself *had* in 3:21–22, 27, 31; Lambrecht and Thompson, *Justification by Faith*, 58–59. Romans 4 then goes on to defend the Mosaic law in its broader scriptural witness to righteousness and faith. Paul's play on words is only possible by using "law" (νόμος) and not "Scripture" (γραφή), a crucial point that escapes Lambrecht and Thompson. Paul's rhetorical play seems designed to open up the possibility of a new understanding. The key phrase for this new understanding in v. 31 is διὰ τῆς πίστεως.

[24] See, for instance, Otfried Hofius, "Das Gesetz des Mose und das Gesetz Christi," *ZNW* 80 (1983): 278–80.

[25] Moo, *Romans*, 253–54, but Moo already answers his own objection: Paul never uses νόμος by itself to refer to the Mosaic law's scriptural witness. He employs qualifying phrases. Hence Paul specifies πίστεως in v. 27. The use of νόμος in v. 31 depends on v. 27. Moo also objects that Paul does not use γάρ in 4:1 as Rhyne's pattern would expect. Perhaps the γάρ Moo is looking for comes in 4:3. Moo (p. 253) himself admits that this is not the "more serious" problem.

contrasts the "promise" with the "Law" in 4:13–14?"[26] Räisänen and Westerholm question whether Paul has been developing a twofold sense of the law, since the distinction is completely absent in Rom 4? Räisänen questions why Paul treats the law "as a unified whole" in 3:31 had he been thinking in terms of a twofold distinction in v. 27. Therefore, he reasons, the twofold distinction in the law must be false, and Paul must have had in mind something other than the Mosaic law by the distinction.[27] Yet Rom 3:31 *does* in fact reflect the distinctions made in Rom 3:27: it speaks of the law as both abolished and upheld. The use of "promise" instead of the positive phrase "law of faith" in Rom 4 is not all that troublesome either.[28] In Rom 4 Paul is simply guided by the language of the Genesis narratives that had used the word "promise."[29] One should not expect Paul to continue using "law of faith" in ch. 4. Romans 4 neatly supports Paul's argument in 3:27–31: the Mosaic law, understood in the sense of Torah/Scripture, had pointed to salvation by faith all along.[30]

Räisänen's favorite argument against taking νόμος in v. 27 as the Mosaic law is that it is difficult to see how boasting could be excluded by the Mosaic law.[31] Romans 3:21–26 speak of *God's* activity. What *God* is doing in Christ, and not the Mosaic law, excludes boasting. Verse 27 uses the passive ἐξεκλείσθη ("it is excluded") and implies that God is the agent. How would God exclude boasting "by means of" the law? Only God's new act of salvation in Christ could accomplish that.[32] Räisänen's reasoning, in the end, fails to convince. While it is true that the law does not exclude boasting, that is, "the law of works," the "law of faith," on the other hand, *does* exclude boasting insofar as it is a law that witnesses to the righteousness *of God* that is through faith. The law viewed from the standpoint of faith testified long ago to God's impending action in Christ.[33]

---

[26] Westerholm, *Israel's Law and the Church's Faith*, 125; who again follows Räisänen, "The 'Law' of Faith and the Spirit," 58.

[27] Räisänen, "The 'Law' of Faith and the Spirit," 58.

[28] The opposite of the "promise" (as with the "law of faith") would be the "law of works."

[29] Friedrich reminds his readers that the "promise" (ἐπαγγελία) itself is also in the law (νόμος), and this promise testifies to a righteousness based on faith; "Das Gesetz," 416.

[30] Eduard Löhse, "ὁ νόμος τοῦ πνεύματος τῆς ζωῆς Exegetische Anmerkungen zu Röm 8,2," in *Neues Testament und christliche Existenz: Festschrift für Herbert Braun zum 70, Geburtstag am 4. Mai 1973* (ed. Hans Dieter Betz and Luise Schottroff; Tübingen: J.C.B. Mohr [Paul Siebeck], 1973), 281–83.

[31] Räisänen, "The 'Law' of Faith and the Spirit," 59–62.

[32] Thus following 3:21–26.

[33] One finds the same dual role for "Scripture" (γραφή) in Gal 3:8, 22. Räisänen mentions Gal 3:8's *positive* personification of the Scripture with respect

Peter von der Osten-Sacken and Hans Hübner have argued that "law of faith" (3:27) should not be understood in terms of Rom 3:21–22 but rather in terms of Rom 8:2: "the law of the Spirit of life." According to Osten-Sacken and Hübner, Paul is speaking not of the law understood from the point of view of the Scriptures' witness to faith but rather as the law freed from carnal misuse, that is, the right response to the law.[34] But Rom 3 nowhere indicates a carnal misuse of the law. Paul uses "law of works" and "the law" interchangeably.[35] For example, 3:20 says that no one is justified "b*y the works of the law*." Verse 21 clearly responds to that dilemma by asserting a justification that takes place "apart from *the law*." A distinction between "law" and "law of works"—the one referring to the law per se and the other a misuse of the law—would ruin the flow of logic.[36] When Hübner says that a right attitude toward the law excludes boasting (in v. 27), he is forced to ignore the divine passives in the text; the divine passives emphasize the activity of God and not that of human individuals.[37] The reference to "law of faith" is best understood in the light of the verses immediately preceding in 3:21–22, even as the "law of the Spirit of life" (8:2) builds on the positive uses of the law in Rom 7. Understanding νόμος in v. 27 to mean the Mosaic law unifies 3:27–30 with the discussion of the law that preceded (3:21–22). Verse 27 also prepares for v. 31. In all three places, vv. 21–22, v. 27, and v. 31, Paul speaks of the law in both a positive and negative way. The negative elements indicate the law from the perspective of the works that it requires. The positive elements all point to the law from the vantage point of faith. In Rom 4 Paul shows precisely how the law testifies to faith in the person of Abraham. "The Law of faith, then, is the Law in its function of calling for and facilitating the same sort of trust in God as that out of which Abraham lived."[38]

---

to the Abrahamic promise but does not make too much of it. He prefers, instead, to emphasize the negative reference in Gal 3:22, which he sees as paralleling the law's condemning role in Rom 3:19–20. Note the instrumental role of "Scripture" in 3:22. God acts *through* Scripture, even as God acts in Rom 3:27–28 *through* the "law of faith" (cf. the positive reference in Gal 3:8).

[34] Peter von der Osten-Sacken, *Römer 8 als Beispiel paulinischer Soteriologie* (Göttingen: Vandenhoeck & Ruprecht, 1975), 245–50; Hans Hübner, *Law in Paul's Thought* (trans. James C. G. Greig; Edinburgh: T&T Clark, 1984), 116–17, 138–40.

[35] Westerholm, *Israel's Law and the Church's Faith*, 125.

[36] See the discussions of "works of the law" vis-à-vis "law" in chs. 6 and 7.

[37] Hübner, *Law*, 116–17; Räisänen, "The 'Law' of Faith and the Spirit," 60. Better candidates for the exclusion of boasting would include the law in its broader context as scriptural witness to faith, or to God's action in Christ.

[38] Dunn, "The Law of Faith," 68–69. It is more than coincidental that Paul says in Rom 14:23 "everything that is not from faith is sin," hence "the law of faith"; Dunn, "The Law of Faith," 69 n. 23; idem, *Romans 9–16*, 828–29.

II. The Implications of Romans 4:4–5 for the Law

Romans 4:2, 4–6 speak of "works" (ἐξ ἔργων, τῷ ἐργαζομένῳ). Ἔργα corresponds neatly to the same word in 3:27. Paul's comments in Rom 4 illumine and ground his comments in ch. 3. Paul builds on the tension internal to the law—between its requirements and its witness to faith—that he had introduced in ch. 3. Romans 3:31, a transitional verse, paved the way for the example of Abraham as an instance of the law's own testimony to the need for faith.[39] Many of the motifs in the early part of Rom 4 mirror the end of Rom 3. Paul continues the discussion of "justification" (δικαιοσύνη, 3:20–22, 24–26, 28, 30; 4:2–3, 5–6). This justification is likewise according to "grace" (χάρις, 3:24; 4:4, 16). The concept of faith hearkens back to what preceded (πιστεύω, 3:22, 26–27 [assuming the latter two do not refer to Christ's faithfulness]; 4:3, 5, 11–13, 16–17).[40] The matter of circumcision (or uncircumcision) recurs (3:20; 4:9–12). The christological dimension in 4:25 corresponds to 3:25–26. The concern about rendering the promise void in 4:14 parallels the law, which was in similar danger in 3:31. In 4:2 Paul returns to the idea of boasting, which the law of faith (as opposed to the law of works) had excluded in 3:27.[41] The argument of Rom 4 must therefore be seen as a development of the end of Rom 3.

The connection regarding "boasting" deserves elaboration since it affects Paul's line of thought regarding the law and works. The use of the definite article (ἡ καύχησις, 3:27) likely specifies this boasting as that referred to in Rom 2.[42] Boasting in 2:23 was defined as "in the law." Paul

---

[39] G. N. Davies (*Faith and Obedience*, 141) rightly disagrees with Abraham J. Malherbe ("*Me Genoito* in the Diatribe and Paul," in *Paul and the Popular Philosophers* [Minneapolis: Fortress, 1989], 30) for seeing Rom 3:31 as an exception to the μὴ γένοιτο pattern that Malherbe himself had identified. In this pattern, μὴ γένοιτο acts as a transitional device. See the independent discussion of this pattern in Rhyne (*Faith*, 30–59, esp. 58–59).

[40] Should one see πίστις as a reference to Christ's own faith or faithfulness, the argument would be significantly altered. The law would function as a witness not to the need for faith but rather to the faith(fulness) of Christ himself. For an analysis from this perspective, see especially Hays, " 'Have We Found Abraham to Be Our Forefather according to the Flesh?' A Reconsideration of Rom 4:1," *NovT* 27 (1985): 76–98.

[41] For a similar listing, see Thomas H. Tobin, "What Shall We Say That Abraham Found? The Controversy behind Romans 4," *HTR* 88 (1995): 442 n. 12. With respect to boasting, see especially Rhyne (*Faith*, 78) and Käsemann (*Commentary on Romans*, 106).

[42] Chae, *Paul As Apostle*, 167.

criticizes those who boast in their Jewish identity (2:17) and circumcision (2:25) as a people subject to the law. He asserts that the law provides no special advantage before God's judgment but rather forms the basis for God's strict judgment of the Jew alongside the Gentile according to works. Romans 3:9–18 then claims that "all" are under the power of sin. If *everyone* is sinful and lacking the deeds that God requires, then 3:27 may seem surprising. When Paul asks, "By what sort of law is boasting excluded?" surely it would be by the "[law] of works." A sinful people have failed to live up to its standards (3:9–18). But Paul does not draw this conclusion. Lambrecht and Thompson conclude that Paul is saying that the law *in theory* does not exclude boasting since one might possibly perfectly obey it. Thus it must be faith in Christ (3:21–26) that ultimately excludes boasting. They conclude that 3:27 follows 3:21–26 and not 1:18–3:20 for this reason.[43] While the key to the interpretation of 3:27 does lie in its placement after 3:21–26, Lambrecht and Thompson's conclusion does not necessarily follow. Although Paul suggested in Rom 2 that Jewish obedience to the law had been less than perfect (a point stated more explicitly in Rom 3), the lack of requisite obedience did not prevent the Jews from boasting in their Jewish heritage in ch. 2, so why should it in 3:27?[44] Boasting is excluded only when the Jew views the law from the perspective of faith. Then they see that the law itself never offered a valid boast, since it never saved (3:21–26). From that perspective the advantage of the Jew over the Gentile on the basis of mere possession of the law dissipates. God never justified on the basis of the law but rather on the basis of faith. Verse 28 thus serves very naturally as support for the conclusion in v. 27.[45] Modern scholarship has been right to high-

---

[43] Lambrecht and Thompson, *Justification by Faith,* 21–29; so also G. N. Davies, *Faith and Obedience,* 132–33. Despite Davies's further comments, his thesis seems to be the exact opposite of Rom 3:27: "For it is not the adoption of the νόμος of faith that excludes glorying; rather, it is the *failure* to adopt the νόμος of faith that excludes glorying" (my translation).

[44] Just because a boast does not measure up to reality does not in itself prevent one from boasting, even if the boast is misguided. Note especially Paul's question in 2:23 to the Jew who is boasting in the law—he asks if the Jew is *at the same time* dishonoring God with transgression. It is faith in Christ that changes the situation and illumines the true situation under the law; the law cannot save.

[45] Neil Elliot (*Rhetoric,* 214–15) misses the fact that 3:27 must follow 3:21–26 because it is only God's action *in Christ* that decisively shows the law's real inability to save and so eliminates the Jews' boast in the law. The Jew who adopts the perspective of this faith will find his/her prior boast excluded. Elliot does not adequately take into account the Jewish ethnic perspective throughout 3:27–30. The link to what is universally and impartially true will come in vv. 4–8 as Paul broadens his language to "works" in general. Because the Jewish law ulti-

light the ethnic implications of Paul's reasoning. That Rom 3:27–28 ought to be understood in light of the ethnic advantages of the Jews in Rom 2 is confirmed by v. 29. Paul rhetorically asks: "Is God the God of Jews only?" Paul J. Achtemeier summarizes the point:

> The point of the question is this: if it were not true that a person is made righteous by trust apart from works of the law, but rather one could be righteous by works of the law, then God would be the God of the Jews alone, since only Jews can perform the "works of the law." That Paul then expressly denies: God is indeed also the God of the gentiles.[46]

The traditional Reformation understanding of Romans mistakenly took justification by faith as the central point of this section and entirely ignored the question of the Gentiles and the Jewish law. Verse 28 shows how πίστις eliminates the boasting mentioned in v. 27. Verse 29 then tells what happens as a result of this elimination of the boast that arises out of the Jewish law: the division of humanity is dissolved and begins to reflect God's oneness (v. 30).[47] By asserting that the Gentiles are included in God's plan by faith apart from the law, Paul has departed from

---

mately is a merely human activity, the Jews' situation is no different from anyone else's and requires God's divine intervention. One sees in 4:2–8 how *no one* may boast apart from God's sovereign action, not even the Jew! In other words, one may grant that 3:27–30 remain focused on Jewish ethnocentrism in the law without jeopardizing Elliot's main point that God deals with both the Jews and the Gentiles impartially.

[46] "Unsearchable Judgments," 533. This point has been underscored by Richard W. Thompson, who shows how Paul's statements about justificaion are used to support the inclusion of the Gentiles; "The Inclusion of the Gentiles in Rom 3,27–30," *Bib* 69 (1988): 543–46.

[47] Further support for this reading is provided by Richard Hays's suggestion that vv. 29–30 may be punctuated differently: ἢ Ἰουδαίων ὁ θεὸς μόμον; οὐχὶ καὶ ἐθνῶν; ναὶ καὶ ἐθνῶν. εἴπερ εἷς ὁ θεὸς ὃς δικαιώσει περιτομὴν ἐκ πίστεως, καὶ ἀκροβυστίαν διὰ τῆς πίστεως. "Or is God the God of Jews only? Is he not the God of Gentiles also? Yes, of Gentiles also. If indeed God, who will justify the circumcised on the basis of faith, is one, he will also justify the uncircumcised through faith." Hays writes:

> Paul assumes without defense or fanfare that "God will justify the circumcised ἐκ πίστεως." Paul did not invent the doctrine of justification by faith. He could assume it as the common conviction of Jewish Christianity, as Gal 2:15–16 unmistakably shows. . . . There, as here, the thrust of Paul's argument is directed against Christians who confess themselves to be justified ἐκ πίστεως Χριστοῦ ("on the basis of Christ's faith") but who fail to draw what Paul sees as the logical corollary of this confession, that Gentiles need not come under the law in order to be justified. There lies the disputed issue ("Have We Found Abraham," 85).

On the tight connection between vv. 29–30 and what precedes, see Terence L. Donaldson's summary:

the Jewish point of view. The law is clearly in jeopardy of abrogation. It is one thing for the Jew to be justified by faith, but another for the Gentile to be justified by faith apart from the law. Rom 4 addresses this dilemma.

Romans 4 provides the testimony of the law itself to the primacy of faith for all humanity. Paul picks Abraham as an example of faith precisely because Abraham suits the need of his argument for a righteous *uncircumcised* believer. Abraham, prior to his circumcision, was justified by faith just as the Gentiles. If this is the case with the Jews' own "forefather according to the flesh" (4:1; understood along the lines of 3:29—is God the God only of the Jews?), then the Jews may no longer object to the Gentiles. A precedent was set long ago. The abrupt appearance of Abraham in the argument of Romans is no longer baffling. Paul's thinking revolves around the implications of justification by faith for the Gentiles and Jewish ethnocentrism. Rightly understood, the Genesis narratives speak of a right standing with God on the basis of faith prior to circumcision (4:10–11). Abraham's *faith* truly makes him "our forefather." He is the father of both the circumcised and the uncircumcised (4:10–18) and not just those whose identity is determined by possession of the Mosaic law (4:14: οἱ ἐκ νόμου; cf. v. 16).

Jewish ethnocentrism therefore forms the backdrop for Paul's discussion of Abraham in ch. 4 as well. Recent scholarship has understandably concluded that the problem with the Mosaic law is that it wrongly limited salvation to the Jews and fostered Jewish superiority and ethnic division. There is only one problem—Rom 4:4–8. Paul Achtemeier recognizes the problem posed by these verses: "It is I think one of the ironies of interpreting Romans that the passage that most clearly points to works of the law as a Jewish boundary marker is juxtaposed to the passage (4:4–5) that seems most clearly to point to works as human accomplishment about which one may boast."[48] Hays criticizes the traditional reading of 3:27–4:25 for ignoring the issue of Jewish ethnocentrism and yet all but ignores 4:4–8. He admits that vv. 4–8 speak of justification by faith as opposed to justification by works but is content merely to point

---

> [Verse 29] is tied to what precedes by means of the connective ἤ ["or"]. Verse 29a, then, introduces a new line of argumentation in service of the claim "a person is justified by faith apart from works of law" (v. 28). The premise implied by v. 29a is: (1) If justification is by works of law, God is the God of Jews only. Then the argument continues: but (2) God is God of Jews and Gentiles (since God is one); therefore (3) circumcised and uncircumcised alike will be justified on the basis of faith, and not works of law (*Paul and the Gentiles*, 82).

[48] Achtemeier, "Unsearchable Judgments," 533 n. 44.

out that this motif remains subsidiary to the larger issue of Jewish ethnocentrism in the surrounding context.[49] Likewise, Achtemeier dismisses the problem by simply reasserting that Paul is concerned with the issue of relying on one's own ethnic heritage in the passage. Since Rom 4:4–8 are embedded in a broader context that is addressing the matter of Jewish ethnic heritage as embodied in the law, the better question would be how vv. 4–8 function within that broader argument. Paul poses "works" as the antithetical opposite to "faith" in 4:4–5 in a section that immediately follows and echoes 3:27–30's contrast between the "law of faith" and the "law of works." How Paul understands "works" in 4:4–5 must therefore influence how one understands the "law of works."[50]

The role of Abraham in Jewish tradition must be considered in order to appreciate the significance of these verses. Abraham was the exemplar of the true Jew. The Jews saw him as a model of obedience to God. Abraham had kept the then-unwritten Mosaic law: "He kept the law of the Most High . . . and when he was tested he proved faithful" (Sir 44:20). *Second Baruch* 57:1–2 says that the unwritten law was available in the time of Abraham and that he fulfilled its works. The book of *Jubilees* develops Abraham's obedience to the law at length. *Jubilees* 23:10 says that Abraham kept the law even before it was written. In *Jub.* 11–12 Abraham breaks with pagan idolatry and leaves for Canaan. Abraham thus warns Isaac against the deeds of the children of men. Isaac must avoid walking in their ways since there is no righteousness with them (*Jub.* 21:21–22). In *Jub.* 6:19; 14:1–2, 20; 15:1–2; 22:1–12, Abraham participates in the Feast of Weeks. In *Jub.* 16:20–31 Abraham participates in the Feast of Booths. Mattathias in 1 Macc 2:52 reminds his sons: "Was not Abraham found faithful [εὑρέθη πιστός] when tested [i.e., his willingness to sacrifice Isaac in Gen 22], and it was reckoned [ἐλογίσθη] to him as righteousness [εἰς δικαιοσύνην]?" Judith 8:25–27 reminds the Israelites how God tested Abraham's heart. For his faithfulness and

---

[49] Hays, "Have We Found Abraham," 89, 92–93.

[50] Barclay (*Obeying the Truth,* 246) rightly recognizes how the traditional interpretation of Romans took Rom 4:4–5 as the key to Paul's entire critique of the law and failed to recognize that the issue had been with *Jewish* works and not works in general. Barclay, however, sides with the "new perspective" position of Dunn and Sanders and sees Rom 4:4–5 (along with 4:16–17) as "some subsidiary generalized comments about 'faith as such' and 'works as such.'" Paul is showing that the "absence or insufficiency of works underlines human inadequacy" (p. 247). The problem with Barclay's view is that he has marginalized Rom 4:4–5 and severed it from its context. As demonstrated above, this section of Romans is closely tied to the preceding argument. Paul is here demonstrating *another,* related reason why the Jewish law and its works are inadequate.

willingness to sacrifice Isaac, Abraham becomes a model for martyrdom in 4 Macc 16:19–20. Abraham is often said to have been *perfect* in his observance of the law: "Abraham was perfect in all of his actions with the LORD and was pleasing through righteousness all of the days of his life" (*Jub.* 23:10). "And all of the nations of the earth will bless themselves by your seed *because your father obeyed me and observed my restrictions and my commandments and my laws and my ordinances and my covenant.* And now, obey my voice, and dwell in this land" (*Jub.* 24:11). "Abraham . . . was counted as a friend for keeping God's precepts and not following the desire of his spirit" (CD 3.2–3). "You, therefore, O Lord, God of the righteous, did not appoint grace for the righteous, such as Abraham, Isaac, and Jacob, those who did not sin against you" (*Pr. Man.* 8). In *T. Ab.* 10:13 a voice comes down from heaven attesting that up to that point "Abraham has not sinned."[51] *Mishnah Qiddushin* 4:14 says: "And we find that Abraham our father *had performed the whole Law* before it was given." A consistent motif, then, in Jewish treatments of Abraham was his perfect or nearly perfect obedience to God's law.[52]

Although Jews looked to Abraham as a model of faithful (πιστός) and law-abiding conduct, Paul denies any significance to Abraham's faithfulness. He interprets "faith" (πίστις) in terms of belief (or trust) apart from human activity (ἔργον, ἐργάζομαι).[53] After repeatedly asserting justification apart from works in Rom 3:21–31 and 4:2, Paul says in 4:4–5: "Now to one who works, wages are not reckoned as a gift but as something due." Paul here defines "works" *not* in terms of Jewish ethnic identity or nationalism but rather in the broader framework of human activity: this is a "work" in order to merit wages and reward as opposed to God's free grace (cf. 3:24, δωρεάν). As Westerholm writes (in his critique of Dunn): "Since the issue ('works of law' *versus* 'faith in Jesus Christ') permits restatement in terms of a general distinction between

---

[51] See also Wis 10:5. Nevertheless, *Gen. Rab.* 60:2 says that Abraham did occasionally fall short.

[52] Francis Watson restricts his analysis to texts emphasizing Abraham's separation from the Gentiles (e.g., *Jubilees*); *Paul, Judaism and the Gentiles,* 137. However, Abraham's exemplary obedience is stressed at least as much as his separation from the Gentiles. Further, it was *because* Abraham was obedient to God that he had to separate from Gentiles involved in idolatry and sin. Ethnic separation is subordinate to one's overall obedience of God. Nor does the data permit, with Cranford, a limiting or subordinating of Abraham's obedience to those aspects of the law that marked his distinctiveness; "Abraham in Romans 4," 76–77. See ch. 1 on this point.

[53] For a similar analysis of Gal 3 in relation to the faith/faithfulness of Abraham, see In-Gyu Hong, "Does Paul Misrepresent the Jewish Law? Law and Covenant in Gal. 3:1–14," *NovT* 36 (1994): 165–73.

'works' and 'faith,' the point of the attack cannot be limited to statutes in the law which served as Jewish 'identity markers.'"[54] The same problem emerges in Rom 3:20, where Paul says that by the "works (ἔργα) of the law" no one will be justified; the law merely provides the knowledge of sin. In this verse Paul means far more than merely Jewish markers of identity. Glenn Davies writes: "It is not merely circumcision and laws pertaining to ethnic exclusivity which bring knowledge of sin, but all the demands of God as they are embodied in the law (cf. 7.8). Obedience to the law is that which is denied any causal relationship to justification, not mere badges of national righteousness."[55] For Davies, the use of νόμος in v. 20, in relation to the knowledge of sin, helps define νόμος in the phrase ἐξ ἔργων νόμου. As the second part of the verse involves far more than the ethnic aspects of the law, so also does the first part.[56] The entire verse remains focused on the matter of *doing* what the law requires. If this understanding of 3:20 is correct, the verse would correspond to Paul's point in Rom 4 on "works." God's justifying activity is entirely apart from any human activity or achievement. As Achtemeier and Hays show, this conclusion cannot be avoided, but some have tried.

Sanders tries to avoid this conclusion by noting that Paul does not actually identify the Mosaic law in Rom 4:4. The problem with this argument is that the "works" of 4:2, 4, 6 are placed in an antithetical relationship to righteousness by faith, even as the "works of the law" had stood in the same relation in Rom 3:21–26, 28. Paul is continuing his critique of "works." Paul uses the term (ἔργα) without νόμος because he wants to generalize at this point to human versus divine activity ("works" versus grace). Paul's general principle regarding "works" and grace will impact how "works of the law," a subcategory, should be taken.[57] Dunn suggests that Paul employs the commercial language of "wages" and "work" in 4:4–5 in order to clarify what God's "reckoning" (λογίζομαι) is *not;* God's reckoning of faith for righteousness is not what one would expect on the basis of a business transaction, as λογίζομαι might initially

---

[54] Westerholm, *Israel's Law and the Church's Faith,* 119.

[55] G. N. Davies, *Faith and Obedience,* 118.

[56] The ethnic dimension, though, is never far from Paul's mind, as 3:29 shows (and 3:19, with ἐν τῷ νόμῳ). The proximity of 3:19 shows that the ethnic and legal elements are inextricably interwoven throughout Paul's argument. The import of this connection will be made clear in a moment.

[57] At the other extreme is the position of Reinhold Liebers, who thinks that the "works" of 4:4–5 refer specifically to the Mosaic law's "works"; *Das Gesetz als Evangelium: Untersuchungen zur Gesetzeskritik des Paulus* (ATANT 75; Zürich: Theologischer, 1989), 31–40, 71–73. By failing to take seriously Paul's avoidance of the term νόμος, Liebers misses the more generalized sense of the argument.

suggest.[58] But even if Paul were using commercial language, God's reckoning of faith for righteousness would still be a matter of grace/faith apart from human effort.[59] Advancing Dunn's research, Michael Cranford thinks that Abraham's "work" in 4:4–5 should be understood as the patriarch's circumcision (4:9). Cranford concludes that Paul would not be talking about "mere human effort."[60] A shortcoming of Cranford's

---

[58] Dunn, "Yet Once More," 112; idem, *Romans 1–8,* 203, against C. E. B. Cranfield, " 'The Works of the Law' in the Epistle to the Romans," *JSNT* 43 (1991): 96–97. Thomas R. Schreiner objects:

> Even if Dunn is correct regarding the reason for the illustration, he hardly goes far enough. Why does Paul think it is necessary to explain that *reckon* is different in divine-human relations? This is not merely a point of scholarly interest to his readers. More likely he makes the point because some might mistakenly think that one's status with God is reckoned on a commercial basis, that is, on the basis of works (*The Law and Its Fulfillment,* 100).

Cf. Cranfield, *Romans,* 1:231–32.

[59] Further, Dunn ignores the tension in Judaism between God's grace to those within the covenant and his strict judgment according to deeds. Cranford, building on the work of Dunn, writes:

> However God reckoned Abraham righteous, it was not in the same fashion that a worker is reckoned his pay at the end of the day. Paul draws on the workman imagery for the specific purpose of explaining the term λογίζεσθαι, not the term ἔργα, as traditional interpreters typically assume. "Working" is an accidental aspect of the analogy, and therefore does not form the basis for Paul's inclusion of the metaphor in his argument ("Abraham in Romans 4," 80).

Nevertheless, vv. 4–5 do in fact contrast a reckoning according to "works" (ἐξ ἔργων), "working" (ἐργάζομαι), or "according to debt" (κατὰ ὀφείλημα), and a reckoning "according to grace" (κατὰ χάριν) by "faith" (ἡ πίστις). The same antithesis recurs repeatedly throughout this section of Romans (for example, 3:20–22, 27; 4:4–5). The antithesis is hardly "accidental." Achtemeier and Hays are more candid about the difficulties of these two verses for a thoroughly ethnic reading of Paul's argument.

Cranford continues:

> Verse 4 suggests a works analogy well enough, but we would expect v. 5 to balance the analogy by stating something like, "but to the one who does not work and yet receives a payment, his reward is according to grace and not because of his own effort." This parallelism never occurs, however, though traditional commentators assume it as if it was clearly expressed ("Abraham in Romans 4," 81).

But this sort of parallelism *is* present. The image of "one who works" (τῷ ἐργαζομένῳ) is clearly contrasted with "one who does not work" (τῷ μὴ ἐργαζομένῳ). The contrast between "grace" (κατὰ χάριν) and "debt" (κατὰ ὀφείλημα) is already clear in v. 4 and need not be restated. Already Paul is preparing for the re-inclusion of Israel in Rom 9–11: salvation does not depend upon anyone wanting it or running hard after it, but upon God.

[60] "Abraham in Romans 4," 81.

analysis is that he must read the text backward from v. 9, rather than forward from vv. 4–5.[61]

Paul's handling of Abraham contrasts sharply with the patriarch's description in Jewish literature. Where the Jews saw Abraham as having been rewarded for his obedience, Paul disagrees and says in 4:4–5 that God reckons on the basis of grace/faith and not obligation.[62] Paul emphasizes Abraham's believing apart from his works/accomplishments.[63] The verses that follow strongly imply that Abraham was, in fact, "ungodly." Abraham's God is described in v. 5 as one who "justifies the ungodly" (τὸν ἀσεβῆ). This implies that when he received the promise and believed, Abraham was "ungodly."[64] The psalm Paul cites in Rom 4:7–8 speaks of the sinner whose sins are covered and are not reckoned but forgiven. Paul applies the psalmist's language to "those to whom God reckons righteousness apart from works" (v. 6).[65] In vv. 9–10 Paul ap-

---

[61] Cranford ("Abraham in Romans 4," 83) admits that the ethnic dimension of Paul's argument is "somewhat obscured in the metaphors and citations of 4.4–8" but then "made clear in v. 9." It would make better sense to see it reemerging in v. 9 but absent per se in vv. 4–8. Verse 9's οὖν marks a new stage in the discussion. The advantage of the reading offered in this chapter is that it integrates the plain meaning of the text (an antithesis in vv. 4–5 between grace and human activity) into the surrounding logic of Paul's inclusion of the Gentiles in spite of the Mosaic law. Verses 9–10 do begin to narrow Paul's discussion of human effort in general in vv. 4–5 to those aspects of the law that distinguish the Jews. If the law has been relegated to a human activity and performance, then the same would apply to those aspects of the law that had marked the Jews as a distinct people from the Gentiles; hence, God can include the Gentiles in his salvation apart from membership in ethnic Israel under the law. This takes the logic of vv. 4–5 forward to vv. 9–10, rather than backward as Cranford prefers; "Abraham in Romans 4," 83.

[62] Contra Dunn. Given this tradition of interpretation in Judaism, Paul's clarification in vv. 4–5 may have been absolutely necessary.

[63] Consequently, the Jew who relies on the law would be relying on his own faithful accomplishments.

[64] Anthony Tyrrell Hanson, "Abraham the Justified Sinner," in *Studies in Paul's Technique and Theology* (London: SPCK, 1974), 53.

[65] Cranford ("Abraham in Romans 4," 83) claims, following Howard, that the antithesis of faith and works does not occur in vv. 6–8. Paul is instead "concerned with forgiveness apart from ethnic Israel." However, nothing in vv. 6–8 points to membership in ethnic Israel. The ethnic dimension will resume in v. 9. Nor should one expect the faith-works antithesis to continue in vv. 6–8. The point had already been satisfactorily made in vv. 4–5, which closed with faith being reckoned to "the ungodly." This mention of the "ungodly" paves the way for the Davidic citation, with its mention of "lawlessness" and "sinfulness." Paul's logic in moving from vv. 4–5 to vv. 6–8 is essentially that God does not reckon according to works since, left to one's own, there would be only "impiety" (ἀσεβῆ), "lawlessness" (ἀνομίαι), and "sinfulness" (ἁμαρτίαι).

plies the language of the psalm to *Abraham*. The implication is that Abraham is one whose sins have been forgiven and not reckoned to him.[66] The psalm speaks of sins of a moral nature, and its citation implies that Abraham may have been guilty of such sins as well.[67] The many parallels between Rom 4 and Ps 32 suggest that Abraham ought to be understood in terms of the psalm.[68] If this understanding is correct, then even "faithful Abraham" was not faithful enough (cf. Gal 3:10 and

---

[66] Hanson, "Abraham the Justified Sinner," 53. Verses 4–9a are sandwiched between references to Abraham and his faith in vv. 2 and 9b. Paul's language is general in vv. 4–9a. "His" faith in 4:5 is not properly Abraham's but "the ungodly person's"; Chae, *Paul As Apostle*, 184–85. Nevertheless, Paul boldly gives the impression that Abraham is ἀσεβής. Paul emphasizes that Abraham's faith was reckoned to him for righteousness, suggesting that Abraham was credited with a righteousness that he himself did not actually possess. This understanding of Abraham would definitely advance Paul's argument: "Gentiles, who have neither their own actual righteousness nor covenant-righteousness, *can be* and *are to be nevertheless counted as righteous* when they exercise the faith which Abraham had while he was in uncircumcision"; Chae, *Paul As Apostle*, 185 (with Dodd).

[67] As Cranfield ("The Works of the Law," 97) emphasizes, this is a further problem for Dunn's position. The psalm quote indicates that Paul has in mind more general failures at this point, inclusive of morality. In v. 5 the author of Ps 32 (presumed to be David) confesses his sin to the Lord. This confession forms the context for the verses Paul quotes (Ps 32:1–2). One need only consider the sins that David confessed: sins of adultery with Bathsheba and murder of her husband.

Cranford ("Abraham in Romans 4," 82) and Liebers (*Das Gesetz als Evangelium*, 32–33) force the data into a preconceived mold of Jewish ethnocentrism when they equate Abraham's "ungodliness" with uncircumcision. Cranford contends that αἱ ἀνομίαι ("lawless deeds") and αἱ ἁμαρτίαι ("sins") are terms "typically associated with Gentiles" and approvingly quotes Dunn (*Romans 1–8*, 206) that ἀνομία and ἁμαρτωλός indicate actions "outside the covenant." What Cranford (and Dunn) ignore is that these terms can also be used in reference to "sinfulness" in general and could characterize a Jew (as is clear when Ps 32 uses such terminology for the author himself). Cranford ("Abraham in Romans 4," 82) follows Dunn (*Romans 1–8*, 204–5) in interpreting the word τὸν ἀσεβῆ in Rom 4:5 as a reference to those "excluded from the covenant," "Gentiles." But Paul's condemnation of ἀσέβεια in Rom 1:18–32 included the Jews (see esp. Rom 1:23 and the discussion in ch. 7). The list of sins at the end of Rom 1 includes several of a more generally *moral* nature that would include both Jews and Gentiles. Romans 11:26 cites the Old Testament to the effect that God would remove ἀσεβείας ἀπὸ Ἰακώβ (from Jacob)! In other words, Paul can use this language for Israel as well as the Gentiles. The use of ἀσέβεια should therefore be taken as a general indictment of sin that could apply to both Gentiles and Jews.

[68] Hanson, "Abraham the Justified Sinner," 55–56. ἀσεβής in v. 5 is a rare word in Paul but may be occasioned by Ps 32:5 in the LXX. Verse 3 says "my body wasted away," cf. Rom 4:19. In Ps 32:10 "steadfast love surrounds those who trust in the LORD"; cf. Rom 4:18.

the requirement of perfect obedience). God therefore justifies *apart* from human activity or faithfulness.

Scholarship has a long history of thinking in terms of "either/or." Either Paul's problem with the law concerns its preoccupation with Jewish ethnic identity, or the problem is with the law as a human accomplishment. While Rom 4:4–5 clearly emphasize that the problem with "works" is that they remain human accomplishments, Rom 3:28–29 and 4:9–15 speak of the inclusion of the Gentiles vis-à-vis the Jewish law. Schreiner writes: "Jewish nationalism and exclusivism cannot be neatly separated from Jewish obedience to the law. Jewish nationalism was intimately and inextricably tied up with devotion to Torah."[69] The real question, according to Hays and others, is the relationship of vv. 4–5 to the surrounding verses that speak of the relationship of Gentiles to the law.[70] Thus, to my way of thinking, the point of vv. 4–5 would be that God saves by his free grace through faith rather than by works which are based on human accomplishment. Thus, the Mosaic law must be excluded from God's justifying activity since it is based on the Jews' accomplishment and merit. If the Mosaic law is excluded, then the Gentiles are no longer excluded by that law from God's saving plan (since the law had divided the Jews from the Gentiles by the works that it demanded of the Jews). If my reading is correct, vv. 4–5 provide a supporting argument for the inclusion of the Gentiles in God's salvation.[71]

---

[69] T. R. Schreiner, *The Law and Its Fulfillment,* 102; so also Silva, "The Law and Christianity," 351–53.

[70] N. T. Wright, for example, says that "Paul's critique of 'works' . . . functions *within* his critique of 'national righteousness'" (as quoted from his unpublished dissertation by B. W. Longenecker, *Eschatology and Covenant,* 212).

[71] Paul favors ἔργον cognates in 4:1–8 and avoids the term νόμος. This discussion of works in general then forms the basis for Paul's conclusions in 4:9 (οὖν) with regard to circumcision, i.e., the implications for ethnocentrism; Thomas R. Schreiner, *Romans* (Baker Exegetical Commentary on the New Testament; Grand Rapids: Baker, 1998), 218.

Romans 3:27–4:12 offer support for the Gentile mission with the Torah as a key step in the reasoning; contra Donaldson, *Paul and the Gentiles,* 173–84. An elimination of any *soteriological* advantage for ethnic Judaism in and of itself does not mean that there are not other significant (even potentially *saving*) advantages for the Jews so long as one finds the key to those advantages *in Christ.* In other words, in Donaldson's words " 'Not Torah' does not imply 'not Israel, and therefore no distinction' " (p. 184). But "not Torah" means no automatic path to salvation for ethnic Jews apart from Christ and, consequently, no exclusion of the Gentiles apart from the Torah. Also, Donaldson needs to distinguish the Torah's demand from the Torah as a potential alternative path to salvation inclusive of God's election and covenant.

The Mosaic law, which had previously divided humanity, is fundamentally a human endeavor with no saving significance. The example of Abraham shows that if God can justify him as a sinner apart from works by faith, surely God can justify the uncircumcised, Gentile sinner on the basis of the same faith.[72]

The denial of any saving significance to the law is grounded in Paul's Christology. One of Dunn's students, Bruce Longenecker, offers a similar appraisal of Paul's logic in Rom 3:27–4:8:

> As we have seen, *4 Ezra* demonstrates that, when God's grace is removed from ethnocentric definitions of the covenant, ethnocentrism is replaced by legalism. The same would be true of Paul's charge in Rom 4.1–5, following on from 3.21–31 where he demonstrated that God's grace is upon the christocentric community, not upon the ethnic group of the Jews *per se.* Outside the christian community of faith, any "pursuers" (9.31) of righteousness are simply spinning their wheels, acting on their own accord, to no avail. . . . Outside the christian community the Jew who thinks himself to respond to God's grace by his nomistic practice is, in Paul's eyes, attempting to earn salvation through works, thereby cutting himself off from God's promise to establish for/through Abraham a worldwide family by means of faith.[73]

The law is not God's provision for sin. Paul had discovered that in Christ. If the sacrifices and atonement of the law are of no avail in and of themselves as a means of grace, then the law is reduced to the realm of human achievement and doing.[74] If even faithful Abraham and David

---

[72] This removal of human activity from the realm of God's saving action is crucial to Paul's argument. If all people are under sin (3:19–20), such sin and failure, particularly on the part of Israel, might place God's promises in jeopardy. But God's faithfulness to his promises far surpasses human failure and unfaithfulness. As Elliot writes:

> When Paul asks whether Abraham is "our forefather according to the flesh", he is taking up again the theme in 3.1–8 and 3.21–26 of God's unswerving loyalty to the divine purposes. Again and again that theme has involved affirming God's sovereignty against possible compromise through human sinfulness. . . . By showing that the promise to Abraham was not made dependent on Abraham's prior performance, Paul safeguards the promise to Israel and to the Gentiles alike (*Rhetoric,* 220).

Since God's saving action does not rest on human activity or performance but on God's own faithfulness to the promises, the Jews may be saved in spite of their sinfulness, and God can include the Gentiles in salvation without compromising Israel's priority.

[73] B. W. Longenecker, *Eschatology and Covenant,* 213–14.

[74] Even as Paul's critique of the law has a twofold dimension, so also does the law itself. It was never enough in Judaism to be born a Jew or to boast in one's

fell short of the law's demands, how much more would the rest of the Jews fall short, let alone the Gentiles? That is the essence of Paul's critique in Rom 4:2–8. Paul can speak of the law as a mere human work and achievement only because the law has already been emptied of any saving significance in 3:21–26.[75] Because of human sin and unfaithfulness, God acts in Christ to save both Jew and Gentile.

III. Conclusion

Romans 3:27–31 again delves into the Mosaic law. Paul treats the law from two very different perspectives: from the perspective of the works that it requires, and from the perspective of faith. Paul's discussion of the faith of Abraham in Rom 4 helps explicate the law from the perspective of faith in 3:27. Paul's discussion in 4:4–5 of "works" and "wages"/"reward" elaborates on "[the law] of works." Romans 4:4–5 show that Paul has in mind more than just those aspects of the law that divide the Jew from the Gentile but the very performance of the law as a whole. The law involves a demand. One must labor under it in order to receive its "wages" and "reward." Yet even Abraham and David, as exemplars of Judaism, did not attain the law's ideal. God must justify the ungodly apart from the law. And if that is the case, then the path is open for the salvation of the ungodly Gentile. For Paul, God's law had pointed to the necessity of faith all along, a faith that now finds its fulfillment in Jesus Christ. While Rom 3:28–29 do highlight Jewish ethnocentrism

---

possession of the law. One also had to live as a Jew, which entailed doing all that the law required. On the necessity of doing what the law required, see chs. 1 and 2. The Jews therefore claimed to possess a superior morality (see, for instance, Wis 14:12–31; *T. Naph.* 3:3–4:1; as well as the discussion in ch. 9).

[75] See chs. 3–5 on the failure of election, covenant, and sacrifice to offer God's saving mercy or grace to the Jewish people. God's saving action in Christ (vv. 21–26) should make clear that the law cannot (and did not) save. The law's activities are therefore human "works" and nothing more, even as vv. 4–5 maintain. They can be placed in opposition to God's grace in a way few Jews would recognize simply because of Paul's *Christology.* A law that does not avail and attest to the Jew's right relationship with God is already itself a law few Jews would recognize. Once the law is relegated to the realm of mere human activity, Paul can turn to the ethnic components; thus v. 9. Circumcision is therefore not the basis for God's blessing. Seen in the light of what precedes, it becomes a mere human action that cannot save. In fact, v. 11 will complete the circle back to 3:21–22. Circumcision is actually a sign of righteousness through faith. Paul will then particularize this faith in 4:24–25.

(the one God is the God of *all*), Rom 4:4–5 highlight *another* problem: apart from the plan of God, the works the law prescribes are a matter of merely human effort. Paul's critique is two-sided. Traditional interpreters neglected the ethnic dimension to Paul's argument, while more recent interpreters neglect the critique of law-observance as merely human achievement. Yet human achievement is what is left of the law when grace has been shown to be in Christ and not the law (Rom 3:21–26).[76]

---

[76] Is such a move on Paul's part comprehensible in the context of Judaism? Too much recent Pauline scholarship has emphasized the law as the boundary marker of an elect people to the exclusion of God's strict judgment according to people's works. When the grace of the system is questioned, the other side of the equation comes into play: a strict judgment according to works. The law becomes a matter of human performance to be evaluated at the judgment according to God's strict standards. Again, one finds an emphasis on the necessity of rigorous obedience in Philo, Qumran, and *Jubilees*. See chs. 1 and 2, especially the various carefully balanced formulations in intertestamental literature such as Sir 16:11–12. The positions taken in post-70 C.E. literature independently bear witness to what happens when the framework collapses and the balance shifts toward a judgment according to works.

Chapter Nine

Life under the Law according to Philippians 3:2–9 and Romans 7

Philippians 3:2–9 occupy a pivotal place in any understanding of Paul and the law and almost inevitably raise questions about Rom 7. The two passages are often treated side by side since they both include potentially autobiographical material, and yet they offer apparently contradictory conclusions regarding human potential to obey the law. Whereas "blameless" law-observance is a viable possibility according to the Philippians passage, in Rom 7 Paul describes an agonizing struggle to do what the law requires. What role would these two seemingly contradictory passages play in a schema where Paul sees doing the Mosaic law as difficult, if not virtually impossible?

I. Philippians 3:2–9

If Paul thinks that there is a "plight" involved for those who would live according to the law (as I have maintained in the last three chapters), how could he have considered himself "blameless" with respect to the righteousness of the law in Phil 3:6? Since Paul judges his previous law-observance blameless, doing the law must not be all that problematic. Paul certainly does not indicate that he had felt any anxiety about his own fulfillment of the law.[1] He even considers his achievement in the law a matter of

[1] Paul Achtemeier writes: "Paul was quite sure that the law could be fulfilled. He surely implies that he had done just that as a Pharisee" (*Romans*, 127). Or with Peter T. O'Brien: "Clearly this is no pessimistic self-portrait or recollection of one tortured by an unattainable ideal, a conclusion that has often been

boast. Recent Pauline interpreters have concluded from Phil 3:2–9 that Paul did not consider perfect obedience of the law impossible.

One can be considered "righteous" even while not perfectly doing doing all that the law requires. Sanders tracks the term *righteousness* throughout intertestamental and Tannaitic literature in *Paul and Palestinian Judaism.* According to Sanders, the biblical commandments "are nevertheless difficult or even impossible fully to obey."[2] With respect to the Tannaim, Sanders writes: "Although the term 'righteous' is primarily applied to those who obey the Torah, the Rabbis knew full well that even the righteous did not obey God's law perfectly."[3] "Human perfection was not considered realistically achievable by the Rabbis."[4] The Sipra relates the incident in the Hebrew Scriptures of Nadab and Abihu as an example of human imperfection. Nadab and Abihu were killed by fire for an unholy offering of fire before the Lord, and yet they were not exposed or humiliated in death.[5] The Sipra comments: "how much the more so [will God show pity to] *other righteous persons*!" (emphasis mine). Abihu and Nadab were considered among the righteous even though their sin warranted punishment by death. "Righteousness" for a Jew never meant that one had been sinless and had perfectly done all that God commanded in the law. The "righteous" are those who attempt to obey the law in its entirety and who seek atonement for sin or failure.[6]

---

drawn from Rom. 7. Here is a man well satisfied, reminiscent of the rich young ruler in the Gospel story (Lk. 18:21) who claims to have kept all the commandments from his youth" (*Commentary on Philippians* [NIGTC; Grand Rapids: Eerdmans, 1991], 379). Likewise Ben Witherington III, *Friendship and Finances in Philippi: The Letter of Paul to the Philippians* (New Testament in Context; Valley Forge, Pa.: Trinity Press International, 1994), 92.

Nothing in the text indicates that Phil 3:6 is to be limited to Paul's "pre-Christian evaluation of himself." He is writing from a Christian vantage point in his life. He considers his former observance of the law to be σκύβαλα (v. 8); thus Don B. Garlington, *Faith, Obedience and Perseverance: Aspects of Paul's Letter to the Romans* (WUNT 79; Tübingen: J.C.B. Mohr [Paul Siebeck], 1994), 140–41. And yet nowhere does Paul, from his Christian standpoint, qualify his boasts; contra T. R. Schreiner, "Paul and Perfect Obedience," 262.

[2] Sanders, *Paul and Palestinian Judaism,* 115; see also p. 137. Moore writes: "He [God] did not expect an impossible perfection of creatures in whom he himself implanted the 'evil impulse,' and therefore, in foresight of their failure, provided repentance as the remedy for their shortcomings" (*Judaism,* 2:94).

[3] Sanders, *Paul and Palestinian Judaism,* 203.

[4] Ibid., 137.

[5] Shemini Mekhilta deMiluim 22–27 (on Lev 10:1–5; Neusner, *Sifra,* 2:130–32).

[6] As Sanders puts its: "the *righteous are those who obey the Torah and atone for transgression*" (*Paul and Palestinian Judaism,* 204). Or with Moore: "Righ-

The ultimate criterion is faithfulness to the covenant relationship. As Sanders summarizes the views of the Qumran sect: "from the point of view of the halakah, one is required to walk perfectly. From the point of view of the individual in prayer or devotional moments, he is unable to walk perfectly and must be given perfection of way by God's grace." To walk perfectly is never to transgress (1QS 3.9–11). According to 1QH[a] 12 (= 4).29–32, no one is "righteous" or follows the "perfect path." Such "righteousness" belongs only to God. But God graciously confers a divine "righteousness" on community members. In 1QH[a] 19 (=11).29–32 God's "righteousness" purifies sinful people and proffers mercy. In 1QS 11.12 the sinner finds salvation by God's own righteousness. Because of God's conferral of righteousness and mercy, the community member can be called "righteous."[7] The Qumran hymns continually implore God for the forgiveness of sins even while the author strives toward a perfection that is impossible for people on their own. Philo offers the same understanding:

> Having performed all this religiously, he ordered a calf and two rams to be brought. The calf he purposed to offer to gain remission of sins, showing by this figure that *sin is congenital to every created being,* even the best, just because they are created, and this sin requires prayers and sacrifices to propitiate the Deity, lest His wrath be roused and visited upon them (*Mos.* 2.147; emphasis mine).[8]

Philo judges sacrifices and prayer as necessary to propitiate God for one's sins in order to maintain a right relationship with the Lord.

The term *blameless* functions in a similar manner. For example, 2 Chr 15:17 describes Asa as "blameless," only to be followed with a catalogue of his sins in 2 Chr 16. Zechariah and Elizabeth are "blameless" in Luke 1:6, and yet Zechariah is rebuked in 1:18–20 for his unbelief. Job is "blameless" but still struggles with sin (Job 1:8; 2:3; 33:9; cf. 15:14, 15; 22:3).[9] Christians are to be "blameless," according to 1 Thess 3:13, 5:23,

---

teousness, in the conception of it which Judaism got from the Scriptures, had no suggestion of sinless perfection. Nor are the sins of the righteous all venial; the gravest moral lapses may befall them, as they did David. What distinguishes the righteous man who has fallen into sin is his repentance" (*Judaism,* 1:494–95).

[7] Thus Sanders, *Paul and Palestinian Judaism,* 305–12. He concludes from the data: "On the one hand, there is the sense of human inadequacy before God . . . ; no one can be righteous or perfect before God; no one, on his own, has 'righteous deeds'. On the other hand, there is the consciousness of being elect; thus some are righteous *(tsaddiq, yitsdaq),* but only by the grace of God" (pp. 311–12).

[8] See also *Fug.* 158.

[9] Job's "blamelessness" is affirmed at various points in the book (1:8; 2:3; 33:9; 34:6). Elihu challenges Job's claim to be blameless. Eliphaz points out in

and 1 Cor 1:8.[10] "Blameless" can describe Christians at the judgment (1 Thess 3:13) or in the present (1 Thess 2:10, and Paul's own activity among the Thessalonians). In Phil 2:15 Paul admonishes the Christians at Philippi to strive to be blameless and pure. While Paul urges Christians to be blameless, he never once intimates that Christians are completely free from sin.[11] "Blameless" is a *cultic* term.[12] Paul admonishes the Philippians to be "blameless" and "without blemish" while he describes himself as a libation being poured over the sacrifice and offering of their faith (Phil 2:14–17).

From the narrow point of view of God's commands, no one is able to do perfectly what the law requires. From the broader perspective inclusive of God's election and mercy, one can be blameless and righteous before God. A "blameless" Jew is one who attempts to avoid sin and takes advantage of repentance and the sacrificial system for failure. Sanders concludes from the availability of sacrifices and atonement that perfect achievement of the law is not required.[13] A Jew need only remain

---

15:14–16 that *no one* is righteous. He questions Job's status in 22:3. Bildad asks in 25:4 how an individual can be righteous before God and how one born of woman can be pure. Even Job asks at one point whether what is pure can come from what is impure (14:1, 4). God's speech at the end does not deny that all people are sinful, as the friends of Job repeatedly claim, but neither does God condemn Job as a sinner (as the friends do). Scholars have questioned whether Job remains blameless throughout the book. If so, the apparent conflict with the statements of his friends may find resolution in the same manner as Paul's statements in Phil 3. Blamelessness before God may not be the same as sinlessness, since blamelessness depends on a right *relationship* with God.

[10] Sanders, *Paul, the Law,* 23.

[11] Romans 3:19–20; 5:12 and the entirety of Rom 7 all directly state or presuppose human sinfulness; with Sanders, *Paul, the Law,* 23–24. Sin remains a power in this age, as Rom 5–7 makes clear. Until the eschaton Christians must still struggle against sin with the power of the Spirit (Rom 8:1–10).

[12] Michael Newton emphasizes this point. "Blamelessness" allows one to stand before God in cultic worship; *The Concept of Purity at Qumran and in the Letters of Paul* (SNTSMS 53; Cambridge: Cambridge University Press, 1985), 74, 84–86. In Ps 101:6: "whoever walks in the way that is blameless shall minister to me." So also Sanders, who places it in the context of Christian sanctification and cultic holiness before God; *Paul and Palestinian Judaism,* 450–53, 470–72, 493–95; idem, *Paul, the Law,* 63 n. 138.

[13] Sanders cites the talmudic baraita that even the patriarchs could not stand God's reproof if he judged strictly (*b.* ʿ*Arak.* 17a, top; Sanders, *Paul and Palestinian Judaism,* 203). If God judged strictly, no one would live; ibid., 181, 203–4. Moore writes: "With the multitudinous and minute regulations of the laws, it was inevitable that they should often be infringed in ignorance, or mistake, or pure accident. For such cases the law itself creates a special category of sins committed 'unwittingly' (בשגגה), or through inadvertence" (*Judaism,*

faithful to the covenant. Sanders confuses the entire system, inclusive of mercy and sacrifice, with the command to do everything that God has commanded.[14] Perfect obedience of the law is indeed enjoined in Jewish literature of the period even while embedded within a system of grace and atonement.[15] Individuals are evaluated in this literature either from the vantage point of the entire system (hence blamelessness) or from the vantage point of the law's strict demand (where sin and failure is a commonplace).[16]

Paul reflects the same tension in his writings: he can call himself blameless with respect to the righteousness of the law and yet affirm that all people are sinners. What Sanders has to say on this matter cannot be stressed enough: "It would be hazardous to suppose that Paul must have held one position as his true view, while using the other only for the sake of argument. He could quite easily have held both, without ever playing them off against each other so that he became aware that they are mutually exclusive."[17] Rabbi Eliezer (*b. Sanh.* 101a) asserted that "there is none that is righteous" and on another occasion was surprised that he

---

1:463). While freedom from sin was extremely difficult, the rabbis did allow for the possibility with certain exceptional individuals. In *Mek. Vayassa'* 3 (on Exod 16:10; Lauterbach, *Mekilta de-Rabbi Ishmael,* 2:106), Rabbi Eliezer of Modi'im thought that the patriarchs were free from sin. Rabbinic views therefore varied. At times, not even the patriarchs were sinless. At other times, certain exceptional individuals could remain free from sins. See A. Büchler, *Studies in Sin and Atonement: In the Rabbinic Literature of the First Century* (Library of Biblical Studies; New York: Ktav, 1967), 331–35.

[14] This was demonstrated in ch. 1 of this work; Sanders does not always keep the two perspectives clearly defined.

[15] Thus R. Gamaliel in *m. ʾAbot* 3:16 could be concerned about his failure to obey perfectly the law. Philo and *Jubilees* could present as models of piety certain individuals who had perfectly obeyed God's decrees. The Qumran community strove toward "perfection of way."

[16] *Fourth Ezra* 7:68–69 expresses a skepticism about human ability to refrain from sin: "For all who have been born are entangled in iniquities, and are full of sins and burdened with transgressions. And if after death we were not to come into judgment, perhaps it would have been better for us." In *4 Ezra* 9:36: "For we who have received the law and sinned will perish, as well as our hearts that received it." Rabbi Gamaliel could despair over the necessity of perfect obedience, while R. Akiba consoled him on the basis of a more merciful judgment based on a majority of deeds. Elsewhere the rabbis generally considered a variety of means effective for the atoning of sin. Gamaliel's despair in *m. ʾAbot* is therefore unusual. Most rabbis were confident that "all Israelites" have a share in the world to come. Gamaliel is valuable as an example of the need for "perfection of way" within the system as a whole.

[17] Sanders, *Paul, the Law,* 24.

had committed a sin for which he had to suffer.[18] The key lies in the fact that Paul describes his prior status as "blameless." He never says that he was without sin as a Pharisee. To assume that to be "blameless" is the same as to be sinless and innocent of any violation of the Mosaic law would be an error.[19] The "new perspective" interpretation of Paul and the law has been wrong to cite Phil 3 as proof that Paul did not have a problem with perfect obedience of the law.

So how "blameless" *is* Paul with respect to the law if one grants that he still could have been guilty of sin? Paul claims to be circumcised and an Israelite of the tribe of Benjamin. He is a Pharisee, a Hebrew of Hebrews, and has manifested his zeal in a public persecution of the church. Several commentators have noted that each point on Paul's list in Phil 3 concerns what is publicly verifiable.[20] These are the observable marks of an *outward* "blamelessness" in personal accomplishments. Paul is countering Jewish-Christian missionaries by citing his own credentials in the form of "accessible, objectively verifiable claims."[21] The Qumran community offers a helpful parallel. Members had to be perfect in their *publicly observable* behavior with respect to the law; their private sins were an entirely different matter.[22]

In Phil 3 Paul speaks of both his Jewish identity and his accomplishment of the Jewish law. Paul begins with three accolades of Jewish identity. He was circumcised on the eighth day, he is an Israelite, and he is from the tribe of Benjamin. For a law-observant Jew, such markers of Jewish identity guarantee privilege and a right status before God. The issue in Phil 3 is therefore not "works-righteousness" but whether Jewish identity (at least regarding the first three items on Paul's list) brings a right standing before God. On the other hand, Paul does not stop there but cites three accolades of publicly observable achievement. With respect to the law, he was a Pharisee; with respect to zeal, a persecutor of the church; with respect to righteousness in the law, blameless. The Jews

---

[18] The rabbis could be surprised that they had sinned to the point that they merited suffering or death (*Mek. Nezikin* 18 [to 22:22 (23); Lauterbach, *Mekilta de-Rabbi Ishmael,* 3:141–2]; *b. Sanh.* 101a [on R. Eliezer]).

[19] The mistaken connection is understandable, since "blameless" is a cultic term associated with the Mosaic law.

[20] P. T. O'Brien, *Commentary on Philippians,* 380; Robert H. Gundry, "The Moral Frustration of Paul Before His Conversion: Sexual Lust in Romans 7:7–25," in *Pauline Studies* (ed. Donald A. Hagner and Murray J. Harris; Grand Rapids: Eerdmans, 1980), 234.

[21] Moisés Silva, *Philippians* (Wycliffe Exegetical Commentary; Chicago: Moody, 1988), 175.

[22] Sanders, *Paul and Palestinian Judaism,* 286–93.

never saw the law as strictly a matter of identity; the second three items Paul lists all involve *accomplishment.* The Jewish law demands obedience.[23] Paul's former "righteousness" was clearly based on his performance of the law. The closer a Jew came to perfect observance, the greater was his or her boast with respect to the law. In other words, the law always involves accomplishment and not just identity. A high status in Judaism for Paul requires not only membership in the covenant people but also excellence in law-observance.

In light of the revelation of God's righteousness in Christ (Phil 3:9), Paul views his former righteousness and accomplishment as "rubbish" (to put it mildly). A profound irony ensues. Once Paul used to think that he possessed righteousness through his Jewish identity and performance of the law, but now he knows that he had achieved only his "own" righteousness.[24] A "blameless" Jew would have relied upon God's election and a merciful system of atonement and sacrifice.[25] If such grace and mercy are located only in Christ, the whole system of Jewish thought breaks down.[26] The law's observance becomes a merely human

---

[23] Gundry, "Grace," 13; O'Brien, *Commentary on Philippians,* 369. T. R. Schreiner observes that Dunn's thesis cannot account for Paul's accomplishments; it is not a matter of merely being a Jew or Pharisee. It is also a matter of exemplary living:

> If Sanders and Dunn are correct, and the only issues troubling Paul are that some Jews fail to see that salvation is now through Christ or that the Jews possess no covenantal advantage, why does Paul confuse the issue by comparing himself to his adversaries, arguing that he was more devoted to practicing the law than they? He should say plainly that salvation through Christ is apart from the law. Instead, Paul inserts the idea of the depth of his devotion to law observance. Presumably he does this because his opponents thought they were right with God because of their own devotion to God, manifested in their observance of the law (*The Law and Its Fulfillment,* 113).

[24] P. T. O'Brien (*Commentary on Philippians,* 394) observes that Paul's wording of ἐμήν without the article draws attention to itself and emphasizes that the righteousness being spoken of is Paul's own, a righteousness that he had acquired. Unfortunately, O'Brien goes further to argue that this indicates that Paul was attempting to establish a claim upon God by his own self-righteousness. Likewise Gundry sees an attitudinal self-righteousness at work in this passage; "Grace," 13–14. The problem with Gundry's understanding is that Paul sees his own righteousness as a "gain." There is nothing wrong with his fulfillment of the law in itself. The problem is that it is not *God's* means of righteousness.

[25] T. R. Schreiner ("Paul and Perfect Obedience," 261), In-Gyu Hong (*Law in Galatians,* 138) and others (for example, Garlington, *Faith,* 141) highlight the sacrificial system. Given Sanders's portrait of Judaism as covenantal nomism, this suggestion would be on target.

[26] For example, Michael Cranford appeals to the sacrificial system of Judaism as proof that perfect obedience of the law would not have been an issue for

endeavor offering a worthless righteousness.[27] The framework of Judaism has been supplanted by a new framework: God's action in Christ. Severed from the gracious framework of God's electing and saving activity, the law can offer only an empty promise, "rubbish."

II. Romans 7:14–25 in Context

Romans 7 is full of vexing issues. Scholars have been particularly perplexed by the identity of the "I." Is Paul speaking about Christian existence under the law? Or is he speaking about his prior experience as a non-Christian? Is Paul's discussion autobiographical or typical?[28] Regardless of the position one takes on these matters, all would agree that Paul is speaking about existence under the law. Rather than get distracted by the perennial conundrums of this chapter, the purpose of the discussion that follows is much narrower. What does Paul see as problematic about existence under the law?

In Rom 7:7 Paul asks: "Is the law sin?" The question cannot be isolated from the chapters and verses that immediately precede. In Rom

---

Paul; "Possibility of Perfect Obedience," 257. On this point he follows James D. G. Dunn, who writes on Gal 3:10: "Paul was able to describe himself as 'blameless' before his conversion (Phil. iii.6; see also on i.14); *not* because he committed no sin, *not* because he fulfilled every law without exception, but because the righteousness of the law included use of the sacrificial cult and benefit of the Day of Atonement" (*Galatians,* 171).

[27] John M. G. Barclay expresses the point well:

> the items in Paul's lists are not "loss" because Paul has achieved them (in self-righteous pride) but because they are *merely his own human characteristics* which do not count as truly significant before *God.* This is why he talks of boasting "in the flesh" (3.3–4): they are indications of status and achievement *on a merely human level,* rather than what really counts before God (*Obeying the Truth,* 244).

Only faith in Christ could create such a shift in Paul's thinking to see these things as worthless. As a Jew he would have seen them as ordained and sanctioned by God. However, Barclay is wrong to rule out any notion of achievement. The latter three accolades in Phil 3 are precisely that—Paul's achievements. There is more at work in Paul's critique of the law than what Barclay sees (following Dunn). It is not just Jewish cultural identity but *also* the observance of the law itself that have been downgraded to merely human accomplishment of no value in God's scheme of things. This is a radical position!

[28] Almost any one of the plethora of articles and monographs on the "I" in Rom 7 surveys the various positions. For a recent study advancing Dunn's perspective that the chapter refers to *Christian* existence, see Garlington, *Faith,* 110–43. For a succinct expression of the opposing viewpoint, see Achtemeier, *Romans,* 118–30.

5:20–21 Paul introduces personified, apocalyptic forces that dominate human existence: the law, sin, and grace. In 6:13 the Christian is exhorted to present his or her body to God and not to sin. Sin and death are powers that exercise dominion and "rule" (6:9, 12, 14). In 6:12 sin is obeyed. Paul traces sin's entry into the cosmos to the actions of one man, Adam, and with sin came death (5:12, 17). As Adam brought sin and death into the world, another man, Jesus Christ, brought a third cosmic power, the power of grace. For those in Christ there is a change of lordship. Sin and death are *enslaving* powers (e.g., 6:6, 18), and only Christ can bring about deliverance from this bondage (6:7).[29] Believers in Christ are released from one age and its powers into another. Death's rule is broken (6:9).

The various relationships between the three cosmic "forces" of sin, the law, and grace structure the ensuing chapters. In Rom 6:1 Paul asks about the relationship between sin and grace. May Christians continue sinning in order that grace may abound? In Rom 6:15 Paul turns to a second combination of elements. He asks whether a Christian may sin since he or she is under grace and not the law? Paul turns to the final combination in Rom 7:7, where he asks if the law is sin.[30] The law too can be an enslaving power! In 6:15 Paul speaks of being "under" grace rather than the law. By this language Paul suggests that individuals must be liberated from the law (see 6:9, 14). This narrower focus on the law as a ruling power begins in 7:1. Even as one must die to sin (6:2), so one must die to the law (7:4). Death frees one from both sin (6:7, 18) and the law (7:2–3, 6), and this freedom allows the Christian to serve in the newness of life (6:4) and the Spirit (7:6).[31] Only by sharing in Christ's death can the Christian be freed from the enslaving powers of the old age.[32] It

---

[29] Christians have been freed from the enslaving power of sin in order that they might present their members as servants of a new master, righteousness (6:19–20), in order to serve God (6:22). As Tannehill points out, almost every verse in 6:10–23 is structured by this contrast between opposing powers, between sin, death, and the law on one side as opposed to grace, obedience, righteousness, and God on the other; *Dying and Rising with Christ,* 16. Dunn (*Romans 1–8,* 335) likewise maps out the antitheses of this chapter; cf. 1QS 3.13–4.26 on "the two spirits."

[30] P. J. Achtemeier, *Romans,* 102.

[31] Anders Nygren, *Commentary on Romans* (Philadelphia: Fortess, 1949), 268.

[32] Räisänen, *Paul and the Law,* 58. Paul's analogy is a woman bound by the law to her husband until his death frees her from the legal obligation. Similarly, a death must take place in order to free one from the power of the law. This death took place when the Christian was buried and raised with Christ in baptism (6:3–13). Dying permits the believer to live! On the sequential flow of logic in

may be surprising to find God's holy law listed as an enslaving power from which one must be released. What is it about the law that enslaves? Romans 5:14 has already provided a provocative hint: the law causes trespass to increase. Romans 7:5–6 elaborates. The law holds people captive by sentencing those who sin to death. In fact, the law *provoked* sin. This close connection between the law and sin leads very naturally to v. 7: is the law sin? Romans 7:5–6 are therefore programmatic for the discussion that follows.[33]

Upon posing the question whether the law is sin in v. 7, Paul answers by saying that no one would know what coveting was apart from the command. The law reveals sin for what it is (7:8, 19, 23). This echoes Rom 3:20. Paul continues in ch. 7 by explaining that the law is sin's innocent victim. Sin uses the law's commandment, which was intended to bring life, to multiply itself and bring death instead (7:8, 10–11).[34] Thanks to sin, the real culprit, the law too enslaves and pronounces death upon the sinner (7:13–25).[35] The law, then, is good, just, and holy (7:12), but sin took the law that was good and brought about a totally different result (7:13). While the law is indeed "spiritual" (7:14) and "good" (7:16; see also vv. 22 and 25), the power of sin turns out to be far stronger than the desire to do what the law commands. People under the law find themselves in the "wretched" position of being unable to do

---

this text, see Joyce A. Little, "Paul's Use of Analogy: A Structural Analysis of Romans 7:1–6," *CBQ* 46 (1984): 82–90.

[33] Structurally, 7:6d's "oldness of the letter" is taken up in 7:7–25, even as 7:6c's "newness of the Spirit" acts as a heading for Rom 8. Romans 7 is clearly discussing existence under the law apart from the Spirit. The Spirit in Rom 8 brings a release from this oppressive situation under the law; Günther Bornkamm, "Sin, Law and Death: An Exegetical Study of Romans 7," in *Early Christian Experience* (New York: Harper & Row, 1969), 88–89, 100; James Dunn (*Romans 1–8*, 358) and others—for instance, S. Voorwinde ("Who Is the 'Wretched Man' in Romans 7:24?" *VR* 54 [1990], 21–22)—see 7:7–25 explicating v. 5 while Rom 8 expands v. 6. Bornkamm points to the recurrence of νύνι in Rom 8:1, corresponding to its use in Rom 7:6. Romans 8:2 then speaks of "liberation," a liberation from the law and death, even as in 7:6. Romans 8:2 announces the Spirit and new life, even as 7:6. What 8:2 adds to 7:6 is the liberation from *sin* and the law, the connection that occupies Paul in 7:7–25. While recognizing these features, Jan Lambrecht does not account for the γάρ in Rom 8:2, which would place the beginning of the new unit in 8:1; "Man Before and Without Christ: Rom 7 and Pauline Anthropology," *LS* 5 (1974–1975): 21–22.

[34] One is reminded of the law's curse in Gal 3:10, 13.

[35] That sin is the ultimate enslaving power for Paul is clear already from 3:9, which states that all are under sin. Sin reigns with death in 6:14, 17, and 32. So also 6:18; Tannehill, *Dying and Rising with Christ*, 16.

good; they do what they hate instead (7:15) because of the tyranny and power of sin (7:14, 17, 20, 24). Three times Paul cycles through an admission that the "I" is unable to accomplish what the law demands (7:15–16, 18–20, 21–23).[36] Paul finds one commandment epitomizing the futile struggle to obey the law: "Do not covet." Of all the commandments the prohibition against coveting exposes the problem of a sinful heart. The battle against sin penetrates to the inner core of human existence to secret, sinful desires and motives that stand in the way of obedience of God's holy law.[37]

Michael Winger has drawn attention to Paul's use of ἐντολή.[38] Paul may have in mind the command οὐκ ἐπιθυμήσεις ("Do not covet") in Rom 7:7. A second possibility is that Paul is referring to νόμος from the point of view of all of its commands.[39] In either case, Paul's choice of ἐντολή in the midst of his discussion of νόμος places the emphasis squarely on the law's command.[40] The varied terminology that Paul uses to express the same point makes it clear that *doing* the law is the key issue. Eleven times he repeatedly uses three synonyms to make his point in vv. 15–21: πράσσω (vv. 15, 19), ποιέω (vv. 15, 16, 19, 20, 21), and

---

[36] On the logic of this section as a whole, see Mark A. Seifrid, "The Subject of Rom 7:14–25," *NovT* 34 (1992): 326–31. On the parallelism and repetition between vv. 15–17 and vv. 18–20, see also Paul W. Meyer, "The Worm at the Core of the Apple: Exegetical Reflections on Romans 7," in *The Conversation Continues: Studies in Paul and John in Honor of J. Louis Martyn* (ed. Robert T. Fortna and Beverly R. Gaventa; Nashville: Abingdon, 1990), 76–78.

For Greco-Roman parallels to the conflict between willing and doing, see Hildebrecht Hommel, "Das 7. Kapitel des Römerbriefs im Licht antiker Überlieferung," in *Theologia Viatorum VIII: Jahrbuch der Kirchlichen Hochschule Berlin, 1961/1962* (ed. Fritz Maass; Berlin: Walter de Gruyter, 1962), 90–116; and Gerd Theissen, *Psychological Aspects of Pauline Theology* (trans. John P. Galvin; Philadelphia: Fortress, 1987), 211–19. The most extensive treatment has been Stowers, *A Rereading of Romans*, 260–64.

[37] "Do not covet" in Rom 7:7 is the most private and interior of the commandments. Philippians 3 spoke of a public, observable blamelessness, saying little or nothing about the possibility of an internal struggle with sin and desire. The only distinguishing characteristic of the tenth commandment from the others is its unique focus on interiority; J. A. Ziesler, "The Role of the Tenth Commandment in Romans 7," *JSNT* 33 (1988): 47–48.

[38] *By What Law? The Meaning of* Νόμος *in the Letters of Paul* (SBLDS 128; Atlanta: Scholars Press, 1992), 166–67.

[39] Paul is certainly not using the word as a synonym for νόμος. Why would Paul vary his terminology for the Mosaic law here and nowhere else?

[40] For a similar alternation of νόμος and ἐντολή, see 13:8–10. The doing of God's will that was impossible prior to Christ and the Spirit finally proves possible. In loving one's neighbor as oneself one does what the law had been after all along.

κατεργάζομαι (vv. 15, 17, 18, 20).[41] The "problem" or "plight" of the law according to Rom 7:14–25 is that that those who know what the law demands are unable to "do" it.[42] Romans 8:3–4 will turn to the work of Christ as the solution to fleshly humanity's inability (τὸ ἀδύνατον) to do what God requires in the law. Through Christ the law's "righteous decree" (τὸ δικαίωμα τοῦ νόμου) is fulfilled in believers.[43]

---

[41] This creates a powerful rhetorical effect; Käsemann, *Commentary on Romans,* 202. John M. Espy's distinctions between the three terms seem overly subtle; "Paul's 'Robust Conscience' Re-examined," *NTS* 31 (1985): 184–85 n. 62.

[42] Such an analysis does not require an autobiographical reference here. Nevertheless, Paul himself had been under the law prior to the Damascus road. In light of the Jewish parallels, Paul could describe his former existence under the law as "blameless" even while admitting a "plight" of failure to do what it requires (whether personally or in general). Another possibility is that Paul may have come to see the full extent of his sin only after the fact in light of his persecution of the church. Paul mentions his persecuting activity in 1 Cor 15 as the reason why he is the least among the apostles. Quite possibly lurking behind Paul's statements in Rom 7 is the recognition that despite all his best intentions he still ended up doing what he did not want to do. He ended up working *against* the very God he thought he was serving by persecuting the church; see, for example, Achtemeier, *Romans,* 123; Kim, *The Origin of Paul's Gospel* (WUNT 2/4; Tübingen: J. C. B. Mohr [Paul Siebeck], 1981), 280–81, 287, 345–46. Sin used the law to further its own sinful purposes despite Paul's best intentions. Only in Christ does the full extent of the "plight" under the law become apparent. These two possibilities need not be mutually exclusive. Certainly a reduction of the law to a struggle with its requirements is only possible when its gracious framework has been redefined in terms of Christ. This would also explain why Paul's contemporaries would not have felt this plight as acutely as Rom 7 describes it. The Jews thought that it was within the power of every individual to choose to do what is good or not (Sir 15:11–22; *Pss. Sol.* 9:4–5; *2 Bar.* 54:15, 19; 85:7). The Jews did not see themselves as having been born slaves to sin (contra Rom 5:12–19; 6:15–22; 8:5–8). They could always appeal to their election and sacrifice. On this point, see Timo Laato *(Paul and Judaism),* who shows that Rom 7 is typical of a much more negative anthropology in Paul. In other words, Paul's negative anthropology is a symptom of something more fundamental going on in Paul's theology, the shift from covenantal to christological nomism. At precisely the point the Jew would have invoked the election and atonement, Paul finds the solution in Christ (thus Rom 7:24–25).

[43] E. P. Sanders (*Paul, the Law,* 74) admits that in Rom 7 "humans are depicted as unable to fulfill it [the law] because of sin and the flesh." He adds (pp. 74–75): "Its 'fault,' rather, is that it does not bear within itself the power to enable people to observe it." Sanders is then quick to qualify his comments on Rom 7. He says with respect to Pauline material outside of Rom 7: "It is worth observing that in none of these passages does Paul argue that the law is too hard to be fulfilled adequately" (p. 78). Romans 7 is therefore the exception where Paul *does* say that people are unable to accomplish the law. The problem, though, is that Gal 3:10 confirms what Paul says in Rom 7 (see ch. 6). The necessity of doing the

One ought to note that absolutely nothing in Rom 7 suggests that Paul's problem with the law is that it leads to national righteousness or ethnic pride.[44] On the contrary, possession of the law is good as long as one can translate possession of the law into the concrete action that the law demands. Winger observes that ἐντολή is never used in a way that would clearly demarcate Jews from Gentiles.[45] Paul sees the law as setting forth a demand that must be successfully accomplished by the individual. The interplay of pronouns in Rom 6 and 7 suggests that Jewish ethnocentrism is one of the least of Paul's concerns in this section. Sanders points out that it is impossible to divide the oscillating pronouns in 6:1–7:6 into "we Jews" versus "you Gentiles": " 'You' are not under the law (6:14); 'we' are not under the law (6:15); 'you' were slaves of sin (6:20); 'you' have died to the law (7:4); 'we' were in the flesh (7:5); 'we' are discharged from the law (7:6). It is not possible to divide the pronouns up, 'you' referring to Gentiles and 'we' to Jews; all were previously under sin, all were in the flesh, all were under the law."[46] The "plight" under the law in Rom 6 and 7 appears to involve both Jews and Gentiles. Paul prepares for this radical conclusion in Rom 2:14–16. Although the Gentiles do not have the law, they are a law to themselves as their consciences accuse or defend them on the basis of their deeds. A law is at work among them that corresponds to the Jewish law and renders them accountable before God. The law as an expression of God's will for human conduct can therefore be understood in a special sense as a universal, cosmic power that stands over *all* humanity.[47] The law

---

law has been a motif in Rom 2–4, and these chapters pave the way for the critique here in Rom 7. What seems obvious to Sanders in Rom 7 need not be a contradiction of what Paul says elsewhere. Paul will continue his critique in Rom 9–11 (as will become clear in the following chapter). There is nothing "extreme" about Paul's "presentation of human inability" here; contra Sanders (p. 78).

[44] James D. G. Dunn has championed the perspective that the law enslaves in Rom 7 (and 6) through the sin of "national righteousness," "national self-righteous judgment on others," and "unself-critical presumption of God's favor" (Dunn, *Romans 1–8,* 352; cf. p. 387). In other words, Paul's point, for Dunn, has little to do with struggling with the law's commands but rather concerns the Jews' mistaken understanding of the law in overly nationalistic terms.

[45] Winger, *By What Law?* 166–67.

[46] Sanders, *Paul, the Law,* 72; so also Räisänen, *Paul and the Law,* 18–23.

[47] Paul leaves this conclusion, through the device of mixed pronominal references, at the level of inference. He would never want to say that Gentiles stand under the law per se. He can speak of the Gentiles as under the law only in a *special* sense, the sense of Rom 2:14–16. Interestingly, in Gal 3:19–4:10 there is a similar switching of pronouns that has proven utterly vexing. Like Rom 6–7, the Galatians passage is in the context of slavery or domination. Sanders concludes:

demands that all people live according to the standards of a holy and righteous God and that they will be judged accordingly (Rom 1:18–2:29).

Romans 7 therefore elaborates on what Paul sees as the fundamental "problem" in the law. Analysis of Paul's critique of the law ought to begin with Rom 7, where Paul directly addresses the issue. Dunn's suggestion that the problem with the law is that it leads to a mistaken *understanding* of the law as a source of Jewish national righteousness can hardly account for the language of oppression and existential struggle that characterizes this chapter. The law places a demand on people that individuals are unable to satisfy because of sin. The failed daily struggle to do what the law requires leads to bondage and enslavement.

III. Excursus on *Nomos* in Romans 7

Many scholars think that Paul is playing on the word νόμος in Rom 7:14–25 and that νόμος does not always refer to the Mosaic law. The debate over νόμος does not affect in any way Paul's assertion in Rom 7 that

---

"Although Paul has shown in Gal 2:15 that he knew the standard distinction between being a Gentile 'sinner' and a righteous Jew, his general tendency, in evidence in Rom 6:1–7:4 as well as in Gal 3:19–4:10, was to universalize the human plight. All were under sin and in need of redemption; all were under the law" (*Paul, the Law,* 72); likewise Räisänen, *Paul and the Law,* 18–23. Most recently, J. Louis Martyn's commentary on *Galatians* (pp. 334–36) has called attention to the alternation of pronouns in Galatians. In Gal 3:13–14: Christ redeemed "us" (presumably *the Jews*) from the law's curse in order that Abraham's blessing would pass to the Gentiles so that "we" (*Jews and Gentiles* at this point) might receive the promised Spirit through faith. So also Gal 3:23–29 and 4:5b–7. Terence L. Donaldson has proposed a theory to try to demonstrate an underlying consistency; "The 'Curse of the Law' and the Inclusion of the Gentiles: Galatians 3.13–14," *NTS* 32 (1986): 94–112. While N. T. Wright tries to improve upon Donaldson's work, Wright still thinks that the reception of the Spirit was promised to "us Jews" and not the Gentiles; *Climax,* 143–44. See Brice L. Martin's refutation of such schemes in *Christ and the Law in Paul* (NovTSup 62; Leiden: E. J. Brill, 1989), 100–104. After explaining why the various attempts to sort out the pronouns into tidy groupings of Jew versus Gentile fail, J. L. Martyn concludes: "Before the advent of Christ humanity was an enslaved monolith; in Christ humanity is becoming a liberated unity" (*Galatians,* 336). In a special sense the law is an enslaving power over *all* humanity. Such a move is foreshadowed already in the Old Testament; see Sidney Greidanus, "The Universal Dimension of Law in the Hebrew Scriptures," *SR* 14 (1985): 43–50. Paul's play with the pronouns does not allow the subject of those in relation to the law to be limited to the Jews (nor to the Gentiles, as Stowers would contend).

humans futilely struggle to do what the law requires. Nevertheless, a consistent usage of νόμος for the Mosaic law in this chapter would support a similar consistency in Rom 3:27–31, when the apostle speaks of νόμος πίστεως, the Mosaic law from the vantage point of its witness to faith.

Throughout Rom 7:14–25 Paul remains focused on the Mosaic law. Verse 7's question "Is the law sin?" acts as a heading for the rest of the chapter. Nevertheless, Paul could be playing on the word νόμος at certain points in the discussion and mean a general "principle" and not the Mosaic law. The key verses cited in support of this conclusion are 7:21–23:

> [21] So I find it to be a law that when I want to do what is good, evil lies close at hand. [22] For I delight in the law of God in my inmost self, [23] but I see in my members another law at war with the law of my mind, making me captive to the law of sin that dwells in my members.

This translation of νόμος in v. 21 (NRSV) could very well be taken to mean "principle": "I find it to be a principle that when I want to do what is good, evil lies close at hand."[48] Paul also contrasts in vv. 22–23 the "law of God" with "another law", the "law of sin." Douglas Moo points out that ἕτερος ("another"), unlike ἄλλος, does not always mean "another of a different kind," but "it always means 'another,' distinguishing two separate entities."[49] "The law of God" would be the Mosaic law (cf. 7:7, 12, 14). Thus the "other" law cannot be the same as the "law of God." "The other law" must be "the law of sin," or the "principle" of sin's power that is waging war against the "law of my mind."

But on closer analysis the case for νόμος as "principle" in Rom 7:22–23 is not compelling. Paul has been using νόμος in Rom 5–7 consistently for the Mosaic law. Romans 5:12–14 define an era from Adam until Moses, prior to the Mosaic law. The entry of the Mosaic law onto the stage of human history, according to Rom 5:20, only increased transgressions (similarly Rom 7:13). The elements of sin, grace, and the Mosaic law in Rom 5:20 then become the governing concepts in the three rhetorical questions of 6:1; 6:15; and 7:7. Even the "law of the husband" in 7:2 ought to be understood in terms of the Mosaic law. Verse 2 is part of a chain of reasoning leading to v. 7's question regarding the Mosaic law. Verse 2 must be referring to "the (Mosaic) law with respect to the

---

[48] If so, the ὅτι-clause would stand in apposition to τὸν νόμον; thus Winger, *By What Law?* 81–82 n. 74.

[49] Moo, *Romans*, 463 n. 72.

husband," a genitive of reference.[50] The focus on the Mosaic law is undisputed until vv. 21–23.[51]

To understand νόμος ἁμαρτίας in v. 23 as something other than "the law in the hands of sin" is to miss totally the point of Paul's argument in Rom 7. In 7:10 the command that was intended for life has become a means of death because of the distorting effects of sin. The whole point of 7:7–12 is that the law is not sin, but sin used the law to bring about death instead of life. Although the law is "spiritual" (7:14) and "holy and just and good" (7:12), it stands in tension with itself since it also leads to death because of sin.[52] Paul Meyer concurs that one cannot interpret the "other law" in vv. 22–23 apart from 8:1–2: "The phrase 'the law of sin and death' in 8:2 can only be intended as a shorthand summary of the whole point of 7:7–25: It is the law that has been used by sin to produce death. But that means that not only the 'law of God' (v. 22) but also this 'different law' (v. 23) is the Mosaic law!"[53] Once one sees that "the law of sin" phrase in 7:23 and 8:2 summarizes what Paul said about sin using the law in vv. 7–12, the path is clear for a similar understanding of the genitives with νόμος elsewhere in Rom 7 and 8. Snodgrass explains that the way the law functions depends directly upon the sphere in which it is operating. In the realm of sin, the law functions very differently from the law in the hands of Christ and the Spirit.[54] The

---

[50] That Paul is describing the Mosaic law and not the Roman system, see Dunn, *Romans 1–8*, 360; Fitzmyer, *Romans*, 457; see also 1 Cor 7:39.

[51] Osten-Sacken cannot conceive of Paul using νόμος in vv. 21–23 for "rule" or "principle" after Paul has so extensively used νόμος for the Mosaic law elsewhere in the chapter; *Römer 8*, 209–10.

[52] Wilckens, *Der Brief an die Römer*, 2:90. N. T. Wright says that to take νόμος in these verses as anything other than the Mosaic law is "to escape the deep rush of Paul's argument and paddle off into a shallow and irrelevant backwater" (*Climax*, 199). Räisänen completely misses the mark when he suggests that the strict understanding of νόμος as Mosaic law in these verses involves a "divided Torah"; "Paul's Word-Play," 89. The problem is not a divided Torah but rather a single Torah being used by sin in a way completely contrary to what God intended, as the "inner person" or the "mind" recognized. Nevertheless, the law, like the "I," has been forced by sin to act in a way contrary to God's intended plan for it. It is a "divided law"; Dunn, *Romans 1–8*, 409. The law has been so distorted under the influence of sin that Paul can call it "another law."

[53] Paul W. Meyer, "Worm at the Core," 79; contra Winger, *By What Law?* 43–44, 185–89, who is forced to see four separate and distinct "nomoi" in Rom 7:22–23, even though Paul has referred consistently to the Mosaic law in the preceding verses. Winger (p. 186) summarizes well himself the problems with seeing the uses of νόμος as something other than the Mosaic law: "there are so many νόμοι that they can scarcely be kept straight."

[54] Snodgrass, "Spheres of Influence," 99–101.

disputed phrase ὁ νόμος τοῦ πνεύματος τῆς ζωῆς in 8:2 would be the law in the hands of the Spirit of life.[55] The Spirit of life works through the law itself to resolve the "plight" under the Mosaic law caused by sin in Rom 7.[56] Räisänen objects that 8:2's νόμος τοῦ πνεύματος cannot be the Mosaic law since that would mean that the law itself frees the individual from the law (ὁ νόμος τῆς ἁμαρτίας καὶ τοῦ θανάτου).[57] But a different agent is handling the law in Rom 8:2 with very different results: the Spirit. Paul showed in Rom 3:27–4:25 how the law as Scripture *in the hands of faith* testifies to Jesus Christ. This is a very different function for the law than its more typical function to express the works that God requires ("the law of works"). Likewise the law in the hands of the Spirit would surely testify to the righteousness found in Christ. The Mosaic law stands in tension with itself in Rom 7–8 just as earlier in the letter (and as will be the case again in Rom 9:30–10:8).[58]

"I find it to be a law/principle that when I want to do good" (vv. 21–22) may also be translated: "I find with respect to the law that when I want to do good." Several scholars point out that the object of εὑρίσκω cannot be τὸν νόμον since the object is supplied by the ὅτι clause. What the "I" has found is that evil lies close at hand whenever the "I" wishes to do good. τὸν νόμον must be an accusative of respect. Paul makes this discovery with respect to the Torah: "That is, whenever the ἐγώ seeks to do the good as understood and defined in the Torah, the result is the opposite, namely the doing of evil."[59] The parallels between v. 21 and v. 10 reinforce the conclusion that νόμος in v. 21 must refer to the Mosaic law:

---

[55] Romans 7:14 says that the Mosaic law is "spiritual." One should not be surprised then by Paul's qualification of νόμος with the Spirit in 8:2; Hübner, *Law,* 144.

[56] The connections of Rom 8:2 to v. 3 (γάρ) and v. 4 (ἵνα), where Paul is clearly speaking of the Mosaic law, requires that νόμος be taken as the Mosaic law in 8:2 as well; there is an "engste syntaktische Zusammenhänge" (Osten-Sacken, *Heiligkeit,* 16); contra Räisänen, "The 'Law' of Faith and the Spirit," 64–67.

[57] Räisänen, "The 'Law' of Faith and the Spirit," 65.

[58] As Eduard Lohse put so well, the law is a way of salvation (Heilsweg) since it testifies about Christ; it is ὁ νόμος τοῦ πνεύματος τῆς ζωῆς (p. 281). Lohse adds that Christ is precisely the one who has fulfilled the demands of the Mosaic law.

[59] P. J. Achtemeier, "Unsearchable Judgments," 532–33; so also P. W. Meyer, "Worm at the Core," 79, and N. T. Wright, *Climax,* 198. Räisänen ("The 'Law' of Faith and the Spirit," 88–89 n. 3) criticizes Wilckens and Zahn on this matter, but on the possibility of an accusative of reference, as suggested by Klyne Snodgrass ("Spheres of Influence," 93–113, esp. 105), Räisänen's critical pen goes silent.

v. 10: εὑρέθη μοι ἡ ἐντολὴ . . . εἰς ζωὴν . . . εἰς θάνατον

v. 21: εὑρίσκω τὸν νόμον . . . τὸ καλόν . . . τὸ κακὸν[60]

Just as v. 10 refers to the Mosaic law (see vv. 7–9 and ἡ ἐντολή), so also v. 21. Verse 21 also closely parallels several motifs in the preceding verses. καλόν parallels ἀγαθόν in vv. 12–13, 16, 18–19 (as opposed to κακόν in vv. 19, 21). παράκειμαι parallels 7:18. The close ties between v. 21 and the preceding verses that are focused on the Mosaic law (e.g., 7:16b) indicate that 7:21 must also be referring to the Mosaic law.[61]

Many point to the phrase ἕτερον νόμον in v. 23. Since ἕτερος ("another") modifies νόμος, it is thought that this νόμος cannot be the same as "the law (νόμος) of God" and must be "another law/principle." This reasoning is not compelling when considered in the context of the situation Paul is describing. The ἕτερος νόμος is "the Torah as it has been taken over and used by sin operating through the foothold which is the flesh."[62] Dunn adds:

> But whether such a distinction between ἕτερος and ἄλλος was intended is far from certain, since the two are often used interchangeably (BGD, ἕτερος 1βγ), and the "difference" could be simply the different way in which the law was experienced when it was used by sin (vv. 8, 11, 13), so different from the law acknowledged as good (vv. 16, 22).[63]

One may grant, with Moo, a distinction between "another law" and the "law of God" without concluding that ἕτερος νόμος is something other than the Mosaic law. Paul would simply be saying that the law has been so distorted in the hands of sin that one can speak of it as if it were actually "another law." Paul does not assert that there are two different νόμοι at issue here. Paul says that the "I" *perceives* "another law" (βλέπω). The "I" does not see the law manifested as truly the law of God, but rather the "I" sees the law clothed in an unrecognizable shape because of sin.[64]

---

[60] Noted by both N. T. Wright (*Climax,* 198) and Dunn (*Romans 1–8,* 392). Dunn (p. 392) writes of this parallel: "in both cases what is in view is the harsh discovery through personal experience of how the law, which should be for life and should promote the good, actually helps bring about the opposite."

[61] Dunn, *Romans 1–8,* 392

[62] N. T. Wright, *Climax,* 198.

[63] Dunn, *Romans 1–8,* 395.

[64] Similarly, "the law of my mind" in v. 23 is to be understood alongside v. 22, which says that the "I" delights in the "law of God according to the inner man." The "inner man" would be the same as the "mind" of v. 23. The "inner man," or the "mind," recognizes the law to be spiritual, holy, just, and good, but sin uses the flesh in order to bring about a different result (7:14; 8:7); Wilckens, *Der Brief an de Römer,* 2:90.

IV. Conclusion

Romans 7 clearly develops the plight of the individual under the law who finds himself or herself unable to do what the law requires. Sin prevents the possibility of successful performance of the law's demands. This is why the law "of life" cannot save. Salvation must be found instead in the law's testimony in the hands of the Spirit to Jesus Christ. The blamelessness of which Paul speaks in Phil 3 does not undermine such a reading of Rom 7 (and Gal 3:10 for that matter), since Paul does not claim to have obeyed the law without ever sinning. The Qumran literature offers a helpful parallel to the relationship between Phil 3 and Rom 7. Members of the Qumran community could strive toward perfect righteousness among their peers even while privately confessing their sins and failures before God.[65] Whereas Phil 3 addresses Paul's legal blamelessness relative to his peers, Rom 7 speaks to the situation of an individual under God's law considered in itself.

---

[65] E. P. Sanders observes that, unlike the relatively abundant devotional material from Qumran, very few Tannaitic prayers have survived; *Paul and Palestinian Judaism*, 223–33. The few surviving Tannaitic prayers parallel those from Qumran. The Tannaim, even while admonishing strict obedience of the law, went before God in prayer to seek forgiveness for their sins and failures.

Chapter Ten

Romans 9:30–10:8: Israel's Pursuit of the Law

Romans 9:30–10:21 is yet another passage where Paul discusses the Mosaic law in terms of human striving and achievement. The rhetorical question in 9:30 marks the beginning of a new section. Like 9:30 a rhetorical question flags a structural break at 11:1 (cf. 5:1; 6:1; 7:7; 8:31; 9:14). Although God's sovereign right to choose dominates Paul's discussion in the bulk of Rom 9:6–29, a motif that is still evident in 9:30–10:21, in v. 30 Paul begins to address humanity's response. This shift in emphasis is accompanied by a shift in vocabulary. In 9:30–10:21 Paul reprises the language of faith and righteousness. Paul leaves righteousness and faith behind (with the exception of a brief backward glance at the role of faith in 11:20) in the next section of the letter in Rom 11.[1] Romans 9:30–10:21 is also distinguished by an *inclusio* that frames the discussion. Both 9:30–32 and 10:19–21 contrast ethnic Israel with the Gentiles' inclusion into God's people (Paul's quotation of Hosea in 9:24–26 had introduced this motif).[2] While the *inclusio* in 9:30–32 and 10:19–21 helps set the tone for 9:30–10:21 as a whole, the following discussion will be limited to 9:30–10:8, since 10:8 marks the end of Paul's treatment of the law.[3]

---

[1] This faith (πίστις) is contrasted with Israel's "unfaithfulness"/"unbelief" (ἀπιστία) in vv. 20, 23, but the language of believing faith is certainly not as marked as it was in ch. 10.

[2] See Wilckens (*Der Brief an die Römer,* 2:210) for additional connections to 9:1–29; also Moo, *Romans,* 617. Wilckens sees the theme of righteousness marking 9:30–33 as a transitional section to what follows in ch. 10.

[3] The conclusion of the chapter will briefly discuss Rom 10:9–21, the remainder of the literary unit.

I. The New Perspective on Romans 9:30–10:21

Having agreed with Sanders that first-century Jews did not consider a right status before God something they had to merit or earn, most interpreters prefer a strictly ethnic approach to Rom 9–11. Interpreters of Rom 9–11 prior to Sanders typically read Paul against a backdrop of Jews striving to merit salvation by means of their good works.[4] Romans 9:30–31 says: "Gentiles, who did not strive for righteousness, have attained it, that is, righteousness through faith; but Israel, who did strive for the righteousness that is based on the law, did not succeed in fulfilling that law." In 10:3 Paul continues: "For, being ignorant of the righteousness that comes from God, and seeking to establish their own, they have not submitted to God's righteousness." The problem with the more traditional, pre-Sanders view is the location of these verses in the middle of a discussion of Jewish ethnic identity and privileges vis-à-vis the Gentiles. Paul's entire discussion has been motivated out of a concern for the Jewish people in light of God's promises and election of them (9:1–5). Then in Rom 9:24–29 Paul begins to speak of the Gentiles' enjoying entry into God's people as a result of the "hardening" of the Jews. In Rom 10:10–13 Paul asserts that there is no distinction between Jew and Gentile. In Rom 11:25–32, the climax of Paul's argument in chs. 9–11, Paul predicts the salvation of *all* Israel, that is, all ethnic Israel in the end times.[5]

What drives Paul's argument throughout these chapters is the Jews' consciousness of their status as a special people chosen by God. "Their own" righteousness in 10:3 must therefore refer not to self-achievement but rather to ethnic distinction. As N. T. Wright puts it: "The 'meta-level' of Israel's problem with the Torah is 'national righteousness.'"[6] Israel is guilty of turning the law "into a charter of racial

---

[4] For example, Schlier, *Der Römerbrief,* 306–12; Cranfield, *Romans,* 2:509–10; idem, "Some Notes on Romans 9:30–33," in *Jesus und Paulus: Festschrift für Werner Georg Kümmel zum 70. Geburtstag* (ed. E. Earle Ellis and Erich Gräßer; Göttingen: Vandenhoeck & Ruprecht, 1975), 40, 42–43; Rhyne, *Faith,* 101; Moo, *Romans,* 626, 634–36; T. R. Schreiner, *The Law and Its Fulfillment,* 104–12; idem, "Israel's Failure to Attain Righteousness in Romans 9:30–10:3," *TJ* 12 NS (1991): 214, 216. Badenas (*Christ,* 105) straddles the fence on the issue, refusing to decide between "reliance on ancestry or merits": "Israel relied so much on ethnic belonging to the people of God and on its own merits that it overlooked that the basic relation of man to God can only be based on faith." For a traditional articulation see, for instance, p. 112.

[5] See ch. 4.

[6] *Climax,* 243.

privilege."[7] The Jews were *presuming* that they enjoyed God's grace. Such a presumption of grace is quite the opposite of trying to *earn* God's favor by works. Paul counters this presumption in Rom 9 with the idea that God has always elected a remnant *within* national Israel. Not all ethnic Israel is true Israel. Just as God works with a chosen remnant within Israel, so God has sovereignly decided to bring the Gentiles to salvation by means of Christ.

If the Jews' "own righteousness" is understood as their racial and ethnic privilege, their "works" (ἔργα) must correspondingly be taken as "the way of life confined to the Jewish community."[8] N. T. Wright understands "works" as a shorthand for the "works of the law," that is, "the badges of Jewish membership (Sabbath, dietary laws, circumcision) which kept Jews separate from Gentiles."[9] Dunn writes: "Israel's mistake was not that they had understood righteousness as obedience to the law . . . , but that they had understood obedience to the law too much in terms of specific acts of obedience like circumcision, sabbath observance, and ritual purity."[10]

The Jews' confidence in their own "automatic national privilege" and righteousness led them to misconstrue their Scriptures and to reject Jesus as the Messiah.[11] They did not recognize that by faith in him the way to salvation was opened to *all* people. Not surprisingly, 10:4 parallels 1:16's "to everyone who has faith." In 10:11–13 Paul uses the word "all" four times![12] Paul's citations from Isa 28:16 and Joel 3:5 emphasize everyone. "This suggests that in v. 5 [Rom 10:5] the emphasis is not on 'doing' per se, but on 'doing *them*', i.e., living the way of life which is confined to the Jewish community, in contrast to the universality of faith."[13] As Dunn summarizes in his commentary on Romans:

---

[7] Ibid., 241.

[8] Watson, *Paul, Judaism and the Gentiles,* 165; see the full discussion on pp. 164–68.

[9] N. T. Wright, *Climax,* 240. Or: "Christ is the 'end' of the Torah in terms of the use of 'works' (Sabbath, food, circumcision) to bolster national privilege." (*Climax,* 242).

[10] Dunn, *Romans 9–16,* 593.

[11] N. T. Wright, *Climax,* 240; Wright continues on p. 244: "Israel's fault was her rejection of God's plan; which manifested itself in her 'national righteousness' . . . ; which expressed itself in her rejection of the crucified Messiah."

[12] Dieter Zeller, *Juden und Heiden in der Mission des Paulus: Studien zum Römerbrief* (2d ed.; FB 8; Katholisches Bibelwerk, 1976), 124. On the significance of the word "all," see Williams, "Righteousness of God," 247.

[13] Watson, *Paul, Judaism and the Gentiles,* 165. George E. Howard suggested this understanding already in 1969: "Beginning with vs. 3 Paul says that the Jews are ignorant of the righteousness of God and are seeking to establish

> The trouble with Israel is that they have confused the law and the righteousness it speaks of with works like circumcision which serve to make righteousness a function of Jewish identity rather than of God's gracious outreach to and through faith. This failure came to eschatological expression and climax in their refusal to recognize Christ as Messiah (vv. 30–33). . . . Paul's thesis then is of the law misunderstood and abused to give a concept of righteousness restricted to those living according to Jewish tradition and custom (the equivalent of the law abused and corrupted by sin in chap. 7).[14]

II. Problems with the New Perspective

The growing consensus that Paul is confronting a presumption based on Jewish ethnic identity (or national righteousness) has led many interpreters to conclude that this passage has absolutely nothing to do with individual achievement and the doing of the law. That conclusion may have been premature. Interestingly, many of the issues in 9:30–10:8 parallel those that came to the fore in Rom 3:27–4:8. The debate once again revolves around the term ἔργα. Does it mean those aspects of the law that distinguish Jews from Gentiles, or does it refer to the demands of the Mosaic law in general? While the broader context of Rom 9–11 does indeed speak of the future of ethnic Israel, Paul is not necessarily viewing ἔργα as exclusively those acts that distinguish the Jews from the Gentiles.[15] On the contrary, Paul's flow of thought in these chapters indicates a much more generalized use of ἔργα as human activity and achievement per se, quite apart from any special emphasis on national

---

their own. This means that they are unaware that God's righteousness is one which includes all nations. They are seeking to establish *their own* righteousness, i.e., collective righteousness, to the exclusion of the gentiles. Consequently, they are not subject to God's righteousness" ("Christ the End of the Law: The Meaning of Romans 10:4ff.," *JBL* 88 [1969]: 336).

[14] Dunn, *Romans 9–16*, 576–77. See also his "new perspective" reading in " 'Righteousness from the Law' and 'Righteousness from Faith': Paul's Interpretation of Scripture in Romans 10:1–10," in *Tradition and Interpretation in the New Testament: Essays in Honor of E. Earle Ellis for His 60th Birthday* (ed. Gerald F. Hawthorne and Otto Betz; Grand Rapids: Eerdmans, 1987), 216–28.

[15] One ought to stress the word "exclusively," since νόμος in this passage is indeed the unique possession of the Jews. It is the Jews who strive for the righteousness of the law and not the Gentiles, a fact that confirms that νόμος refers to the Mosaic law. Then in 10:5 Paul quotes Moses with regard to the righteousness of the law, which again confirms that 9:30–32 is speaking of the Mosaic law. The problem with the law, however, does not primarily lie in its national exclusiveness.

boundary markers (but certainly inclusive of them). Several distinct lines of evidence lead to this conclusion.

The key word ἔργα refers to human activity throughout Rom 9–11 (as was the case in Galatians and Rom 2–4). Whenever ἔργα is used with νόμου or in relation to the law, there is nothing to indicate that Paul has only ethnic boundary markers in mind. Paul uses the language of ἔργα νόμου to indicate the deeds or works that the Mosaic law requires *in general.* In Rom 9:12 Paul's uses ἔργα in his discussion of God's choice of Jacob over Esau. According to vv. 10–13, God chose Jacob (κατ' ἐκλογὴν) before either of the two brothers were even born or before either had "done anything good or bad" (πραξάντων τι ἀγαθὸν ἢ φαῦλον). From this exclusion of individual deeds Paul concludes that the divine choice was "not by works [οὐκ ἐξ ἔργων] but by his [God's] call." Human activity plays no role in God's election. Absolutely nothing in these verses indicates the badges of Israel's national identity. Paul concludes in v. 15 that God will have mercy on whom he has mercy. Mercy is a divine prerogative. "Therefore" (ἄρα—v. 16), "it depends not on human will or exertion, but on God who shows mercy" (οὐ τοῦ θέλοντος οὐδὲ τοῦ τρέχοντος).[16] The language of "works" (ἔργα) and striving (διώκω) in Rom 9:30–32 echoes the earlier discussion and contrast of human achievement and divine prerogative in 9:6–29. Paul speaks of "pursuing" (διώκω) and not "attaining" (φθάνω) the law.[17] Commentators generally identify this as the language of racing.[18] Paul then speaks in 9:32b of the

[16] 9:15–16 mirrors 9:11: God's choice does not depend on the human will or striving.

[17] Given Paul's use of νόμος for the Mosaic law in the prior chapters of Romans, it is hardly likely νόμος suddenly means "principle" in this text, as John Murray (*The Epistle to the Romans* [2 vols.; NICNT; Grand Rapids: Eerdmans, 1965], 2:43) and Sanday and Headlam (William Sanday and Arthur Headlam, *A Critical and Exegetical Commentary on the Epistle to the Romans* [5th ed.; ICC; Edinburgh: T&T Clark, 1896], 279) suppose (citing 3:27 and 7:21). The case for νόμος as something other than the Mosaic law did not prove compelling earlier in the letter.

[18] For instance, Badenas (*Christ,* 101–2) interprets the entire passage along these lines: διώκων refers to the pursuit of the goal; κατέλαβεν refers to attaining the goal; οὐκ ἔφθασεν refers to stumbling over an obstacle; καταισχύνω refers to disappointment and the shame of defeat; and τέλος is the goal, winning post, or finish line. So also Schlier, *Der Römerbrief,* 306; Wilckens, *Der Brief an die Römer,* 2:211–12; Stowers, *A Rereading of Romans,* 303–6; Thielman, *Paul and the Law,* 205; T. R. Schreiner, *The Law and Its Fulfillment,* 108 n. 54. See the discussion of τέλος in 10:4. Some have questioned whether Paul has in mind a Hellenistic athletic background. Students with a grammar school and basic rhetorical school training were familiar with Homer's *Iliad,* which included the footrace between Antilochus, Ajax, and Odysseus. The language of pursuing and running was also

stone of "stumbling." The imagery is therefore that of human striving and effort.[19] For Paul, human striving stands in sharp contrast to the God who elects apart from any human activity. In light of vv. 6–29 the "works" of 9:32 must likewise refer to human activity and performance of the Mosaic law. Just as God has mercy on whomever he will, God sovereignly chooses to include the Gentiles among his people. The logic of 9:30–10:8 is interwoven with the logic of what preceded in ch. 9.[20] Similarly, Rom 11:6 uses the language of "works" (ἐξ ἔργων). Like Rom 9:12, 11:6 is situated in the midst of a contrast between divine choice and human activity/performance. Paul may even be drawing upon racing language again in 11:11–12 when he speaks of "stumbling" and "falling."[21] Although Rom 11:6 is embedded within a discussion of Israel's

---

used in Judaism for the performance of the law (see Ps 119 [LXX: 118]:32; *b. Ber.* 28b); Piper, *Justification,* 152–55. What is undisputed, in either case, is the element of human exertion.

[19] As Stowers puts it: "Races are about will, effort, achievement, and well-earned rewards" (*A Rereading of Romans,* 305).

[20] Stephen Westerholm, "Paul and the Law in Romans 9–11," in *Paul and the Mosaic Law* (ed. James D. G. Dunn; WUNT 89; Tübingen: J.C.B. Mohr [Paul Siebeck], 1996), 228; Westerholm adds that Paul's discussion of works in general earlier in Rom 9 prepares for the more specific discussion in terms of *Israel's* "pursuit" and "works" in 9:32–10:8. As E. E. Johnson puts it:

> The imagery of the race course that dominates the argument of 9:30–33 and was hinted at already in 9:16 (ὁ τρέχων) gets turned on its head at 10:4 when the achieved goal is a divine accomplishment rather than a human one. To pursue God's righteousness by works is to consider that it is accomplished by human πράξαντες (9:11), θέλοντες, or τρέχοντες (9:16) rather than by God who is ὁ καλῶν (9:12), ὁ ἐλεῶν (9:16), [ὅς] θέλει (9:18; cf. 9:22), ὁ πλάσας (9:20), ὁ κεραμεύς (9:21), [ὅς] ἐκάλεσεν ἡμᾶς οὐ μόνον ἐξ Ἰουδαίων ἀλλὰ καὶ ἐξ ἐθνῶν (9:24) (*Function of Apocalyptic,* 155).

Jan Lambrecht has criticized Michael Cranford for downplaying the very clear references to human effort *in general* throughout Rom 9:11–13. Lambrecht shows that there is a contrast between human activity and God's sovereign choice; "Paul's Lack of Logic," 55–60. Cranford sees God's election in Rom 9 as irrespective of Jewish ethnic and national identity; "Election and Ethnicity," 27–41. What should one conclude from this debate? Paul is already developing in Rom 9 what will become clearer in 9:30–10:21. It is God's sovereign right to choose a people, and that choice is irrespective of what people have done or any merit on their part. Ethnic identity in Paul's reasoning is not exclusive of the issue of merit. As an exposition of Paul's logic in Rom 9 *as a whole,* Cranford is right ("Election and Ethnicity," 40): "Paul clearly associates nomistic service with human effort, and therefore *any argument which undercuts deeds* will serve to undermine reliance on works of the law" (emphasis mine).

[21] παράπτωμα may perhaps be taken as "false step." See Stowers (*A Rereading of Romans,* 312–16) for an explication of the significance of this imagery in light of Paul's Gentile audience.

national election and privilege (see 11:1–2), Paul's use of ἔργα may still refer to human activity and striving. Paul recounts the days of Elijah. Even in those days, God had been working salvation on the basis of a remnant and not the nation as a whole. God revealed to Elijah that there were seven thousand, a remnant, who had not bowed the knee to Baal. Paul sees a remnant in his own day. While Elijah's seven thousand deserved acclamation for not having bowed the knee to Baal, Paul says that they were "chosen by grace" (v. 5). He elaborates in v. 6 that "if it is by grace, it is no longer on the basis of works, otherwise grace would no longer be grace." In other words, God's choice of the seven thousand was made completely apart from their own faithfulness in avoiding idolatry (compare this with 9:10–13's apart from doing "anything good or bad"). God's grace and election are clearly contrasted and set apart from human activity and faithfulness.[22] Faithful actions did not (and do not) merit God's election.

In Rom 9:32 Paul says that the Jews did not attain to the law: "because they did not strive for it on the basis of faith, but as if it were based on works." The antithesis of "faith" versus "works" hearkens back to Paul's critique of the law in Rom 3:27–4:8. Romans 3:27–4:8's "boasting" motif in turn is based on Rom 2: it is not enough for the Jews to possess God's law. That law has to be obeyed. National privilege in the law is of no value apart from the corresponding obedience (2:13, 25). Since all people sin (including the Jews), Paul could say in Rom 3:20 that no one is justified by the works of the law. Then in Rom 4:4–5 Paul elaborated on the "works" of the law in 3:27 and explained that "works" are a matter of human activity and achievement as opposed to God's sheer, unmerited grace. In juxtaposing faith and works in relation to the law again in Rom 11, Paul hearkens back to his earlier discussion in 3:27–4:5, which had placed human activity in antithesis with divine grace through faith (3:27; 4:4–5).[23]

---

[22] Certainly the works involved here are those performed by Israelites. Nevertheless, the logic of the passage parallels Rom 9: works of *any* kind simply do not influence God's act of election. Any influence of human activity at all would compromise the divine prerogative in election; Westerholm, "Paul and the Law in Romans 9–11," 229.

[23] So also Westerholm, "Paul and the Law in Romans 9–11," 229–30. Barclay, while citing the material from Rom 9 and 11, did not consider the implications for his "new perspective" reading; *Obeying the Truth*, 249–50. These texts parallel Rom 4:4–5 and prove that 4:4–5's contrast between grace and human efforts was no "subsidiary argument." Sanders, on the other hand, recognized the difficulty of Rom 11:6 for his understanding of Paul's theology (*Paul, the Law*, 166 n. 40): "We should note that in Rom. 11:6 Paul actually does contrast grace

In Rom 10:5 Paul cites Lev 18:5. He cited this same OT passage in Gal 3:10–12. Galatians applies Lev 18:5 in terms of the necessity to do the law;[24] Paul's understanding of Lev 18:5 in terms of human activity and performance of the law in Galatians lends credence to a similar understanding in Rom 10:5, and consequently 9:30–32. Romans 9:30–10:8 nowhere mentions circumcision, Sabbath, or other national identity markers. Nothing in these verses indicates that Paul has in mind only those aspects of the law that distinguish Jews from Gentiles.[25] Even if Paul had in mind the boundary-marking aspects of the law, national identity is never divorced from the individual's own doing of the law (as was clear in Phil 3, where national identity stands alongside human performance of the law).[26]

In conclusion, the language and imagery of 9:30–32 within the context of Rom 9–11 require that "works" (ἔργα) be understood in the very general terms of doing the law. Paul says that the righteousness of the law is not God's own righteousness but a merely human sort of righteousness and achievement (10:2–3).[27] The Jews treasured the law as a gift of God and a sign of their election, but in the course of Rom 10 Paul shows that God's grace and mercy are bound up in the work of Jesus Christ.[28] The law's works, then, are merely human activity; God's grace

---

with works, so that doing the law can be regarded as a rejection of grace on the assumption that election can be earned." G. N. Davies wants to go further, suggesting that the οὐκέτι in 11:6 indicates a temporal shift away from a system of "works-righteousness" legalism to a system of grace—a critique that is emerging only in 9:30–10:3 and 11:6 (but prepared for by what came before in Romans); *Faith and Obedience*, 123–26. But Paul does not criticize the Jews for their zeal per se. The performance of the law is simply a human endeavor that does not bring about God's election or grace.

[24] See ch. 6 on the problem Paul identifies with the law in Gal 3:10: the law requires perfect obedience. Note also the emphatic placement of Lev 18:5's ὁ ποιήσας αὐτά. The law is based on a principle of doing what it requires (which dovetails with Gal 3:10).

[25] "The burden of proof is on those who want to assign a more specific meaning to the word ἔργα in this context, since semantically the broader meaning of the term is preferred unless there are decisive reasons in the context for limiting it" (T. R. Schreiner, "Israel's Failure," 217). God's own activity and election takes precedence over *any* human activity, including those works that demonstrate ethnic particularity; Westerholm, "Paul and the Law in Romans 9–11," 229.

[26] See ch. 9.

[27] On the relationship between the law and faith, see the following discussion of 9:30–33.

[28] The importance of the Gentiles being included in salvation would be the natural consequence of salvation by faith instead of by the requirements of the law. Certainly national righteousness would be one aspect of the law's

stands apart from human involvement.[29] This sketch of Paul's logic on the relationship between Israel's national privilege and a critique of the law as a merely human endeavor would be strengthened by retracing in detail Paul's line of thought in 9:30–10:8.

II. A Reading of Romans 9:30–10:8

A. Romans 9:30–33

Romans 9:30–32a literally reads: "What then shall we say? Although the Gentiles were not pursuing righteousness, they attained righteousness, namely a righteousness that is on the basis of faith. But Israel, although they were pursuing a law of righteousness [νόμον δικαιοσύνης] did not attain the law.[30] Why? Because they [pursued it (διώκω)] not on the basis of faith but as (if) on the basis of works."[31] What is the meaning of the

---

requirements, but it would be included in any discussion of the law per se. One need not overspecify Paul's argument, particularly given the broader context's emphasis on human activity and performance; contra Howard, "Christ the End," 336–37. The law was not just a matter of possession; it was a matter of possession and practice (as in Phil 3).

[29] The issue is not just a lack of faith in Christ but also a dependence on doing the law's precepts (or national righteousness, for those who agree with Sanders). However, there is a relationship between these two problems. For many, the issue is one of cause and effect: pursuing one's own righteousness ended up in neglecting God's righteousness in Christ; thus, among others, Laato, *Paul and Judaism,* 198; Käsemann, *Commentary on Romans,* 277–83; Murray, *Romans,* 2:42–49. As I have maintained, I think the problem runs in the opposite direction; it is not works-righteousness driving Paul's thought, but Christology emptying the law of its gracious significance.

[30] A concessive translation is suggested by the contrast between not pursuing and yet attaining, and pursuing and yet not attaining. Causal participles are not likely since the cause is suggested by the answer to the ensuing διὰ τί.

[31] Text-critically, ἔργων ("works") at the end of v. 32a should be read without νόμου, since ἔργων νόμου would be an assimilation to Rom 3:20, 28; Gal 2:16; 3:2, 5, 10; Cranfield, *Romans,* 2:509. The understood verb in v. 32 is best taken as διώκω, thereby paralleling the same verb used in the previous verses. Ulrich Wilckens thinks that the understood verb should be φθάνω ("attained"/*erlangen*); *Der Brief an die Römer,* 2:210, 212. The suggestion has not been met with enthusiasm, since it renders the logic obscure: Israel's attaining on the basis of works explains why they did *not* attain the law. T. David Gordon has suggested that the understood verb is from εἰμί ("to be"): "Israel did not attain the law? Why? Because *it [the law] is not characterized by* faith but as by works"; "Why Israel Did Not Obtain Torah-Righteousness: A Translation Note on Rom 9:32,"

phrase "law of righteousness" (νόμον δικαιοσύνης)? Is this a law that *demands* righteousness? Or is it a law that *promises* righteousness (whether as a witness to righteousness by faith or as a promise to those who do the law)?[32] Or could it be the law falsely understood as a way of righteousness?[33] An important clue is the antithesis between faith and works (ἐκ πίστεως and ἐξ ἔργων) in v. 32. One finds the same antithesis in Rom 3:27–31.[34] In that passage Paul had contrasted the law understood from the perspective of the works that it demands (thus 4:4–5) with the law understood from the perspective of the faith to which it bears witness (e.g., 3:21 and the testimony to Abraham's faith in Rom 4).[35] Could it be that Paul is playing on the same two different aspects of νόμος here?

Cranfield believes that "law of righteousness" (νόμον δικαιοσύνης) refers to the law as Mosaic Scripture—the law as it testifies to the righteousness of faith (Rom 3:21–22; 10:6–13).[36] The Jews would have attained the law and righteousness if they had pursued it on the basis of the faith to which the Law testifies. Badenas also thinks that Paul means the Torah in the revelatory sense: "the law from the perspective of the

---

WTJ 54 (1992): 163–66. Unfortunately, Gordon does not account for the presence of the word ὡς ("as") in the phrase "as by works." This word suggests a statement about the misunderstanding of the Jews rather than a critique of the law itself. The ὡς makes excellent sense with διώκω ("pursue") as the understood verb. Israel pursued the law not on the basis of faith but rather as on the basis of works. They pursued the law, understood from their point of view *as if* it were based on their deeds. On ὡς signalling a subjective element, see also Sanday and Headlam, *Romans,* 280; Käsemann, *Commentary on Romans* 278; Moo, *Romans,* 626 n. 43.

[32] On the law as demanding righteousness, see Schlier, *Der Römerbrief,* 307. For the law promising righteousness, see Käsemann, *Commentary on Romans,* 277; Cranfield, *Romans,* 507–8; and Lietzmann, *An die Römer,* 94, followed by Osten-Sacken, *Römer 8,* 252 n. 25.

[33] C. K. Barrett, *The Epistle to the Romans* (BNTC; London: Adam & Charles Black, 1957), 193. Another possibility suggested by Barrett is the adjectival sense "righteous" law; "Romans 9.30–10.21: Fall and Responsibility of Israel," in *Essays on Paul* (Philadelphia: Westminster, 1982), 140. But given the use of δικαιοσύνη for the Gentiles' right relationship with God in v. 30, δικαιοσύνη is unlikely to have a different meaning here in terms of the Jews. T. R. Schreiner writes: "the Gentiles have obtained the very thing (a right relation with God) that Israel sought" ("Israel's Failure," 212). One expects "righteousness" itself in the parallelism and not an adjective.

[34] Rhyne recognizes the importance of 3:27–4:25 for the interpretation of Rom 9:30–32, although he opts for only one of the nuances of the law as determinative here, νόμος πίστεως; *Faith,* 99–101.

[35] See ch. 8.

[36] *Romans,* 2:508.

δικαιοσύνη it promises, aims at, or bears witness to (cf. 3:21)."[37] Westerholm poses the main objection to taking νόμον δικαιοσύνης in the sense of revelatory Torah; the law insofar as it testifies to faith does not make a very good object of verbs of pursuing (διώκω) and attaining (φθάνω).[38] Westerholm points out that Paul's focus is on the law in terms of the works that it demands (thus the quote from Lev 18:5 in Rom 10:5). While Westerholm is right to emphasize the deeds that the law requires (as argued in the preceding section), such an emphasis need not rule out other nuances in Paul's understanding of the law. Romans 3:27–4:8 shows how the law can be understood from differing perspectives.

The way Paul phrases vv. 31–32a lends support to the possibility that the apostle is playing on the same two aspects of the law as in 3:27: the law from the perspective of the works that it demands and the law as a witness to righteousness and faith. Note the various elements of parallelism. The Gentiles did not pursue. The Jews did pursue.[39] The Gentiles attained where the Jews did not.[40] Yet the parallelism is disrupted at certain key points. The Gentiles did not pursue a *righteousness* based on faith, whereas the Jews pursued the *law* of righteousness. One would have expected that Israel pursued a "*righteousness* based on the law" (δικαιοσύνην τὴν ἐκ νόμου) to parallel the Gentiles' nonpursuit of the "righteousness based on faith." Whereas the Gentiles obtain *righteousness,* the Jews do not attain *the law.*[41] The parallelism leads one to expect *righteousness* where one finds, instead, the law. Both disruptions draw attention to the law as the culprit.

---

[37] Badenas, *Christ,* 104; see also p. 143.

[38] Westerholm, *Israel's Law and the Church's Faith,* 127. From Westerholm's standpoint, Rhyne (*Faith,* 100) is wrong to rule out the law from the point of view of the works that it demands. It was just such works that the Israelites were engaged in pursuing.

[39] Nothing in this text indicates that the Jews were wrong to pursue the law, as Wilckens supposes; *Der Brief an die Römer,* 2:212. It is the paradoxical fact that the group that was *not* pursuing it attained it while the group that *was* pursuing it did not. Rightly Steven Richard Bechtler, "Christ, the Τέλος of the Law: The Goal of Romans 10:4," *CBQ* 56 (1994): 292.

[40] Although Paul uses synonyms for "attain" (καταλαμβάνω, φθάνω).

[41] T. R. Schreiner maintains the parallelism with the Gentiles (who attain righteousness) by saying that the Jews did not attain [*righteousness*] *with respect to the law* (εἰς νόμον as an adverbial accusative of general reference); "Israel's Failure," 213. Whereas the Gentiles obtain righteousness, the Jews do not attain righteousness. The problem is that εἰς νόμον cannot be an adverbial accusative of reference here. φθάνω εἰς τι is an idiomatic phrase for "attain to something," in this case, the law.

Consider the first disruption: Paul's use of νόμον δικαιοσύνης ("law of righteousness") where one would have expected δικαιοσύνην τὴν ἐκ νόμον ("righteousness that is based on law"). Paul uses the latter wording in Rom 10:5 when he quotes Lev 18:5 to the effect that the righteousness of the law is based on doing its precepts. The break in the anticipated parallelism of 9:30–31 created by νόμον δικαιοσύνης indicates a deliberate play on terms. The law ought to be understood here differently from what the Jews (or the reader) might initially have supposed (given Israel's pursuit of the law). In other words, had Paul wished to speak unequivocally of the law from the perspective of the works that it demands, he could have used the same phraseology as in 10:5 and as would be expected by the parallelism.[42] He chooses, instead, to disrupt the parallelism with conspicuously different wording, thereby leading the reader to consider a different understanding of νόμος. Given the precedent of 3:27–4:25 (and the νόμος + genitive phrases earlier in the letter), an answer is not far from hand: Paul is speaking of the law as a witness to righteousness.[43] The Jews are pursuing a law that witnesses to righteousness as if it were based on their active pursuit and performance of its works. The Jews do not perceive the law in its inner connection to righteousness: righteousness is based on faith and not the doing of what the law prescribes.[44]

---

[42] Contra Schlier, *Der Römerbrief*, 307.

[43] Badenas, *Christ*, 103, is absolutely right: "If Paul has νόμον δικαιοσύνης in 9.30 while he has τὴν δικαιοσύνην τὴν ἐκ νόμου in 10.5, the most probable reason is that he meant νόμον δικαιοσύνης in 9.30 and τὴν δικαιοσύνην τὴν ἐκ νόμου in 10.5"; contra Sanders, *Paul, the Law*, 63 n. 130. Räisänen says:

> One would have expected Paul to write that Israel was striving at "the righteousness of the law", but did not attain "righteousness". Instead, the text as we have it reads: Israel, striving at the "law of righteousness", did not "arrive at the law". In view of these striking reversals of the genitive relationship it is difficult not to think of the realisation or otherwise of the true purpose of the Torah (*Paul and the Law*, 53–54).

One must therefore rule out that Paul means the "righteousness that is based on (doing) the law, or that the law requires." The phrase must refer to the law in its testimony or promise of righteousness, a righteousness on the basis of faith; with Osten-Sacken, *Römer 8*, 253; Rhyne, *Faith*, 101; and Badenas, *Christ*, 103–4. Paul elsewhere says that there is no righteousness available on the basis of the law (Gal 3:21–22). Yet the law still testifies to the righteousness found by faith (Gal 4:21; Rom 3:27).

[44] Thus Paul draws attention to νόμος in the phrase νόμον οὐκ ἔφθασεν, where one would have expected an article of previous reference, the full phrase "law *of righteousness*," or the word ἐκεῖνον ("that law").

Bechtler explains that if Paul had said that Israel failed to attain the righteousness reached by the Gentiles, "his readers could have inferred a radical

So why did the Jews not "attain" the law? Westerholm and T. R. Schreiner believe that the Jews did not attain the law because the Jews did not perfectly do the law. Westerholm recognizes that Paul does not expressly state this. Since Paul belabored the Jews' disobedience of the law in Rom 2, 3, and 7, he had no reason to revisit those points again. The problem with Westerholm and Schreiner's thinking is that Paul does say why the Jews did not attain the law. The words "attain" in v. 31b, the understood "pursue" in v. 32a, and the stone of "stumbling" in v. 32b are all related. They are all part of the racing imagery, and they form a coherent sequence of thought:

> v. 31b: Israel did not attain the law.
>
> v. 32a: Why? Because they did not pursue it on the basis of faith but as if on the basis of works,
>
> v. 32b: they stumbled on the stone of stumbling.[45]

Regardless of the exact punctuation of v. 32, the thought is clear.[46] In pursuing the law as if on the basis of works/human activity, the Jews stumbled on the stone of stumbling and did not attain the law. The ὡς of v. 32a bears its full force. It indicates the false perspective in which the Jews pursued the law in its testimony to righteousness. They had pursued the law as if its righteousness were based on human effort rather than faith.[47] Consequently, they stumbled on the stone.

---

discontinuity between the righteousness of Torah and the righteousness of God defined christologically and disclosed, *independently of the observance of Torah,* to all who believe." Rather "Because Israel has not attained *the goal* of the Torah, namely, righteousness, neither has it in fact attained the Torah itself, the law that leads to righteousness" (Bechtler, "Christ," 294). The reason Israel did not realize the true goal of the Torah in Christ was that they were concerned with its requirements. This is a false path (thus the ὡς); contra Bechtler, "Christ," 293.

[45] T. R. Schreiner, "Israel's Failure," 214, reverses the logic: stumbling is the *result* of not attaining righteousness in the pursuit of the law. Surely stumbling is the *cause* of not reaching that goal.

[46] Placing a comma after ἔργων and inserting the participial form of διώκω (διώκοντες) would render the entirety of v. 32 the response to the initial "Why?" (διὰ τί). See Badenas, *Christ,* 105–6, 241 n. 157.

[47] Thus Rhyne (*Faith,* 101, 167 n. 42) and G. N. Davies (*Faith and Obedience,* 123–24), who argue that ὡς indicates the Jews' subjective attitude and perception that they could attain the law on the basis of their works. On the subjective element signalled by ὡς, see note 31. Paul therefore understands the Mosaic law to teach faith and not salvation by mere works (see ch. 8). As Felix Flückiger explains, it is a misunderstanding to think that one can attain the law apart from the faith to which the law testifies; "Christus, des Gesetzes τέλος," *TZ* 11 (1955): 154.

Paul is not primarily concerned with the Jews' disobedience of the law at this point in his letter. What he is concerned with is the fact that human pursuit of the law is in principle opposed to God's actions on the basis of election. God's election is based on faith and not human merit or activity.[48] Likewise, it would be wrong to say that the problem with the Jews is only that they did not believe. Paul places faith and works into an antithesis. It is *because* they were involved in the doing of the law that they failed to believe. They understood the law from the perspective of its demands rather than from the perspective of faith. The irony is that the Jews failed to attain their own special possession, a law that was intended for righteousness, whereas the Gentiles without the law attained righteousness. The Jews missed out on the inner meaning of the law in its testimony to righteousness because of their rush to pursue the law's demands.[49] Consequently, they stumbled over the stone of stumbling (v. 32b).[50] The racing imagery continues in v. 32b, tying that verse to what preceded by means of content (if not also grammar).

B. Romans 10:1–3

Räisänen thinks that the address to the "brethren" (ἀδελφοί) in 10:1 marks a new phase in the argument.[51] The use of ἀδελφοί, however—as a survey of Rom 1:13; 7:4; 8:12; 1 Cor 1:11; 7:24, 29 shows—is not determinative for a new section.[52] The discussion of the Jews seeking their "own righteousness" as opposed to the righteousness of God clearly hearkens back to Israel's pursuit of righteousness in 9:30–33.[53] Paul

---

[48] See the close connection to 9:24–29. As T. R. Schreiner writes on the connection between 9:30 and what precedes: the only way the Gentiles could enter into a right relationship with God and possess faith is through God's own electing activity apart from human will or effort (9:6, 16); "Israel's Failure," 211. The thought will be explicit by 10:17. The true source of faith is God's powerful word (recall Rom 4:17).

[49] Badenas (*Christ,* 105) is wrong to deny any reference to human performance of the law in this passage. That is precisely what ἐξ ἔργων means given the context of its usage in Rom 9 and 11. Badenas's thinking seems to be in the process of formation on this matter. On p. 240 n. 153, he reverts to seeing the contrast as one of "human merits" versus "divine grace."

[50] See the discussion of the identity of the stone of stumbling in the notes to ch. 4.

[51] After arguing a break at 10:1, Räisänen concludes that τέλος in 10:4 must mean "end" since the racing imagery would be limited by the break to 9:30–32 (thereby ruling out "goal" as a possible translation); *Paul and the Law,* 54. In answering this structural question, one is already looking forward to 10:4.

[52] Dunn, *Romans 9–16,* 579.

[53] T. R. Schreiner, "Israel's Failure," 215.

returns in 10:3 to the aorist third person plural used in 9:32. Romans 10:3 must be referring to the same event(s): righteousness.[54] The failure of recognition in 10:2–3 (ἐπίγνωσις, ἀγνοεῖν) parallels Israel's failure to recognize the true meaning of the law in 9:32 (they pursued it ὡς ἐξ ἔργων). The use of Isa 28:16 in 10:11 ties the argument from 9:33 together into a unit.

The Jews' misunderstanding of the law's inner nature in 9:32 is confirmed by 10:2–3.[55] The Jews had a "zeal" for God but were lacking "knowledge" (ἐπίγνωσις). Verse 3 explains v. 2.[56] Because they were ignorant (ἀγνοοῦντες) of God's righteousness and because they were striving to establish (ζητοῦντες στῆσαι) their own (τὴν ἰδίαν) righteousness, the Jews did not subordinate themselves to the righteousness of God. The language of "striving" in 10:3 also develops 9:30–32 and confirms that the issue here is human accomplishment (even as in 9:30–32). The Jews failed because they sought a righteousness of their own, their own achievement, instead of God's righteousness. Paul never criticizes zeal for the law per se. The problem for Paul is not with striving to do what the law says. The problem lies in the bigger picture. If Christ is the key to God's righteousness, as Paul's letter to the Romans has asserted in Rom 1:16–17 (and will assert in Rom 10:4), then, even though the law is good in itself, striving after the law will not yield a righteousness before God. Such effort will be reduced to human activity. In fact, the law could become a liability if one were to focus on doing its works and miss its inner meaning—its testimony to God's righteousness in Christ.[57]

Many have noted parallels between Rom 10:1–3 and Phil 3:4–11. The Jews' "zeal for God" parallels Paul's own "zeal" as a persecutor of the church. Israel's "ignorance" of God's righteousness stands in contrast

---

[54] Paul W. Meyer, "Romans 10:4 and the 'End' of the Law," in *The Divine Helmsman: Studies in God's Control of Human Events, Presented to Lou H. Silberman* (ed. James L. Crenshaw and Samuel Sandmel; New York: Ktav, 1980), 65.

[55] P. W. Meyer also notes the return in 10:3 of the aorist third person plural (as in 9:32), which indicates that Paul has in mind "the same event or sequence of events" ("Romans 10:4," 65).

[56] Perhaps the ἐπί functions as an intensive; the Jews lacked *true* knowledge; Badenas, *Christ,* 109.

[57] "Their own righteousness" is also less than perfect. One need only recall Deut 9:4, 6 in the light of Deut 7:8 and 8:11–18. Thielman disagrees with Sanders (*Paul, the Law,* 38), N. T. Wright (*Climax,* 241), and Watson (*Paul, Judaism and the Gentiles,* 165), who all see the Jews' "own" righteousness as national righteousness: "If Paul is thinking biblically, however, and the biblical language of 10:5–13 shows that he is, then he is probably echoing Deuteronomy's references to Israel's 'own' inadequate 'righteousness'" (Thielman, *Paul and the Law,* 300 n. 52). Paul had explicitly made this point earlier in the letter (see Rom 3:9–18).

with Paul's own "knowledge" of Christ Jesus in Phil 3:8. Israel's establishing its "own righteousness" parallels Paul's "own righteousness" in Phil 3:9. Philippians 3 (properly construed) argues that the righteousness of God in Christ reveals the righteousness of the law to be one's "own" righteousness—a righteousness of one's own doing.[58] Because of the revelation of God's righteousness in Christ, to pursue righteousness through any other means than Christ is to pursue something other than God's righteousness. It is to pursue a righteousness of one's own doing.[59] In their unenlightened zeal for God, the Jews of Rom 10:1–3 were ignorant of the true righteousness of God.

C. Romans 10:4

"For Christ is the end of the law so that there may be righteousness for everyone who believes" (10:4). This verse grounds Paul's assertions in vv. 2–3 (γάρ). A righteousness apart from Christ is a merely human righteousness.[60] The word τέλος has proven difficult to translate. Christ could be the "goal" of the law; Christ would be what the law had pointed to and its fulfillment. Christ could also be the "end" of the law, its termination point. Many who favor translating τέλος as "goal" point to the racing imagery in 9:30–32. Since Räisänen's case for a sharp break at 10:1 is less than convincing, the possibility of τέλος as "goal" remains viable. If 10:1–3 are closely related to 9:30–33, then 10:4 would be related to 9:30–33, since 10:4 functions as support for 10:2–3. Many have therefore found the racing imagery of 9:30–32 carried through to 10:4, which favors "goal" as the proper translation.[61] On the other hand, one cannot be absolutely

---

[58] See the discussion of Phil 3 in ch. 9.

[59] The aorist verb "did not submit" in 10:3 already looks ahead to 10:4, the rejection of Christ, the true end/goal of the Torah; Cranfield, *Romans,* 2:515.

Romans 2, 3, 7, and Gal 3:10–12 have adequately shown the human incapacity to do what God requires in the law; cf. ch. 1 and the Jewish sense of the extreme difficulty of doing all that God requires. The focus here, however, is on the failure to recognize God's righteousness in Christ.

[60] Since early on in the letter, Paul has connected the righteousness of God to the gospel of Jesus Christ (1:17; 3:5, 25–26; cf. 1 Cor 1:30; 2 Cor 5:21). The use of righteousness alongside Torah has intensified expectation of a christological connection up to this point. By 10:4 that expectation is relieved. Refusal to submit to God's righteousness means rejecting Christ, the embodiment of that righteousness; Badenas, *Christ,* 110–11.

[61] Flückiger, "Christus," 154–55; Thielman, *Paul and the Law,* 205, 299 n. 45; Badenas, *Christ,* 101–2. Badenas (p. 115) argues that since the Jews missed the goal of the race, they stumbled and kept on running, but in the wrong direction.

Thomas H. Tobin takes the racing imagery further than Badenas; "Romans 10:4: Christ the Goal of the Law," in *The Studia Philonica Annual: Studies in*

certain that Paul intends an allusion to the race in 10:4. Bechtler cautions that 10:4 comes after an interval of three verses without racing imagery.[62] Moo thinks that the language is too general to suggest racing.[63]

Even if Paul is not continuing the motif of racing in 10:4, τέλος could still mean "goal."[64] The primary consideration pointing toward τέλος as "goal" is the play on terms in 9:30–32. Paul had disrupted the reader's expectations by suggesting two different aspects of the Mosaic law: the law as something to be pursued on the basis of the works that it requires, and the law as a witness to righteousness based on faith. The latter strongly suggests that Paul has "goal" in mind in 10:4. Israel did not attain righteousness because they pursued it in ignorance and wrongly thought that righteousness could be achieved on the basis of the law's works. Israel failed to see that righteousness is based on *faith*—a faith grounded in *the Messiah*.[65] Thus when the Jews did not submit to the righteousness that God had prepared for them, they established their own righteousness instead. They failed to see that Christ is the *goal* of the law, the one to whom the law had been pointing all along. Another important consideration for taking τέλος as "goal" comes in Rom 10:6–8. Paul takes a passage from the Torah and interprets it in terms of Christ. This sort of rhetorical move reinforces Paul's point that the Torah, properly understood, attests to God's righteousness found in Christ.

Badenas and Rhyne, who have both argued for Christ as the "goal" of the law, emphasize that there is nothing negative about the relationship between righteousness and the law.[66] However, there *is* a negative relationship if one understands the law from the point of view of the works it demands. Christ is the "end" of the law in the sense of a pursuit

---

Hellenistic Judaism (vol. 3, ed. David T. Runia; Atlanta: Scholars Press, 1991), 276–79. He sees the same language in, among other places, Phil 3:12–16, 1 Cor 9:24. Philo too speaks of the "goal" (τέλος) of the law in the midst of racing imagery. Tobin concludes that Paul is drawing on a Hellenistic *topos* of racing imagery. See J. Duncan M. Derrett for a possible OT precursor to this motif; " 'Running' in Paul: The Midrashic Potential of Hab 2,2," *Bib* 66 (1985): 560–67. See also note 18 above.

[62] Thomas R. Schreiner, "Paul's View of the Law in Romans 10:4–5," *WTJ* 55 (1993): 120; Räisänen, *Paul and the Law,* 54 n. 54; Bechtler, "Christ," 292 n. 15. Bechtler also points out that the word καταισχύνω ("disappoint") does not refer to the "agony of defeat" in a race since its occurrence here is motivated entirely by Isa 28:16 (LXX).

[63] Moo, *Romans,* 621 n. 22.

[64] Bechtler, "Christ," 301.

[65] "Christ" should be taken as the "Messiah"; see 9:5 and 10:9 (cf. 10:6, 7, 17, 21).

[66] Badenas, *Christ,* 114; Rhyne, *Faith,* 103.

of righteousness based on its demands.[67] Translating τέλος as "end" also dovetails with v. 5, which is connected to v. 4 by γάρ. Räisänen points out that since Paul speaks in v. 5 of righteousness based on doing what the law requires, Paul must be concluding in 10:4 that the law—with respect to a righteousness on the basis of its demands—has come to an end in Christ.[68] Certainly striving after the law in the attempt to do what it requires has been a major factor in Israel's failure to "attain" the law and the establishment, instead, of "their own" righteousness (v. 3).[69] On the other hand, Paul seems to be demolishing a "straw man" when he claims that the Jews are pursuing the law on the basis of its works. The Jews of Paul's day would not have seen their relationship with God as achieved through the doing of the law. They would have pointed (at least in large measure) to God's election and mercy, as Sanders has shown. The problem is that Paul views the matter from a radically christological perspective. God's election and mercy are operative *in Christ*. The law had pointed to Christ and faith in him as its "goal" (cf. 3:21). If so, then faith in Christ eliminates any saving value in the law. In the *Pauline* framework of understanding, the law without Christ is a merely human endeavor.[70] In Paul's perspective, Christ is the "end," the termination of the law as a human pursuit of righteousness.

One therefore sees a dual perspective at work in τέλος. Just as the law can be viewed from either of two perspectives in Rom 9:30–32, one finds the same dual perspective on τέλος in 10:4. Some have objected to seeing τέλος as a play on words in 10:4. Although he later modified his position, Räisänen once claimed that an understanding of τέλος as both

---

[67] Bechtler ("Christ," 302) no doubt echoes the sentiments of many when he denies "end" as a possible translation since he sees no role for human striving and achievement in the passage but only national righteousness. Apart from the considerations in favor of human striving, even national righteousness and ethnic division come to an "end" with Christ (thus Gal 3:28).

[68] Räisänen, *Paul and the Law,* 54.

[69] T. R. Schreiner rightly connects vv. 3–4: "[Paul] is responding to the specific problem raised in v. 3 of people wrongly using the law to establish their own righteousness. In v. 4 Paul points out that those who believe in Christ cease using the law as a means of establishing their own righteousness" ("Paul's View of the Law," 122). Schreiner would go further and deny any possibility of the law as "goal," that is, as a testimony to faith. He too quickly dismisses an important layer in the argument: that if Israel had used the law rightfully and knowledgeably, they would have recognized Christ as the goal of the law (and as such, the end of its wrong use).

[70] It is not that Jewish theology was a theology driven by human achievement of the law. It is just that human achievement of the law is all that is left of Jewish theology once its gracious framework has been torn down and reconstructed in Christ.

"end" *and* "goal" is "the most dubious of all."[71] Dunn warns against being led astray into "either/or" thinking, since τέλος is ambiguous.[72] Thielman disagrees with Räisänen as well: to reach the "goal" of a race signals that one has reached the *end* of the race.[73] The possibility that Paul has in mind both senses is therefore realistic and defensible.[74] Paul is deliberately ambiguous in his use of τέλος in 10:4. Yet the deliberate ambiguity is not limited to 10:4. Paul prepares for the rhetorical move already in 9:30–32 as well as in 3:27–4:25.

Another problem is what the following words, εἰς δικαιοσύνην, modify. Dunn thinks that εἰς δικαιοσύνην in 10:4 must modify νόμος, since these two words are connected in 10:5 (see also νόμον δικαιοσύνης in 9:31).[75] Christ would be the end of the law-as-a-way-to-righteousness, that is, the mistaken pursuit of national righteousness. The primary problem with Dunn's analysis is that the prepositional phrase should have come right after νόμου, were that the case.[76] However, one could maintain the sense of Dunn's translation even if the prepositional phrase modified the entirety of what precedes. Sam Williams paraphrases Rom 10:4: "with respect to the attaining of righteousness Christ is the end of the law" (but in no other sense).[77] Williams's paraphrase too has been grammatically disputed.[78] For Schreiner, the prepositional

---

[71] Räisänen, *Paul and the Law,* 53 (first edition). By the second edition he decided that this is a viable option after all. E. E. Johnson (*Function of Apocalyptic,* 152 n. 127) concurs with Räisänen's initial dissent.

[72] Dunn, *Romans 9–16,* 589.

[73] Thielman, *Paul and the Law,* 299 n. 45.

[74] Thus also Ragnar Bring, "Die Gerechtigkeit Gottes und das Alttestamentliche Gesetz: Eine Untersuchung von Röm 10,4," in *Christus und das Gesetz: Die Bedeutung des Gesetzes des Alten Testaments nach Paulus und Sein Glauben an Christus* (Leiden: E. J. Brill, 1969), 43–44. Unfortunately, Bring (p. 44) wrongly goes on to associate "doing the law" with believing in Christ (and incorporation into Christ's righteousness) in Gal 3:10, 12 and Rom 10:5. The error of the Jews (p. 45) was that they confused "doing the law" with the "works of the law" when they did not believe. They thought the precepts of the law could lead to righteousness (p. 46).

[75] Dunn, *Romans 9–16,* 590.

[76] Badenas, *Christ,* 115–16; Cranfield, *Romans,* 2:519–20 n. 2. Only 77 of the 1800 NT occurrences of εἰς modify a noun, and 56 of these instances immediately precede or come after the noun it modifies. Of the remaining twenty-two instances, the prepositional phrase is never separated from its noun by the subject of the sentence; Moo, *Romans,* 637 n. 34. This assumes that Χριστός is the subject.

[77] Sam K. Williams, "The 'Righteousness of God' in Romans," *JBL* 99 (1980): 284.

[78] Mark A. Seifrid points out that "a survey of NT nouns and/or pronouns linked by ἐστίν (or ἐστίν understood) and followed by a preposition, shows that

phrase modifies the predicate nominative (adverbial of general reference): Christ is the *end* of the law *with respect to* (establishing) righteousness.[79] Schreiner's approach would permit Dunn's line of thought as well. Schreiner's translation and argument show that the mistaken attempt to establish righteousness could just as easily refer to doing what the law requires, quite apart from any emphasis on national righteousness. Sanders suggests yet another reading with the prepositional phrase taken as final or consecutive: "with a view to" or "resulting in."[80] In other words, the prepositional phrase is ambiguous and could work with a translation of τέλος as *either* "end" *or* "goal." Viewed from one perspective, Christ could be the "end" of the law *with respect to* establishing righteousness. Alternatively, Christ could be the true "goal" and meaning of the law *resulting in* righteousness for all who believe. The ambiguity surrounding νόμος in 9:30–32 and τέλος in 10:4 is paralleled by a similar ambiguity with εἰς δικαιοσύνην. In each instance, Paul contrasts a perspective from the vantage point of the law's works with a perspective based upon the law's testimony to a righteousness through faith in Christ. Romans 10:5–8 juxtapose these two perspectives yet again.

D. Romans 10:5[81]

In Rom 10:5 Paul cites Lev 18:5: "The person who does these things will live by them." The focus of Leviticus seems to be entirely on doing the

---

virtually all have the prepositions related to the predicate nominative alone" ("Paul's Approach to the Old Testament in Rom 10:6–8," *TJ* 6 NS [1985]: 9 n. 30). If so, the phrase could not modify the entire preceding phrase but only the predicate nominative τέλος νόμου. On the separation of τέλος and εἰς δικαιοσύνην, τέλος is thrust forward for emphasis, and so the separation would not be a factor.

[79] T. R. Schreiner, "Paul's View of the Law," 122–23. Cf. εἰς in Rom 16:19; 2 Cor 2:9; Rom 8:7 (?). As with Dunn, Paul would be speaking here experientially. Paul does not see the law as *ever* having been a way of righteousness (Gal 2:21; 3:21; Rom 4). While Paul sees the Jews as having misunderstood the law on that point (9:31; 10:3), that misunderstanding should come to an "end" with Christ.

[80] Sanders, *Paul, the Law,* 39–40; see Rom 5:18; Phil 1:19; Rom 10:1, 10. Seifrid too asserts that the phrase has a telic force; "Paul's Approach," 9 n. 29. Whereas Sanders takes the prepositional phrase with all of what precedes, taking the prepositional phrase with the predicate nominative would not jeopardize the overall sense. Paul Meyer ("Romans 10:4," 68) takes the prepositional phrase with τέλος: Christ is the "intent and goal of the law, to lead to righteousness for everyone who believes."

[81] Several scholars have suggested emending the Nestle-Aland text of Rom 10:5; thus Rhyne, *Faith,* 104–5, 170 nn. 70–71; Badenas, *Christ,* 118–19. The

law; it is concerned with the law from the perspective of the works that it demands. George Howard disagrees, since the law itself included a component of grace in the form of atoning sacrifices (in Leviticus).[82] To do what the law required, Howard concludes, would not have been a burden. On the other hand, the immediate context of Lev 18:5 does not mention any gracious elements. Leviticus 18:1–30 is generally considered a literary unit.[83] Verses 1–5 introduce a series of sexual laws that require irrevocable expulsion from the people when violated (cf. 18:28–29; 20:22–24). There is no sacrifice for these sins (18:29; 26:31).[84] The regulations of 18:7–23 are repeated in 20:9–21, where death is required for violators. In the context of Lev 18 and 20, "do this and live" (Lev 18:5) must mean

---

Nestle-Aland reading is more difficult and more likely the original. The problem with the alternative readings in the textual tradition is that they all eliminate the awkward grammar in the more difficult reading (τὴν δικαιοσύνην as an adverbial accusative of respect modifying γράφει). The other textual variants result from the shift of ὅτι to a position after γράφει (an assimilation to Rom 3:10–12; 4:17; 8:36; 9:12; 1 Cor 14:21; 2 Cor 6:16; Gal 3:10). With "the righteousness based on the law" as the object of ποιήσας, the former direct object (αὐτά) would be dropped, and the neuter plural ἐν αὐτοῖς would be changed to αὐτῇ in view of the new feminine, singular direct object. Note how the same group of texts has these changes. Further, Paul is likely to have quoted the LXX here as in Gal 3:12. A scribe would not likely *introduce* grammatical awkwardness in an attempt to conform the quote to the LXX (τὴν δικαιοσύνην as an adverbial accusative of respect). On leaving the text as it stands, see Andreas Lindemann, "Die Gerechtigkeit aus dem Gesetz: Erwägungen zur Auslegung und zur Textgeschichte von Römer 10:5," *ZNW* 73 (1982), 232–37, 246–50; Dunn, *Romans 9–16*, 599; Seifrid, "Paul's Approach," 13. Bandstra (*Law*, 103 n. 128a) thinks that the variants within the OT citation (the mention of αὐτά; αὐτοῖς for αὐτῇ) reflect a scribal harmonization with Lev 18:5 (LXX) and Gal 3:12. Inserting αὐτά as object of ποιήσας would call for moving the ὅτι to after γράφει. It is easier to explain how the textual variants could arise from the reading of the Nestle-Aland text than the reverse.

[82] Howard, "Christ the End of the Law," 334; followed by Walter C. Kaiser Jr., "Leviticus 18:5 and Paul: Do This and You Shall Live (Eternally?)," *JETS* 14 (1971): 25. Leviticus 18:5 is quoted in Ezek 20:11, 13, 21 as referring to the law as God's great life-giving gift to Israel. Nehemiah 9:29 quotes it in reference to the covenant relationship of God and his people and thus as a promise of life. See also Deut 4:1; 5:32–33; 8:1; 30:15–20; Ezek 18:9, 21; 33:19, which all refer to "do and live." The law is a "law of life" (Sir 17:11; 45:5). James Dunn sees this living by the law in terms of "covenantal nomism," a way of life within the Jewish covenant; "Righteousness from the Law," 219.

[83] Gordon J. Wenham, *The Book of Leviticus*, 249–50; R. K. Harrison, *Leviticus: An Introduction and Commentary* (TOTC; Downers Grove, Ill.: InterVarsity Press, 1980), 183–84. Both authors outline the chapter according to a covenant-treaty form. Harrison, 183, treats vv. 18–20 as a larger literary context.

[84] Contra also G. N. Davies, *Faith and Obedience*, 192–93.

more than living "in" these commandments, that is, in their sphere (as Howard suggests).[85] A person lives by *doing* these commands or else the individual must die or be expelled from the people.[86] God's blessings depend on successfully obeying what has been commanded (Lev 26:1–13). Disobedience brings God's punishment and expulsion (26:14–39). Howard believes that the law in Paul's writings includes the elements of Judaism's gracious framework, that is, the notion of atoning sacrifice, but Paul can treat the law as a series of empty obligations because he views the law apart from Judaism's gracious context.[87]

The ethnic dimension of Paul's comments in 9:30–10:3 has led many scholars to conclude that Paul is concerned with "national righteousness" and not individual behavior. They point to a corresponding corporate dimension in Leviticus. According to Lev 18:24–28 the land of Israel will "vomit" evildoers out even as the prior inhabitants had been expelled. Leviticus 18:5, as part of this section of Leviticus, became associated with the exile (Neh 9:29; Ezek 20:11, 13, 21). However, the warning of national exile (18:24–28) comes at the end of a section regarding individual behavior.[88] In other words, the corporate fate of the nation cannot be abstracted from individual obedience. By an *individual's* doing these commands he or she avoids death or banishment, that is, "lives." Paul's use of Lev 18:5 conforms with the context of Lev 18: Christ is the "end" of the law (Rom 10:4) insofar as anyone need establish righteousness (i.e., "live") through doing its commands (Rom 10:5; Lev 18:5).[89]

Bandstra interprets Rom 10:5 in light of Phil 2:7–10 as a reference to what *Christ* has done; Rom 10:5 does not speak of what people do in general but of what *the man* did.[90] The word ἄνθρωπος, however, is

---

[85] Kaiser, "Leviticus 18:5," 19–28.

[86] Martin Noth, *Leviticus: A Commentary* (rev. ed.; OTL; Philadelphia: Westminster, 1977), 134; Harrison, *Leviticus,* 185. "Life" is the reward dependent on obedience in the Pentateuch (Lev 26:3–13; Deut 4:1–2, 40; 5:33; 6:1–3; 7:12–16; 8:1; 28:1–14). The "life" of Lev 18:5 depends on the faithful observance of the law. So also Neh 9:29; Ezek 20:13, 21; and CD 3.14–16.

[87] See ch. 5 on Paul's opinion of the atoning sacrifices of Judaism.

[88] The regulations of 18:7–23 are repeated in 20:9–21. The context of Lev 17–20 includes many regulations that affect the individual Israelite.

[89] In particular, those who see an allusion to "covenantal nomism" here fail to take into account that the *"doing"* of the law in Lev 18:5 would, in Paul's context, dovetail with the contrast in Rom 9 and 10 up to this point between *God's saving activity and righteousness* and *human activity and pursuit of righteousness.* Israel's "doing" is not a positive element in this context.

[90] Bandstra, *Law,* 103–5. So also Stowers, *A Rereading of Romans,* 308–9; Cranfield, *Romans,* 2:521–22. Bandstra relies too heavily on Johannes Munck's case for parallels with Phil 2:7–11; *Christ and Israel: An Interpretation of Romans*

hardly an obvious reference to Christ. If Paul were referring to Christ, he would surely have made his point more explicitly, as he does in the case of the Deuteronomy citation in the ensuing verses.[91] The parallel to Phil 3:9 does not help Bandstra's case either. Phil 3:9 refers negatively to the "righteousness of the law," which renders a positive use of the phrase in Rom 10:5 unlikely.[92]

Bring thinks that the righteousness of the law in 10:5 is the *explanation* of the righteousness of faith (and not its opposite). Since righteousness is available only through faith in Christ, faith in Christ fulfills the necessity to "do the law." "Doing" means "believing."[93] Romans 9:30–10:5 juxtaposes the true way of righteousness through Christ (attested in the law) with Israel's failure to submit to that true way of righteousness because of their pursuit of the law's righteousness through its works (9:30–32; cf. 10:3).[94] Paul cites Lev 18:5 to show that the righteousness that stems from the law itself is based on *doing* what it requires. This is a very different righteousness from what *God* has done in Christ. Christ is the end of the law as a means of trying to establish one's own righteousness.[95]

9–11 (trans. Ingeborg Nixon; Philadelphia: Fortress, 1967), 86–89. The parallels are hardly impressive.

[91] G. N. Davies (*Faith and Obedience,* 198) adds: "the christological dimension in 10.6–8 is different from that offered by Cranfield in 10.5. In the former Christ is the object of faith, whereas in the latter he is supposed to be the subject of the action."

[92] T. R. Schreiner, "Paul's View of the Law," 126, 129.

[93] Bring, "Die Gerechtigkeit Gottes," 42–49, 52, 54; idem, "Paul and the Old Testament: A Study of the Ideas of Election, Faith and Law in Paul, with Special Reference to Romans 9:30–10:30," *ST* 25 (1971): 47–52. See also G. N. Davies, *Faith and Obedience,* 189–98; Badenas, *Christ,* 118–25; Daniel B. Fuller, *Gospel and Law: Contrast or Continuum? The Hermeneutics of Dispensationalism and Covenant Theology* (Grand Rapids: Eerdmans, 1980), 65–88.

[94] Badenas, *Christ,* 120. Paul posits a *contrast* between doing and believing. This contrast will continue in vv. 6–8 as Paul omits any reference to works in his citations from Deuteronomy; Rhyne, *Faith,* 170 n. 76 (see discussion below). "τὴν δικαιοσύνην τὴν ἐκ νόμου ποιεῖν (10:5) corresponds to διώκειν νόμον δικαιοσύνης . . . ὡς ἐξ ἔργων (9:32) and τὴν ἰδίαν (δικαιοσύνην) ζητεῖν στῆσαι (10:3), while ἡ ἐκ πίστεως δικαιοσύνη (10:6) corresponds to διώκειν νόμον δικαιοσύνης . . . ἐκ πίστεως (9:30, 32) and (πᾶς) ὁ πιστεύων (9:33; 10:4)"; Rhyne, *Faith,* 105; cf. Osten-Sacken, *Römer 8,* 255.

One ought also to note that nowhere does Paul speak positively of the "righteousness that comes from/is based on the law." Paul contrasts that sort of righteousness with the righteousness from God in Phil 3:9. The negative reference to "my own righteousness" in Phil 3:9 parallels "their own" righteousness in Rom 10:3; T. R. Schreiner, *The Law and Its Fulfillment,* 110.

[95] Badenas writes:

E. Romans 10:6–8

In Rom 10:6–8 Paul cites Deut 9:4 and 30:12–13 as the words of ἡ ἐκ πίστεως δικαιοσύνη. Paul's ascribing these verses to "the righteousness of faith" and not to Moses (cf. Deut 5:1; 29:1–2) prepares for his unusual exegesis of these texts.[96] Paul shows how the Mosaic law teaches *another* righteousness, a righteousness based on faith. In its original context Deut 30:12–14 asserted that the law's requirements were not too difficult.[97] The message of Deut 30:12–14 would have agreed with Lev 18:5

> For by quoting Moses in Lev 18.5 as teaching righteousness by works, Paul would be—in a certain sense—excusing Israel's "pursuit of law righteousness ἐξ ἔργων" (9.31–32). If this was the way of righteousness taught by Moses, the Jews could not be accused of "establishing their own way of righteousness" (10.3). They were, vis-à-vis Moses, theologically right! They were doing what the law commanded, and their understanding of the law would be correct! But this is the contrary to what Paul says. One of Paul's charges against Israel is precisely their wrong understanding of Scripture (*Christ,* 121).

Again, the text has to be understood within *Paul's* logic. In light of Paul's critique of their obedience earlier in the letter, the way of righteousness prescribed by the deeds of the law became a curse instead of a blessing. Now Paul explains that the Jews stumbled over the law's inner meaning, which is based on *faith* apart from the works that it prescribes (9:33). The law itself witnesses to a different sort of righteousness, one found *in* Christ (Rom 10:6–8). If the blessings the Torah speaks of are found in Christ, then the works of the Torah cannot convey those blessings and are relegated to a matter of precepts.

[96] There is good reason to believe that Paul is directly interacting with Deuteronomy. The ten verses or so preceding and following 10:6–8 all involve actual quotations. The citation generally follows the LXX of Deut 30:14. The alteration of crossing the sea to descending into the depths is attested in *Targum Neofiti* on Deut 30:13. See also Ps 139:8–9. The "sea" (יָם) was frequently referred to as the abyss (ἄβυσσος, also used for the Hebrew תְּהוֹם); Gen 49:25; Deut 33:13; Ps 36:7(6); Prov 33:20; 8:27–30; Seifrid, "Paul's Approach," 18–19. ἀλλὰ τί λέγει is probably an abbreviation of ἀλλὰ τί λέγει ἡ γραφή (see Gal 4:30; Rom 4:3; 11:2, 4, as well as the scribal emendation of this verse). Finally, the Pauline preface, beginning with τοῦτ' ἔστιν, is used in the NT elsewhere only in Rom 9:7–8; Heb 7:5; and 1 Pet 3:20 (see also 1QS 8.14–15; 4QFlor 1.11; 4QpIsa^{b} 2.6–7). Paul is not merely alluding to Deuteronomy but actually working with the text; M. Jack Suggs, " 'The Word Is Near You': Romans 10: 6–10 within the Purpose of the Letter," in *Christian History and Interpretation: Studies Presented to John Knox* (ed. W. R. Farmer, C. F. D. Moule, and R. R. Niebuhr; Cambridge: Cambridge University Press, 1967), 300–302; Dunn, "Righteousness from the Law," 216–18; Seifrid, "Paul's Approach," 17–18.

[97] "This commandment" and "the word" refers to the entirety of the covenant stipulations (4:2; 6:1; 17:20; 30:11; 31:5; 32:47). The covenant requirements are not too difficult since God's word is "very near to you."

on the need to obey the law.[98] Yet Paul prefaces Deut 30:12–14 with Deut 9:4 (and 8:17): μὴ εἴπῃς ἐν τῇ καρδιᾳ σου. He carefully omits all references to the central theme of doing (ποιεῖν) the law and its commandments. He omits καὶ ἀκούσαντες αὐτὴν ποιήσομεν (Deut 30:12). He omits καὶ ἀκουστὴν ἡμῖν ποιήσει αὐτὴν καὶ ποιήσομεν (v. 13). He also omits καὶ ἐν ταῖς χερσίν σου αὐτὸ ποιεῖν (v. 14).[99] Whereas Deut 30:12–14 had referred to the attainability of the law's commandments apart from superhuman effort, Paul interprets the verses (τοῦτ' ἔστιν) in a very different manner. Instead of the accessibility of the law and its commandments, Paul speaks of the accessibility of *Christ* and *faith*. He uses the "word of faith" (τὸ ῥῆμα τῆς πίστεως) instead of ῥῆμα as commandment (in Deuteronomy). "In your mouth and in your heart" no longer refer to the readiness to do the law's commandment but rather to the Christian confession of faith.[100] From Paul's point of view, the law witnesses to faith in Christ, that is, its "goal." Romans 10:6–8 therefore grounds the words of 10:4.[101]

Paul seems to have altered radically what Deut 30 was saying. Paul generally uses the OT as a *proof* of his own position, and it is not likely that such a radical departure would have served his case.[102] One possible rationale for Paul's approach is that he is building on the current Jewish tradition in his day that personified the Torah of Deut 30:12–14 in terms of Wisdom (e.g., Bar 3:29–30). Paul could be extending this Torah-equals-Wisdom equation to Christ.[103] In Christ one finds the blessings that Baruch attributed to Wisdom and the Torah.[104] Baruch 3:29–30 says:

---

[98] As Suggs put it:

> To Paul's "Moses writes that the man who practises the righteousness which is based on the law shall live by it", the proper Jewish rebuttal might run: "But Moses also writes, 'This commandment which I command you this day is not too hard for you, neither is it far off, etc. . . . The word is near you.'" But it is just because it is a text of that kind that we should be hesitant to assume that Paul's interpretation is completely out of contact with contemporary Jewish tradition ("The Word Is Near You," 303).

[99] Rhyne, *Faith,* 170 n. 76; Badenas, *Christ,* 125. Christ essentially replaces the commandment, and faith replaces the performance of the commandment; L. T. Johnson, *Reading Romans,* 160.

[100] Rhyne, *Faith,* 106–8; Koch, *Die Schrift,* 129–32, 157, 295–96.

[101] Rhyne, *Faith,* 111.

[102] Badenas, *Christ,* 126–27.

[103] Thus Suggs, "The Word Is Near You," 304.

[104] In Prov 30:1–4 is the question: "Who has ascended to heaven and come down?" following the confession, "I have not learned wisdom" (but contrast the LXX). See also Job 15:7–8. It was common for Wisdom to be considered inaccessible (Eccl 7:23–24). Job 28 asks where wisdom may be found and concludes that it

> Who has gone up into heaven, and taken her,
>   and brought her down from the clouds?
> Who has gone over the sea, and found her,
>   and will buy her for pure gold?[105]

In light of Bar 4:1's identification of Wisdom with the commandments of God and the law that endures forever, Suggs calls Bar 3:9–4:4 the "gospel of the Torah" since the commandments of the law/Wisdom are considered a source of life.[106] Paul simply adds a third term to this equation: Christ. Christ and righteousness by faith in him are thereby seen to be the true goal of the Torah.[107] The equation of Christ = Wisdom = Torah is not without problems.[108] James Dunn emphasizes that Deut

---

is beyond the reach of humans (vv. 13–14; cf. Job 11:5–12). Wisdom is then personified in Prov 1–9 and granted special status relative to creation (Prov 8:22–30; Wis 9:1–4). Wisdom is the revealer of hidden mysteries (see Wis 7:27; Sir 51:13–30). Wisdom was therefore connected to the law in Jewish tradition; thus Wis 6:4, 9; 9:9, "keeping the law" means "learning wisdom and not transgressing." Wisdom and the Torah are set in parallel in *2 Bar.* 38:1–39:1; 48:24; 51:3–4, 7. Wisdom is virtually equated with the Torah in Sir 24:23 on the "Praise of Wisdom," or in Bar 4:1; Suggs, "The Word Is Near You," 304–8.

[105] Cf. Wisdom in Sir 24:5, 23.

[106] Suggs, "The Word Is Near You," 309. Suggs (pp. 309–10) sees this tradition reflected in the Amoraic period in *Midrash Rabbah, Deuteronomy.*

[107] E. E. Johnson follows Suggs in viewing 10:6–8 as dependent on Baruch; *Function of Apocalyptic,* 133–39. Although Paul in his citation alters Deut 30:12a differently, Johnson sees Paul dependent on Baruch's use of Deut 30:12a. Neither Paul nor Baruch cite Deut 30:13a, but both resume again with Deut 30:13b, and both change διαπεράζω to a βαίνω verb. While Paul goes on to quote Deut 30:14 (unlike Baruch), both make reference to ζωή (4:1; 10:5; Lev 18:5). Like the Torah, Christ brings the distant word near. Gerald T. Sheppard points out that the alterations of Deut 30:12–13 in Baruch avoid reference to obedience and doing in favor of finding, bringing, and purchasing; "Wisdom and Torah: The Interpretation of Deuteronomy Underlying Sirach 24:23," in *Biblical and Near Eastern Studies: Essays in Honor of William Sanford LaSor* (ed. Gary A. Tuttle; Grand Rapids: Eerdmans, 1978), 173–74. This would parallel Paul's own movement away from the language of obedience and doing.

[108] First, Paul stands much closer to Deuteronomy than to the Wisdom tradition attested in Baruch. Baruch 3:15–31 speaks of the futility of the search for Wisdom among the nations. No one has discovered it (3:31). In 3:32–38 God is the answer to the problem of Wisdom's *inaccesibility* and God has granted Wisdom to Israel. The issue in Baruch had been the inaccessibility of Wisdom to general humanity, whereas for Paul the point is Christ's *accessibility.* Seifrid, "Paul's Approach," 21; W. D. Davies, *Paul and Rabbinic Judaism,* 154. Note the generalization to all human experience in Baruch's emendation of Deuteronomy; Sheppard, "Wisdom and Torah," 172–73. Second, the equation of Wisdom and Torah is not convincing in *Midr. Deut.* 7:7, where Wisdom is not actually

30:12–14 was being used in Paul's day in a *variety* of ways. The common denominator in Jewish interpretations was a reference to something "higher."[109] For example, in Philo's case the passage pointed to "the good," which was the goal of ethical discipline.[110] Dunn writes: "Deut 30:11–14 was widely regarded as looking beyond the Torah to some transcendent category of more universal appeal, particularly in the diaspora."[111] He adds:

> Paul evidently shares the same intuition. But for him the something more, of cosmic scope and universal significance, can only be an allusion to Christ. So just as these others saw in Deut 30 a reference to a grander theme which nevertheless comes to clearest articulation in the law, so Paul sees in Deut 30 a reference to Christ who comes to clearest expression in the gospel, the word of faith which defines the deeper meaning of Deuteronomy's "commandment," at the level of the heart.[112]

If Dunn's analysis is correct, the two questions (Who has gone up? Who has come down?) of Deuteronomy virtually beg for an interpretation in terms of Christ's humiliation and exaltation.[113]

Badenas believes that the key to Rom 10:6–8 is found in the OT context of Deut 30:12–14. Paul's ascription of the Deuteronomy citation to the righteousness of faith was simply a rhetorical device to emphasize that the Torah itself speaks of the righteousness of faith.[114] Paul intro-

---

mentioned. In Sir 24:5 there is a connection of Wisdom and Torah, but no clear reference to Deut 30:12–13. Seifrid, "Paul's Approach," 23. Badenas (*Christ*, 127) notes that the key phrase "the word is near," in Romans and Deuteronomy, is lacking in Baruch. Third, the language of ascending to heaven and crossing the sea (or going down to the abyss) had become somewhat proverbial (see *Jub.* 24:31; *4 Ezra* 4:8; *b. B. Meṣiʿa* 59b); Moo, *Romans*, 653 n. 34. The use of this language does not secure a reference to Baruch. Fourth, as Seifrid ("Paul's Approach," 22–23) points out, Paul's language is closer to Deuteronomy. Finally, even if certain sectors of Judaism may have equated the law with wisdom, is it likely that the Gentiles reading Paul's letter would have recognized this notion? More likely, they would have been, at best, familiar with the Deuteronomy passage. Hays (*Echoes*, 81–82), while sympathetic toward an allusion to Wisdom, points out (p. 81) that the identification of Christ and Wisdom is a little subtle: "This fusion occurs in the cave of echo, not at the overt discursive level."

[109] Dunn, *Romans 9–16*, 604–5.

[110] *Post.* 84–85; *Mut.* 236–237; *Virt.* 183; *Praem.* 80, as well as allusions in *Somn.* 2.180; *Spec.* 1.301; Dunn, *Romans 9–16*, 614.

[111] Dunn, "Righteousness from the Law," 220.

[112] Dunn, *Romans 9–16*, 614.

[113] Ibid., 614–15; Hays, *Echoes*, 79–80. The order of the questions in Paul probably reflects Deuteronomy.

[114] A point corresponding to Rom 3:27–4:25 and 9:30–33.

duces Deut 30:12–14 by means of the words of Deut 8:17 and 9:4–6. These two passages "warn against the human tendency to forget the absolute initiative of the divine mercy."[115] Both passages warn against claiming "because of *my* righteousness" (LXX: διὰ τὰς δικαιοσύνας μου), which is reminiscent of Rom 10:3. The danger for Israel was attributing the actions of God's divine mercy and initiative to "their own righteousness," their doing of the law. Deuteronomy 8:17 and 9:4–6 warn the Israelites against thinking that God's blessings and mercy were in any way dependent on their doing of the law.[116] The immediate context of Deut 30:12–14 is also significant. These verses are bracketed by Deut 30:6 and 16, which speak of the promise of "circumcision of the heart." Jeremiah 31:33; 32:39–40; Ezek 11:19–20; 36:26–27 all draw upon the Deuteronomy phrase.[117] Paul too sees within the Torah the need for a circumcision of the heart (as opposed to the doing of its precepts). A circumcision of the heart points to the divine, not human action.[118] Paul deletes all references to the doing of the Torah to emphasize his point. In fact, by the language of ascent and descent in Deut 30:12–14, Paul can show what is *not* required of human beings by God (cf. the athletic imagery of 9:30–32). Paul sees in Deuteronomy a denial of the necessity of human effort and an emphasis on what God has done.[119] The broader context of Deuteronomy coheres with Badenas's reading as well. Deuteronomy is grounded in God's choice of Israel and the patriarchs (4:28, 32; 10:14–15). God chose Israel on the basis of his love for the people and the oath sworn to the Fathers (7:7–8). The statutes were an expression of Israel's elevated status before God (4:6–8; 29:29) and were

---

[115] Badenas, *Christ,* 129; see also I. Howard Marshall, "Salvation, Grace and Works in the Later Writings in the Pauline Corpus," *NTS* 42 (1996): 350–51.

[116] Hays writes:

> Implicitly, however, the intertextual echoes created by Paul's evocation of Deut. 9:4 and of the Wisdom tradition suggest hauntingly that Paul's reading is less arbitrary than it sounds. From Deuteronomy, Paul echoes the idea that the covenant depends on grace from start to finish rather than on Israel's own righteousness (*Echoes,* 82).

Hays, though, limits Israel's "own righteousness" to their ethnic identity as opposed to the emphasis in Paul on doing (or rather, *not* doing).

[117] See ch. 3 on the importance of these texts to Paul's reflections on his gospel ministry in 2 Cor 3. Given Paul's use of these prophetic texts, he must see in Deut 30:12–14 a promise of the new age in Christ.

[118] Badenas, *Christ,* 129–30.

[119] Paul's emphasis is clearly on the word being "near" (ἐγγύς), which he thrusts to the fore of the sentence for added (christological) emphasis; Badenas, *Christ,* 131.

meant to bring about divine blessing through obedience (28:1–14). Paul sees that blessing and election embodied in the person of Jesus Christ.[120]

To conclude: the divine grace made accessible by God in the Torah is to be understood in terms of Christ. Christ is the Torah's true inner substance and meaning. The "word" of the Torah in Deut 30:14 (ῥῆμα) is therefore interpreted by Paul in terms of the Christian proclamation of Christ. The Torah witnesses to the righteousness of faith found in Christ as its "goal."[121] Paul is saying to those with ears to hear that the Word of God did indeed come near from the heights of heaven and the depths of the abyss. The Word came near in the person of Jesus Christ.

F. The Relationship between Romans 10:5 and Romans 10:6–8

If Rom 10:5 is treating a righteousness of the law based on doing its works, and Rom 10:6–8 is discussing the law's witness to a righteousness apart from its works, then v. 5 and vv. 6–8 are expressing antithetical perspectives on the law. Several difficulties stand in the way of such a reading and require a response. First, if Paul intended a contrast between vv. 5 and 6–8, he might have used a stronger word such as ἀλλά rather than δέ. But Paul's use of γάρ . . . δέ may or may not involve antithetical contrast, depending upon the context. For γάρ . . . δέ involving contrast, see Rom 2:25; 4:3–4; 5:7–8, 13, 16; 6:10, 23; 7:2.[122] For δέ itself signaling an adversative relationship, see, for example, 1 Cor 2:15–16.The construction γάρ . . . δέ is used in Rom 7:8–9; 10:10; and 11:15–16 for a *non*antithetical relationship (e.g., 10:10: "*for* with the heart *and* the mouth").[123] Second, Paul would not likely pit Scripture against Scripture in contrasting two different ways to righteousness.[124]

---

[120] So Seifrid, "Paul's Approach," 34–36.

[121] Badenas, *Christ,* 132–33. Paul's use of the text implies the very *opposite* of what Deuteronomy says. Whereas Deuteronomy emphasized that the law was capable of fulfillment, the text in Paul's hands says that the law *does* require superhuman effort, which effort is excluded not by the law but by *Christ.* Hence, doing the commandments is not so easy after all! It is faith in Christ that is near and easy. See ch. 1 on how the Jews saw obeying the law perfectly as extremely difficult, if not impossible.

[122] In fact, this sequence occurs twenty-two times in Rom 1–8. In three instances it is continuative (Rom 4:15; 7:8–9; 8:24), and in fifteen instances contrastive (see also Rom 7:14, 18b, 22–23; 8:5, 6, 13, 22–23, 24–25); Moo, *Romans,* 650 n. 23. The evidence favors a contrast.

[123] Howard, "Christ the End," 335–36, followed by Kaiser, "Leviticus 18:5," 27; Badenas, *Christ,* 122–23.

[124] Flückiger, "Christus," 155. For other examples, see above on Rom 10:5.

However, Paul need not be construed as citing Moses against Moses here.[125] The apostle is citing two distinct aspects in the witness of the law: the law understood from the point of view of the work that it demands and the law from the point of view of its testimony to faith. Paul does not deny that the law offers righteousness to those who do what it requires (Rom 2). The problem is sin (Rom 3; 7). Thus, Rom 9:30–10:13 speaks of the law's witness to a *different* sort of righteousness. The relationship between vv. 5 and 6–8 is one of contrast but not a strong antithesis. Moses is not wrong on the need to do the law. The righteousness of faith does not rule out the need to do the law. It is just that doing the law cannot save. Third, many of those who have advocated the "goal" interpretation of τέλος in Rom 10:4 see v. 5 as *complementary* to vv. 6–8. For example, Flückiger agrees with those who think that Paul is speaking in 10:5–8 of the *obedience of faith (der Glaubensgehorsam)* that Christ brings about in believers, an obedience that leads to life. In Flückiger's approach, the Deut 30:12–14 citation speaks of successful observance of the law and agrees with Lev 18:5.[126] Flückiger's approach is one of many that construe v. 5 in harmony with vv. 6–8, several of which were critiqued in the discussion of Rom 10:5.[127] The ultimate problem is that these approaches are not able to account for the *contrast* that runs through this passage between the law as an object of pursuit/works and the law as a testimony to God's righteousness in Christ. Romans 10:5 expresses Christ as the "end" of the law (perceived as a way to righteousness). When the law in v. 5 is understood from the perspective of the works it requires rather than from the perspective of its witness to righteousness, the contrast with vv. 6–8 would remain.

William S. Campbell offers a reading where Rom 10:6–8 could be antithetical as well as complementary with v. 5. Verse 5 could be a mirror image of v. 4. Just as 10:4 could refer to "goal" and have the sense of "end," a both/and option may be at work in 10:5–8. Romans 10:5 would support 10:4 as "goal" if *Christ* were the person who had actually lived

---

[125] Even if that were the case, the use of citations in apparent tension with other citations *(leges contrariae)* was a common technique in Greco-Roman and Jewish literature; see Philo and Hillel. One would arbitrate between the positions based on the citations by showing that the opposing citations can be harmonized within one's own position. J. S. Vos takes this approach with Rom 10:5–10; "Die Hermeneutische Antinomie bei Paulus (Galater 3.11–12; Römer 10.5–10)," *NTS* 38 (1992): 254–70, esp. 258–60.

[126] Flückiger, "Christus," 155.

[127] See the critique of Bring by Seifrid, "Paul's Approach," 14–15, especially Seifrid's point that doing is clearly set in opposition with believing all through this passage.

the life the law required.[128] Then Rom 10:6–8 would be complementary to 10:5 and supportive of 10:4. Moses would no longer be the author of a wrong kind of righteousness. However, to the individual who does not have eyes to see Christ as the goal of the Torah, 10:5 points to human performance and doing the law (the very issue of 9:30–10:3 as the Jews stumbled over the law from the perspective of its works).[129] The law from the wrong perspective of its demand for human accomplishment to attain salvation comes to an "end" with Christ. The law wrongly understood from the perspective of the works that it requires leads the non-Christian into a position where Scripture is pitted against Scripture with two different ways of righteousness. In Christ the scriptural witness (10:5 and 10:6–8) coheres and becomes complementary. A "both/and" reading of vv. 5–8 (unlike τέλος in v. 4) is not as compelling. Several elements in these verses indicate a contrast between vv. 5 and 6–8. Paul attributes Lev 18:5 in v. 5 to Moses but the Deuteronomy citation in vv. 6–8 to a personified righteousness. Dunn writes:

> Although Moses elsewhere is cited as the author of the Torah quotation (9:15; 10:19; 1 Cor 9:9), in none of these cases is he set alongside a concept like "righteousness", as here. In this case the better parallels are Rom 5:14, 1 Cor 10:2 and 2 Cor 3:7–15, where Moses is put forward as characterizing the old epoch now superseded by Christ. The implication is that Lev 18:5 speaks for the old epoch before Christ, represented by Moses, while Deut 30:12–14 speaks for the new age of God's wider grace introduced by Christ, characterized by "the righteousness from faith" (3:21–26; 10:4).[130]

Not only is there a contrast between different subjects in the respective clauses (Moses versus the δικαιοσύνη ἐκ τοῦ νόμου), but the modifiers of δικαιοσύνη also contrast (ἐκ τοῦ νόμου versus ἐκ πίστεως). Whenever Paul juxtaposes righteousness "from faith" with righteousness "from" (ἐκ) another source with δέ linking the two righteousnesses, he intends to make a contrast (e.g., Rom 4:16; 9:30, 32; Gal 2:16; 3:21–22).[131] In Phil 3:9 Paul contrasts the same two "righteousnesses" as in Rom 10:5–8.[132] Even the actions (doing the commandments versus confess-

---

[128] William S. Campbell, "Christ the End of the Law: Romans 10:4," in *Papers on Paul and Other New Testament Authors* (vol. 3 of *Studia Biblica 1978;* ed. E. A. Livingstone; JSNTSup 3; Sheffield: JSOT Press, 1980), 77–78.

[129] W. S. Campbell recognized the possibility of this twofold function of 10:5 (ibid., 78).

[130] Dunn, "Righteousness from the Law," 218–19; cf. idem, *Romans 9–16,* 602.

[131] Dunn, "Righteousness from the Law," 218; idem, *Romans 9–16,* 602.

[132] Westerholm writes that if one reads Rom 10:5 in agreement with 10:6–8, one must believe "that, whereas Paul contrasts the righteousness of the

ing the Lord Jesus and believing that God has raised him) stand in antithesis.[133] Bechtler concludes: "There is clearly a contrast, therefore, between human 'doing' in v. 5 and God's action in Christ in vv. 6–9."[134] Paul carefully altered the Deuteronomy citation to get rid of any notion of "doing," the very idea that he expresses in Lev 18:5. Paul's wording therefore indicates a contrast between "doing" and "believing."[135] Verses 5–8 act as support for v. 4's double entendre with τέλος by contrasting two ways of looking at the law. The law can be understood (wrongly) as a means to attain righteousness through the law's demands (v. 5). Faith in Christ puts an end to the law understood from this perspective. Or the law can be seen as a witness to righteousness in Christ (thus vv. 6–8).[136] Christ would be the "goal" of the law when understood from this perspective.

---

law and that of faith in Phil. 3:9, he identifies them here; . . . that, whereas in Phil. 3:9, Paul identifies his own righteousness with that which is based on law, here he distinguishes between Israel's own righteousness (Rom. 10:3) and the righteousness which is based on the law (v. 5)" (*Israel's Law and the Church's Faith,* 128). Westerholm's objection continues, "whereas [Paul] quotes Lev. 18:5, without elaborating on it, as a self-evident demonstration that 'the law does *not* rest on faith' in Gal 3:12, he quotes the same verse, without elaboration, as a self-evident demonstration that the law *does* rest on faith in Rom 10:5" (ibid.). Finally, on scriptural passages in tension, see Vos, "Hermeneutische Antinomie," 254–70, esp. 258–60.

133 Bechtler, "Christ," 304.

134 Bechtler, "Christ," 305. But Bechtler goes on to contend that there is no polemic against "works-righteousness" here. Paul's focus is strictly "Israel's exclusivistic understanding of its privilege as the people of God's covenant." Nevertheless, contra Bechtler, it is because the law in *all that it demands* has been denied a role in righteousness that the Gentiles may be included in God's salvation. So why do arguments against "doing" the law crop up embedded in discussions of Israel versus the Gentiles (see here and Rom 3:27–28)? The answer is simply that if Israel could attain salvation by their performance of the law, then salvation would be through the law and the Gentiles would have to observe the law with the Jews. Since salvation is *not* achieved through the works the law requires, but rather through the faith it points toward, the Gentiles may be included (as Israel itself) *apart* from the law's works. Thus one finds a critique of the doing of the law in passages addressing the Jews and Gentiles, but for a different reason than Bechtler (p. 305 n. 63) supposes.

135 With Seifrid, "Paul's Approach," 14–15; T. R. Schreiner, "Paul's View of the Law," 129. See the contrast between Hab 2:4 and Lev 18:5 in Gal 3:10–12, again a contrast between doing and believing; Rhyne, *Faith,* 105; T. R. Schreiner, *The Law and Its Fulfillment,* 110.

136 The support for v. 4 need not be limited to v. 5 alone but could entail the entirety of vv. 5–8; Seifrid, "Paul's Approach," 13.

IV. Conclusion

Throughout Rom 9:6–29 Paul says that God's election and salvation are based on a sovereign, divine choice whether to have mercy or to harden. Human effort plays no role in God's decision. Paul's discussion in 9:30–10:8 builds on this contrast between divine prerogative and human achievement and extends the discussion to include the Mosaic law. Righteousness before God is determined on the basis of faith in Christ and not accomplishment of what the law requires. By denying that the accomplishment of the law results in righteousness, Paul opens the door for God to save apart from a particular ethnic group in possession of that law, namely, Israel. Since performance of the law is not a factor, God can include Gentiles who do not observe the law among the righteous on the same terms as Jews. At the same time, if God is saving through Christ and not the works of the law, then the law's precepts are relegated to mere human activity with no potential to justify. The ironic tragedy, for Paul, is that in seeking God's righteousness through the law, the Jews are left only with a righteousness of "their own." Their zeal for the law is commendable, but God's path to righteousness is in Christ (10:3). Christ is the "goal" of the Torah; those who realize this fact will be freed from a wrong conception of it as a way of righteousness based on its works. Such a misunderstanding comes to an "end." A similar contrast between the law from the perspective of its works and from the perspective of its witness to righteousness in Christ dominates vv. 5 and 6–8.

Paul's unit of thought continues on from Rom 10:8 to the end of the chapter. Verses 9–18 show a renewed emphasis on salvation being entirely apart from human activity and accomplishment. In vv. 10–13 Paul traces saving faith to the preaching about Christ. Verse 17 adds that this faith comes from the word of Christ. Saving faith is entirely a miracle of God through the word. Paul then returns to the ethnic aspects of his discussion in 10:19–21. Since salvation comes through faith in the word about Christ (vv. 9–18), the distinction between ethnic Israel and the Gentiles is no longer applicable with respect to God's method of salvation. Faith in Christ determines whether an individual Israelite is among the obedient or disobedient (v. 21). Romans 10:9–21 would therefore dovetail with the results of this chapter. Sanders was right to emphasize that the Jews' overall approach to the law was not legalistic, but Paul's understanding empties the law of any saving value. To seek salvation in the law's works, from Paul's vantage point, would be to engage in a sort of works-righteousness since the law's works are simply a human activity. God's salvation is in Christ. Paul's conclusions with regard to the law's works would also apply to other attempts at currying God's favor through human achievement. From a theological perspective, Paul's antithesis between God's plan in Christ and human effort still eliminates the path of "works-righteousness." Nevertheless, this elimination of human works is the result of Paul's christological reasoning and is not itself an emperical claim that Jews approached the law in a legalistic fashion.

Conclusion

In *Paul and Palestinian Judaism* E. P. Sanders defined "covenantal nomism" as an underlying pattern of religion in intertestamental (Palestinian) and Tannaitic Judaism. The Jews were obligated to obey the Mosaic law's requirements, but their endeavor to observe the law did not render them guilty of "works-righteousness." Jewish literature from this period typically placed the observance of the law within the context of God's election and covenant with Israel and God's forgiveness manifested in a system of atonement and sacrifice. After reviewing much of the literature that had formed the basis for Sanders's model, in ch. 1 I have proposed a modified "covenantal nomism." In his exposé of mistaken caricatures of Judaism prevalent in NT scholarship, Sanders had wrongly dismissed or downplayed references to perfect obedience of the law. Chapter 1 overviewed several examples in intertestamental and Tannaitic literature that assert that God's law enjoins perfect obedience even while that requirement is embedded within a covenantal framework of grace and forgiveness. Chapter 2 discussed several instances, primarily from apocalyptic literature, where that gracious framework was compromised either by the loss of the temple in 70 C.E. or by a setting in the Diaspora. When God's election and sacrifice play little or no role or are radically challenged in the wake of disturbing events, Jewish thought drifts toward legalism. The Jewish apocalypticists envision a divine Judge determining who is to be saved on the basis of either perfect obedience or a majority of good deeds outweighing the bad. Such an unmitigated emphasis on rigorous obedience in this literature is an understandable outgrowth of a breakdown of the gracious framework of Judaism. Insofar as the apocalypses radically question or ignore the saving efficacy of God's election and mercy toward ethnic Israel, this literature provides a useful and important point of comparison for Paul.

Chapters 3–5 compared the key motifs of covenant, election, and sacrifice in Paul and in covenantal nomism. Paul does not consider the Mosaic covenant to offer any saving benefits to the Jews (ch. 3). Ethnic Israel's election does not automatically avail for a place in the world to come (ch. 4). The Jews' election as a people was bound up with the necessity of faith in Christ. Since faith in Christ is the crucial element, Paul can also speak of Gentile Christians as God's elect. Nowhere does Paul allow a role for the traditional atoning sacrifices (ch. 5). If he speaks of atoning sacrifice at all, he denies its atoning benefits and speaks instead of the atoning benefits available through faith in Christ. Paul nullifies the gracious framework of covenant, election, and sacrifice in favor of a very different framework centered on Christ.

Paul's denial of the saving efficacy of Judaism's gracious framework coheres with his emphasis on doing the law (chs. 7–10). Paul says that the law pronounces a curse upon those who are not perfectly obedient (ch. 6). An emphasis in Paul on the necessity and difficulty of doing what God requires in the law can stand alongside an appreciation of the law as a unique possession of the Jewish people. Previous Pauline scholarship has been too quick to think in "either/or" terms. To see Paul's problem with the law exclusively in terms of its wrongful exclusion of the Gentiles from salvation (as Dunn's Romans commentary asserts) does not recognize the consistency with which Paul critiques the law as requiring strict accomplishment. Apart from Christ, the law is a merely human endeavor (chs. 7–8, 10, in respect to Rom 2:17–29; 3:27–4:8; 9:30–10:8). The law becomes a "work," a futile struggle for humans to achieve its strict demands (chs. 6, 9, and 10, regarding Gal 3:10; Rom 7; 9:30–10:8).

The advantages of this "newer perspective" on Paul and the law are manifold. Prior to his conversion, Paul maintained a position that conforms to the definition of covenantal nomism (Phil 3:3–7). He believed that he was "blameless" with respect to the law and did not doubt his place in the world to come (even if he may have struggled with sin, depending on one's view of Rom 7). Paul's opponents at Galatia and his imaginary dialogue partner in Rom 2 adhere to a position that can be labeled covenantal nomism. A proper approach to Paul and the law must recognize the validity of covenantal nomism as a description of Paul's Jewish background and of the milieu of his Jewish-Christian dialogue partners (with the "new perspective"). A "newer perspective" must also account for passages that have proven difficult in the "new perspective" paradigm. Passages emphasizing the need to do the law or the strictness of the law's demand stand alongside other passages that highlight the ethnic dimension of the law. A Jew would not have seen the law's requirement of obedience and its function as a charter of ethnic identity as exclusive. Scholarship on Paul and the law today is wrongly polarized on this point. A proper analysis of Paul and law must explain how Paul can see the law as an enslaving power over the Jews (e.g., Rom 7). The law enslaves precisely in regard to the difficulty of doing what God requires in it. More importantly, a proper view of Paul and the law ought to compare covenantal nomism, Paul's former viewpoint, with Paul's current position as a believer in Christ. The dynamics of such a shift in Paul's understanding of where God's grace is located accounts for his negative view of the law, a perspective that would sound strange to many Jewish readers who treasured the "law of life."

If this "newer perspective" is right, it ought to conform with the evidence available beyond Paul's letters. Although such a discussion is beyond the purview of this work, it may be helpful to offer suggestions on how this approach to Paul and the law might compare with the views of the authors of the Synoptic Gospels and with Paul's earliest interpreters (if not Paul himself). With respect to the Synoptic Gospels, E. P. Sanders concludes in *Jesus and Judaism* that Jesus did not dispute any of the tenets of Jewish covenantal nomism.[1] Sanders's Jesus understood his mission to be to the elect people of Israel in the name of the God of Israel. Jesus did not stress the nomism of the system, nor did he dwell on the covenant or sacrifices. Jesus' orientation was *eschatological* and *assumed* the framework of covenantal nomism. Dale Allison has offered a corrective to Sanders's thinking.[2] Allison concludes that the Gospels' lack of any real discussion of the key conceptual elements of covenantal nomism is "not because Jesus assumed its truth but precisely because he rejected it (or at least the common understanding of it)."[3] In the sayings attributed to John the Baptist in Matt 3 and Luke 3 (sayings typically assigned to Q and deemed most probably authentic), the Baptist rejects any saving benefit to Abrahamic ancestry (Matt 3:9 par. Luke 3:8).[4] When John threatens his Jewish listeners with the fires of judgment, he does not assume that "all Israelites" have a share in the world to come.[5] On the contrary, being a faithful Jew did not itself ensure membership in the covenant community. John therefore baptized the Jews. The implications of this action are profound when one considers that the Jews

---

[1] E. P. Sanders, *Jesus and Judaism* (Philadelphia: Fortress, 1985), 336–37.

[2] Dale C. Allison Jr., "Jesus and the Covenant: A Response to E. P. Sanders," *JSNT* 29 (1987): 57–78.

[3] Ibid., 58.

[4] Ibid., 58–59.

[5] Ibid., 60.

required proselytes to be baptized as part of their entry into the elect community of Israel.[6] In the eucharistic tradition (attested already in 1 Cor 11:25) Jesus formulates the benefits of his saving work in terms not of the old, Mosaic covenant but of a "new covenant."[7] The Gospel Jesus also indicates that salvation in the world to come depends not on Judaism's covenantal framework but on people's response *to him* (e.g., Luke 12:8–9 par. Matt 10:32–33).[8] Instead of beginning with Israel's election and seeing the "wicked" saved by their joining of Israel, Jesus required that all people—including "sinners"—accept him as God's eschatological representative (e.g., Matt 22:1–10 par. Luke 14:15–24). As Allison writes: "Salvation was no longer viewed as faithfulness to God's covenant and obedience to the Torah. Salvation was rather acceptance of and faithfulness to Jesus' way. 'He who acknowledges me before man.'"[9] In other words, an excursion into the Synoptic Gospels would confirm that Paul is by no means unique in denying the salvific benefits of Judaism's gracious framework. One finds a similar collapse of covenantal nomism in favor of a christological framework. Membership in ethnic Israel offers no saving benefit in itself for the Synoptic Gospel writers.

If this "newer perspective" is right, it ought to conform with the evidence available from Paul's later writings (or those of his earliest interpreters). Scholars working with Paul and the law sometimes fail to consider that either Paul or one of his early disciples, the author of Ephesians, understood "works" as a matter of human accomplishment and not ethnic identity. The author of Eph 2:8–9 juxtaposes salvation by faith with works (διὰ πίστεως . . . οὐκ ἐξ ὑμῶν . . . οὐκ ἐξ ἔργων). This parallels the undisputed letters where Paul places salvation by faith in contrast with the works of the law (ἔργων νόμου), or "works" for short (see Gal 2:16; 3:2–5, 9, 10; Rom 3:27, 28; 4:2, 3, 5; 9:32). The author of Ephesians even mentions "boasting," which in Paul's undisputed letters meant pride in one's possession of the law and Jewish heritage (see Rom 3:27, particularly in the light of Rom 2). Yet in Ephesians this boasting is clearly interpreted in terms of a claim before God. Whereas modern, "new perspective" interpreters of Paul see "works" as having nothing to do with human achievement of the law, the author of Ephesians understands

---

[6] Ibid., 59–60.

[7] Ibid., 65–66. Jesus uses *sacrificial language* for his *own* work in Mark 14:24. Further, Jesus submitted to John's baptism, a baptism by a preacher who denied the saving efficacy of the Jews' covenant privileges.

[8] Ibid., 66–67. In other words, the framework of covenantal nomism has been replaced (or modified) by God's covenantal faithfulness *in Christ.* A proper response to Christ is essential to salvation.

[9] Ibid., 73.

"works" in the sense of *human effort in general.* Andrew Lincoln's summary of the importance of Eph 2:8–9 relative to the "new perspective on Paul" is worth quoting at length:

> The writer wishes to exclude any notion of earning salvation by human efforts which lead to self-congratulation. There has been a trend in recent Pauline interpretation either to play down his polemic against works of the law or to reinterpret it. On the one hand, it has been played down in the interests of stressing both contemporary Judaism's witness to itself in terms of covenantal nomism and Paul's own starting-point for his criticism of the law in the exclusiveness of salvation by faith in Christ. On the other hand, it has been reinterpreted by arguing that Paul is attacking simply national righteousness not legal righteousness, the notion of pride in possessing the law and the badge of circumcision rather than the notion of keeping the law to gain God's approval. Could it be that Eph 2:8–10, in taking up works and boasting as major Pauline themes and interpreting them in terms of human performance, has not totally distorted Paul's perspective but serves as a reminder of the centrality and significance of Paul's criticism of works of the law and the boasting they involve in such passages as Rom 3:27, 28; 4:1–5; 9:30–10:13; Gal 3:10–14; Phil 3:3–9?[10]

Critics claim that advocates of the more traditional approach have viewed Paul through the lenses of Augustine and Luther. This is a facile critique. Long before Augustine and Luther, the author of Ephesians already interpreted the Pauline phrases "works of the law" and "works" in terms of general human accomplishment.[11] The author of Ephesians

---

[10] Andrew T. Lincoln, "Ephesians 2:8–10: A Summary of Paul's Gospel," *CBQ* 45 [1983]: 628–29; see also Andrew T. Lincoln, "The Theology of Ephesians," in *The Theology of the Later Pauline Letters*, by Andrew T. Lincoln and A. J. M. Wedderburn (New Testament Theology; Cambridge: Cambridge University Press, 1993), 131–32, 135–36; so also Räisänen, *Paul and the Law,* 197–98; Andrew T. Lincoln, *Ephesians* (WBC 42; Dallas: Word, 1990), 112–13. Even James Dunn recognizes this as the apparent meaning of Eph 2:8–9; *The Theology of Paul the Apostle,* 371.

Nor is the evidence limited to Eph 2:8–9. In the disputed Pauline literature, one ought to take into consideration Titus 3:3–7 as well. There the writer asserts that God "saved us not because of any works of righteousness that we had done," but rather "according to his mercy" we were "justified by his grace." Again, "works" (ἔργων) are taken in the general sense of "doing" (ἃ ἐποιήσαμεν). Likewise 2 Tim 1:9. See the discussion of these two passages in I. Howard Marshall, "Salvation, Grace and Works in the Later Writings in the Pauline Corpus," *NTS* 42 (1996): 348–54.

[11] In the words of Andrew Lincoln:

> What we have seen, however, is that Ephesians has already clearly interpreted Paul in this way by generalizing the discussion of Romans to make it one about salvation by grace as opposed to human effort in general rather than works of the law in

understood an aspect of Paul's thinking that "new perspective" readers have missed. Paul's critique of Jewish pride in the possession of the law was never exclusive of his critique of the need, and difficulty, to accomplish that law.

Traditional scholarship was not entirely off the mark in its analysis of Paul and the law. The law does indeed require accomplishment and serves as a mirror to human failure. Yet the path to this conclusion was often fraught with a critical error: first-century Judaism was never the culprit. The error was to foist on first-century Judaism what was an essential step in *Paul's own* reasoning corresponding to his transition from a law-observant Jew to the apostle to the Gentiles. Paul's newfound faith in Christ forced him to place the law's requirements into a new framework of understanding. This created an artificial problem for Paul with the law, a problem that a Jew (or Jewish Christian!) subscribing to a system of covenantal nomism would not have recognized. But for the apostle, it was a problem that should have been clear to anyone in Christ.

The time has come to recognize that the "new perspective" went astray in limiting Paul's critique of the law to its ethnic, boundary-marking features. While Sanders's work certainly paved the way for a proper recognition of the intensely ethnic component of Paul's reasoning, that reasoning was never exclusive of a critique of the law's observance as a failed, human endeavor. As Paul the Christian apostle reconciled himself with his new faith, he found himself unable to affirm the law as a source of life. Even as Paul moved beyond covenantal nomism in his own thinking, modern scholarship must confront the question of whether it is time to move beyond the "new perspective" impasse to a "newer perspective."

---

particular. . . . Well before the time of Augustine, the generalization of justification and the focus on grace have an unmistakable precedent within the New Testament and within the Pauline corpus itself, as Ephesians sees works as human effort and performance which can obscure the gracious activity of God in providing a complete salvation ("The Theology of Ephesians," 135–36).

Selected Bibliography

Aageson, James W. "Scripture and Structure in the Development of the Argument in Romans 9–11." *CBQ* 48 (1986): 265–89.

Abbott, T. K. *A Critical and Exegetical Commentary on the Epistles to the Ephesians and to the Colossians.* ICC. Edinburgh: T&T Clark, 1897.

Abegg, Martin G. Jr. "Exile and the Dead Sea Scrolls." Pages 111–25 in *Exile: Old Testament, Jewish, and Christian Conceptions.* Edited by James M. Scott. JSJSup 56. Leiden: E. J. Brill, 1997.

Achtemeier, Elizabeth. *Nahum–Malachi.* IBC. Atlanta: John Knox, 1986.

Achtemeier, Paul J. *1 Peter.* Hermeneia. Minneapolis: Fortress, 1996.

———. *Romans.* IBC. Louisville: John Knox, 1985.

———. "St. Paul, Accommodation or Confrontation: A Tradition- and Context-Analysis of Romans 1.18–32 and 2.14–15, Attempting to Determine Whether or Not Paul Is Seeking to Accommodate the Thought of These Verses to the Hellenistic Mentality." Th.D. diss., Union Theological Seminary, New York, 1957.

———. " 'Some Things in Them Hard to Understand': Reflections on an Approach to Paul." *Int* 38 (1984): 254–67.

———. "Unsearchable Judgments and Inscrutable Ways: Reflections on the Discussion of Romans." In *SBL Seminar Papers, 1995,* 521–34. Atlanta: Scholars Press, 1995. Repr. with corrections in *Looking Back, Pressing on.* Edited by E. Elizabeth Johnson and David M. Hay. Vol. 4 of *Pauline Theology.* SBLSymS. Atlanta: Scholars Press, 1997.

Albeck, H. *Shishshah Sidre Mishnah.* 6 vols. Jerusalem: Bialik Institute and Dvir, 1952–1959.

Aletti, Jean-Noël. "Rm 1,18–3,20: Incohérence ou cohérence de l'argumentation paulinienne?" *Bib* 69 (1988): 47–62.

———. "Romains 2. Sa cohérence et sa fonction." *Bib* 77 (1996): 153–77.

Alexander, T. D. "The Passover Sacrifice." Pages 1–24 in *Sacrifice in the Bible.* Edited by Roger T. Beckwith and Martin J. Selman. Grand Rapids: Baker, 1995.

Allison, Dale C. Jr. "Jesus and the Covenant: A Response to E. P. Sanders." *JSNT* 29 (1987): 57–78.

Alt, Albrecht. "The Origins of Israelite Law." *Essays on Old Testament History and Religion.* Translated by R. A. Wilson. Garden City, N.Y.: Doubleday, 1966.

Amadi-Azuogu, Chinedu Adolphus. *Paul and the Law in the Argument of Galatians.* BBB 104. Weinheim: Beltz Athenäum, 1996.

Andersen, F. I. "2 (Slavonic Apocalypse of) Enoch." Pages 91–100 in *Apocalyptic Literature and Testaments.* Vol. 1 of *The Old Testament Pseudepigrapha.* Edited by James H. Charlesworth. Garden City, N.Y.: Doubleday, 1983.

Anderson, Megory, and Philip Culbertson. "The Inadequacy of the Christian Doctrine of Atonement in Light of Levitical Sin Offering." *AThR* 68 (1986): 303–28.

Antwi, Daniel Jacobson. "The Death of Jesus As Atoning Sacrifice: A Study of the Sources and Purpose of New Testament Soteriology, with Particular Reference to Selected Texts." Ph.D. diss., University of Aberdeen, 1980.

Appel, Gersion. *A Philosophy of Mitzvot': The Religious-Ethical Concepts of Judaism, Their Roots in Biblical Law and The Oral Tradition.* New York: Ktav, 1975.

Aus, Roger D. "Paul's Travel Plans to Spain and the 'Full Number of the Gentiles' in Rom. XI 25." *NovT* 21 (1979): 232–62.

Bachmann, D. Philipp. *Der zweite Brief des Paulus an die Korinther.* 3d ed. Leipzig: A. Deichertsche Verlagsbuchhandlung Werner Scholl, 1918.

Badenas, Robert. *Christ the End of the Law: Romans 10.4 in Pauline Perspective.* JSNTSup 10. Sheffield: JSOT Press, 1985.

Bailey, Jon Nelson. "*Metanoia* in the Writings of Philo Judaeus." In *SBL Seminar Papers, 1991,* 135–41. Atlanta: Scholars Press, 1991.

Bandstra, Andrew John. *The Law and the Elements of the World: An Exegetical Study in Aspects of Paul's Teaching.* Kampen: J. H. Kok, 1964.

Barclay, John M. G. *Jews in the Mediterranean Diaspora: From Alexander to Trajan (323 BCE–117 CE).* Edinburgh: T&T Clark, 1996.

———. *Obeying the Truth: Paul's Ethics in Galatians.* Minneapolis: Fortress, 1988.

Barrett, Charles Kingsley. "The Allegory of Abraham, Sarah, and Hagar in the Argument of Galatians." Pages 154–70 in *Essays on Paul.* Philadelphia: Westminster, 1982. Originally pages 1–16 in *Rechtfertigung: Festschrift für Ernst Käsemann zum 70. Geburtstag.* Edited by Johannes Friedrich, Wolfgang Pohlmann, and Peter Stuhlmacher. Tübingen: J.C.B. Mohr (Paul Siebeck), 1976.

———. *A Commentary on the Second Epistle to the Corinthians.* New York: Harper & Row, 1973.

———. *The Epistle to the Romans.* Black's New Testament Commentaries. London: Adam & Charles Black, 1957.

———. *Essays on Paul.* Philadelphia: Westminster, 1982.

———. *Paul: An Introduction to His Thought.* Louisville: Westminster John Knox, 1994.

———. "Romans 9.30–10.21: Fall and Responsibility of Israel." In *Essays on Paul.* Philadelphia: Westminster, 1982.

Bartchy, S. Scott. ΜΑΛΛΟΝ ΧΡΗΣΑΙ*: First-Century Slavery and 1 Corinthians 7:21.* SBLDS 11. Missoula, Mont.: Scholars Press, 1973.

Barth, Markus. *The People of God.* JSNTSup 5. Sheffield: JSOT Press, 1983.

Bassler, Jouette M. *Divine Impartiality: Paul and a Theological Axiom.* SBLDS 59. Chico, Calif.: Scholars Press, 1982.

Baumgarten, Joseph M. "Does *tlh* in the Temple Scroll Refer to Crucifixion?" *JBL* 91 (1972): 472–81.

———. "Sacrifice and Worship among the Jewish Sectarians of the Dead Sea (Qumran) Scrolls." *HTR* 46 (1953): 141–59.

Bechtler, Steven Richard. "Christ, the Τέλος of the Law: The Goal of Romans 10:4." *CBQ* 56 (1994): 288–308.

Bell, Richard H. *No One Seeks for God: An Exegetical and Theological Study of Romans 1.18–3.20.* WUNT 106. Tübingen: J.C.B. Mohr (Paul Siebeck), 1998.

Bellefontaine, Elizabeth. "The Curses of Deuteronomy 27: Their Relationship to the Prohibitives." Pages 256–68 in *A Song of Power and the Power of Song.* Edited by Duane L. Christensen. Winona Lake, Ind.: Eisenbrauns, 1993.

Belleville, Linda L. "A Letter of Apologetic Self-Commendation: 2 Cor. 1:8–7:16." *NovT* 31 (1989): 142–63.

———. "Paul's Polemic and the Theology of the Spirit in Second Corinthians." *CBQ* 58 (1996): 281–304.

———. *Reflections of Glory: Paul's Polemical Use of the Moses-Doxa Tradition in 2 Corinthians 3.1–18.* JSNTSup 52. Sheffield: Sheffield Academic Press, 1991.

Bernstein, Moshe J. "כי קללת אלהים תלוי (Deut. 21:23): A Study in Early Jewish Exegesis." *JQR* 74 (1983): 21–45.

Betz, Hans Dieter. *Galatians.* Hermeneia. Philadelphia: Fortress, 1979.

Bieringer, Reimund. "2 Kor 5,19a und die Versöhnung der Welt." *ETL* 63 (1987): 295–326. Repr. pages 429–59 in *Studies on 2 Corinthians.* By R. Bieringer and J. Lambrecht. BETL 112. Leuven: Leuven University Press, 1994.

Bligh, John. *Galatians: A Discussion of St Paul's Epistle.* London: St. Paul Publications, 1969.

Boccaccini, Gabriele. *Middle Judaism: Jewish Thought, 300 B.C.E. to 200 C.E.* Minneapolis: Fortress, 1991.

Bogaert, Pierre. *Apocalypse de Baruch.* 2 vols. Sources chrétiennes 144. Paris: Cerf, 1969.

Bonneau, Normand. "The Logic of Paul's Argument on the Curse of the Law in Galatians 3:10–14." *NovT* 39 (1997): 60–80.

Bornkamm, Günther. "Gesetz und Natur. Röm 2:14–16." In *Studien zu Antike und Urchristentum.* Vol. 2. BEvT 28. Munich: Chr. Kaiser, 1959.

———. "Sin, Law and Death: An Exegetical Study of Romans 7." In *Early Christian Experience.* New York: Harper & Row, 1969.

Böttrich, Christfried. *Weltweisheit, Menschheitsethik, Urkult: Studien zum slavischen Henochbuch.* WUNT. Second Series 50. Tübingen: J.C.B. Mohr (Paul Siebeck), 1992.

Boyarin, Daniel. *A Radical Jew: Paul and the Politics of Identity.* Berkeley and Los Angeles: University of California Press, 1994.

Brandenburger, Egon. *Die Verborgenheit Gottes im Weltgeschehen: Das Literarische und Theologische Problem des 4. Esrabuches.* ATANT 68. Zürich: Theologischer Verlag, 1981.

Braswell, Joseph P. " 'The Blessing of Abraham' versus 'The Curse of the Law': Another Look at Gal 3:10–13." *WTJ* 53 (1991): 73–91.

Bratcher, Dennis Ray. "The Theological Message of Habakkuk: A Literary-Rhetorical Analysis." Ph.D. diss., Union Theological Seminary in Virginia, 1984.

Braulik, Georg. "The Development of the Doctrine of Justification in the Redactional Strata of the Book of Deuteronomy." Pages 151–64 in *The Theology of Deuteronomy: Collected Essays of Georg Braulik, O. S. B.* Translated by Ulrika Lindblad. N. Richland Hills, Tex.: BIBAL, 1994.

Braun, Herbert. "Beobachtungen zur Tora-Verschärfung im häretischen Spätjudentum." *TLZ* 79 (1954): 347–52.

Breech, Earl. "These Fragments I Have Shored against My Ruins: The Form and Function of 4 Ezra." *JBL* 92 (1973): 267–74.

Breytenbach, C. "Versöhnung, Stellvertretung und Sühne: Semantische und Traditiongeschichtliche Bemerkungen am Beispiel der Paulinischen Briefe." *NTS* 39 (1993): 59–79.

Brichto, Herbert Chanan. "The Worship of the Golden Calf: A Literary Analysis of a Fable on Idolatry." *HUCA* 54 (1983): 1–44.

Bring, Ragnar. *Commentary on Galatians.* Translated by Eric Wahlstrom. Philadelphia: Muhlenberg, 1961.

———. "Die Gerechtigkeit Gottes und das Alttestamentliche Gesetz: Eine Untersuchung von Röm 10,4." *Christus und das Gesetz: Die Bedeutung des Gesetzes des Alten Testaments nach Paulus und Sein Glauben an Christus.* Leiden: E. J. Brill, 1969. Reprinted from *ST* 20 (1966).

———. "Paul and the Old Testament: A Study of the Ideas of Election, Faith and Law in Paul, with Special Reference to Romans 9:30–10:30." *ST* 25 (1971): 21–60.

Brooke, George. Review of E. P. Sanders, *Paul and Palestinian Judaism. JJS* 30 (1979): 247–50.

Bruce, F. F. *Commentary on Galatians.* NIGTC. Grand Rapids: Eerdmans, 1982.

———. "The Curse of the Law." Pages 27–36 in *Paul and Paulinism: Essays in Honour of C. K. Barrett.* Edited by M. D. Hooker and S. G. Wilson. London: SPCK, 1982.

Büchler, A. *Studies in Sin and Atonement: In the Rabbinic Literature of the First Century.* Library of Biblical Studies. New York: Ktav, 1967.

Buckel, John. *Free to Love: Paul's Defense of Christian Liberty in Galatians.* Grand Rapids: Eerdmans, 1993.

Bultmann, Rudolf. "Neueste Paulusforschung." *TRu* 8 (1936): 1–22.

———. *Theology of the New Testament.* Vol. 1. Translated by Kendrick Grobel. New York: Charles Scribner's Sons, 1951.

Burton, Ernest De Witt. *A Critical and Exegetical Commentary on the Epistle to the Galatians.* ICC. Edinburgh: T&T Clark, 1921.

Byrne, Brendan. *'Sons of God'—'Seed of Abraham': A Study of the Idea of the Sonship of God of All Christians in Paul against the Jewish Background.* AnBib 83. Rome: Biblical Institute, 1979.

Cambier, J.-M. "Le jugement de tous les hommes par Dieu seul, selon la vérité, dans Rom 2.1–3.20." *ZNW* 67 (1976): 187–213.

Campbell, Douglas A. *The Rhetoric of Righteousness in Romans 3.21–26.* JSNTSup 65. Sheffield: Sheffield Academic Press, 1992.

———. "A Rhetorical Suggestion Concerning Romans 2." In *SBL Seminar Papers, 1995,* 140–67. Atlanta: Scholars Press, 1995.

Campbell, William S. "Christ the End of the Law: Romans 10:4." Pages 73–81 in *Papers on Paul and Other New Testament Authors.* Vol. 3 of *Studia Biblica 1978.* Edited by E. A. Livingstone. Journal for the Study of the New Testament: Supplement Series 3. Sheffield: JSOT Press, 1980.

———. "Favoritism and Egalitarianism: Irreconcilable Emphases in Romans?" In *SBL Seminar Papers, 1998,* vol. 1, pages 12–32. Atlanta: Scholars Press, 1998.

———. "Salvation for Jews and Gentiles: Krister Stendahl and Paul's Letter to the Romans." Pages 65–72 in *Papers on Paul and Other New Testament Authors.* Vol. 3 of *Studia Biblica 1978.* Edited by E. A Livingstone. JSNTSup 3. Sheffield: Sheffield Academic Press, 1980.

Caneday, Ardel. "'Redeemed from the Curse of the Law': The Use of Deut 21:22–23 in Gal 3:13." *TJ* 10 New Series (1989): 185–209.

Carmignac, Jean. "L'Utilité ou L'Inutilité des Sacrifices Sanglants dans la *Regle de la Communauté* de Qumrân." *RB* 63 (1956): 524–32.

Carras, George P. "Romans 2,1–29: A Dialogue on Jewish Ideals." *Bib* 73 (1992): 183–207.

Cavallin, H. C. C. "'The Righteous Shall Live by Faith': A Decisive Argument for the Traditional Interpretation." *ST* 32 (1978): 33–43.

Cerfaux, L. *The Church in the Theology of St. Paul.* Translated by Geoffrey Webb and Adrian Walker. Freiburg: Herder, 1959.

Chae, Daniel J.-S. *Paul As Apostle to the Gentiles: His Apostolic Self-Awareness and Its Influences on the Soteriological Argument in Romans.* Paternoster Biblical and Theological Monographs. Carlisle, Cumbria, U.K.: Paternoster, 1997.

Charles, R. H. *The Apocalypse of Baruch.* London: Adam & Charles Black, 1896.

Charlesworth, James H. "The SNTS Pseudepigrapha Seminars at Tübingen and Paris on the Books of Enoch." *NTS* (1978–1979): 315–23.

———, ed. *The Old Testament Pseudepigrapha.* 2 vols. Garden City, N.Y.: Doubleday, 1983, 1985.

Childs, Brevard. *The Book of Exodus: A Critical, Theological Commentary.* Old Testament Library. Philadelphia: Westminster, 1974.

Chilton, Bruce. *A Feast of Meanings: Eucharistic Theologies from Jesus through Johannine Circles.* NovTSup 72. Leiden: E. J. Brill, 1994.

Christiansen, Ellen Juhl. *The Covenant in Judaism and Paul: A Study of Ritual Boundaries As Ethical Markers.* AGJU 27. Leiden: E. J. Brill, 1995.

Clements, Ronald E. "'A Remnant Chosen by Grace' (Romans 11:5): The Old Testament Background and Origin of the Remnant Concept." Pages 106–21 in *Pauline Studies.* Edited by Donald A. Hagner and Murray J. Harris. Grand Rapids: Eerdmans, 1980.

Coats, George W. "The King's Loyal Opposition: Obedience and Authority in Exodus 32–34." Pages 91–109 in *Canon and Authority: Essays in Old Testament Religion and Theology.* Edited by George W. Coats and Burke O. Long. Philadelphia: Fortress, 1977.

Cohen, Naomi G. "The Jewish Dimension of Philo's Judaism—An Elucidation of de Spec. Leg. IV 132–150." *JJS* 38 (1987): 165–86.

Cohen, Shaye J. D. *From the Maccabees to the Mishnah.* Library of Early Christianity 7. Philadelphia: Westminster, 1987.

Collange, J.-F. *Enigmes de la Deuxieme Épitre de Paul aux Corinthiens: Étude Exégetique de 2 Cor. 2:14–7:4.* SNTSMS 18. Cambridge: Cambridge University Press, 1972.

Collins, John J. *The Apocalyptic Imagination: An Introduction to Jewish Apocalyptic Literature.* 2d ed. Grand Rapids: Eerdmans, 1998.

———. *Between Athens and Jerusalem: Jewish Identity in the Hellenistic Diaspora.* New York: Crossroad, 1983.

Conzelmann, Hans. *1 Corinthians.* Translated by James W. Leitch. Edited by George W. MacRae. Philadelphia: Fortress, 1975.

Corriveau, Raymond. *The Liturgy of Life: A Study of the Ethical Thought of St. Paul in His Letters to the Early Christian Communities.* Studia Travaux de recherche 25. Paris: Desclée de Brouwer, 1970.

Cosgrove, Charles H. *The Cross and the Spirit: A Study in the Argument and Theology of Galatians.* Macon, Ga.: Mercer University Press, 1988.

———. *The Elusive Israel: The Puzzle of Election in Romans.* Louisville: Westminster John Knox, 1997.

———. "The Mosaic Law Preaches Faith: A Study in Galatians 3." *WTJ* 41 (1978–1979): 146–64.

Courtman, Nigel B. "Sacrifice in the Psalms." Pages 41–58 in *Sacrifice in the Bible.* Edited by Roger T. Beckwith and Martin J. Selman. Grand Rapids: Baker, 1995.

Cranfield, C. E. B. *A Critical and Exegetical Commentary on the Epistle to the Romans.* 2 vols. ICC. Edinburgh: T&T Clark, 1975, 1979.

———. "Giving a Dog a Bad Name: A Note on H. Räisänen's *Paul and the Law.*" *JSNT* 38 (1990): 77–85.

———. "Some Notes on Romans 9:30–33." Pages 35–43 in *Jesus und Paulus: Festschrift für Werner Georg Kümmel zum 70. Geburtstag.* Edited by E. Earle Ellis and Erich Gräßer. Göttingen: Vandenhoeck & Ruprecht, 1975.

———. "'The Works of the Law' in the Epistle to the Romans." *JSNT* 43 (1991): 96–97.

Cranford, Michael. "Abraham in Romans 4: The Father of All Who Believe." *NTS* 41 (1995): 71–88.

———. "Election and Ethnicity: Paul's View of Israel in Romans 9.1–13." *JSNT* 50 (1993): 27–41.

———. "The Possibility of Perfect Obedience: Paul and an Implied Premise in Galatians 3:10 and 5:3." *NovT* 36 (1994): 242–58.

Dabelstein, Rolf. *Die Beurteilung der 'Heiden' bei Paulus.* Beiträge zur biblischen Exegese und Theologie, 14. Frankfurt: Peter D. Lang, 1981.

Dahl, Nils Alstrup. "The Future of Israel." In *Studies in Paul.* Minneapolis: Augsburg, 1977.

Dalton, W. J. "Expiation or Propitiation? (Rom. iii. 25)." *ABR* 8 (1960): 3–18.

Daly, Robert J. *Christian Sacrifice: The Judaeo-Christian Background Before Origen.* Studies in Christian Antiquity 18. Washington, D.C.: Catholic University of America Press, 1978.

Das, A. Andrew. "1 Corinthians 11:17–34 Revisited." *Concordia Theological Quarterly* 62 (1998): 187–208.

———. "Oneness in Christ: The *Nexus Indivulsus* between Justification and Sanctification in Paul's Letter to the Galatians." *Concordia Journal* 21 (1995): 173–86.

Davies, Glenn N. *Faith and Obedience in Romans: A Study in Romans 1–4.* JSNTSup 39. Sheffield: Sheffield Academic Press, 1990.

Davies, P. R., and B. D. Chilton. "The Aqedah: A Revised Tradition History." *CBQ* 40 (1978): 514–46.

Davies, R. E. "Christ in Our Place—The Contribution of the Prepositions." *TynBul* 21 (1970): 71–91.

Davies, W. D. *Christian Origins and Judaism.* London: Darton, Longman & Todd, 1962.

———. *Jewish and Pauline Studies.* Philadelphia: Fortress, 1984.

———. *Paul and Rabbinic Judaism: Some Rabbinic Elements in Pauline Theology.* London: SPCK, 1955.

———. "Paul and the Dead Sea Scrolls: Flesh and Spirit." Pages 157–82, 276–82 in *The Scrolls and the New Testament.* Edited by Krister Stendahl. New York: Harper & Brothers, 1957.

———. "Paul and the Law: Reflections on Pitfalls in Interpretation." Pages 4–16 in *Paul and Paulinism: Essays in Honour of C. K. Barrett.* Edited by M. D. Hooker and S. G. Wilson. London: SPCK, 1982.

Davis, Dale Ralph. "Rebellion, Presence, and Covenant: A Study in Exodus 32–34." *WTJ* 44 (1982): 71–87.

Deissmann, Adolf. *Bible Studies.* 2d ed. Translated by Alexander Grieve. Edinburgh: T&T Clark, 1909.

———. "ΙΛΑΣΤΗΡΙΟΣ und ΙΛΑΣΤΗΡΙΟΝ." *ZNW* 4 (1903): 193–212.

———. *Light from the Ancient Near East.* Translated by Lionel R. M. Strachan. New York: George H. Doran, 1927.

Delcor, Mathias. *Le Testament d'Abraham: Introduction, Traduction du Texte Grec et Commentaire de la Recension Grecque Longue.* Studia in Veteris Testamenti pseudepigraphica. Leiden: E. J. Brill, 1973.

Derrett, J. Duncan M. "'Running' in Paul: The Midrashic Potential of Hab 2,2." *Bib* 66 (1985): 560–67.

Desjardins, Michel. "Law in 2 Baruch and 4 Ezra." *SR* 14 (1985): 25–37.

Dewey, Arthur H. *Spirit and Letter in Paul.* Lewiston, N.Y.: Edwin Mellen, 1996.

Dodd, C. H. "ΙΛΑΣΚΕΣΘΑΙ, Its Cognates, Derivatives, and Synonyms, in the Septuagint." *JTS* 32 (1930–1931): 352–60.

Donaldson, Terence L. "The 'Curse of the Law' and the Inclusion of the Gentiles: Galatians 3.13–14." *NTS* 32 (1986): 94–112.

———. "Israelite, Convert, Apostle to the Gentiles: The Origin of Paul's Gentile Mission." Pages 62–84 in *The Road from Damascus: The Impact of Paul's Conversion on His Life, Thought, and Ministry.* Edited by Richard N. Longenecker. Grand Rapids: Eerdmans, 1997.

———. *Paul and the Gentiles: Remapping the Apostle's Convictional World.* Minneapolis: Fortress, 1997.

———. "'Riches for the Gentiles' (Rom 11:12): Israel's Rejection and Paul's Gentile Mission." *JBL* 112 (1993): 81–98.

Donfried, Karl P. "The Theology of 1 Thessalonians." Pages 28–63 in *The Theology of the Shorter Pauline Letters* (with I. Howard Marshall). Cambridge: Cambridge University Press, 1993.

Dülmen, Andrea van. *Die Theologie des Gesetzes bei Paulus.* SBM 5. Stuttgart: Katholisches Bibelwerk, 1968.

Dumbrell, William J. "Paul's Use of Exodus 34 in 2 Corinthians 3." Pages 179–94 in *God Who is Rich in Mercy.* Edited by Peter T. O'Brien and David G. Peterson. Homebush West NSW, Australia: Lancer Books, 1986.

Dunn, James D. G. *Christology in the Making: A New Testament Inquiry into the Origins of the Doctrine of the Incarnation.* 2d ed. Grand Rapids, Eerdmans, 1989.

———. *The Epistle to the Galatians.* Black's New Testament Commentaries. Peabody, Mass.: Hendrickson, 1993.

———. "4QMMT and Galatians." *NTS* 43 (1997): 147–53.

———. *Jesus, Paul, and the Law: Studies in Mark and Galatians.* Louisville: Westminster John Knox, 1990.

———. " 'The Law of Faith,' 'the Law of the Spirit' and 'the Law of Christ.' " Pages 62–82 in *Theology and Ethics in Paul and His Interpreters.* Edited by Eugene H. Lovering Jr. and Jerry L. Sumney. Nashville: Abingdon, 1996.

———. "Paul and Justification by Faith." Pages 85–101 in *The Road from Damascus: The Impact of Paul's Conversion on His Life, Thought, and Ministry.* Edited by Richard N. Longenecker. Grand Rapids: Eerdmans, 1997.

———. "Paul's Understanding of the Death of Jesus." Pages 125–41 in *Reconciliation and Hope: New Testament Essays on Atonement and Eschatology.* Edited by Robert Banks. Exeter: Paternoster, 1974.

———. " 'Righteousness from the Law' and 'Righteousness from Faith': Paul's Interpretation of Scripture in Romans 10:1–10." Pages 216–28 in *Tradition and Interpretation in the New Testament: Essays in Honor of E. Earle Ellis for His 60th Birthday.* Edited by Gerald F. Hawthorne and Otto Betz. Grand Rapids: Eerdmans, 1987.

———. *Romans 1–8.* WBC 38A. Dallas: Word, 1988.

———. *Romans 9–16.* WBC 38B. Dallas: Word, 1988.

———. *The Theology of Paul the Apostle.* Grand Rapids: Eerdmans, 1998.

———. *The Theology of Paul's Letter to the Galatians.* Cambridge: Cambridge University Press, 1993.

———. "Was Paul against the Law? The Law in Galatians and Romans: A Test-Case of Text in Context." Pages 455–75 in *Texts and Contexts: Biblical Texts in Their Textual and Situational Contexts.* Edited by Tord Fornberg and David Hellholm. Oslo: Scandinavian University Press, 1995.

———. "Yet Once More—'The Works of the Law': A Response." *JSNT* 46 (1992): 99–117.

Ebeling, Gerhard. *The Truth of the Gospel: An Exposition of Galatians.* Translated by David Green. Philadelphia: Fortress, 1985.

Eckert, Jost. "Das letzte Wort des Apostels Paulus über Israel (Röm 11,25–32) – eine Korrektur seiner bisherigen Verkündigung?" Pages 57–84 in *Schrift und Tradition: Festschrift für Josef Ernst zum 70. Geburtstag.* Edited by Knut Backhaus and Franz Georg Untergaßmair. Paderborn: Ferdinand Schöningh, 1996.

Eckstein, Hans-Joachim. *Verheißung und Gesetz: Eine exegetische Untersuchung zu Galater 2,15–4,7.* WUNT 86. Tübingen: J.C.B. Mohr (Paul Siebeck), 1996.

Elert, Werner. "Redemptio ab hostibus." *TLZ* 72 (1947): 264–70.

Elliot, Neil. *The Rhetoric of Romans: Argumentative Constraint and Strategy and Paul's Dialogue with Judaism.* JSNTSup 45. Sheffield: Sheffield Academic Press, 1990.

Endres, John C. *Biblical Interpretation in the Book of Jubilees.* Washington, D.C.: Catholic Biblical Association of America, 1987.

Epp, Eldon Jay. "Jewish-Gentle Continuity in Paul: Torah and/or Faith? (Romans 9:1–5)." *HTR* 79 (1986): 80–90.

Esler, Philip F. "The Social Function of *4 Ezra*." *JSNT* 53 (1994): 99–123.

Espy, John M. "Paul's 'Robust Conscience' Re-examined." *NTS* 31 (1985): 161–88.

Evans, Christopher. "Romans 12.1–2: The True Worship." Pages 7–33 in *Dimensions de la Vie Chrétienne (Rm 12–13)*. Edited by Lorenzo De Lorenzi. Série Monographique de "Bendedicta" 4. Rome: Abbaye de S. Paul h.l.m., 1979.

Evans, Owen E. "New Wine in Old Wineskins: XIII. The Saints." *ExpTim* 86 (1974–1975): 196–200.

Farrar, Austin. "The Ministry in the New Testament." Pages 113–82 in *Apostolic Ministry, Essays on the History and the Doctrine of the Episcopacy*. Edited by K. E. Kirk. London: Hodder & Stoughton, 1946.

Fee, Gordon D. *The First Epistle to the Corinthians*. NICNT. Grand Rapids: Eerdmans, 1987.

———. *Paul's Letter to the Philippians*. NICNT. Grand Rapids: Eerdmans, 1995.

Feldman, Louis H. "The Concept of Exile in Josephus." Pages 145–72 in *Exile: Old Testament, Jewish, and Christian Conceptions*. Edited by James M. Scott. JSJSup 56. Leiden: E. J. Brill, 1997.

Fischer, Ulrich. *Eschatologie und Jenseitserwartung im hellenistischen Diasporajudentum*. BZNW 44. Berlin: Walter de Gruyter, 1978.

Fitzer, Gottfried. "Der Ort der Versöhnung nach Paulus: Zu der Frage des Sühnopfers Jesu." *TZ* 22 (1966): 161–83.

Fitzmyer, Joseph A. "Crucifixion in Ancient Palestine, Qumran Literature, and the New Testament." *CBQ* 40 (1978): 493–513.

———. " '4QTestimonia' and the New Testament." Pages 58–89 in *Essays on the Semitic Background of the New Testament*. London: Geoffrey Chapman, 1971.

———. *Paul and His Theology: A Brief Sketch*. 2d ed. Englewood Cliffs, N.J.: Prentice Hall, 1989.

———. "Paul's Jewish Background and the Deeds of the Law." Pages 18–35, 125–30 in *According to Paul: Studies in the Theology of the Apostle*. Mahwah, N.J.: Paulist, 1993.

———. *Romans*. AB 33. New York: Doubleday, 1993.

Flückiger, Felix. "Christus, des Gesetzes τέλος." *TZ* 11 (1955): 153–57.

———. "Die Werke des Gesetzes bei den Heiden (nach Röm. 2, 14 ff.)." *TZ* 8 (1952): 17–42.

Flusser, David. "From the Essenes to Romans 9:24–33." *Judaism and the Origins of Christianity*. Jerusalem: The Magnes Press, The Hebrew University, 1983.

Forbes, Nevill, and R. H. Charles. "The Book of the Secrets of Enoch." Pages 425–30 in vol. 2 of *The Apocrypha and Pseudepigrapha of the Old Testament*. Edited by R. H. Charles. 2 vols. Oxford: Clarendon, 1913.

Freeman, Hobart E. "The Problem of the Efficacy of Old Testament Sacrifices." *Bulletin of the Evangelical Theological Society* 5 (1962): 73–79.

Friedrich, Gerhard. "Das Gesetz des Glaubens Röm. 3,27." *TZ* 10 (1954): 401–17.

———. *Die Verkündigung des Todes Jesu im Neuen Testament.* Biblisch Theologische Studien 6. Neukirchen-Vluyn: Neukirchener Verlag, 1982.

Fryer, Nico S. L. "The Meaning and Translation of *Hilasterion* in Romans 3:25." *EvQ* 59 (1987): 99–116.

Füglister, Notker. *Die Heilsbedeutung des Pascha.* SANT 8. Munich: Kösel-Verlag, 1963.

Fuller, Daniel P. *Gospel and Law: Contrast or Continuum? The Hermeneutics of Dispensationalism and Covenant Theology.* Grand Rapids: Eerdmans, 1980.

———. "Paul and 'The Works of the Law.'" *WTJ* 38 (1975–1976): 28–42.

Fuller, Reginald. *The Mission and Achievement of Jesus: An Examination of the Presuppositions of New Testament Theology.* London: SCM Press, 1954.

Fung, Ronald Y. K. *The Epistle to the Galatians.* NICNT. Grand Rapids: Eerdmans, 1988.

Furnish, Victor Paul. *II Corinthians.* AB 32A. New York: Doubleday, 1984.

Gager, John R. *The Origins of Anti-Semitism: Attitudes toward Judaism in Pagan and Christian Antiquity.* Oxford: Oxford University Press, 1983.

García Martínez, Florentino. *The Dead Sea Scrolls Translated: The Qumran Texts in English.* Translated by Wilfred G. E. Watson. 2d ed. Leiden: E. J. Brill, 1996.

———. "4QMMT in a Qumran Context." Pages 15–27 in *Reading 4QMMT: New Perspectives on Qumran Law and History.* Edited by John Kampen and Moshe J. Bernstein. Society of Biblical Literature Symposium Series. Atlanta: Scholars Press, 1996.

Garlington, Don B. *Faith, Obedience and Perseverance: Aspects of Paul's Letter to the Romans.* WUNT 79. Tübingen: J.C.B. Mohr (Paul Siebeck), 1994.

Garnet, Paul. *Salvation and Atonement in the Qumran Scrolls.* WUNT. Second Series 3. Tübingen: J.C.B. Mohr (Paul Siebeck), 1977.

Gärtner, Bertil. *The Temple and the Community in Qumran and the New Testament: A Comparative Study in the Temple Symbolism of the Qumran Texts and the New Testament.* SNTSMS 1. Cambridge: Cambridge University Press, 1965.

Gaston, Lloyd. *Paul and the Torah*. Vancouver: University of British Columbia Press, 1987.

———. "Paul and the Torah." In *Antisemitism and the Foundations of Christianity*. Edited by Alan Davies. New York: Paulist, 1979.

———. "Works of Law As a Subjective Genitive." *SR* 13 (1984): 39–46.

Gaylord, H. E., Jr. "3 (Greek Apocalypse of) Baruch." Pages 653–61 in *Apocalyptic Literature and Testaments*. Vol. 1 of *The Old Testament Pseudepigrapha*. Edited by James H. Charlesworth. Garden City, N.Y.: Doubleday, 1983.

Georgi, Dieter. *The Opponents of Paul in Second Corinthians*. Philadelphia: Fortress, 1986.

Gese, Hartmut. "The Atonement." In *Essays on Biblical Theology*. Translated by Keith Crim. Minneapolis: Augsburg, 1981.

Getty, Mary Ann. "Paul and the Salvation of Israel: A Perspective on Romans 9–11." *CBQ* 50 (1988): 456–69.

Ginzberg, Louis. "Baruch, Apocalypse of (Greek)." Pages 549–51 in *The Jewish Encyclopedia*. Edited by Isidore Singer et al. New York: Funk & Wagnalls, 1902, 1916.

Goldingay, John. "Old Testament Sacrifice and the Death of Christ." Pages 3–20 in *Atonement Today: A Symposium at St John's College, Nottingham*. Edited by John Goldingay. London: SPCK, 1995.

Goodwin, D. R. " Ἐὰν μή, *Gal.* ii. 16." *JBL* 6 (1886): 122–27.

Gordon, T. David. "Why Israel Did Not Obtain Torah-Righteousness: A Translation Note on Rom 9:32." *WTJ* 54 (1992): 163–66.

Gowan, Donald E. *Theology in Exodus: Biblical Theology in the Form of a Commentary*. Louisville: Westminster John Knox, 1994.

Gräßer, Erich. *Der Alte Bund im Neuen*. WUNT 35. Tübingen: J. C. B. Mohr (Paul Siebeck), 1985.

———. "Zwei Heilswege? Zum theologischen Verhältnis von Israel und Kirche." Pages 411–29 in *Kontinuität und Einheit: Für Franz Mußner*. Edited by Paul-Gerhard Müller and Werner Stenger. Freiburg: Herder, 1981.

Greenfield, Jonas C. Prolegomenon to *3 Enoch or The Hebrew Book of Enoch*, by Hugo Odeberg. New York: Ktav, 1973.

Greenwood, David. "Jesus As Hilasterion in Romans 3:25." *BTB* 3 (1973): 316–22.

Greidanus, Sidney. "The Universal Dimension of Law in the Hebrew Scriptures." *SR* 14 (1985): 39–51.

Grobel, Kendrick. "A Chiastic Retribution-Formula in Romans 2." Pages 255–61 in *Zeit und Geschichte. Dankesgabe an Rudolf Bultmann zum 80. Geburtstag*. Edited by Erich Dinkler. Tübingen: J.C.B. Mohr (Paul Siebeck), 1964.

Guerra, Anthony J. "Romans 4 As Apologetic Theology." *HTR* 81 (1988): 251–70.

Gundry, Robert H. "Grace, Works, and Staying Saved in Paul." *Bib* 66 (1985): 1–38.

———. "The Moral Frustration of Paul Before His Conversion: Sexual Lust in Romans 7:7–25." Pages 228–45 in *Pauline Studies.* Edited by Donald A. Hagner and Murray J. Harris. Grand Rapids: Eerdmans, 1980.

Gunkel, H. "Das Vierte Buch Esra." Pages 331–401 in vol. 2 of *Die Apokryphen und Pseudepigraphen des Alten Testaments.* Translated and edited by E. Kautzsch. Tübingen: J.C.B. Mohr (Paul Siebeck), 1900.

Gunton, Colin. "Christ the Sacrifice: Aspects of the Language and Imagery of the Bible." Pages 229–38 in *The Glory of Christ in the New Testament: Studies in Christology in Memory of George Bradford Caird.* Edited by L. D. Hurst and N. T. Wright. Oxford: Oxford University Press, 1987.

Guttmann, Alexander. "Tractate Abot—Its Place in Rabbinic Literature." *JQR* 41 (1950–1951): 181–93.

Habel, Norman. "The Form and Significance of the Call Narratives." *ZAW* 77 (1965): 297–323.

Hafemann, Scott J. "Paul and the Exile of Israel in Galatians 3–4." Pages 329–71 in *Exile: Old Testament, Jewish, and Christian Conceptions.* Edited by James M. Scott. JSJSup 56. Leiden: E. J. Brill, 1997.

———. *Paul, Moses, and the History of Israel.* WUNT 81. Tübingen: J.C.B. Mohr (Paul Siebeck), 1995. Repr. Peabody, Mass.: Hendrickson, 1996.

———. "The Salvation of Israel in Romans 11:25–32: A Response to Krister Stendahl." *Ex auditu* 4 (1988): 38–58.

———. *Suffering and the Spirit: An Exegetical Study of II Cor. 2:14–3:3 within the Context of the Corinthian Correspondence.* WUNT. Second Series 19. Tübingen: J.C.B. Mohr (Paul Siebeck), 1986.

Hagner, Donald A. "Paul and Judaism—The Jewish Matrix of Early Christianity: Issues in the Current Debate." *Bulletin for Biblical Research* 3 (1993): 111–30.

Hahn, Ferdinand. "Zum Verständnis von Römer 11.26a: '. . . und so wird ganz Israel gerettet werden.'" Pages 221–36 in *Paul and Paulinism: Essays in Honour of C. K. Barrett.* Edited by M. D. Hooker and S. G. Wilson. London: SPCK, 1982.

Hainz, Josef. *Ekklesia: Stukturen paulinischer Gemeinde-Theologie und Gemeinde-Ordnung.* Regensburg: Friedrich Pustet Regensburg, 1972.

Hammer, Reuven, trans. *Sifre: A Tannaitic Commentary on the Book of Deuteronomy.* Yale Judaica Series 24. New Haven: Yale University Press, 1986.

Hanse, Hermann. "ΔΗΛΟΝ (Zu Gal 3^{11})." *ZNW* 34 (1935): 299–303.

Hansen, G. Walter. *Abraham in Galatians: Epistolary and Rhetorical Contexts.* JSNTSup 29. Sheffield: JSOT Press, 1989.

Hanson, Anthony Tyrrell. "Abraham the Justified Sinner." In *Studies in Paul's Technique and Theology.* London: SPCK, 1974.

Haran, Menahem. "The Shining of Moses' Face: A Case Study in Biblical and Ancient Near Eastern Iconography." Pages 159–73 in *In the Shelter of Elyon: Essays on Ancient Palestinian Life and Literature in Honor of G. W. Ahlström.* Edited by W. Boyd Barrick and John R. Spencer. JSOTSup 31. Sheffield: JSOT Press, 1984.

Harlow, Daniel C. *The Greek Apocalypse of Baruch (3 Baruch) in Hellenistic Judaism and Early Christianity.* SVTP 12. Leiden: E. J. Brill, 1996.

Harnisch, Wolfgang. "Die Ironie der Offenbarung: Exegetische Erwägungen zur Zion vision im 4. Buch Esra." In *SBL Seminar Papers, 1981,* 79–104. Edited by Kent Harold Richards. Chico, Calif.: Scholars Press, 1981.

———. "Der Prophet as Widerpart und Zeuge der Offenbarung Erwägungen zur Interdependenz von Form und Sache im IV. Buch Esra." Pages 461–93 in *Apocalypticism in the Mediterranean World and the Near East: Proceedings of the International Colloquium on Apocalypticism, Uppsala, August 12–17, 1979.* Edited by David Hellholm. Tübingen: J.C.B. Mohr (Paul Siebeck), 1983.

———. *Verhängnis und Verbeißung der Geschichte: Untersuchungen zum Zeit- und Geschichtsverständnis im 4. Buch Esra und in der syr. Baruchapokalypse.* FRLANT 97. Göttingen: Vandenhoeck & Ruprecht, 1969.

Harrelson, Walter. "Ezra among the Wicked in 2 Esdras 3–10." Pages 21–40 in *The Divine Helmsman: Studies on God's Control of Human Events, Presented to Lou H. Silberman.* Edited by James L. Crenshaw and Samuel Sandmel. New York: Ktav, 1980.

Harris, Murray J. *Jesus As God: The New Testament Use of Theos in Reference to Jesus.* Grand Rapids: Baker, 1992.

Harrison, R. K. *Leviticus: An Introduction and Commentary.* Tyndale Old Testament Commentaries. Downers Grove, Ill.: InterVarsity Press, 1980.

Harvey, A. E. *Jesus and the Constraints of History.* Philadelphia: Westminster, 1982.

Hasel, Gerhard F. *The Remnant: The History and Theology of the Remnant Idea from Genesis to Isaiah.* Berrien Springs, Mich.: Andrews University Press, 1972.

Hayman, A. P. "The Problem of Pseudonymity in the Ezra Apocalypse." *JSJ* 6 (1975): 47–56.

Hays, Richard B. "Christology and Ethics in Galatians." *CBQ* 49 (1987): 268–90.

———. *Echoes of Scripture in the Letters of Paul.* New Haven: Yale University Press, 1989.

———. *The Faith of Jesus Christ: An Investigation of the Narrative Substructure of Galatians 3:1–4:11.* SBLDS 56. Chico, Calif.: Scholars Press, 1983.

———. "'Have We Found Abraham to Be Our Forefather according to the Flesh?' A Reconsideration of Rom 4:1." *NovT* 27 (1985): 76–98.

———. *The Moral Vision of the New Testament: A Contemporary Introduction to New Testament Ethics.* New York: HarperCollins, 1996.

———. "Three Dramatic Roles: The Law in Romans 3–4." Pages 151–64 in *Paul and the Mosaic Law.* Edited by James D. G. Dunn. WUNT 89. Tübingen: J.C.B. Mohr (Paul Siebeck), 1996.

Heiligenthal, Roman. *Werke als Zeichen: Untersuchungen zur Bedeutung der menschlischen Taten im Frühjudentum, Neuen Testament und Frühchristentum.* WUNT. Second Series 9. Tübingen: J.C.B. Mohr (Paul Siebeck), 1983.

Hendel, Ronald S. "Sacrifice As a Cultural System: The Ritual Symbolism of Exodus 24,3–8." *ZAW* 101 (1989): 366–90.

Hengel, Martin. *The Atonement: The Origins of the Doctrine in the New Testament.* Philadelphia: Fortress, 1981.

Henten, Jan Willem van. "The Tradition-Historical Background of Romans 3.25: A Search for Pagan and Jewish Parallels." Pages 101–28 in *From Jesus to John: Essays on Jesus and New Testament Christology in Honour of Marinus de Jonge.* Edited by Martinus C. De Boer. JSNTSup 84. Sheffield: Sheffield Academic Press, 1993.

Hilgert, Earle. "A Review of Previous Research on Philo's *De Virtutibus.*" In *SBL Seminar Papers, 1991,* 103–15. Atlanta: Scholars Press, 1991.

Hill, David. *Greek Words and Hebrew Meanings: Studies in the Semantics of Soteriological Terms.* SNTSMS 5. Cambridge: Cambridge University Press, 1967.

Hofius, Otfried. "'All Israel Will Be Saved': Divine Salvation and Israel's Deliverance in Romans 9–11." *Princeton Seminary Bulletin* Suppl. 1 (1990): 19–39.

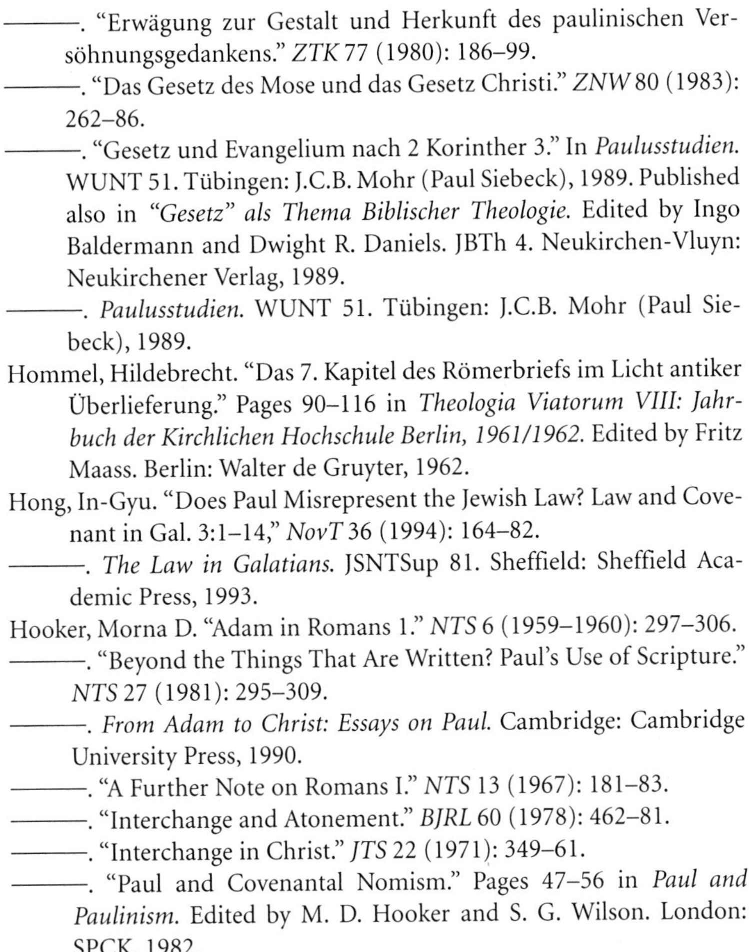

———. "Erwägung zur Gestalt und Herkunft des paulinischen Versöhnungsgedankens." *ZTK* 77 (1980): 186–99.

———. "Das Gesetz des Mose und das Gesetz Christi." *ZNW* 80 (1983): 262–86.

———. "Gesetz und Evangelium nach 2 Korinther 3." In *Paulusstudien.* WUNT 51. Tübingen: J.C.B. Mohr (Paul Siebeck), 1989. Published also in *"Gesetz" als Thema Biblischer Theologie.* Edited by Ingo Baldermann and Dwight R. Daniels. JBTh 4. Neukirchen-Vluyn: Neukirchener Verlag, 1989.

———. *Paulusstudien.* WUNT 51. Tübingen: J.C.B. Mohr (Paul Siebeck), 1989.

Hommel, Hildebrecht. "Das 7. Kapitel des Römerbriefs im Licht antiker Überlieferung." Pages 90–116 in *Theologia Viatorum VIII: Jahrbuch der Kirchlichen Hochschule Berlin, 1961/1962.* Edited by Fritz Maass. Berlin: Walter de Gruyter, 1962.

Hong, In-Gyu. "Does Paul Misrepresent the Jewish Law? Law and Covenant in Gal. 3:1–14," *NovT* 36 (1994): 164–82.

———. *The Law in Galatians.* JSNTSup 81. Sheffield: Sheffield Academic Press, 1993.

Hooker, Morna D. "Adam in Romans 1." *NTS* 6 (1959–1960): 297–306.

———. "Beyond the Things That Are Written? Paul's Use of Scripture." *NTS* 27 (1981): 295–309.

———. *From Adam to Christ: Essays on Paul.* Cambridge: Cambridge University Press, 1990.

———. "A Further Note on Romans I." *NTS* 13 (1967): 181–83.

———. "Interchange and Atonement." *BJRL* 60 (1978): 462–81.

———. "Interchange in Christ." *JTS* 22 (1971): 349–61.

———. "Paul and Covenantal Nomism." Pages 47–56 in *Paul and Paulinism.* Edited by M. D. Hooker and S. G. Wilson. London: SPCK, 1982.

Horne, Charles M. "The Meaning of the Phrase 'and Thus All Israel Will Be Saved' (Romans 11:26)." *JETS* 21 (1978): 329–34.

Hort, Fenton John Anthony. *Epistle of St. James.* London: Macmillan, 1909.

Howard, George E. "Christ the End of the Law: The Meaning of Romans 10:4ff." *JBL* 88 (1969): 331–37.

———. "Romans 3:21–31 and the Inclusion of the Gentiles." *HTR* 63 (1970): 223–33.

Hübner, Hans. *Law in Paul's Thought.* Translated by James C. G. Greig. Edinburgh: T&T Clark, 1984.

———. "Rechtfertigung und Sühne bei Paulus: Eine Hermeneutische und Theologische Besinnung." *NTS* 39 (1993): 80–93.

Hughes, H. Maldwyn. "The Greek Apocalypse of Baruch or III Baruch." Pages 527–32 in vol. 2 of *The Apocrypha and Pseudepigrapha of the Old Testament.* Edited by R. H. Charles. 2 vols. Oxford: Clarendon, 1913.

Hughes, Philip Edgcumbe. *Paul's Second Epistle to the Corinthians.* NICNT. Grand Rapids: Eerdmans, 1962.

Hultgard, Anders. "The Burnt-Offering in Early Jewish Religion: Sources, Practices and Purpose." Pages 83–91 in *Gifts to the Gods: Proceedings of the Uppsala Symposium 1985.* Edited by Tullia Linders and Gullög Nordquist. Uppsala Studies in Ancient Mediterranean and Near Eastern Civilizations 15. Uppsala: Almquist & Wiksell, 1987.

Hultgren, Arland J. *Paul's Gospel and Mission.* Philadelphia: Fortress, 1985.

Huntjens, Johannes A. "Contrasting Notions of Covenant and Law in the Texts from Qumran." *RevQ* 8 (1974): 361–80.

Hurtado, Larry W. *One God, One Lord: Early Christian Devotion and Ancient Jewish Monotheism.* 2d ed. Edinburgh: T&T Clark, 1998.

Hvalvik, Reidar. "A 'Sonderweg' for Israel: A Critical Examination of a Current Interpretation of Romans 11.25–27." *JSNT* 38 (1990): 87–107.

Hyldahl, Niels. "A Reminiscence of the Old Testament at Romans i. 23." *NTS* 2 (1956): 285–88.

Ito, Akio. "Romans 2: A Deuteronomistic Reading." *JSNT* 59 (1995): 21–37.

Jackson, Bernard S. "Legalism." *JJS* 30 (1979): 1–22.

Janssen, Enno. *Testament Abrahams. JSHRZ.* Third Series 2. Gütersloh: Mohn, 1975.

Jaubert, Annie. *La Notion D'Alliance dans le Judaïsme: Aux Abords de L'Ère Chrétienne.* Patristica Sorbonensia 6. Paris: Cerf (Editions du Seuil), 1963.

Jenson, Philip P. "The Levitical Sacrificial System." Pages 25–40 in *Sacrifice in the Bible.* Edited by Roger T. Beckwith and Martin J. Selman. Grand Rapids: Baker, 1995.

Jeremias, Joachim. "Zu Rm 1.22–32." *ZNW* 45 (1954): 119–21.

Jervell, Jacob. *Imago Dei: Gen 1,26f. im Spätjudentum, in der Gnosis und in den paulinischen Briefen.* FRLANT 76. Göttingen: Vandenhoeck & Ruprecht, 1960.

Jewett, Robert. "Honor and Shame in the Argument of Romans." Pages 258–73 in *Putting Body and Soul Together: Essays in Honor of Robin Scroggs.* Edited by Virginia Wiles, Alexandra Brown, and Graydon F. Snyder. Valley Forge, Pa., Trinity Press International, 1997.

Johnson, Dan. "The Structure and Meaning of Romans 11." *CBQ* 46 (1984): 91–103.

Johnson, E. Elizabeth. *The Function of Apocalyptic and Wisdom Traditions in Romans 9–11.* SBLDS 109. Atlanta: Scholars Press, 1989.

———. "Romans 9–11: The Faithfulness and Impartiality of God." Pages 211–39 in vol. 3 of *Pauline Theology.* Edited by David M. Hay and E. Elizabeth Johnson. Minneapolis: Fortress, 1995.

Johnson, H. Wayne. "The Paradigm of Abraham in Galatians 3:6–9." *TJ* 8 New Series (1987): 179–99.

Johnson, Luke Timothy. *Reading Romans: A Literary and Theological Commentary.* New York: Crossroad, 1997.

Johnson, S. Lewis Jr. "Paul and the 'Israel of God': An Exegetical and Eschatological Case-Study." *Mishkan* 6–7 (1987): 49–65.

Johnson, Sherman E. "Paul and the Manual of Discipline." *HTR* 48 (1955): 157–65.

Kaiser, Walter C., Jr. "Leviticus 18:5 and Paul: Do This and You Shall Live (Eternally?)." *JETS* 14 (1971): 19–28.

Kaminsky, Joel S. *Corporate Responsibility in the Hebrew Bible.* JSOTSup 196. Sheffield: Sheffield Academic Press, 1995.

Kampen, John. "4QMMT and New Testament Studies." Pages 129–44 in *Reading 4QMMT: New Perspectives on Qumran Law and History.* Edited by John Kampen and Moshe J. Bernstein. Society of Biblical Literature Symposium Series. Atlanta: Scholars Press, 1996.

Käsemann, Ernst. *Commentary on Romans.* Translated and edited by Geoffrey W. Bromiley. Grand Rapids: Eerdmans, 1980.

———. "The Faith of Abraham in Romans 4." In *Perspectives on Paul.* Philadelphia: Fortress, 1971.

———. "Justification and Salvation History." In *Perspectives on Paul.* Philadelphia: Fortress, 1971.

———. "Some Thoughts on the Theme 'The Doctrine of Reconciliation in the New Testament'." Pages 49–64 in *The Future of Our Religious Past: Essays in Honour of Rudolf Bultmann.* Edited by James M. Robinson. Translated by Charles E. Carlston and Robert P. Scharlemann. New York: Harper & Row, 1971.

———. "The Spirit and the Letter." *Perspectives on Paul.* Philadelphia: Fortress, 1971.

———. "Zum Verständnis von Römer 3.24–26," *ZNW* 43 (1950–1951): 150–54. Reprinted in *Exegetische Versuche und Besinnungen.* Vol. 1. Göttingen: Vandenhoeck & Ruprecht, 1960.

Kaylor, R. David. *Paul's Covenant Community: Jews and Gentiles in Romans.* Atlanta: John Knox, 1988.

Keck, Leander E. "Justification of the Ungodly and Ethics." Pages 199–209 in *Rechtfertigung: Festschrift für Ernst Käsemann zum 70. Geburtstag.* Edited by Johannes Friedrich, Wolfgang Pöhlmann, and Peter Stuhlmacher. Tübingen: J.C.B. Mohr (Paul Siebeck), 1976.

———. *Paul and His Letters.* 2d ed. Philadelphia: Fortress, 1988.

Kertelge, Karl. *"Rechtfertigung" bei Paulus: Studien zur Struktur und zum Bedeutungsgehalt des paulinischen Rechtsfertigungsbegriff.* NTAbh. New Series 3. Münster: Aschendorff, 1967.

Kim, Seyoon. "God Reconciled His Enemy to Himself: The Origin of Paul's Concept of Reconciliation." Pages 102–24 in *The Road from Damascus: The Impact of Paul's Conversion on His Life, Thought, and Ministry.* Edited by Richard N. Longenecker. Grand Rapids: Eerdmans, 1997.

———. *The Origin of Paul's Gospel.* WUNT. Second Series 4. Tübingen: J.C.B. Mohr (Paul Siebeck), 1981.

Kittel, Gerhard, and Gerhard Friedrich. *Theological Dictionary of the New Testament.* Translated by Geoffrey W. Bromiley. 10 vols. Grand Rapids: Eerdmans, 1964–1976.

Kiuchi, N. *The Purification Offering in the Priestly Literature: Its Meaning and Function.* Sheffield: Sheffield Academic Press, 1987.

Klijn, A. F. J. "2 (Syriac Apocalypse of) Baruch." Pages 615–20 in *Apocalyptic Literature and Testaments.* Vol. 1 of *The Old Testament Pseudepigrapha.* Edited by James H. Charlesworth. Garden City, N.Y.: Doubleday, 1983.

Klinzing, Georg. *Die Umdeutung des Kultus in der Qumrangemeinde und im Neuen Testament.* Göttingen: Vandenhoeck & Ruprecht, 1971.

Klostermann, E. "Die adäquate Vergeltung in Rm 1:22–31." *ZNW* 32 (1933): 1–6.

Knibb, Michael A. "The Second Book of Esdras." *The First and Second Books of Esdras.* Edited by R. J. Coggins and M. A. Knibb. CBC. Cambridge: Cambridge University Press, 1979.

Knight, George A. F. *Theology As Narration: A Commentary on the Book of Exodus.* Grand Rapids: Eerdmans, 1976.

Knowles, Michael P. "Moses, the Law, and the Unity of 4 Ezra." *NovT* 31 (1989): 257–74.

Koch, Dietrich-Alex. *Die Schrift als Zeuge des Evangeliums: Untersuchungen zur Verwendung und zum Verständnis der Schrift bei Paulus.* BHT 69. Tübingen: J.C.B. Mohr (Paul Siebeck), 1986.

Kolenkow, Anitra. "The Ascription of Romans 4:5." *HTR* 60 (1967): 228–30.

König, Adrio. "Gentiles or Gentile Christians? On the Meaning of Romans 2:12–16." *Journal of Theology for Southern Africa* 15 (1976): 53–60.

Kraus, Wolfgang. *Der Tod Jesu als Heiligtumsweihe: Eine Untersuchung zum Umfeld der Sühnevorstellung in Römer 3.25–26a.* WMANT 66. Neukirchen-Vluyn: Neukirchener Verlag, 1991.

Kruse, Colin G. *Paul, the Law, and Justification.* Peabody, Mass.: Hendrickson, 1996.

Kuhr, Friedrich. "Römer 2.14f. und die Verheissung bei Jeremia 31.31ff." *ZNW* 55 (1964): 243–61.

Kümmel, Werner Georg. "Πάρεσις und ἔνδειξις: Ein Beitrag zum Verständnis der paulinischen Rechtfertigungslehre." *ZTK* 49 (1952): 154–67. Reprinted in *Heilsgeschehen und Geschichte: Gesammelte Aufsätze, 1933–1964.* Vol. 1. Marburg: N. G. Elwert, 1965.

Kuss, Otto. *Der Römerbrief übersetzt und erklärt.* Vol. 1. Regensburg: Friedrich Pustet, 1957.

Kutsch, Ernst. *Neues Testament—Neuer Bund? Eine Fehlübersetzung wird korrigiert.* Düsseldorf: Neukirchener Verlag, 1978.

Laato, Timo. *Paul and Judaism: An Anthropological Approach.* Translated by T. McElwain. South Florida Studies in the History of Judaism 115. Atlanta: Scholars Press, 1995.

Lagrange, M.-J. *Saint Paul Épitre aux Romains. Etudes bibliques.* Paris: Librairie Lecoffre, 1950.

Lambrecht, Jan. "Curse and Blessing: A Study of Galatians 3,10–14." In *Pauline Studies.* Leuven: Leuven University Press, 1994.

———. "Man Before and Without Christ: Rom 7 and Pauline Anthropology." *Louvain Studies* 5 (1974–1975): 18–33.

———. "Paul's Lack of Logic in Romans 9,1–13: A Response to M. Cranford's 'Election and Ethnicity.'" Pages 55–60 in *Pauline Studies.* Leuven: Leuven University Press, 1994.

———. "Why Is Boasting Excluded? A Note On Rom 3,27 and 4,2." *ETL* 61 (1985): 365–69.

Lambrecht, Jan, and Richard W. Thompson. *Justification by Faith: The Implications of Romans 3:27–31.* Zacchaeus Studies. Wilmington, Del.: Michael Glazier, 1989.

Lane, William L. "Covenant: The Key to Paul's Conflict with Corinth." *TynBul* 33 (1982): 3–29.

Laporte, Jean. "The High Priest in Philo of Alexandria." In *The Studia Philonic Annual: Studies in Hellenistic Judaism.* Vol. 3, ed. David T. Runia, 71–82. Atlanta: Scholars Press, 1991.

———. "Sacrifice and Forgiveness in Philo of Alexandria." Pages 34–42 in volume 1 of *The Studia Philonica Annual: Studies in Hellenistic Judaism.* Edited by David T. Runia. Atlanta: Scholars Press, 1989.

Lauterbach, Jacob Z., trans. *Mekilta de-Rabbi Ishmael.* 3 vols. Philadelphia: Jewish Publication Society of America, 1933–1935.

Levenson, Jon D. "Covenant and Commandment." *Tradition* 21 (1983): 42–51.

Levertoff, Paul P., trans. *Midrash Sifre on Numbers: Selections from Early Rabbinic Scriptural Interpretations.* London: SPCK, 1926.

Levine, Baruch A. "An Essay on Prophetic Attitudes toward Temple and Cult in Biblical Israel." Pages 202–25 in *Minḥah le-Naḥum: Biblical and Other Studies Presented to Nahum M. Sarna in Honour of His 70th Birthday.* Edited by Marc Brettler and Michael Fishbane. JSOTSup 154. Sheffield: JSOT Press, 1993.

———. *In the Presence of the Lord: A Study of Cult and Some Cultic Terms in Ancient Israel.* SJLA 5. Leiden: E. J. Brill, 1974.

Lichtenberger, Hermann. "Atonement and Sacrifice in the Qumran Community." Pages 159–71 in vol. 2 of *Approaches to Ancient Judaism.* Edited by William Scott Green. Brown Judaic Studies 9. Chico, Calif.: Scholars Press, 1980.

Liddell, Henry George, and Robert Scott. *A Greek-English Lexicon.* 9th ed. Oxford: Oxford University Press, 1940.

Liebers, Reinhold. *Das Gesetz als Evangelium: Untersuchungen zur Gesetzeskritik des Paulus.* ATANT 75. Zürich: Theologischer, 1989.

Lietzmann, Hans. *Einführung in die Textgeschichte der Paulusbriefe an die Römer.* 4th ed. HNT 8. Tübingen: J.C.B. Mohr (Paul Siebeck), 1933.

Lieu, Judith M. "Reading in Canon and Community: Deuteronomy 21.22–23, a Test Case for Dialogue." Pages 317–34 in *The Bible in Human Society: Essays in Honour of John Rogerson.* Edited by M. Daniel Carroll R., David J. A. Clines, and Philip R. Davies. JSOTSup 200. Sheffield: Sheffield Academic Press, 1995.

Lincoln, Andrew T. *Ephesians.* WBC 42. Dallas: Word, 1990.

———. "Ephesians 2:8–10: A Summary of Paul's Gospel." *CBQ* 45 (1983): 617–30.

———. "The Theology of Ephesians." Pages 75–166 in *The Theology of the Later Pauline Letters.* By Andrew T. Lincoln and A. J. M. Wedderburn. New Testament Theology. Cambridge: Cambridge University Press, 1993.

Lindemann, Andreas. "Die Gerechtigkeit aus dem Gesetz: Erwägungen zur Auslegung und zur Textgeschichte von Römer 10:5." *ZNW* 73 (1982): 231–50.

Linss, Wilhelm C. "Exegesis of Telos in Romans 10:4." *BR* 33 (1988): 5–12.

Little, Joyce A. "Paul's Use of Analogy: A Structural Analysis of Romans 7:1–6." *CBQ* 46 (1984): 82–90.

Lodge, John G. *Romans 9–11: A Reader-Response Analysis.* University of South Florida International Studies in Formative Christianity and Judaism 8. Atlanta: Scholars Press, 1996.

Lohse, Eduard. *Märtyrer und Gottesknecht: Untersuchungen zur urchristlichen Verkündigung vom Sühnetod Jesu Christi.* 2d ed. Göttingen: Vandenhoeck & Ruprecht, 1963.

———. "ὁ νόμος τοῦ πνεύματος τῆς ζωῆς Exegetische Anmerkungen zu Röm 8,2." Pages 279–87 in *Neues Testament und christliche Existenz: Festschrift für Herbert Braun zum 70. Geburtstag am 4. Mai 1973.* Edited by Hans Dieter Betz and Luise Schottroff. Tübingen: J.C.B. Mohr (Paul Siebeck), 1973.

Longenecker, Bruce W. "Contours of Covenant Theology in the Post-Conversion Paul." Pages 125–46 in *The Road from Damascus: The Impact of Paul's Conversion on His Life, Thought, and Ministry.* Edited by Richard N. Longenecker. Grand Rapids: Eerdmans, 1997.

———. "Different Answers to Different Issues: Israel, the Gentiles and Salvation History in Romans 9–11." *JSNT* 36 (1989): 95–123.

———. *Eschatology and Covenant: A Comparison of 4 Ezra and Romans 1–11.* JSNTSup 57. Sheffield: JSOT Press, 1991.

———. *2 Esdras.* Guides to Apocrypha and Pseudepigrapha. Sheffield: Sheffield Academic Press, 1995.

Longenecker, Richard N. *Galatians.* WBC 41. Dallas: Word, 1990.

———. *Paul: Apostle of Liberty.* New York: Harper & Row, 1964.

Lucas, Ernest C. "Sacrifice in the Prophets." Pages 41–58 in *Sacrifice in the Bible.* Edited by Roger T. Beckwith and Martin J. Selman. Grand Rapids: Baker, 1995.

Lührmann, Dieter. *Galatians.* Translated by O. C. Dean Jr. Minneapolis: Fortress, 1992.

Luz, Ulrich. *Das Geschichtsverständnis des Paulus.* BEvT 49. Munich: Chr. Kaiser, 1968.

Lyonnet, Stanislas. "L'emploi paulinien de ἐξαγοράσειν au sens de "redimere" est-il attesté dans la littérature grecque?" *Biblica* 42 (1961): 85–89.

Lyonnet, Stanislas, and Leopold Sabourin. *Sin, Redemption, and Sacrifice: A Biblical and Patristic Study.* AnBib 48. Rome: Biblical Institute Press, 1970.

Maccoby, Hyam. *Early Rabbinic Writings.* Cambridge Commentaries on the Writings of the Jewish and Christian World 200 BC to AD 200, 3. Cambridge: Cambridge University Press, 1988.

Malherbe, Abraham J. "*Me Genoito* in the Diatribe and Paul." In *Paul and the Popular Philosophers.* Minneapolis: Fortress, 1989. Reprinted from *HTR* 73 (1980): 231–40.

Manson, T. W. " ἹΛΑΣΤΗΡΙΟΝ." *JTS* 46 (1945): 1–10.

Marshall, I. Howard. "Salvation, Grace and Works in the Later Writings in the Pauline Corpus." *NTS* 42 (1996): 339–58.

Martens, John W. "Philo and the 'Higher' Law." In *SBL Seminar Papers, 1991,* 309–22. Atlanta: Scholars Press, 1991.

———. "Romans 2.14–16: A Stoic Reading." *NTS* 40 (1994): 55–67.

———. "Unwritten Law in Philo: A Response to Naomi G. Cohen." *JJS* 43 (1992): 38–45.

Martin, Brice L. *Christ and the Law in Paul.* NovTSup 62. Leiden: E. J. Brill, 1989.

Martin, Ralph P. *2 Corinthians.* WBC 40. Dallas: Word, 1986.

Martyn, J. Louis. "Covenant, Christ, and Church in Galatians." Pages 137–51 in *The Future of Christology: Essays in Honor of Leander E. Keck.* Edited by Abraham J. Malherbe and Wayne A. Meeks. Minneapolis: Fortress, 1993.

———. "The Covenants of Hagar and Sarah." Pages 160–92 in *Faith and History: Essays in Honor of Paul W. Meyer.* Edited by John T. Carroll, Charles H. Cosgrove, and E. Elizabeth Johnson. Atlanta: Scholars Press, 1990.

———. "Events in Galatia: Modified Covenantal Nomism versus God's Invasion of the Cosmos in the Singular Gospel." Pages 160–75 in *Thessalonians, Philippians, Galatians, Philemon.* Edited by Jouette M. Bassler. Vol. 1 of *Pauline Theology.* Minneapolis: Fortress, 1991.

———. *Galatians.* AB 33A. New York: Doubleday, 1997.

———. "A Law-Observant Mission to Gentiles: The Background of Galatians." *SJT* 38 (1985): 307–24.

———. *Theological Issues in the Letters of Paul.* Nashville: Abingdon, 1997.

Mason, Rex. *Zephaniah, Habakkuk, Joel.* Old Testament Guides. Sheffield: JSOT Press, 1994.

Matera, Frank J. *Galatians.* Sacra pagina 9. Collegeville, Minn.: Liturgical Press, 1992.

Mayes, A. D. H. *Deuteronomy.* NCB. London: Marshall, Morgan & Scott, 1979.

McCready, Wayne O. "A Second Torah at Qumran?" *SR* 15 (1985): 5–15.

McKeating, Henry. "Divine Forgiveness in the Psalms." *SJT* 18 (1965): 69–83.

McLean, Bradley Hudson. "The Absence of Atoning Sacrifice in Paul's Soteriology." *NTS* 38 (1992): 531–53.

———. *The Cursed Christ: Mediterranean Expulsion Rituals and Pauline Soteriology.* JSNTSup 126. Sheffield: Sheffield Academic Press, 1996.

———. "The Interpretation of the Levitical Sin Offering and the Scapegoat." *Studies in Religion* 20 (1991): 345–56.

Mendelson, Alan. *Philo's Jewish Identity.* Brown Judaic Studies 161. Atlanta: Scholars Press, 1988.

Merklein, Helmut. *Studien zu Jesus und Paulus.* WUNT 43. Tübingen: J. C. B. Mohr (Paul Siebeck), 1987.

Metzger, Bruce M. "The Punctuation of Romans 9:5." Pages 95–112 in *Christ and the Spirit in the NT.* Edited by Barnabas Lindars and Stephen S. Smalley. Cambridge: Cambridge University Press, 1973.

Meyer, Ben F. "The Pre-Pauline Formula in Rom. 3.25–26a." *NTS* 29 (1983): 198–208.

Meyer, Paul W. "Romans." Pages 1130–67 in *Harper's Bible Commentary.* Edited by James L. Mays. New York: Harper & Row, 1988.

———. "Romans 10:4 and the 'End' of the Law." Pages 59–78 in *The Divine Helmsman: Studies in God's Control of Human Events, Presented to Lou H. Silberman.* Edited by James L. Crenshaw and Samuel Sandmel. New York: Ktav, 1980.

———. "The Worm at the Core of the Apple: Exegetical Reflections on Romans 7." Pages 62–84 in *The Conversation Continues: Studies in Paul and John in Honor of J. Louis Martyn.* Edited by Robert T. Fortna and Beverly R. Gaventa. Nashville: Abingdon, 1990.

Middendorf, Michael Paul. *The "I" in the Storm: A Study of Romans 7.* St. Louis: Concordia, 1997.

Milgrom, Jacob. "Concerning Jeremiah's Repudiation of Sacrifice." *ZAW* 89 (1977): 273–75. Reprinted in *Studies in Cultic Theology and Terminology.* SJLA 36. Leiden: E. J. Brill, 1983.

———. *Cult and Conscience: The Asham and the Priestly Doctrine of Repentance.* SJLA 18. Leiden: E. J. Brill, 1976.

———. "Israel's Sanctuary: The Priestly 'Picture of Dorian Gray.'" *RB* 83 (1976): 390–99. Reprinted in *Studies in Cultic Theology and Terminology.* SJLA 36. Leiden: E. J. Brill, 1983.

———. *Leviticus 1–16.* AB 3. New York: Doubleday, 1991.

———. "The *Modus Operandi* of *Ḥaṭṭāʾt:* A Rejoinder." *JBL* 109 (1990): 111–13.

———. "A Prolegomenon to Leviticus 17:11." *JBL* 90 (1971): 149–56. Reprinted in *Studies in Cultic Theology and Terminology.* SJLA 36. Leiden: E. J. Brill, 1983.

———. "Sacrifices and Offerings, OT." Pages 763–71 in *Interpreter's Dictionary of the Bible: Supplementary Volume.* Edited by K. Crim. Nashville: Abingdon, 1976.

———. "Sin-Offering or Purification Offering?" *VT* 21 (1971): 237–39. Reprinted in *Studies in Cultic Theology and Terminology.* SJLA 36. Leiden: E. J. Brill, 1983.

Milik, J. T., ed. *The Books of Enoch: Aramaic Fragments of Qumran Cave 4.* Oxford: Clarendon, 1976.

Milikowsky, Chaim. "Notions of Exile, Subjugation and Return in Rabbinic Literature." Pages 265–96 in *Exile: Old Testament, Jewish, and Christian Conceptions.* Edited by James M. Scott. JSJSup 56. Leiden: E. J. Brill, 1997.

Mitchell, Stephen. *Regional Epigraphic Catalogs of Asia Minor I: The Inscriptions of North Galatia.* Monograph no. 4. B.A.R. International Series 135. Oxford: British Institute of Archaeology at Ankara, 1982.

Moberly, R. W. L. *The Mountain of God: Story and Theology in Exodus 32–34.* JSOTSup 22. Sheffield: JSOT Press, 1983.

Montefiore, C. G. *IV Ezra: A Study in the Development of Universalism.* London: George Allen & Unwin, 1929.

Montefiore, C. G., and H. Loewe. *A Rabbinic Anthology.* London: Macmillan, 1938.

Moo, Douglas J. *The Epistle to the Romans.* NICNT. Grand Rapids: Eerdmans, 1996.

———. "Israel and Paul in Romans 7.7–12." *NTS* 32 (1986): 122–35.

———. " 'Law,' 'Works of the Law,' and Legalism in Paul." *WTJ* 45 (1983): 73–100.

———. Review of Daniel P. Fuller, *Gospel and Law: Contrast or Continuum? TJ* 3 New Series (1982): 99–103.

———. "The Theology of Romans 9–11: A Response to E. Elizabeth Johnson." Pages 240–58 in vol. 3 of *Pauline Theology.* Edited by David M. Hay and E. Elizabeth Johnson. Minneapolis: Fortress, 1995.

Moore, George Foot. *Judaism in the First Centuries of the Christian Era: The Age of the Tannaim.* 3 vols. Cambridge: Harvard University Press, 1927–1930.

Moreland, Kjell Arne. *The Rhetoric of Curse in Galatians.* Emory Studies in Early Christianity 5. Atlanta: Scholars Press, 1995.

Morfill, W. R., and R. H. Charles. *The Book of the Secrets of Enoch.* Oxford: Clarendon, 1896.

Morgenstern, Julian. "Moses with the Shining Face." *HUCA* 2 (1925): 1–27.

Morris, Leon. *The Apostolic Preaching of the Cross.* Grand Rapids: Eerdmans, 1956.

———. " ʾAsham." *EvQ* 30 (1958): 196–210.

———. "The Meaning of ἹΛΑΣΤΗΡΙΟΝ in Romans III. 25." *NTS* 2 (1955–1956): 33–43.

Moule, C. F. D. "Justification in Its Relation to the Condition κατὰ πνεῦμα (Rom. 8:1–11)." Pages 177–87 in *Battesimo e Giustizia in Rom 6 e 8.* Edited by L. de Lorenzi. Rome: St. Paul Abbey, 1974.

Moulton, James Hope, and Wilbert Francis Howard. *Accidence and Word-Formation.* Vol. 2 of *A Grammar of New Testament Greek.* Edinburgh: T&T Clark, 1929, 1960.

Muffs, Yochanan. *Studies in the Aramaic Legal Papyri from Elephantine.* Studia et Documenta ad Iura Orientis Antiqui Pertinentia 8. New York: Ktav, 1973.

Munck, Johannes. *Christ and Israel: An Interpretation of Romans 9–11.* Translated by Ingeborg Nixon. Philadelphia: Fortress, 1967.

Mundle, Wilhelm. "Zur Auslegung von Röm 2,13 ff." *TBl* 13 (1934): 249–56.

Murphy, Frederick James. *The Structure and Meaning of Second Baruch.* SBLDS 78. Atlanta: Scholars Press, 1985.

Murphy-O'Connor, Jerome. "The New Covenant in the Letters of Paul and the Essene Documents." Pages 194–204 in *To Touch the Text: Biblical and Related Studies in Honor of Joseph A. Fitzmyer, S. J.* Edited by Maurya P. Horgan and Paul J. Kobelski. New York: Crossroad, 1989.

———. "*Pneumatikoi* and Judaizers in 2 Cor 2:14–4:6." *ABR* 34 (1986): 42–58.

Murray, John. *The Epistle to the Romans.* Vol. 2. NICNT. Grand Rapids: Eerdmans, 1965.

Mußner, Franz. *Der Galaterbrief.* HTKNT 9. Freiburg: Herder, 1974.

———. " 'Ganz Israel wird gerettet werden' (Röm 11, 26)." *Kairos* 18 (1976): 241–55.

———. *Tractate on the Jews: The Significance of Judaism for Christian Faith.* Translated by Leondard Swidler. Philadelphia: Fortress, 1984.

Myers, Jacob M. *I and II Esdras.* AB 42. Garden City, N.Y.: Doubleday, 1974.

Nanos, Mark D. *The Mystery of Romans: The Jewish Context of Paul's Letter.* Minneapolis: Fortress, 1996.

Neusner, Jacob. "Comparing Judaisms." *HR* 18 (1978): 177–91.

———. *Judaic Law from Jesus to the Mishnah: A Systematic Reply to Professor E. P. Sanders.* South Florida Studies in the History of Judaism 84. Atlanta: Scholars Press, 1993.

———. *The Rabbinic Traditions about the Pharisees before 70.* 3 vols. Leiden: E. J. Brill, 1971.

———. "The Use of the Later Rabbinic Evidence for the Study of Paul." Pages 43–63 in vol. 2 of *Approaches to Ancient Judaism.* Edited by William Scott Green. 5 vols. Chico, Calif.: Scholars Press, 1978–1985.

———, ed. *Sifra: An Analytical Translation.* 3 vols. BJS 138–40. Atlanta: Scholars Press, 1988.

Neusner, Jacob, and Richard S. Sarason, eds. *The Tosefta.* 6 vols. Hoboken, N.J.: Ktav, 1977–1986.

Newman, Barclay M. "Translating 'Seed' in Galatians 3.16, 19." *BT* 35 (1984): 334–37.

Newton, Michael. *The Concept of Purity at Qumran and in the Letters of Paul.* SNTSMS 53. Cambridge: Cambridge University Press, 1985.

Nickelsburg, George W. E. "The Bible Rewritten and Expanded." Pages 89–156 in *Jewish Writings of the Second Temple Period.* Edited by Michael E. Stone. CRINT 2.2. Philadelphia: Fortress, 1984.

———. "Eschatology in the Testament of Abraham: A Study of the Judgment Scenes in the Two Recensions." Pages 23–64 in *Studies on the Testament of Abraham.* Edited by George W. E. Nickelsburg. Society of Biblical Literature Septuagint and Cognate Studies 6. Missoula, Mont.: Scholars Press, 1972, 1976.

———. *Jewish Literature between the Bible and the Mishnah: A Historical and Literary Introduction.* Philadelphia: Fortress, 1981.

———. "Structure and Message in the Testament of Abraham." Pages 85–93 in *Studies on the Testament of Abraham.* Edited by George W. E. Nickelsburg. Society of Biblical Literature Septuagint and Cognate Studies 6. Missoula, Mont.: Scholars Press, 1972, 1976.

Nickelsburg, George W. E., with Robert A. Kraft. *Early Judaism and Its Modern Interpreters.* Atlanta: Scholars Press, 1986.

Nickelsburg, George W. E., and Michael E. Stone. *Faith and Piety in Early Judaism: Texts and Documents.* Philadelphia: Fortress, 1983.

Nicole, Roger R. "C. H. Dodd and the Doctrine of Propitiation." *WTJ* 17 (1954–1955): 117–57.

Nikiprowetzky, Valentin. "La Spiritualisation des Sacrifices et le Culte Sacrificiel au Temple de Jérusalem chez Philon D'Alexandrie." *Semitica* 17 (1967): 97–116.

Noth, Martin. *Exodus: A Commentary.* Translated by J. S. Bowden. Philadelphia: Westminster, 1962.

———. "For All Who Rely on Works of the Law Are under a Curse." Pages 118–31 in *The Laws in the Pentateuch and Other Studies.* Translated by D. R. Ap-Thomas. Philadelphia: Fortress, 1967.

———. *Leviticus: A Commentary.* Rev. ed. Old Testament Library. Philadelphia: Westminster, 1977.

Nygren, Anders. "Christus der Gnadestuhl." Pages 89–93 in *In Memoriam Ernst Lohmeyer.* Edited by Werner Schmauch. Stuttgart: Evagelischen Verlagswerk GmbH., 1951.

———. *Commentary on Romans.* Philadelphia: Fortess, 1949.

O'Brien, Peter T. *Commentary on Philippians.* NIGTC. Grand Rapids: Eerdmans, 1991.

Oegema, Gerbern S. "Versöhnung ohne Vollendung? Römer 10,4 und die Tora der messianischen Zeit." Pages 229–61 in *Bund und Tora: Zur theologischen Begriffsgeschichte in alttestamentlicher, frühjüdischer und urchristlicher Tradition.* Edited by Friedrich Avemarie and Hermann Lichtenberger. WUNT 92. Tübingen: J.C.B. Mohr (Paul Siebeck), 1996.

Oepke, Albrecht. *Der Brief des Paulus an die Galater.* 3d ed. THKNT. Berlin: Evangelische Verlagsanstalt, 1973.

Oesterley, W. O. E. *II Esdras.* London: Methuen & Co., 1933.

Osborne, William L. "The Old Testament Background of Paul's 'All Israel' in Romans 11:26a." *Asia Journal of Theology* 2 (1988): 282–93.

Osten-Sacken, Peter von der. *Christian-Jewish Dialogue: Theological Foundations.* Translated by Margaret Kohl. Philadelphia: Fortress, 1986.

———. *Die Heiligkeit der Tora: Studien zum Gesetz bei Paulus.* Munich: Chr. Kaiser, 1989.

———. *Römer 8 als Beispiel paulinischer Soteriologie.* FRLANT 112. Göttingen: Vandenhoeck & Ruprecht, 1975.

Pannenberg, Wolfhart. *Jesus—God and Man.* 2d ed. Translated by Lewis L. Wilkins and Duane A. Priebe. Philadelphia: Westminster, 1977.

Penna, Romano. *Paul the Apostle: Wisdom and Folly of the Cross.* Translated by Thomas P. Wahl. 2 vols. Collegeville, Minn.: Liturgical Press, 1996.

Philonenko, Marc. "La cosmogonie du 'Livre des Secrets d'Hénoch.'" Pages 109–16 in *Religions en Égypte Hellénistique et Romaine.* Paris: Presses Universitaires de France, 1969.

Picard, Jean-Claude. *Apocalypsis Baruchi Graece.* PVTG 2. Leiden: E. J. Brill, 1967.

———. "Observations sur L'Apocalypse Grecque de Baruch." *Semitica* 20 (1970): 77–103.

Pines, S. "Eschatology and the Concept of Time in the Slavonic Book of Enoch." Pages 72–87 in *Types of Redemption.* Edited by R. J. Zwi Werblowsky and C. Jouce Bleeker. Studies in the History of Religions 18. Leiden: E. J. Brill, 1970.

Piper, John. "The Demonstration of the Righteousness of God in Romans 3:25–26." *JSNT* 7 (1980): 2–32.

———. *The Justification of God: An Exegetical and Theological Study of Romans 9:1–23.* 2d ed. Grand Rapids: Baker, 1993.

Plöger, Josef G. *Literarkritische, formgeschichtliche und stilkritische Untersuchungen zum Deuteronomium.* BBB 26. Bonn: Peter Hanstein, 1967.

Plummer, Alfred. *A Critical and Exegetical Commentary on the Second Epistle of St. Paul to the Corinthians.* ICC. Edinburgh: T&T Clark, 1915.

Pobee, John S. *Persecution and Martyrdom in the Theology of Paul.* JSNTSup 6. Sheffield: JSOT Press, 1985.

Pohlenz, Max. "Paulus und die Stoa." *ZNW* 42 (1949): 69–104.

Ponsot, Hervé. "Et ainsi tout Israel sauvé; Rom., XI, 26a." *RB* 89 (1982): 406–17.

Porter, Calvin L. "Romans 1.18–32: Its Role in the Developing Argument." *NTS* 40 (1994): 210–28.

Porter, J. R. *Leviticus.* London: Cambridge University Press, 1976.

The "Progymnasmata" of Theon. Translated by James R. Butts. Ann Arbor, Mich.: University Microfilms International, 1986.

Quarles, Charles L. "The Soteriology of R. Akiba and E. P. Sanders' *Paul and Palestinian Judaism.*" *NTS* 42 (1996): 185–95.

Räisänen, Heikki. "Faith, Works and Election in Romans 9: A Response to Stephen Westerholm." Pages 239–46 in *Paul and the Mosaic Law.* Edited by James D. G. Dunn. WUNT 89. Tübingen: J.C.B. Mohr (Paul Siebeck), 1996.

———. "Galatians 2.16 and Paul's Break with Judaism." Pages 112–26 in *Jesus, Paul and Torah: Collected Essays.* Translated by David E. Orton. JSNTSup 43. Sheffield: Sheffield Academic Press, 1992. Originally published in *NTS* 31 (1985): 543–53.

———. "The 'Law' of Faith and the Spirit." Pages 48–68 in *Jesus, Paul and Torah: Collected Essays.* Translated by David E. Orton. JSNTSup 43. Sheffield: Sheffield Academic Press, 1992. Originally published in *NTS* 26 (1979–1980): 101–17.

———. "Legalism and Salvation by the Law: Paul's Portrayal of the Jewish Religion As a Historical and Theological Problem." Pages

63–83 in *Die Paulinische Literatur und Theologie*. Edited by Siegfried Pedersen. Göttingen: Vandenhoeck & Ruprecht, 1980.

———. *Paul and the Law*. 2d ed. WUNT 29. Tübingen: J.C.B. Mohr (Paul Siebeck), 1986.

———. "Paul, God, and Israel: Romans 9–11 in Recent Research." Pages 178–206 in *The Social World of Formative Christianity and Judaism: Essays in Tribute to Howard Clark Kee*. Edited by Jacob Neusner, Peder Borgen, Ernest S. Frerichs, and Richard Horsley. Philadelphia: Fortress, 1988.

———. "Paul's Conversion and the Development of His View of the Law." *NTS* 33 (1987): 404–19.

———. "Paul's Word-Play on νόμος: A Linguistic Study." Pages 69–94 in *Jesus, Paul and Torah: Collected Essays*. Translated by David E. Orton. JSNTSup 43. Sheffield: Sheffield Academic Press, 1992. Originally pages 131–54 in *Glaube und Gerechtigkeit: In Memoriam Rafael Gyllenberg*. Edited by J. Kiilunen et al. Helsinki: Finnish Exegetical Society, 1983.

———. "Romans 9–11 and the 'History of Early Christian Religion.'" Pages 743–65 in *Texts and Contexts: Biblical Texts in Their Textual and Situational Contexts*. Edited by Tord Fornberg and David Hellholm. Oslo: Scandinavian University Press, 1995.

Refoulé, François. "Cohérence ou incohérence de Paul in Romains 9–11." *RB* 98 (1991): 51–79.

———. "*. . . Et ainsi tout Israël sera sauvé*": *Romains 11:25–32*. LD 117. Paris: Cerf, 1984.

Renwick, David A. *Paul, the Temple, and the Presence of God*. Brown Judaic Studies 224. Atlanta: Scholars Press, 1991.

Reumann, John. "The Gospel of the Righteousness of God: Pauline Reinterpretation in Romans 3:21–31." *Interpretation* 20 (1966): 432–52.

Rhyne, C. Thomas. *Faith Establishes the Law*. SBLDS 55. Chico, Calif.: Scholars Press, 1981.

———. "*Nomos Dikaiosynēs* and the Meaning of Romans 10:4." *CBQ* 47 (1985): 486–99.

Richardson, Peter. *Israel in the Apostolic Church*. SNTSMS 10. Cambridge: Cambridge University Press, 1969.

Richter, Wolfgang. *Die sogenannten vorprophetischen Berufungsberichte: Eine literaturwissenschaftliche Studie zu 1 Sam 9,1–10, 16, Ex 3f. und Ri 6,11b–17*. Göttingen: Vandenhoeck & Ruprecht, 1970.

Ridderbos, Herman. *Paul: An Outline of His Theology*. Translated by John Richard de Witt. Grand Rapids: Eerdmans, 1975.

Robertson, A. T. *A Grammar of the Greek New Testament in the Light of Historical Research.* 4th ed. Nashville: Broadman, 1934.

Robinson, D. W. B. "The Distinction between Jewish and Gentile Believers in Galatians." *ABR* 13 (1965): 29–48.

———. "The Salvation of Israel in Romans 9–11." *Reformed Theological Review* 26 (1967): 81–96.

Rogerson, J. W. "Sacrifice in the Old Testament: Problems of Method and Approach." Pages 45–59 in *Sacrifice.* Edited by M. F. C. Bourdillon and Meyer Fortes. London: Academic Press, 1980.

Rosenau, Hartmut. "Der Mensch zwischen Wollen und Können: Theologische Reflexionen im Anschluß an Röm 7,14–25." *TP* 65 (1990): 1–30.

Roshwald, Mordecai. "The Perception of Law in Judaism." *Judaism* 34 (1985): 360–66.

Rost, Leonhard. *Die Vorstufen von Kirche und Synangogue im Alten Testament: Eine Wortgeschichliche Untersuchung.* Stuttgart: W. Kohlhammer, 1938.

Rubinstein, Arie. "Observations on the Slavonic Book of Enoch." *JJS* 13 (1962): 1–21.

Sabourin, Leopold. *Rédemption Sacrificielle: Une Enquete Exégétique.* Studia 11. Bruges: Desclée de Brouwer, 1961.

Saldarini, Anthony J. Review of E. P. Sanders, *Paul and Palestinian Judaism. JBL* 98 (1979): 299–303.

Sanday, William, and Arthur C. Headlam. *A Critical and Exegetical Commentary on the Epistle to the Romans.* 5th ed. ICC. Edinburgh: T&T Clark, 1896.

Sanders, E. P. "The Covenant As a Soteriological Category and the Nature of Salvation in Palestinian and Hellenistic Judaism." Pages 11–44 in *Jews, Greeks and Christians.* Edited by Robert Hamerton-Kelly and Robin Scroggs. Leiden: E. J. Brill, 1976.

———. *Jesus and Judaism.* Philadelphia: Fortress, 1985.

———. *Jewish Law from Jesus to the Mishnah: Five Studies.* Philadelphia: Trinity Press International, 1990.

———. *Judaism: Practice and Belief 63 BCE–66 CE.* Philadelphia: Trinity Press International, 1992, 1994.

———. *Paul.* Past Masters. Oxford: Oxford University Press, 1991.

———. *Paul and Palestinian Judaism: A Comparison of Patterns of Religion.* Philadelphia: Fortress, 1977.

———. "Paul on the Law, His Opponents, and the Jewish People in Philippians 3 and 2 Corinthians 11." Pages 75–90 in *Paul and the Gospels.* Vol. 1 of *Anti-Judaism in Early Christianity.* Edited by

Peter Richardson with David Granskou. Waterloo, Ontario, Canada: Wilfrid Laurier University Press, 1986.

———. *Paul, the Law, and the Jewish People.* Philadelphia: Fortress, 1983.

———. "Puzzling Out Rabbinic Judaism." Pages 65–79 in vol. 2 of *Approaches to Ancient Judaism.* Edited by William Scott Green. 5 vols. Chico, Calif.: Scholars Press, 1978–1985.

———. "Testament of Abraham." Pages 671–81 in *Apocalyptic Literature and Testaments.* Vol. 1 of *The Old Testament Pseudepigrapha.* Edited by James H. Charlesworth. Garden City, N.Y.: Doubleday, 1983.

———. "Testament of Abraham." Pages 56–70 in *Outside the Old Testament.* Edited by M. De Jonge. Cambridge Commentaries on the Writings of the Jewish and Christian World 200 BC to AD 200 4. Cambridge: Cambridge University Press, 1985.

Sandnes, Karl Olav. *Paul—One of the Prophets?* WUNT. Second Series 43. Tübingen: J.C.B. Mohr (Paul Siebeck), 1991.

Sänger, Dieter. "Rettung der Heiden und Erwählung Israels: Einige vorläufige Erwägungen zu Römer 11,25–27." *KD* 32 (1986): 99–119.

Sayler, Gwendolyn B. *Have the Promises Failed? A Literary Analysis of 2 Baruch.* SBLDS 72. Chico, Calif.: Scholars Press, 1984.

Schechter, Solomon. *Aspects of Rabbinic Theology.* 1909. Repr., Woodstock, Vt.: Jewish Lights, 1993.

Schiffman, Lawrence H. *From Text to Tradition: A History of Second Temple and Rabbinic Judaism.* Hoboken, N.J.: Ktav, 1991.

———. "The Rabbinic Understanding of Covenant." *RevExp* 84 (1987): 289–98.

Schlier, Heinrich. *Der Brief an die Galater.* 14th ed. Kritisch-exegetischer Kommentar über das Neue Testament 7. Göttingen: Vandenhoeck & Ruprecht, 1971.

———. *Der Römerbrief.* HTKNT 6. Freiburg: Herder, 1977.

Schmeller, Thomas. *Paulus und die 'Diatribe': Eine vergleichende Stilinterpretation.* Neutestamentliche Abhandlungen. New Series 19. Münster: Aschendorf, 1987.

Schnabel, Eckhard J. *Law and Wisdom from Ben Sira to Paul: A Tradition Historical Enquiry into the Relation of Law, Wisdom, and Ethics.* Tübingen: J.C.B. Mohr (Paul Siebeck), 1985.

Schnackenburg, Rudolf. *The Church in the New Testament.* Translated by W. J. O'Hara. New York: Herder & Herder, 1965.

Schneider, Bernardin. "The Meaning of St. Paul's Antithesis 'The Letter and the Spirit.'" *CBQ* 15 (1953): 163–207.

Schoeps, Hans Joachim. *Paul: The Theology of the Apostle in the Light of Jewish Religious History.* Translated by Harold Knight. Philadelphia: Westminster, 1961.

———. "The Sacrifice of Isaac in Paul's Theology." *JBL* 65 (1946): 385–92.

Scholem, Gershom. *Ursprung und Anfänge der Kabbala.* Studia Judaica: Forschung zur Wissenschaft des Judentums 3. Berlin: Walter de Gruyter, 1962.

Schreiner, Josef. "Das 4. Buch Esra." *Apokalypsen. JSHRZ* 5.4. Gütersloh: Gerd Mohn, 1981.

Schreiner, Thomas R. "The Church As the New Israel and the Future of Ethnic Israel in Paul." *Studia Biblica et Theologica* 13 (1983): 17–38.

———. "Did Paul Believe in Justification by Works? Another Look at Romans 2." *Bulletin for Biblical Research* 3 (1993): 131–58.

———. "Is Perfect Obedience to the Law Possible? A Re-examination of Galatians 3:10." *JETS* 27 (1984): 151–60.

———. "Israel's Failure to Attain Righteousness in Romans 9:30–10:3." *TJ* 12 New Series (1991): 209–20.

———. *The Law and Its Fulfillment: A Pauline Theology of Law.* Grand Rapids: Baker, 1993.

———. "Paul and Perfect Obedience to the Law: An Evaluation of the View of E. P. Sanders." *WTJ* 47 (1985): 245–78.

———. "Paul's View of the Law in Romans 10:4–5." *WTJ* 55 (1993): 113–35.

———. *Romans.* Baker Exegetical Commentary on the New Testament. Grand Rapids: Baker, 1998.

———. "'Works of the Law' in Paul." *NovT* 33 (1991): 217–44.

Schrenk, Gottlob. "Der Segenswunsch nach der Kampfepistel." *Judaica* 6 (1950): 170–90.

Schubert, Paul. *Form and Function of the Pauline Thanksgivings.* BZNW 20. Berlin: Alfred Töpelmann, 1939.

Schulz, Siegfried. "Die Anklage in Röm. 1,18–32." *TZ* 14 (1958): 161–73.

Schürer, Emil. *A History of the Jewish People in the Time of Jesus Christ.* 5 vols. Translated by Sophia Taylor and Peter Christie. 1890. Repr., Peabody, Mass.: Hendrickson, 1994.

Schwartz, Daniel R. "Two Pauline Allusions to the Redemptive Mechanism of the Crucifixion." *JBL* 102 (1983): 259–68.

Schweitzer, Albert. *The Mysticism of Paul the Apostle.* Translated by William Montgomery. New York: Seabury, 1931.

Scott, James M. "'For as Many as Are of Works of the Law Are Under a Curse' (Galatians 3.10)." Pages 187–221 in *Paul and the Scriptures of Israel.* Edited by Craig A. Evans and James A. Sanders. JSNTSup 83. Sheffield: Sheffield Academic Press, 1993.

Seeley, David. *The Noble Death: Graeco-Roman Martyrology and Paul's Concept of Salvation.* JSNTSup 28. Sheffield: Sheffield Academic Press, 1990.

Segal, Alan F. "Covenant in Rabbinic Writings." *SR* 14 (1985): 53–62.
———. *Paul the Convert: The Apostolate and Apostasy of Saul the Pharisee.* New Haven: Yale University Press, 1990.
Seifrid, Mark A. "Blind Alleys in the Controversy over the Paul of History." *TynBul* 45 (1994): 73–95.
———. "Paul's Approach to the Old Testament in Rom 10:6–8." *TJ* 6 New Series (1985): 3–37.
———. "The Subject of Rom 7: 14–25." *NovT* 34 (1992): 313–33.
Sheppard, Gerald T. "Wisdom and Torah: The Interpretation of Deuteronomy Underlying Sirach 24:23." Pages 166–76 in *Biblical and Near Eastern Studies: Essays in Honor of William Sanford LaSor.* Edited by Gary A. Tuttle. Grand Rapids: Eerdmans, 1978.
Siker, Jeffrey S. *Disinheriting the Jews: Abraham in Early Christian Controversy.* Louisville: Westminster John Knox, 1991.
Silva, Moisés. "Is the Law against the Promises? The Significance of Galatians 3:21 for Covenant Continuity." Pages 153–67 in *Theonomy: A Reformed Critique.* Edited by William S. Barker and W. Robert Godfrey. Grand Rapids: Zondervan, 1990.
———. "The Law and Christianity: Dunn's New Synthesis." *WTJ* 53 (1991): 339–53.
———. *Philippians.* Wycliffe Exegetical Commentary. Chicago: Moody, 1988.
Sly, Dorothy I. "Philo's Practical Application of Δικαιοσύνη." In *SBL Seminar Papers, 1991,* 298–308. Atlanta: Scholars Press, 1991.
Smiles, Vincent M. *The Gospel and the Law in Galatia: Paul's Response to Jewish-Christian Separatism and the Threat of Galatian Apostasy.* Collegeville, Minn.: Liturgical Press, 1998.
Snodgrass, Klyne R. "I Peter II. 1–10: Its Formation and Literary Affinities." *NTS* 24 (1977–1978): 97–106.
———. "Justification by Grace—To the Doers: An Analysis of the Place of Romans 2 in the Theology of Paul." *NTS* 32 (1986): 72–93.
———. "Spheres of Influence: A Possible Solution to the Problem of Paul and the Law." *JSNT* 32 (1988): 93–113.
Soucek, Josef B. "Zur Exegese von Röm. 2, 14ff." In *Antwort. Karl Barth zum Siebzigsten Geburtstag am 10. Mai 1956.* Zollikon-Zurich: Evangelischer Verlag, 1956.
Stanley, Christopher D. *Paul and the Language of Scripture: Citation Technique in the Pauline Epistles and Contemporary Literature.* SNTSMS 69. Cambridge: Cambridge University Press, 1992.
———. "'The Redeemer Will Come ἐκ Ζιών: Romans 11.26–27 Revisited." Pages 118–42 in *Paul and the Scriptures of Israel.* Edited by

Craig A. Evans and James A. Sanders. JSNTSup 83. Sheffield: Sheffield Academic Press, 1993.

———. " 'Under a Curse': A Fresh Reading of Galatians 3.10–14." *NTS* 36 (1990): 481–511.

Steck, Odil Hannes. *Israel und das Gewaltsame Geschick der Propheten: Untersuchungen zur Überlieferung des Deuteronomistischen Geschichtsbildes im Alten Testament, Spätjudentum und Urchristentum.* WMANT 23. Neukirchen-Vluyn: Neukirchener Verlag, 1967.

Stendahl, Krister. *Meanings: The Bible As Document and As Guide.* Philadelphia: Fortress, 1984.

———. *Paul among Jews and Gentiles.* Philadelphia: Fortress, 1976.

Stockhausen, Carol Kern. *Moses' Veil and the Glory of the New Covenant.* AnBib 116. Rome: Pontifical Biblical Institute, 1989.

Stone, Michael Edward. *Features of the Eschatology of IV Ezra.* HSS 35. Atlanta: Scholars Press, 1989.

———. *Fourth Ezra.* Hermeneia. Philadelphia: Fortress, 1990.

———. "On Reading an Apocalypse." Pages 65–78 in *Mysteries and Revelations: Apocalyptic Studies since the Uppsala Colloquium.* Edited by John J. Collins and James H. Charlesworth. JSPSup 9. Sheffield: Sheffield Academic Press, 1991.

———. "Reactions to Destructions of the Second Temple." *JSJ* 12 (1981): 195–204.

———. *The Testament of Abraham: The Greek Recensions.* Texts and Translations, Pseudepigrapha Series 2. Missoula, Mont.: Society of Biblical Literature, 1972.

Stowers, Stanley Kent. *The Diatribe and Paul's Letter to the Romans.* SBLDS 57. Chico, Calif.: Scholars Press, 1981.

———. *A Rereading of Romans: Justice, Jews, and Gentiles.* New Haven: Yale University Press, 1994.

———. "Text As Interpretation." Pages 17–27 in *Judaic and Christian Interpretations of Texts: Contents and Contexts.* Edited by J. Neusner and E. Frerichs. Vol. 3 of *New Perspectives on Ancient Judiasm.* Lanham, Md.: University Press of America, 1987.

Strelan, J. G. "A Note on the Old Testament Background of Romans 7:7." *Lutheran Theological Journal* 15 (1981): 23–25.

Stuhlmacher, Peter. "The Apostle Paul's View of Righteousness." In *Reconciliation, Law, and Righteousness: Essays in Biblical Theology.* Philadelphia: Fortress, 1986.

———. "Eighteen Theses on Paul's Theology of the Cross." In *Reconciliation, Law, and Righteousness: Essays in Biblical Theology.* Philadelphia: Fortress, 1986.

———. *Gerechtigkeit Gottes bei Paulus.* Göttingen: Vandenhoeck & Ruprecht, 1965.

———. "Jesus' Resurrection and the View of Righteousness in the Pre-Pauline Mission Congregations." In *Reconciliation, Law, and Righteousness: Essays in Biblical Theology.* Philadelphia: Fortress, 1986.

———. "Recent Exegesis on Romans 3:24–26." In *Reconciliation, Law and Righteousness.* Philadelphia: Fortress, 1986.

Suggs, M. Jack. "'The Word Is Near You': Romans 10: 6–10 within the Purpose of the Letter." Pages 289–312 in *Christian History and Interpretation: Studies Presented to John Knox.* Edited by W. R. Farmer, C. F. D. Moule, and R. R. Niebuhr. Cambridge: Cambridge University Press, 1967.

Sweeney, Marvin A. "Habakkuk." Pages 1–6 in vol. 3 of *Anchor Bible Dictionary.* Edited by David Noel Freedman. 6 vols. New York: Doubleday, 1992.

Sykes, S. W. "Sacrifice in the New Testament and Christian Theology." Pages 61–83 in *Sacrifice.* Edited by M. F. C. Bourdillon and Meyer Fortes. London: Academic Press, 1980.

Talbert, Charles H. "A Non-Pauline Fragment at Romans 3.24–26?" *JBL* 85 (1966): 287–96.

———. *Reading Corinthians: A Literary and Theological Commentary on 1 and 2 Corinthians.* New York: Crossroad, 1989.

Tannehill, Robert C. *Dying and Rising with Christ: A Study in Pauline Theology.* Berlin: Alfred Töpelmann, 1967.

Taylor, Vincent. *The Atonement in New Testament Teaching.* London: Epworth, 1940.

———. "Great Texts Reconsidered." *ExpTim* 50 (1938–1939): 295–300.

Theissen, Gerd. *Psychological Aspects of Pauline Theology.* Translated by John P. Galvin. Philadelphia: Fortress, 1987.

Thielman, Frank. *From Plight to Solution: A Jewish Framework for Understanding Paul's View of the Law in Galatians and Romans.* NovTSup 61. Leiden: E. J. Brill, 1989.

———. *Paul and the Law: A Contextual Approach.* Downers Grove, Ill.: InterVarsity Press, 1994.

Thompson, Alden Lloyd. *Responsibility for Evil in the Theodicy of IV Ezra.* SBLDS 29. Missoula, Mont.: Scholars Press, 1977.

Thompson, Richard W. "The Inclusion of the Gentiles in Rom 3,27–30." *Bib* 69 (1988): 543–46.

———. "Paul's Double Critique of Jewish Boasting: A Study of Rom 3,27 in Its Context." *Bib* 67 (1986): 520–31.

Thornton, T. C. G. "The Meaning of καὶ περὶ ἁμαρτίας in Romans viii. 3." *JTS* 22 (1971): 515–17.

———. "Propitiation or Expiation? ἱλαστήριον and ἱλασμός in Romans and 1 John." *ExpTim* 80 (1968–1969): 53–55.

Thrall, Margaret E. *A Critical and Exegetical Commentary on the Second Epistle to the Corinthians.* 2 vols. ICC. Edinburgh: T&T Clark, 1994.

Tobin, Thomas H. "Controversy and Continuity in Romans 1:18–30." *CBQ* 55 (1993): 298–318.

———. "Romans 10:4: Christ the Goal of the Law." In *The Studia Philonica Annual: Studies in Hellenistic Judaism.* Vol. 3, ed. David T. Runia, 272–80. Atlanta: Scholars Press, 1991.

———. "What Shall We Say That Abraham Found? The Controversy behind Romans 4." *HTR* 88 (1995): 437–52.

Toews, John E. *The Law in Paul's Letter to the Romans: A Study of Romans 9.30–10.13.* Ann Arbor, Mich.: University Microfilms, 1977.

Tomson, Peter J. *Paul and the Jewish Law: Halakha in the Letters of the Apostle to the Gentiles.* Compendia rerum iudaicarum ad Novum Testamentum 3.1. Minneapolis: Fortress, 1990.

Travis, Stephen H. "Christ As Bearer of Divine Judgment in Paul's Thought about the Atonement." Pages 21–38 in *Atonement Today: A Symposium at St John's College, Nottingham.* Edited by John Goldingay. London: SPCK, 1995.

Turner, Nigel (and James Hope Moulton). *Syntax.* Vol. 3 of *A Grammar of New Testament Greek.* Edinburgh: T&T Clark, 1963.

Tyson, Joseph B. "'Works of Law' in Galatians." *JBL* 92 (1973): 423–31.

Unnik, W. C. van. "La conception paulinienne de la nouvell alliance." *Litterature et Theologie Pauliennes.* RechBib 5. Bruges: Desclée De Brouwer, 1960.

Vaillant, A. *Le Livre des Secrets d'Hénoch, texte slave et traduction française.* Textes publiés par l'Institute d'Études Slaves 4. Paris: Institut d'Études Slaves, 1952.

Van Seters, John. "The Place of the Yahwist in the History of the Passover and Massot." *ZAW* 95 (1983): 167–82.

VanderKam, James C. "Exile in Jewish Apocalyptic Literature." Pages 89–109 in *Exile: Old Testament, Jewish, and Christian Conceptions.* Edited by James M. Scott. JSJSup 56. Leiden: E. J. Brill, 1997.

Vaux, Roland de. *Les Sacrifices de L'Ancien Testament.* Cahiers de la Revue biblique 1. Paris: Gabalda, 1964.

———. *Studies in Old Testament Sacrifice.* Cardiff: University of Wales Press, 1964.

Vermes, Geza. *The Dead Sea Scrolls in English.* 4th ed. New York: Penguin Books, 1995.

Vinson, Richard B. "A Comparative Study of the Use of Enthymemes in the Synoptic Gospels." Pages 119–41 in *Persuasive Artistry: Studies in New Testament Rhetoric in Honor of George A. Kennedy.* Edited by Duane F. Watson. JSNTSup 50. Sheffield: Sheffield Academic Press, 1991.

Vollenweider, Samuel. *Freiheit als neue Schöpfung: Eine Untersuchung zur Eleutheria bei Paulus und in seiner Umwelt.* FRLANT 147. Göttingen: Vandenhoeck & Ruprecht, 1989.

Voorwinde, S. "Who Is the 'Wretched Man' in Romans 7:24?" *Vox reformata* 54 (1990): 11–26.

Vos, J. S. "Die Hermeneutische Antinomie bei Paulus (Galater 3.11–12; Römer 10.5–10)." *NTS* 38 (1992): 254–70.

Wagner, Volker. *Rechtssätze in gebundener Sprache und Rechtssatzreihen im israelitischen Recht: Ein Beitrag zur Gattungsforschung.* BZAW 127. Berlin: Walter de Gruyter, 1972.

Walker, Rolf. "Die Heiden und das Gericht. Zur Auslegung von Römer 2, 12–16." *EvT* 20 (1960): 302–14.

Walker, William O. "Translation and Interpretation of ἐὰν μὴ in Galatians 2:16." *JBL* 116 (1997): 515–20.

Wallis, Gerhard. "Der Vollbürgereid in Deuteronomium 27, 15–26." *HUCA* 45 (1974): 47–63.

Walton, Steve. "Sacrifice and Priesthood in Relation to the Christian Life and Church in the New Testament." Pages 136–56 in *Sacrifice in the Bible.* Edited by Roger T. Beckwith and Martin J. Selman. Grand Rapids: Baker, 1995.

Watson, Francis. *Paul, Judaism and the Gentiles: A Sociological Approach.* SNTSMS 56. Cambridge: Cambridge University Press, 1986.

Weber, Ferdinand. *System der altsynagogalen palästinischen Theologie oder Die Lehren des Talmud.* 1880. Republished in *Jüdische Theologie auf Grund des Talmud und verwandter Schrifen.* Edited by Franz Delitzsch and Georg Schnedermann. 2d ed. Leipzig: Dörffling Franke, 1897.

Wedderburn, A. J. M. "Paul and the Law." *SJT* 38 (1985): 613–22.

Weiss, Meir. "Concerning Amos' Repudiation of the Cult." Pages 199–214 in *Pomegranates and Golden Bells: Studies in Biblical, Jewish, and Near Eastern Ritual, Law, and Literature in Honor of Jacob Milgrom.* Edited by David P. Wright, David Noel Freedman, and Avi Hurvitz. Winona Lake, Ind.: Eisenbrauns, 1995.

Wengst, Klaus. *Christologische Formeln und Lieder des Urchristentums.* Gütersloh: Gerd Mohn, 1972.

Wenham, Gordon J. *The Book of Leviticus.* NICOT. Grand Rapids: Eerdmans, 1979.

———. "The Theology of Old Testament Sacrifice." Pages 75–87 in *Sacrifice in the Bible.* Edited by Roger T. Beckwith and Martin J. Selman. Grand Rapids: Baker, 1995.

Wenthe, Dean O. "An Exegetical Study of I Corinthians 5:7b." *Springfielder* 38 (1974): 134–40.

Westerholm, Stephen. *Israel's Law and the Church's Faith: Paul and His Recent Interpreters.* Grand Rapids: Eerdmans, 1988.

———. "Paul and the Law in Romans 9–11." Pages 215–37 in *Paul and the Mosaic Law.* Edited by James D. G. Dunn. WUNT 89. Tübingen: J.C.B. Mohr (Paul Siebeck), 1996.

———. "Response to Heikki Räisänen." Pages 247–49 in *Paul and the Mosaic Law.* Edited by James D. G. Dunn. WUNT 89. Tübingen: J.C.B. Mohr (Paul Siebeck), 1996.

———. "Sinai As Viewed from Damascus: Paul's Reevaluation of the Mosaic Law." Pages 147–65 in *The Road from Damascus: The Impact of Paul's Conversion on His Life, Thought, and Ministry.* Edited by Richard N. Longenecker. Grand Rapids: Eerdmans, 1997.

Whiteley, D. E. H. *The Theology of St. Paul.* Oxford: Basil Blackwell, 1964.

Wilckens, Ulrich. *Der Brief an die Römer.* 3 vols. EKKNT 6.1–3. Neukirchener-Vluyn: Neukirchener Verlag, 1978–1982.

Wilcox, Max. ""Upon the Tree"—Deut 21:22–23 in the New Testament." *JBL* 96 (1977): 85–99.

Willett, Tom W. *Eschatology in the Theodicies of 2 Baruch and 4 Ezra.* JSPSup 4. Sheffield: JSOT Press, 1989.

Williams, Sam K. *Jesus' Death As Saving Event: The Background and Origin of a Concept.* HDR 2. Missoula, Mont.: Scholars Press, 1975.

———. "Justification and the Spirit in Galatians." *JSNT* 29 (1987): 91–100.

———. "The 'Righteousness of God' in Romans." *JBL* 99 (1980): 241–90.

Williamson, Ronald. *Jews in the Hellenistic World: Philo.* Cambridge Commentaries on the Writings of the Jewish and Christian World 200 BC to AD 200 1.2. Cambridge: Cambridge University Press, 1989.

Windisch, Hans. *Der zweite Korintherbrief.* Edited by Georg Strecker. Kritisch-exegetischer Kommentar über das Neue Testament. Göttingen: Vandenhoeck & Ruprecht, 1970.

Winger, Michael. *By What Law? The Meaning of* Νόμος *in the Letters of Paul.* SBLDS 128. Atlanta: Scholars Press, 1992.

———. "Meaning and Law." *JBL* 117 (1998): 105–10.

Winston, David. "Judaism and Hellenism: Hidden Tensions in Philo's Thought." In *The Studia Philonica Annual: Studies in Hellenistic*

Judaism. Vol. 2, Edited by David T. Runia, 1–19. Atlanta: Scholars Press, 1990.

———. "Philo's Doctrine of Repentance." Pages 29–40 in *The School of Moses: Studies in Philo and Hellenistic Religion.* Edited by John Peter Kenney. Atlanta: Scholars Press, 1995.

Wintermute, O. S. "Jubilees." Pages 35–142 in *Expansions of the "old Testament" and Other Legends, Wisdom and Philosophical Literature, Prayers, Psalms, and Odes, Fragments of Lost Judeo-Hellenistic Works.* Vol. 2 of *The Old Testament Pseudepigrapha.* Edited by James H. Charlesworth. Garden City, N.Y.: Doubleday, 1985.

Witherington, Ben, III. *Friendship and Finances in Philippi: The Letter of Paul to the Philippians.* The New Testament in Context. Valley Forge, Pa.: Trinity Press International, 1994.

———. *Grace in Galatia: A Commentary on Paul's Letter to the Galatians.* Grand Rapids: Eerdmans, 1998.

Wolff, Christian. *Jeremia im Frühjudentum und Urchristentum.* Texte und Untersuchungen zur Geschichte der altchristlichen Literatur 118. Berlin: Akademie Verlag, 1976.

Wolfson, Harry Austryn. *Philo: Foundations of Religious Philosophy in Judaism, Christianity, and Islam.* Vol. 2. Cambridge: Harvard University Press, 1947.

Wood, J. Edwin. "Isaac Typology in the New Testament." *NTS* 14 (1967–1968): 583–89.

Wright, David P. "The Gesture of Hand Placement in the Hebrew Bible and in Hittite Literature." *JAOS* 106 (1986): 433–46.

Wright, N. T. *Climax of the Covenant: Christ and the Law in Pauline Theology.* Minneapolis: Fortress, 1991.

———. "The Law in Romans 2." Pages 131–50 in *Paul and the Mosaic Law.* Edited by James D. G. Dunn. WUNT 89. Tübingen: J.C.B. Mohr (Paul Siebeck), 1996.

———. "On Becoming the Righteousness of God: 2 Corinthians 5:21." Pages 200–208 in *1 and 2 Corinthians.* Edited by David M. Hay. Vol. 2 of *Pauline Theology.* SBLSymS. Minneapolis: Fortress, 1993.

Yadin, Y. "Pesher Nahum (4Q pNahum) Reconsidered." *IEJ* 21 (1971): 1–12.

Young, Frances M. *Sacrifice and the Death of Christ.* London: SPCK, 1975.

Young, Norman H. "Did St. Paul Compose Romans III:24f.?" *ABR* 22 (1974): 23–32.

———. " 'Hilaskesthai' and Related Words in the New Testament." *EvQ* 55 (1983): 169–76.

———. "Who's Cursed—And Why? (Galatians 3:10–14)." *JBL* 117 (1988): 79–92.

Zeller, Dieter. "Christus, Skandal und Hoffnung: Die Juden in den Briefen des Paulus." Pages 256–78 in *Gottesverächter und Menschenfeinde? Juden zwischen Jesus und frühchristlicher Kirche.* Edited by Horst Goldstein. Düsseldorf: Patmos, 1979.

———. *Juden und Heiden in der Mission des Paulus: Studien zum Römerbrief.* 2d ed. FB 8. Katholisches Bibelwerk, 1976.

Ziesler, J. A. "The Just Requirement of the Law (Romans 8.4)." *ABR* 35 (1987): 77–82.

———. "The Role of the Tenth Commandment in Romans 7." *JSNT* 33 (1988): 41–56.

Zohar, Noam. "Repentance and Purification: The Significance and Semantics of חטאת in the Pentateuch." *JBL* 107 (1988): 609–18.

Index of Modern Authors

Index of Ancient Sources

1 Corinthians

2 Corinthians

Galatians